Devil's Sanctuary

An Eyewitness History of
Mississippi Hate Crimes

Alex A. Alston Jr. and James L. Dickerson

Lawrence Hill Books

Library of Congress Cataloging-in-Publication Data

Alston, Alex A., 1936–
    Devil's sanctuary : an eyewitness history of Mississippi hate crimes /
Alex A. Alston, Jr. and James L. Dickerson.
        p.   cm.
    Includes bibliographical references and index.
    ISBN 978-1-55652-763-0
        1. Hate crimes—Mississippi.   2. Mississippi—Race relations.
3. African Americans—Civil rights—Mississippi.   I. Dickerson, James L.
II. Title.

    HV6773.53.M7A47   2009
    364.1509762—dc22   2009006245

Interior design: Pamela Juárez

First edition
Published by Lawrence Hill Books
an imprint of Chicago Review Press, Incorporated
814 North Franklin Street
Chicago, Illinois 60610
ISBN: 978-1-55652-763-0
Printed in the United States of America
5 4 3 2 1

To Sarah Jane and our wonderful children, Trace, Alyce, and Sheldon

—ALEX A. ALSTON JR.

In loving memory of Rex and Muriel Turner, and their living son, Rex Jr., treasured family members who made a difference in my life

—JAMES L. DICKERSON

"We speak now against the day when our Southern people who will resist to the last these inevitable changes in social relations, will, when they have been forced to accept what they at one time might have accepted with dignity and good-will, will say, 'Why didn't someone tell us this before? Tell us this in time?'"

—WILLIAM FAULKNER, 1955

Contents

Chronology   vii

PART I: In the Beginning

1   The Rose and the Thorn   1
2   Emmett Till: A Prelude to Terror   17
3   Mississippi Crosses the Line   27
4   The Lynching That Shocked the World   47
5   The Loose Ends of Government   57
6   Hoddy Toddy: The Integration of Ole Miss   73
7   The Assassination of Medgar Evers   93
8   Philadelphia Burning   109
9   Charles Moore and Henry Dee   129

PART II: Complete Breakdown

10   Mississippi's Legal Jungle   147
11   Mississippi Gestapo   169
12   Praise the Lord, but Don't Seat the Blacks   193
13   All the News That's Fit to Print—for White
     Mississippians   213
14   Inside the FBI: The Truth About Mississippi   233

PART III: Justice Delayed

15   Byron De La Beckwith: Ordeal by Trial and Error   259

16   Philadelphia Redux: Edgar Ray Killen Raised
     from the Dead   283
17   James Ford Seale: Time Runs Out for a Killer   301

PART IV: Picking Up the Pieces

18   Atonement in a Haunted Land   319

     Acknowledgments   333
     Notes   335
     Select Bibliography   349
     Index   357

Chronology

1926   Waterboarding, a torture technique used against blacks in Mississippi to obtain confessions, was outlawed by the Mississippi Supreme Court.

1936   Alex A. Alston Jr. is born.

1945   James L. Dickerson is born.

1954   *Brown v. Board of Education*, the landmark school desegregation case.

1955   Emmett Till murder.

Federation for Constitutional Government meets in Memphis, Tennessee.

Clyde Kennard applies for admission to the all-white Mississippi Southern College.

FBI targets civil rights leaders by ordering an investigation of the NAACP.

1956   Creation of Mississippi State Sovereignty Commission.

Byron De La Beckwith offers his services to the Sovereignty Commission.

1957   J. Edgar Hoover orders FBI agents to monitor the activities of Martin Luther King Jr. and the Southern Leadership Conference.

1959   Citizens' Council targets NAACP executive secretary Roy Wilkins.

Lynching of Mack Charles Parker in Poplarville, Mississippi.

Clyde Kennard again applies for admission to Mississippi Southern College; he is framed by the Mississippi State Sovereignty Commission on minor charges and sentenced to seven years in the state penitentiary at Parchman, Mississippi.

1961   Freedom Riders arrive in Mississippi to help register black voters.

1962   Riot at the University of Mississippi when James Meredith enrolls for classes.

1963   Cleve McDowell becomes the second black to attend the University of Mississippi.

Mississippi civil rights leader Medgar Evers is murdered.

1964   Civil rights workers Michael Schwerner, Andrew Goodman, and James Chaney are murdered near Philadelphia, Mississippi.

Charles Moore and Henry Dee are murdered by Klansmen near Meadville, Mississippi.

Byron De La Beckwith is tried for the murder of Medgar Evers; there is a mistrial. He is tried again a few months later; again there is a mistrial.

1966   Robert Kennedy visits the University of Mississippi.

1967   Beth Israel Congregation synagogue in Jackson, Mississippi, is bombed by the Ku Klux Klan.

Seven men are found guilty of violating the civil rights of Schwerner, Goodman, and Chaney; eight men are found not guilty; and the jury is unable to reach decisions on three men, including Edgar Ray Killen, the Baptist minister accused of masterminding the plot.

1973   Mississippi State Sovereignty Commission is disbanded.

1989   Federal judge rules that Sovereignty Commission files must be opened to the public.

1994   Byron De La Beckwith is convicted of the murder of Medgar Evers. It is the first ever murder conviction in Mississippi of a white man for a hate crime committed against an African American.

2005   Edgar Ray Killen is convicted of manslaughter in the murders of Schwerner, Goodman, and Chaney.

2007   James Ford Seale is convicted in the murders of Charles Moore and Henry Dee.

2008   James Ford Seale's conviction is overturned by a federal appeals court.

PART I

In the Beginning

1

The Rose and the Thorn

It was the doomsday option, and they embraced it with a level of apocalyptic fervor usually reserved for the passing of collection plates in revival tents: with a choice between racial integration and state-sponsored ignorance, Mississippi's brain trust went with the latter. Early in 1954 the Mississippi legislature, stoking white racial fears, passed a proposed constitutional amendment that authorized the state to close its public schools rather than allow whites and blacks to attend the same classes.

For more than a year there had been street-corner talk that a pending case before the United States Supreme Court, *Brown v. Board of Education*, could result in the destruction of Mississippi's segregated school system. Indeed, as expected, in May 1954 the High Court ruled that racial segregation was unconstitutional. The ruling stunned whites across the South, where African Americans were required by law to attend separate schools and prohibited to use any state or public facilities that were not designated for "coloreds." Public buildings open to African Americans displayed COLORED signs on separate rest rooms and water fountains, but many other buildings, such as libraries, hotels, and restaurants, were off-limits to citizens of color. African Americans bold enough to enter those buildings were subject to arrest.

Mississippians responded to the High Court ruling by going to the polls in November 1954 to ratify, by a two-to-one majority, the constitutional amendment that empowered the state to close all public schools rather than submit to desegregation. Like most other Southern states, Mississippi has its own moral code, frequently referred to by politicians as "Mississippi Values." On the surface, the code provides a positive approach to life, with references to God, patriotism, and family. But beneath the surface is a dark, brooding, some would say destructive way of thinking that supports a belief that the ends justify the means when it comes to preserving those Mississippi Values that provide a sense of worth to the state's white residents.

Culturally, white Mississippians often have a bipolar view of life: At one extreme is the *rose*, a symbol of the sweetness of life that is characterized by sunny skies, idyllic visions of both the past and the future, and a lingering sense of well-being. At the other extreme is the *thorn*, a symbol of generations of violence, brutality, and oppression of not just African Americans but any group that is different from the white majority.

Mississippians have a long history of being against whatever the rest of the nation is for. It's been that way from the beginning, and it's not likely to change anytime soon. To understand why, you have to look at the state's history. Mississippi was primarily settled by four groups of people: indigenous Native Americans; African American slaves who were brought to the state in chains; a handful of patriotic white Americans who moved to Mississippi after fighting in the Revolution; and a large group of white Americans of English, Scottish, and Irish descent who fled to Mississippi to create an alternate universe because they were opposed to the "liberalism" of George Washington, Thomas Jefferson, and the other Founding Fathers. At the time of statehood, white Mississippians were outnumbered by blacks and Native Americans by a margin of more than two to one. White Mississippians remedied that, with President Andrew Jackson's help, by driving the Native Americans off their land and exiling them to Oklahoma, thus making whites the new majority.

Many of Mississippi's early white settlers were a traitorous lot who wanted no part of the Revolution. They were British loyalists who came to what is now Mississippi to escape the colonies. They were proslavery and procorporation (the Founding Fathers were wary of corporations because of the corrupting influence they'd had on British society), and they did not believe in the new "liberal" government because they felt an allegiance to the conservative British monarchy. *Liberal* was a dirty word. Mississippians cringed whenever they heard, "We hold these truths to be self-evident, that all men are created equal, that they are endowed by their Creator with certain unalienable Rights, that among these are Life, Liberty and the pursuit of Happiness." Early Mississippians wanted nothing so much as they wanted a king or queen to rule them, accepting the British view that some citizens, by virtue of their wealth and social standing, are more equal than others. That way of thinking has been Mississippi's curse since statehood.

Oasis in the Delta

Greenville is an oasis of literary and progressive thinking, the very soul of the Mississippi Delta. It is also a miracle city, having survived, during the 1800s and early 1900s, rampaging floods, raging fires, and terrifying yellow fever epidemics. Somehow, each time the city was knocked flat on its back, it always managed to spring back, just as feisty as ever. During the Civil War the city was once burned to the ground by the U.S. Army after overly optimistic Southern patriots opened fire on passing federal warships. In 1927 it was put under six feet of water when the river overflowed its banks and meandered for more than sixty miles toward Greenwood, a smaller Delta town built in the shadow of the red-clay hills that protected the rest of Mississippi from the rampaging floodwaters. Greenville could kill you, or take away everything you loved, if you let it, or it could teach you lessons about the human condition that you could learn nowhere else in Mississippi.

Throughout the twentieth century, one of Greenville's most admirable qualities was its diversity. By a slight margin, most of the city's inhabitants were African Americans, with the remainder made up of Scots, Irish, Italians, and Syrians. There was a large Chinese population and a number of influential Jews. At a time when country clubs around the nation were excluding Jews as a matter of policy, a Jew was the president of Greenville's country club.

The Mississippi Delta just might be one of the most exotic and fascinating places in the world. By the 1950s it had also become, as had most of the rest of Mississippi, a dark and fearful place, where neither God's nor man's laws were obeyed with any regularity. The Delta, for the most part, was inhabited by dirt-poor blacks and white rednecks, and a few wealthy white planters. Once a prehistoric seabed for the Gulf of Mexico, it surfaced to remain flat as a pancake from the yearly flooding of the Mississippi River, which left rich deposits of black alluvial silt to await the cotton seed that made the Delta the envy of cotton growers the world over.

African Americans constituted the vast majority of those who lived in the Delta and would have found this particular piece of real estate closer to a hell than the paradise that whites like to remember. By the mid-1930s most Delta counties were at least three-quarters black and composed of mainly poor agricultural laborers, tenant farmers, and domestics. They were generally poorer and more suppressed than blacks in the rest of Mississippi. As a result, notes historian Charles M. Payne, "as blacks from other states feared going into Mississippi, blacks from the hill counties or piney woods of Mississippi were frequently reluctant to venture into the Delta."

James L. Dickerson:

My mother, Juanita Turner, did not live in Greenville when the Great Flood of 1927 came—she and her family still lived in Mantachie, or "up in the hills," as people in the Delta called northeast Mississippi—but out of curiosity my mother's father, Audie Turner, drove down to the Delta to witness its destruction. Once he arrived Audie borrowed a boat and paddled out into the floodwaters, where he took photographs of the submerged buildings and the African Americans who were being vaccinated against typhoid fever by the U.S. Army medical corps.

At the time, Audie was co-owner of a Mantachie department store, Turner & White, and he had no ambition to move to the Mississippi Delta. That changed in 1936, when someone backed a truck up to the back door of the store and carted away everything of value. With no insurance to cover the theft, Audie lost everything. Broke and without hope of supporting his family in Depression-ravaged north Mississippi, he used the family's political influence to obtain an appointment as a warden at the Mississippi State Penitentiary in Parchman, located in the upper part of the Delta. Known to Mississippians simply as Parchman Farm, it was probably the most infamous prison in the United States.

After four years at Parchman Farm, Audie moved his family to Greenville in 1940, where he took a job with the Mississippi Highway Department. It was while the family lived in Greenville that Mother met my Virginia-born father, James Luther Dickerson, while he was stationed at the Army Air Corps base on the outskirts of the city. He went by the name Luther when he was growing up, but his army buddies renamed him "Dick" and the name stuck. He was discharged from the army in March 1946, when I was six months of age. By then Audie had taken a job as manager of the May's Cash Store in Hollandale, a small town about thirty minutes away from Greenville. With Audie's help, my father got a job as the manager of a May's store in Greenville. May's was a precursor to Wal-Mart in that it offered a line of clothing, for infants to adults, and a hardware division that also included a large inventory of war surplus materials—canteens, boots, outerwear, tools, and so on.

It was around that time that my mother received a telephone call from the president of the Commercial National Bank in Greenville, Mississippi, where she had worked for several years as a teller. She'd quit her job when she'd learned she was pregnant with me. The bank president pleaded with her to return to work, but she said that she couldn't possibly because she had no one to stay home with her son. As a solution, the banker offered his chauffeur's wife as a babysitter. The black woman arrived for the job interview sitting in the backseat of the bank president's luxury car, with her stoic husband at the wheel, neither person acknowledging that they knew the other. "She came and talked to me and I said okay—and I went back to work," Mother later recalled.

That arrangement worked just fine for a while, but before long a problem developed—every time the babysitter picked me up, I started screaming. Not crying, mind you, like you'd do if you spilled your milk, but hollering at the top of my voice. Mother tried to work things out, but I would have nothing to do with the woman, so she was forced to let her go. She was about to quit her job at the bank, when she got an idea.

We lived on Central Avenue in a house once owned by a prominent judge. As was the custom in the South in those days, the alleys that ran behind the houses contained the shanties where the black families lived. On her way to work each morning, Mother had noticed a young black girl who lived in an alley down the street toward the levee. One day she stopped and asked if she'd ever taken care of babies.

"Not white babies, but I've kept black babies," the young girl explained. "I have a little baby of my own."

Mother asked her to come by the house the following day so that they could talk. Sallie Mae Elle was just eighteen, but she was very mature for her age—and she had a smiling face that radiated love. I took to her right away, and, unlike the previous woman, who frightened me, I allowed Sallie Mae to hold and cuddle me, something she did with a sense of wonderment. She'd never held a white baby in her arms.

Sallie Mae fed me my breakfast each day and prepared lunch for the entire family. Later, when I began to talk—I never said "Mama" or "Dada," but rather refrained from speaking until I could do so in complete sentences—I spoke in a mischievous manner, frequently teasing Sallie Mae and my parents.

Race relations in the 1940s throughout the South were devoid of the soon-to-emerge concept of equal rights. Whites and blacks either had good relationships with each other or they did not. Equal rights never entered into the equation, since it was inconceivable that blacks ever would have the same rights enjoyed by whites—in fact, it was against the law. At the time, Northerners labeled blacks who had good relationships with whites as "Uncle Toms" or "Mammies," and to some extent that attitude has continued to the present day; however, relationships between the races were much more complex than that would suggest.

Sallie Mae was the reason I became the first white to integrate the public parks in Greenville, although you won't find any plaques there celebrating the occasion. That's because the story's never been told until now. Well, technically, I didn't integrate the parks, Sallie Mae did, but I was the vehicle through which the integration took place.

The day my destiny called, I was three. Mother was working at the bank when she spotted one of her neighbors in line at her teller's window. The woman seemed agitated, judging by the way she twisted and turned and straightened her skirt every few moments, kicking her leg out, first one way and then the other, pursing her lips as if she had recently sucked a lemon. Her eyebrows had been shaved and redrawn with a black mascara brush, a custom at the time among some whites.

When the woman reached the window, she didn't lay down a wad of cash or a check. She wasn't there on banking business. She leaned over into the window, her voice low and ominous, whispering, "There's something I need to tell you."

Mother looked at her, not liking the way that sounded.

"What is it?"

The woman's voice bristled with anger. "Did you know that that nigger you hired is bringing her little boy to the city park to play with your baby?"

Stunned, Mother said she didn't know anything about that, which was the truth.

"Well, I thought you ought to know," the woman said; then she turned and left.

When she got home that day, Mother asked Sallie Mae about the neighbor's accusations. "Sallie Mae, have you been letting your little boy come up here to play?"

"Yes, ma'am," answered Sallie Mae. "You don't want me to?"

Sallie Mae had a luminous face. When she smiled, she lit up the room, and when she frowned, it nearly broke your heart. She was more than a sitter; she was a presence in our lives. Mother looked at Sallie Mae, who had been caring for me for two-and-a-half years and who loved me as if I was her own child, and she thought about the morally twisted, self-righteous neighbor standing in line to share the bad news about Sallie Mae—and it was no contest.

"No," Mother said, taken by the extravagant kindness in Sallie Mae's face. "I think it's a good idea—a very good idea."

Thus Sallie Mae and her son and I became the subject of controversy at the city park, a place black children were prohibited from visiting. In my first act of civil disobedience, we played on the swings and slides, and we chased each other across the rich Delta grass, which was soft as a cotton quilt when we tripped and fell into its fragrant folds.

Mother, who could be stubborn and unyielding when she wanted to be, never explained why she went against the grain on that one, other than to say that it felt like the right thing to do. Parents sometimes fall into the trap of thinking it is what they buy for their kids or the schools they send them to that matters most. The reality is that what matters most are the daily decisions parents make about their children.

Mother's decision to allow Sallie Mae to do what seemed reasonable and what felt right, despite the strong cultural and legal prohibition against racial mixing in city parks, had a profound effect on my life, for I grew up with an appreciation of black culture, never fearing blacks or hating them. And it has made all the difference. Fast-forward to 1964, when my college rock 'n' roll band, the Strokers, became the first all-white band to play in a black Memphis nightclub, and the ripple effect of Sallie Mae's and Mother's meeting of the minds becomes apparent and takes on a life of its own, which is how social progress invariably occurs.

Alex A. Alston Jr.:

I was born in 1936 in a motel on Highway 61 in the smack center of this remarkable region. My parents were white, but they were not part of the coalition of white plantation owners who controlled every aspect of the social and economic life in the Delta. In fact, at this time, at the end of the Depression, my dad was desperately trying to make a living to support our family by managing this small motel as cars began moving up and down Highway 61. I remember little about Cleveland, Mississippi, because when I was five years old, my family moved ten miles east to Ruleville, a smaller Delta town, where my dad managed a small brick hotel.

My first memory of an encounter with an African American was in 1942, when I was about seven and living on the top floor of the hotel in Ruleville. I remember it as a rainy summer night. I was sound asleep in my small bed, tucked away in the corner of a large room on the top floor, when I was suddenly awakened by a loud, piercing scream: "Get that nigger!"

A young black man had broken into the hotel, stolen some items, and was attempting to escape down the fire escape when the alarm was sounded. I was so proud of my dad. He'd heard the burglar and was chasing him down the corridor with the guests not far behind in hot pursuit. The burglar started down the fire escape, but some men on the ground heard the commotion and started up the fire escape after him, with my dad coming from the top. There was a horrible fight, which terrified me because I thought the burglar would kill my dad. In the midst of the fighting, the burglar bit a large piece out of my dad's leg, and they both fell to the ground, where they continued fighting.

The posse, now a gang of about twenty-five, gave chase with their guns blazing. Although the posse later told me that they had caught the "nigger" hiding on some upper slats in a small abandoned shack about a mile from the hotel, they didn't tell me what happened to him; but by the manner in which the posse looked, talked, and bragged, even as a young boy I felt sure this guy never again saw the light of day. Although I had a million questions, I never discussed this event with my dad after that night.

Surprisingly, this brutal incident involving my dad and a young black man had almost no impact on my view of blacks. The word *nigger* was commonly used to refer to any African American, and the resulting punishment for striking a white man was not unexpected. We lived in a caste system that tolerated no deviation from the rules. Certainly to strike a white would subject a black to the harshest punishment available. Any future thoughts of this incident during my adolescence would have involved the bravery of my dad and not the plight of the poor black. Following the hotel incident, my family moved about thirty-five miles southwest to Hollandale, after Senator James O. Eastland got my father a real job at the post office.

A Rose Garden of Prickly Thorns

For the latter half of the twentieth century, the town of Hollandale, with a population of less than three thousand, was over 80 percent African American. In many respects it was a typical Delta town. The blacks were desperately poor and worked for the wealthy white plantation owners. The black population included almost no landowners, artisans, or professionals, other than a few teachers at the black school. For the most part, black residents were titleless, almost citizenless, and had no hope of ever escaping the poverty that had been handed down to them from their parents and their parents before them. There were exceptions, of course.

Virtually unknown to the white population, blues legend Sam Chatmon sat on the street corners on Saturday afternoons and played his guitar, dressed like any poor black in town. When he wasn't singing and playing his guitar, he toured the capitals of Europe, where he was hailed as an artistic genius and often presented medals of honor. One of his songs, "Sitting on Top of the World," was a national hit and sold millions of copies. He was the most famous person in town, yet few people were aware of that fame.

Hollandale was a fabulous place for a white child to live. There were frequent cakewalks on Main Street, where for a nominal fee you could walk in a circle marked off with chalk until the music stopped— and hope you landed on a square that'd entitle you to own your favorite dessert. During the fall and spring there were frequent parades that featured the Hollandale High School band and gaily decorated cotton trailers pulled by pickup trucks and tractors, all led through town by a string of leggy majorettes wearing fantasy-provoking uniforms as revealing as any swimsuit you could order from Sears, Roebuck.

It was heaven growing up in the Delta in the 1940s and 1950s for many white boys and girls. Their freedom was unsurpassed. They had the full run of the Delta: the mule barns run by gypsies; the icehouse, where they could get a small piece of ice to cool off; and the slaughter plant, where they watched cows being hit over the head with sledgehammers, with buzzards sitting on each fence post awaiting their share. They learned to drink, party, and dance way too early. In later years Mississippi writer Willie Morris, who never lived in the Delta but was familiar with its uniqueness, reminded us that we "acquired our taste for such partying early on, mainly to the accompaniment of a peregrinating black band out of Vicksburg called the Red Tops." What great fun and camaraderie were felt at the Red Tops dances in Belzoni, Rosedale, Greenwood, and at Mink's in Greenville and Lillo's in Leland. The weather was usually pleasant, and if your skin was the right color, people were genuinely courteous and friendly.

Aside from the cakewalks and parades in Hollandale, there was not much cultural activity one could speak of unless you counted the Bible-thumping revivals that the Methodists and Baptists held every year. The white students were dismissed from school for the daytime sessions, where they were saved several times from hell and damnation by the powerful rhetoric of the spirited revival preachers, who could have moonlighted as fire-eaters at the traveling carnivals, so fiery was their speech.

There were at least two real cultural events that may have been the best in the land. It was one exciting time when the Silas Green, from New Orleans, and the nearby Rabbit Foot Negro minstrels came to town. Each came at separate times around cotton-picking season, when the blacks might have a few coins in their pockets. Usually they erected a gigantic tent, with a capacity of about fifteen hundred people, on A. Lee Ganier's pasture, where Church Street meets Highway 61 and across from Dorman's little grocery store. Preceding each show's appearance, the minstrels placed fabulous posters around town and sent a small band strutting in the streets, musically announcing their arrival.

Saturday Night in the Delta

Although a few white customers came into C. R. Anthony's in the 1950s and 1960s, the overwhelming majority of customers were blacks who came to town on Saturdays to buy overalls, blue jeans, rubber boots, piece goods, fancy dress shoes, nightgowns, white socks, and work shirts. On those days the streets were packed with African Americans.

Navigating the sidewalks without actually touching a black person was always a challenge for whites. However, blacks seldom failed to open up a path for a white person, making room as if it were the parting of the Red Sea. If an African American failed to yield the right of way, more often than not he or she would be slapped across the back of the head with a rolled newspaper, an action that usually evoked an apology from the victim.

Every Saturday night in Hollandale there was a drawing, the town's version of a lottery. For every dollar that a customer spent, he or she would get a numbered ticket. At exactly 8:00 P.M., with the streets packed, a ticket was drawn and the lucky person would win one hundred dollars. The winners probably had never seen one hundred dollars in their life, nor were they likely to see it ever again.

Every Saturday night, at 11:00 P.M., the bell rang down at Jue's Grocery, and the blacks knew they must get across the tracks to "Blue Front," or back to their plantations. They had exactly one hour to get home or they would be arrested. At the stroke of the bell, the streets and sidewalks were invariably filled with black families, who quickly disappeared at the sound of the gong, sometimes dropping their new purchases in their haste to get out of town before their presence was challenged by the police.

Intermingled with the good times associated with growing up in a small town in Mississippi during the 1950s was a profound undercurrent of what, for lack of a more descriptive word, could be termed evil. During the day white citizens went about their business with apparent good humor, glad-handing and backslapping their way through the workday, often interacting with blacks in a friendly manner, only to surrender to their basic instincts once the sun went down. Under the cover of darkness, supposedly upstanding citizens intimidated the black population on those occasions when blacks "talked back" to their overseers or whenever there was public talk of blacks having the right to vote.

No African American was allowed to vote in Hollandale, although there were rumors that Buster, the post office janitor, dearly wanted to vote. There was a lot of talk in those days about the National Association for the Advancement of Colored People (NAACP). If white children asked about the NAACP, they were told that it stood for the National Association for Apes, Coons, and Possums.

Leland: Hellhole of the Delta

About eighteen miles north of Hollandale, at the fabled blues crossroads of Highways 61 and 82, is the small town of Leland, home of bluesman Jimmy Reed and Muppets creator Jim Henson. The town once was characterized by *Collier's Weekly* as the "hellhole of the Delta" because of its passion for gambling, prostitution, and cocaine.

Like all Delta towns, Leland owes its existence to the bountiful cotton plantations that surround it. As late as the 1960s, plantation life throughout the Delta was geared toward perpetuating a rigid class system that was immune to the cultural compromises taking place on a daily basis in the rest of the country.

When Hollis Baugh was growing up in the late 1950s and early 1960s on a plantation outside Leland, he had little knowledge of the outside world. At a time when President John F. Kennedy eloquently urged America to tackle bold new frontiers, Baugh lived in a three-room shotgun house with no indoor plumbing (he would not see an indoor toilet until he started school in 1964). His mother cooked on a wood stove, which also served as a major source of heat in the winter months.

Today Baugh, who is assistant director of the Mississippi State Personnel Board and one of the highest ranked blacks in state government, looks back on those not-so-distant plantation days with a sense of wonderment. "We knew we didn't have some things, but we didn't know what we didn't have. If we were deprived, we didn't know it. Mama carried the load. She was the one who worried about things."

Sometimes the load was too much to bear. One day Hollis spotted his mother kneeling on a river bridge about three hundred yards from their house. Sensing that something was wrong, he ran after her, arms outstretched, something deep inside him churning with fear, shouting, "Mama, what are you doing?"

"Oh, nothing," she said, rising to her feet. "I was just praying."

Wiping a tear from her cheek, she took his hand and walked him back home.

Years later, when Hollis was a student at Mississippi State University, his mother told him the truth about what almost happened that day on the bridge. "She brought it up herself," Hollis later recalled, proud of the trust she put in their relationship. "She told me that having all those kids [Hollis was her sixth of nine children] had gotten her down. She was having a hard time taking care of them. She told me she considered jumping off that bridge that day. She said that when I walked up to her, the urge to jump went away."

Unlike the white children who lived on the plantation, Hollis lived in perpetual fear once the sun went down. The Delta was a scary place on a moonless night. He recalls a time when someone would come to their house late each night and bang against the side of the house. He'd see a face looking through the window into the darkened house, trying to make out something or someone inside. One night a friend hid in the edge of the field in the hopes of catching the intruder. But the visits ended as quickly as they had begun, and they never found out who was terrorizing them in the dead of night.

Hollis's mother worked in the cotton fields, picking cotton and chopping weeds, but she also worked as a housemaid for the family who owned the plantation. One Saturday morning she walked across the field to the big house to carry out her cleaning duties and she found the owner lying in the bathtub. He'd blown his head off with a shotgun. Before calling the authorities, she took a few minutes to clean the blood off the floor and the walls. Many years later Hollis asked why she did that. Her answer spoke to the complicated relationship that existed between plantation owner and servant, a mutually dependent relationship that often created a sense of allegiance that seems incomprehensible in today's society: "Because I didn't want anyone to see him like that."

Growing up, Hollis had very little contact with whites. "You knew your place, but there were times, especially on Saturday afternoons, when we all played football in the yard with the owner's grandchildren. That was the only interaction we ever had with white children. The only time I ever saw a white person in my church was when Daddy died and the plantation owner and his wife came to the service. It was two different worlds. You knew your world, but you didn't know much about the other world."

Like most black children in the Delta, Hollis was pulled from school in the fall to pick cotton. After working all day in the fields, he was expected to do his homework when he got home in the evening. "On Friday morning we'd go to school and take tests, and then return to the fields in the afternoon. We never picked cotton on Sunday."

In 2008 Hollis drove to Leland with a white woman who wanted to see the Muppets exhibit that the town had opened to celebrate the life of Jim Henson. While there, he decided to take her out to the plantation to meet the owner's eighty-one-year-old son. To Hollis's surprise, he greeted them warmly. "He seemed to take pride in the fact that I had left the farm and made something of my life. He took part ownership of that. He was proud of me. It surprised me. I'm glad he is proud."

James L. Dickerson:

Hollandale was a wild and crazy place in which to come of age. It was a town of dark secrets, unrestrained passions, and deep-seated hatreds, a place where heroes were in short supply and the pleasantries of life were abundant to those who could afford them.

Some of my strongest memories as an adolescent in Hollandale involved hanging out with friends late at night, much later than a high school student should have been out, driving around in a car to follow married white men as they backed out the doors of their homes with their shoes in their hands. Sometimes they rode down the road to meet other white women. Other times they crossed the tracks to have sexual encounters with black women, sometimes establishing long-term relationships and raising secret families with them. In those days it was not at all unusual for the older boys in my high school to have sexual relations with black girls.

White boys were not alone in breaking that taboo. As a teen, I once went to the picture show with a beautiful white girl my age who I later learned had sex with adult black men. People gossiped about her and made jokes behind her back, but they took no action against her, something I now find incredible.

Alex left for college nine years ahead of me, going first to Millsaps College in Jackson, Mississippi, and then into the U.S. Marine Corps, where he served for nearly four years, before enrolling in law school at the University of Mississippi.

Taking a different route out of town, I left for the University of Mississippi, where I played in a series of rock 'n' roll bands (Road Runners, Strokers, Dynamics) while getting a degree in psychology, before pursuing careers first in social work and then in journalism. It was during our overlapping "coming of age" experiences that most of the civil rights murders, bombings, and beatings took place in Mississippi—the Emmett Till murder; the Medgar Evers murder; the Mack Charles Parker lynching; the Henry Dee and Charles Moore murders; the murders of Michael Schwerner, Andrew Goodman, and James Chaney; and countless other acts of violence, some of which took decades to make their way into a court of law and some of which have never been prosecuted.

Growing up in Mississippi, we learned that there were people with certain beliefs who were immune to prosecution, regardless of their crimes. Looking the other way was the price one paid to preserve Mississippi Values.

2

Emmett Till:
A Prelude to Terror

Racially, the situation in Mississippi during the summer of 1955 was rancid—and potentially explosive. Into that simmering cauldron, stirred by the Supreme Court's desegregation decision the previous year, walked Emmett "Bobo" Till, a fourteen-year-old black youth from Chicago who traveled to Money, Mississippi, during summer break to visit relatives. Money is located along the eastern edge of the Delta, just outside Greenwood. The crossroads town, with its three stores, filling station, post office, school, and cotton gin, took up less space than a single Chicago block.

At 160 pounds, and standing five feet five, Till looked much older than his age, especially at a time when the average weight for adult American males was 160 pounds and the average height was five feet eight.[1] Although still a child, Till had the appearance of a chubby adult, despite a baby face that seemed out of place on his body.

One evening in late August, Till and eight other black youths around his age piled into a 1946 Ford and drove to one of the stores in Money, Bryant's Grocery and Meat Market, a struggling business owned by a white couple: Roy Bryant, twenty-four, a veteran of the

U.S. Army's 82nd Airborne Division, and his pretty wife, Carolyn, twenty-one, a beauty contest winner who dropped out of high school to marry Roy. Along with their two sons, aged two and three, they lived in the back of the two-story, ramshackle store. On this particular day Roy was out of town, helping a brother ride herd on a load of shrimp they had to transport from New Orleans to San Antonio, Texas.[2]

Till and his friends met about a dozen youths, including two girls, in front of the store, a popular teen hangout for blacks. Bryant had built a checkerboard on the front porch, and some of the youths gathered around to watch two players test their skills. Some of the boys wrestled. Others segregated themselves so that they could talk about girls. Eager to fit in, Till bragged about his white girlfriend. When the others doubted that he had a white girlfriend in Chicago, he produced a photograph from his wallet. Still unconvinced, one of the boys said, "There's a pretty white woman in the store. Since you know how to handle white girls, let's see you go in and get a date with her."

Till entered the store and encountered Carolyn standing behind the candy counter. Carolyn's sister-in-law, Juanita Milam, was in the living quarters with her two sons and Carolyn's two sons. It was customary for Juanita and her children to stay with Carolyn when Roy was out of town. On the days when that happened, after the store closed at 9 P.M., Juanita's husband, J. W. Milam, was in the habit of escorting the women and children back to his house, where Carolyn and her children spent the night.

Till looked over the candy selection and asked for two cents' worth of bubble gum. She handed the candy to him. According to Carolyn's account of what happened, as explained by her husband to a reporter, Till grabbed her outstretched hand and squeezed it, mumbling, "How about a date, baby?"[3] Fifty years later, Till's cousin, Simeon Wright, who was there that evening, contradicted that account in his memoir, saying that Till made a purchase and left without incident.

Whatever happened inside the store, everyone seems to agree that Carolyn followed Till and Wright outside, brushing past them at a full run to Juanita's car, where she knew she could get her hands on a pistol. If nothing happened in the store, as Wright later maintained, it begs the question as to why she went outside if it was not to look for a weapon. It was while she was outside that Till, hustled away by his fearful friends, gave Carolyn a "wolf whistle," a sound that cut through the night air with the urgency of a bloody knife.

After the teens left the store, Carolyn and Juanita agreed that it'd be better if they didn't tell their husbands about the incident, so when J.W. arrived to escort them home that night, the women gave no indication there'd been a problem.

Roy and J.W. had the same mother but different fathers. J.W. was twelve years older than Roy and a great deal larger, standing six feet two and weighing 235 pounds. He was known around Money as Big Milam, a loud, boisterous man who knew how to get a hard day's work from black plantation workers. Like his brother, J.W. had served in the United States Army, a veteran of World War II and an experienced platoon leader who'd taken a bullet in the chest from a German soldier. Both brothers saw themselves as sons of the South who stood tall for Mississippi Values.

When Roy returned home, Carolyn still said nothing to him about the incident, which today would be called sexual harassment. But back then it would have been called an invitation for an ass kicking or even worse. One of the few areas of agreement among the races at that time was that men, white and black, had a God-given right to avenge insults directed against their wives or girlfriends. Most of the killings that took place at that time were over "territorial" issues involving women. White men were equal opportunity avengers: they killed as many men of their own race over women as they did men of other races, whether black, Asian, or Native American. Black men killed other black men over that same territorial issue, though they almost never directed their anger against white men, even when justified, because they understood it would be an invitation for a lynching.

Perhaps Carolyn considered Till's age when she first decided not to mention the incident. Perhaps she simply didn't want to experience the turmoil that would accompany telling her husband the truth. Perhaps she knew the first question out of her husband's mouth would be, "What did you do to encourage him?"

Despite Carolyn and Juanita's conspiracy of silence, Roy found out about the incident from a black field-worker, who told him everything. It was Bobo Till who did it, the field hand explained, and he's staying with his uncle, Preacher Wright. There is no record of what Carolyn said when Roy confronted her with that information, but he must have been accusatory, wondering what else she wasn't telling him. Had she flirted with him? Had she, God forbid, had sex with him in the back room? It must have infuriated him that a black field hand could tell him something about his own wife, something so private that it raised more questions than it answered.

Roy, who was so poor that he didn't own a car or a truck, called Big Milam and, without explaining why, told him he needed a ride first thing in the morning. Big Milam balked. Little brother was asking for a favor on a Sunday, the only day he had to sleep in. Then Roy told him the whole story, something he hadn't really wanted to do on the telephone. Big Milam's only response was "I'll be there."

After he got off the telephone, Big Milam couldn't stop thinking about what his brother had told him. It ate away at him like a cancer. It might be different if the blacks in the community weren't already talking about it. The fact that they knew about it meant that he and his brother had to answer what he perceived to be a challenge to his family's honor. That night he drove to Bryant's Grocery and Meat Market. When he got there, Roy and Carolyn were asleep, the windows all dark. He banged on the back door, the .45 Colt automatic he'd used to kill Germans, stuck in his belt. Roy came to the door, still half asleep. Big Milam told him that he didn't want to wait until morning—he wanted to go right now.

Roy dressed and hurried out the back door, clenching a loaded pistol. Neither man said much as they got into Big Milam's truck and drove the three miles to Preacher Wright's house. There wasn't much to say. Both men were stone-cold sober. In their minds they were on a mission from God. It took less than ten minutes to get to Wright's house. The house was dark when they arrived, so about fifty feet off the road Big Milam turned off the truck lights and eased up beneath a cedar tree.

With a flashlight in one hand and the .45 in the other hand, Big Milam accompanied Roy to the front door and watched as his little brother took charge of the situation. Roy beat his doubled-up fist against the door, pounding the flimsy planking.

"Who is it?" asked a frightened voice on the other side of the door.

"Mr. Bryant from Money."

"All right, sir. Just a minute."

Preacher Wright opened the door and stepped out onto the porch.

"You got a boy in there from Chicago?"

"Yes, sir."

"I want to talk to him."

Wright nodded and took both men into the house. He knew all about the trouble at the store, but he was confident they wouldn't hurt a child, couldn't possibly hurt a child who didn't know any better. He figured they just wanted to give him a good whipping. They found Till asleep in a bed with Simeon, Preacher's youngest son. By then the noise had awakened the boys. Big Milam shone the flashlight into Till's face and asked, "You the nigger who did the talking?"

"Yeah," Till replied.

Irritated by the tone of Till's voice, Big Milam said, "Don't say 'yeah' to me—I'll blow your head off. Get your clothes on."

Wright pleaded with them not to hurt Till, explaining that the boy just didn't have good sense. His wife, Elizabeth, offered to pay them money if they'd just leave the boy alone. By then they knew that Till was in serious trouble.

Big Milam told them to go back to sleep. Then they led Till outside to the truck, with Preacher and Elizabeth halfway following them, wringing her hands, staying far enough behind them so as not to be perceived as a threat. They heard someone in the truck, a third person, speaking in a voice that Preacher later described as "a lighter voice than men," identify Till as the boy who had caused the trouble at the store.

Roy and Big Milam ordered Till into the back of the truck and told him to lie down flat. He did as he was told without protest. They started the truck and drove off into the night. As soon as they were out of sight, Elizabeth ran to the house of a white neighbor and awakened him, telling him what'd happened, speaking in a voice that seemed to outrun the words themselves. The neighbor looked out into the night, allowing his neighbor a respectful pause—he owed her that much—and then when the moment was right, he told her there was absolutely nothing he could do about it.

Elizabeth walked back home, confused about what she should do next. Today she would simply call 911 and ask for help. In the 1950s, African Americans were reluctant to approach white law enforcement officials, because it was not unusual for them to be members of the Ku Klux Klan. Elizabeth and Preacher left the other family members at the house and drove to nearby Sumner, where Elizabeth's brother lived. The brother convinced them that they should drive to Greenwood and report the abduction to the sheriff.

Meanwhile, Roy and Big Milam drove the back roads, looking for a place where they could put a good scare into Till. Big Milam knew of a one-hundred-foot cliff overlooking a river that ran very deep at its base. When they couldn't find it, they drove to Big Milam's house, with the brothers still in the cab and Till stretched out on the floor of the truck, out of sight. They arrived shortly before dawn and escorted Till into a toolshed behind the house. Roy and Big Milam took turns working him over with their pistols, pausing periodically to ask him if he was sorry. According to their confession, the answer was always no. Pistol-whipping a prisoner was a punishable offense in the army because it was considered torture, but Big Milam had done it with German prisoners during the big war, and he'd always found it an effective way to get information.

Till baffled them. Although only a child, he took punishment that'd buckled the knees of German prisoners of war. They beat him with their pistols until they fractured his skull, broke his wrists, and caused breaks in his legs. Still, he wouldn't say he was sorry. Till called them bastards and told them that he was as good as they were.

Exhausted, their arms and hands stinging and aching from the force of their pistols striking his body, the men loaded Till into the truck again and drove down the road to a cotton gin owned by Progressive Ginning Company. By then it was daylight. The gin was in the process of being renovated, and Big Milam had seen workers discard a circular metal fan, about three feet in diameter. They loaded the fan into the back of the truck with Till and drove to the Tallahatchie River, where they crossed the bridge and turned along a dirt road that ran parallel to the river. They drove for about two miles to a place where Big Milam once hunted squirrels. They pulled the truck up to the riverbank and stopped, ordering Till to unload the seventy-four-pound fan and carry it to the riverbank. He did as he was told, dropping the fan into the dirt at the place indicated by Big Milam.

At that point, according to their confession, their plan was to tie the boy to the fan with barbed wire and threaten to throw him into the river if he didn't say he was sorry for what he had done. Again, they asked him if he was sorry. Again, he said he was not.

Big Milam told him to take off all his clothes. Till slipped off his shirt, pants, underwear, shoes, and socks—and stood naked before the two men. Big Milam asked him if he still thought that he was as good as a white man.

"Yeah," was Till's one-word answer.

"And you still say you've had white women?"

"Yeah."

Big Milam pointed his .45 automatic at Till and squeezed the trigger, the bullet striking him in the side of the head. Till dropped hard. The brothers then tied the fan to Till's neck with barbed wire and rolled him and the fan into the river. They gathered up his shoes and clothing and tossed the bundle into the back of the truck.

They arrived at Big Milam's house in time to burn Till's shoes and clothing in the backyard before the rest of the household woke to cook breakfast prior to dressing and going to church. Later in the day, when the sheriff arrived to ask the brothers about Till, they admitted they'd taken him from the house but they said they had only taken him back to Roy's house so that Carolyn could identify him. She had said he wasn't the one, so they turned him loose unharmed. They said they didn't have any idea where he was now, but they thought that he had probably gone back to Chicago. The sheriff left without making an arrest.

Three days later, two boys were fishing on the river when they came across a pair of feet sticking up out of the water. Till's body had surfaced. News of the murder swept through the Delta, prompting Hodding Carter, editor of the *Delta Democrat-Times* in Greenville, to editorialize that the "people who are guilty of this savage crime should be prosecuted to the fullest extent of the law."

Till was not the only black murdered that summer. The Reverend George Washington Lee was killed in the Delta town of Belzoni by a shotgun blast after he became the first black in that community to register to vote. No one was ever arrested for his murder. In Brookhaven a black man named Lamar Smith, who'd been encouraging blacks to vote against a white incumbent, was murdered on the courthouse lawn in broad daylight. The sheriff witnessed the shooting but refused to arrest the killer. Not enough evidence, he explained.

Within days after Till's body was found, Roy Bryant and Big Milam were arrested and charged with murder. Incredibly, they went to trial just four weeks later, only to be acquitted by an all-white, male jury that deliberated for only sixty-seven minutes. Afterward a juror told a reporter that the verdict would have come sooner if they hadn't taken a break to have soft drinks. Defense attorneys had argued that the body found in the river wasn't Till's—photographs of the remains revealed a horribly disfigured corpse that barely seemed human. Since DNA testing had not yet been developed for use in criminal cases, the prosecutor had no court-friendly science with which to counter the defense's argument.

At Till's funeral in Chicago, his mother insisted that the coffin remain open so that everyone could see how horribly abused her son had been in Mississippi. *Jet*, a black-owned and -edited magazine with a national circulation, published photographs of Till's disfigured corpse, sparking an outrage among African Americans over the brutal nature of the crime. The national media responded with horror at events in Mississippi, as did the NAACP. *Life* magazine published a full-page editorial, In Memoriam: Emmett Till, which noted that Till's father had died in Italy fighting for his country during World War II.

Senator James O. Eastland leaked to the *Commercial Appeal* in Memphis, one of the South's highest-circulation newspapers, information obtained from military officials that Till's father, Louis Till, was executed by the U.S. Army in 1945 for rape and murder. In response, the *Jackson Daily News*, one of the most staunchly segregationist dailies in the South, sent a reporter to Chicago to interview Till's mother. Based on that interview, the newspaper ran a story that supported the *Commercial Appeal*'s story. In an editorial written by Major Frederick Sullens, the *Jackson Daily News* described the murder as a "brutal, senseless crime," but in typical fashion it complained that the NAACP was using the incident to "arouse hatred and fear."

The Best Confession That Money Could Buy

In June 1956 *Look* magazine published an article entitled "The Shocking Story of Approved Murder in Mississippi." The story focused on Emmett Till, whose murder had become a catalyst for the emerging civil rights movement. In the article, written by William Bradford Huie, Roy Bryant and Big Milam confessed to Till's murder, protected from prosecution again by the same constitution that they'd so flagrantly trampled on.

To write the article, Huie met with Bryant and Milam in their lawyer's office in Greenwood, where the two men provided the gruesome details of the murder. For their confession, *Look* paid the two men a total of four thousand dollars, a significant sum in the mid-1950s. Milam did most of the talking about the actual murder, with Bryant providing most of the information about the events that led up to the murder.

Neither man showed remorse. Explained Milam:

Well, what else could we do? He was hopeless. I never hurt a nigger in my life. I like niggers—in their place—I know how to work 'em. But I just decided it was time a few people got put on notice. As long as I live and can do anything about it, niggers are gonna stay in their place. Niggers ain't gonna vote where I live. If they did, they'd control the government. They ain't gonna go to school with my kids. And when a nigger gets close to mentioning sex with a white woman, he's tired of living. I'm likely to kill him. Me and my folks fought for this country, and we got some rights.[4]

Not impressed with the jury's verdict was Tallahatchie County sheriff H. H. Dogan, who compiled a list of that county's 1955 murders, indicating that there were four killings, three men and one woman, all African Americans. Two of the murders were committed by blacks; two were committed by whites. Opposite each murder victim were the names of the killer or killers. Listed as the murderers of Emmett Till were J. W. Milam and Roy Bryant.[5] Dogan wasn't the sort of man to mince words.

3

Mississippi Crosses
the Line

With passions running high in Mississippi over the U.S. Supreme Court's desegregation order, nationwide publicity about the Emmett Till murder poisoned race relations in the state and inflamed an already heated gubernatorial campaign. The mood of white voters was clear: Not since the Civil War had their passions been so revved. All across the state, there was an "us against them" mentality.

The top contenders in the governor's race in 1955 were J. P. Coleman and former governor Fielding L. Wright, who had served from 1946 to 1952. Wright, a native of Rolling Fork, the birthplace of blues legend Muddy Waters, had a national reputation as a segregationist. His favorite line was that segregation was an eternal truth that transcended party politics. Of the two candidates, Coleman was the more moderate. He had begun his political career in 1946 as a circuit court judge in Ackerman, a small town ninety miles northeast of Jackson. By the time he ran for governor, he'd already been elected state attorney general, but despite an impressive resume he was nowhere near being the most powerful political leader in the state. That distinction rested with Senator James O. Eastland, or "Big Jim," as he was known to his constituents.

Eastland, the owner of a five-thousand-acre cotton plantation in Sunflower County, was a big man who smoked big cigars. He had a slovenly appearance and an oversized beet-red face that always seemed at full moon. That election year Eastland took to the stump, spreading the word from one end of the state to the other. "You are not required to obey any court which passes out such a ruling," he said, referring to the Supreme Court. "In fact, you are obligated to defy it." The High Court was guilty of a "monstrous crime," Eastland said, and was a "clear threat and present danger to the very foundation of our Republican form of government." In a speech delivered on the floor of the U.S. Senate, Eastland accused the Supreme Court of "participation in the worldwide communist conspiracy."[1]

Eastland's rhetorical bombast left no room for reasoned debate. Coleman didn't agree with Eastland's ranting about defying the U.S. Supreme Court, but he avoided going head-to-head with Eastland during the campaign because he knew it would cost him votes. Remarkably, in one of the biggest election surprises of the decade, Coleman defeated Wright. Early in December 1955, in the weeks leading up to his inauguration, Coleman did an about-face and criticized Eastland's proposals to fight the Supreme Court, calling his ideas "foolish" and "legal poppycock."

An Ominous Gathering

It was the week after Christmas 1955. Memphis, Tennessee, was in one of those gray, winter funks that often precede New Year's Eve celebrations in the city. Somber skies. Intermittent drizzle. Bone-chilling winds sauntering in off the Mississippi River. Together they created a soaring misery index that dampened spirits and wrinkled brows. It was in the midst of that stubborn atmospheric lethargy that James Gunter, an enterprising reporter for the city's morning newspaper, the *Commercial Appeal*, long labeled liberal because of its crusading editorials against the Klan, received a tip from a downtown source that something big was in the works.[2] Senator Eastland had been spotted in the city, along with South Carolina senator Strom Thurmond and dozens of other prominent Southerners, all of whom had reputations as ardent segregationists.

Gunter made a few telephone calls and tracked Eastland and Thurmond to the Peabody Hotel, an upscale inn that author William Faulkner once proclaimed the cornerstone of the Mississippi Delta. Arriving at the posh downtown hotel, Gunter found himself blocked from entering the banquet room where the meeting was taking place. Burly guards, precursors to the muscle shirts that later would become fixtures at rock concerts, told him that the gathering was private. He was pushed back, menacingly warned to keep his distance.

Why Memphis was chosen for the meeting is a mystery, but there was nothing mysterious about why the *Commercial Appeal* was barred from the banquet room: in 1923 the newspaper's editorials and cartoons against the Klan had been awarded the Pulitzer Prize for meritorious public service. Gunter, who had a legacy to protect, stood his ground, taking note of who entered and exited the banquet room. When he cornered one delegate in the hallway and asked who would be speaking that day, one of the organizers punched the delegate before he could answer, a warning to keep his mouth shut. The two men quickly retreated behind closed doors.

Gunter was astonished by what he saw that afternoon. Political leaders from twelve Southern states were at the hotel. It was the largest gathering of its kind since before the Civil War. When the four-hour meeting broke up, Gunter was able to talk to enough people to piece together a story. The group, which named itself the Federation for Constitutional Government, had devised a plan to fight racial desegregation in the South. In the weeks following the Memphis gathering, the group established offices in Louisiana and remained in operation well into the 1960s.

Gunter rushed back to the newsroom with a list of thirty-five men he had recognized at the hotel. In addition to Thurmond and Eastland, the organizer of the meeting, he identified former Mississippi governor Fielding L. Wright, Congressman John Bell Williams of Mississippi, and Mississippi speaker of the house Walter Sillers. The next morning, the *Commercial Appeal* exposed the secret gathering with a page-one story and a headline that read

FEDERATION FOR CONSTITUTIONAL GOVERNMENT IS DESIGNED
TO BUILD UP EFFECTIVE FORCE AGAINST INTEGRATION

The story made much of the fact that the meeting was held in secret, and it identified John U. Barr, a wealthy industrialist from New Orleans, as the chairman. During a brief exchange with Gunter, Barr bragged: "This organization is restricted to the South now, but we have found supporters all over the nation. We've kept this thing under wraps until we knew our strength."

News of the Memphis gathering made its way to New York City, where an editor at the *New York Times* yanked the story off the wire and gave it to an aggressive young reporter, Anthony Lewis, to follow up with telephone interviews. Lewis was able to obtain enough information from Barr and others to write a story that editors felt was good enough to make the front page.[3] In the story, Eastland is quoted as saying that the new group would fight the Supreme Court, the labor unions, and the NAACP. Equally tenacious, Barr barked that the group would "fight anything" that got in its way.

Together the *New York Times* and the *Commercial Appeal* obtained the names of most of those in attendance. Aside from Eastland and his supporters, the two most powerful were Barr, a director of the National Association of Manufacturers, and Leander Perez, a powerful Louisiana segregationist who once crowed that there were two types of blacks: "Bad ones are niggers and good ones are darkies."

FBI director J. Edgar Hoover was particularly interested in the Memphis gathering. Two months earlier his racial prejudices had exploded when he was told by a Memphis source that the NAACP had used a letter he'd written in 1946, praising the organization as one that promoted "equality, freedom, and tolerance," to refute charges that it had a relationship with the Communist Party. Hoover ordered an investigation into NAACP activities. Two days after receiving the order, FBI assistant director Alan Belmont provided Hoover with a report that outlined the NAACP's "subversive agenda." Thus it was in the weeks preceding the Memphis gathering that Hoover launched his secret, Memphis-inspired campaign against the civil rights movement.

Birth of the Sovereignty Commission

By the time J. P. Coleman took office in January 1956, he had only two choices when it came to the Memphis gathering: he was either "for 'em or against 'em." Neutrality was not an option. He confided to friends that he didn't care for either choice, but like most white Mississippians, he was opposed to forced integration—and he didn't have the political strength to stand up to the hatemongers.

In the weeks after the Memphis gathering, Coleman abruptly changed the moderate positions he'd taken during the campaign and embraced the radicalism advocated by Eastland, telling reporters his stand on segregation would provide a "bombshell" that could be heard "from the Atlantic to the Pacific."

Rather than risk losing any of the hard-fought power he'd gained as governor, Coleman came down squarely on the side of Big Jim Eastland, who earlier that year had become chairman of the powerful U.S. Senate Judiciary Committee. It was Eastland's position that states had a legal right to pass "acts of nullification" to void Supreme Court decisions that violated the Constitution. When Eastland advocated the creation of a state commission that would have the power to fight the federal government, Coleman embraced the idea, not willing to risk confrontation with a raging bull like Eastland.

Early in 1956, Coleman sent a bill to the Mississippi legislature to create a super-secret spy agency designed to protect the state from the encroaching power of the federal government. The new agency would be named the Mississippi State Sovereignty Commission. The bill was clearly a product of the gathering that had taken place in Memphis the previous December. Under the provisions of the bill, the commission was empowered to "perform any and all acts and things deemed necessary and proper to protect the sovereignty of the State of Mississippi, and her sister states, from encroachment."[4] The commission was given the authority to examine the records and documents of any citizen or organization, and it was provided with a broad-ranging subpoena power that included the authority to enforce obedience "by fine or imprisonment" at the discretion of the commission. It was designed to operate independently of state government, when necessary, and permitted to solicit and use private funds to carry out covert operations.

Coleman thought that support for the proposal would be unanimous, considering the times they lived in, but he was mistaken. Among the 49 senators and 140 members of the House present for the session that considered the bill were Representative William Winter, who went on to hold several state offices, including tax collector, lieutenant governor, and governor, and Representative George Rogers, who eventually left Mississippi politics to work for the Central Intelligence Agency. "Those of us who were Coleman supporters in the legislature viewed the proposal for the Sovereignty Commission with a lot of misgiving," Winter later said. "It was viewed then, I think, as a body that in the wrong hands could create a lot of mischief."[5]

There was little debate on the bill. Most of the discussion was done in backrooms. When the bill came to a vote, it passed by a margin of 130 to 2, with 8 representatives not voting. Representatives George Rogers and Woody Hewitt cast the only votes in opposition. Rogers voted against the bill because there was talk that public money would be used to finance the activities of the Citizens' Council. "I thought that was an improper—if not unconstitutional—use of public funds," he said. "I wasn't in sympathy with all the activities of the Citizens' Council anyway, so I voted against it."[6]

Rogers's opposition to the bill is interesting because of his later involvement with the CIA, where he worked on the staff of the Intelligence Community, a division of the CIA that coordinated the intelligence-gathering activities of more than thirteen governmental agencies, including the Defense and Justice departments. "I was in the part that dealt with computers," Rogers explained. "It was fascinating work." Whether he read the information or not, subsequent reports on the very commission he voted to defeat surely went through his CIA office.

"After it was passed, some of us talked about it and developed increased misgivings about it," says Winter. Those misgivings resulted in a motion to reconsider. By the time the bill came up for the final vote, forty-nine lawmakers had backed away from it, including Winter, who this time around voted against it. The final vote in the House was 91 in favor of the bill, with 23 against and 26 not voting. It sailed through the Senate without a dissenting vote.

Staffing the Sovereignty Commission

The Mississippi capitol rotunda offers a memorable example of the richness of the architecture afforded public buildings constructed at the turn of the century. In many ways the three-story building, dedicated in 1903 and constructed at the then-unheard-of cost of one million dollars, is a replica of the national Capitol in Washington, D.C. Identical east and west wings for the Senate and the House of Representatives meet beneath a blue and gold dome decorated with colorful stained-glass panels that brighten a rotunda open from the ground floor to the dome's apex.

The governor's office is located on the second floor, set off by eight marble pillars that appear to support the third floor. It was behind the impressive door of the governor's office that J. P. Coleman organized the Mississippi State Sovereignty Commission on May 2, 1956. Four months earlier, while taking the oath of office, Coleman had brought attention to the commission by saying, "I have not the slightest fear that four years hence when my successor assumes his official oath that the separation of races in Mississippi will be left intact." The way the commission was designed, the governor and the lieutenant governor were held responsible for the body's operation. The governor was authorized to appoint an overall director as well as a director of public relations.

For the commission's first director, Coleman chose a member of the legislature, Representative Ney Gore of Quitman County. Leonard Hicks, a former head of the Mississippi Highway Patrol, was put in charge of the investigative department. Former FBI agent Zack Van Landingham was hired as the commission's only investigator. For the post of public relations director, Coleman picked the man who had served as his publicity manager in the 1955 campaign, Hal DeCell, a highly regarded editor of the *Deer Creek Pilot*, a small-circulation weekly in Rolling Fork.

With the creation of the commission, Mississippi once again stepped across that philosophical line that had been drawn in the sand before the Civil War. Mississippians felt they were patriotic—indeed, they would punch you in the mouth if you suggested that they were not—yet they could not in good conscience support the concept that "all men are created equal." For the second time in one hundred years, they retreated to their belief in a caste system that stood in stark opposition to the beliefs of the Founding Fathers. As they'd done in the Civil War, they became obsessed with preserving a way of life that existed only in their own minds.

Most of the race-baiting that occurred in Mississippi that year came from the Jackson Citizens' Council. Under the leadership of William J. Simmons, the son of a prominent Jackson banker, this racist, right-wing organization formed countless terrorist cells in small communities throughout the state. Since 1955 the council had published a four-page tabloid newspaper, the *Citizens' Council*, that regularly attacked African American quests for freedom as "tribal instincts" aroused by "NAACP witch doctors" who wanted to do away with American concepts of justice in order to install African models. Blacks were depicted as depraved, diseased, and prone to a criminal lifestyle.[7]

One of the approaches taken by the Jackson Citizens' Council during this time was to support the allegation that the "racial revolution" taking place in America was the result of a Communist conspiracy hatched in the Soviet Union. Thus to be in favor of integration was to be against Mom, apple pie, and the American flag. The three leaders of the council—Simmons; Medford Evans, editor of the council's newspaper; and Louis Hollis, the council's national director—had a history of supporting far-out causes. All three men were also members of the super-secret John Birch Society, a right-wing organization that had a large national following and a reputation for extremist dialogue.

The Commission Gets Down to Business

On May 16, 1956, ten days after stories about the commission's creation appeared in newspapers across the state, Byron De La Beckwith, a thirty-five-year-old tobacco salesman from Greenwood, Mississippi, typed out a letter to Governor Coleman.[8]

"Nothing I know of would give me greater pleasure than to be allowed to serve as an investigator for the purpose of assisting Chief L. C. Hicks in uncovering plots by the NAACP to integrate our beloved State," said Beckwith in the letter. "I am long and strong for maintaining segregation." As part of his employment application, Beckwith cited his experience as an ex-marine on Guadalcanal, in the Solomon Islands, where he received the Purple Heart; his membership in both the National Rifle Association and the Greenwood Citizens' Council; and his proficiency with firearms. He said he was "expert with a pistol, good with a rifle and fair with a shotgun . . . and RABID ON THE SUBJECT OF SEGREGATION."

Beckwith's letter was typical of the enthusiasm and optimism with which the Sovereignty Commission was greeted by disaffected whites who dreamed of a definitive race war that would settle the racial problem once and for all.

Shortly after starting work on May 15, public relations director Hal DeCell organized a series of out-of-state trips for himself and his wife, Carolyn, for the purpose of getting "our side of the story to the hometown newspapers outside the South."[9] His first trip was to Louisville, Kentucky, where he attended the annual meeting of the

National Editorial Association, handed out commission literature, and networked with editors he thought would be useful to the cause.

That summer, after the Citizens' Council in Clarksdale, Mississippi, complained to the Sovereignty Commission that NBC television had sent a film crew to the city, DeCell learned that the interviews would be broadcast on a program titled *Outlook*. Fearful that NBC would edit the film in such a way as to hurt the commission's efforts, he flew to New York with Carolyn and talked his way into the editing room, where he served as an adviser, frequently asking editors to set aside selected parts of the film. What the editors didn't know was that he secretly stuffed the film clippings into his briefcase.

Back in Jackson, DeCell declared his trip a great success: "When we left New York, the film was scheduled to appear on August 26. However, immediately upon my return I heard from New York that Reuven Frank of NBC had canceled it because he said it would make him look like a segregationist. I imagine it was because he couldn't find the clipped portions of the film."[10]

DeCell made no effort to keep his mission a secret. The *Jackson State Times* praised DeCell for sabotaging the film: "Certainly no showing of the film at all is better than having produced the one intended before DeCell got word of the venture. Much of what the Commission has done and will do, though, can never be told. Its behind-the-scenes investigations into race relations, for example, have nipped some few instances of unrest in the bud. Details must remain secret."

While DeCell was out on the road, director Ney Gore undertook a two-day, 598-mile road trip through Mississippi in an effort to recruit support for the commission. He met with supporters in Greenwood on September 15. It is not known if he spoke with Byron De La Beckwith on that date, but it is likely he did, since Beckwith was on the membership committee of the Greenwood Citizens' Council and his letter to Governor Coleman had been hand-delivered to Gore by the governor's secretary, a gesture that, however intended by Governor Coleman, provided Gore with a contact person in Greenwood.

Alex A. Alston Jr.:

Without telling my parents where I was going, I sneaked out of my house early, in order to get a good seat. There were two rows of seats up front reserved for the whites. Probably a couple of dozen whites would attend, and the rest were blacks. This was the only integrated event I ever attended during my childhood, although it really was not fully integrated because the few whites attending were carefully placed in a few front seats where they wouldn't have to sit by blacks. It never occurred to me at that time to challenge the law that prevented blacks from sitting "up front." This was the way it was. Jim Crow law prevailed, and it was forbidden for a black to sit with a white. Ironically blacks were allowed to stand with whites in some situations, such as in neighborhood grocery stores or in the bank. Even then whites were always served first.

When the band started playing and the show opened, the air would be so filled with excitement you would think it might explode. The Silas Green Show from New Orleans was my favorite. It was part musical, part comedy, part dancing, and part revue, with a solid black company that must have exceeded seventy members. The music was wonderful, and the slapstick comedy was hilarious. The chorus lines of beautiful dancers could shake their scantily clad bodies with a rhythm that was riveting and could very well have the tendency to arouse an adolescent male's prurient interest. The singers, comedy acts, costumes, lights, and the most talented nine- and twelve-piece house bands one could imagine made for the best entertainment I can ever remember.

Of course, it was not standard entertainment. It came like a whirlwind with great excitement among the blacks. It was a unique cultural event with an all-black cast that came lumbering in with a giant tent and bands blaring. Blacks in Hollandale, to this day, remember the shows as the greatest cultural events they'd ever seen.

The same can be said about the Rabbit Foot Minstrels. I liked the fact that they originated from Port Gibson, Mississippi, which was right down the road from Hollandale on Highway 61, fewer than ninety miles. The show was mighty proud of its gigantic sign that ran the whole length of the tent: F. S. WALCOTT'S ORIGINAL RABBIT FOOT MINSTRELS. It performances were spectacular, with colorful lights and elegant costumes and with the greatest music in the world that grew out of this cotton country that spawned blues, gospel, jazz, country, rockabilly, and rock 'n' roll. For a time, the show was home to blues legends Ma Rainey and Bessie Smith.

I didn't experience any racial disturbances at the show or, for that matter, any police presence. All I saw was a congenial atmosphere between the races. Perhaps this was because it was an all-black venue and the whites were treated as special guests. This was consistent with Jim Crow culture, as when whites attended the funeral of a favorite servant. Of course, if blacks ever attended a white event and sat wherever they pleased, there would have been a riot.

Once, when I was about twelve, my friends and I noticed some black kids playing baseball north of town in a large field next to Deer Creek. As we walked by, we started throwing the ball around, and the next thing we knew we were actually playing a ball game with the black kids. Feeling some uneasiness but not realizing that it was a major violation of the social code, we played ball with them on several occasions. When our parents found out, the fun came to a screeching halt. I'd never seen my dad as angry as he was on that day. My dad's reaction didn't bother me in the least. I fully accepted the culture. It was the culture of my parents and my grandparents and any authority I knew. I was more concerned that I may have violated the rigid Jim Crow moral code than I was angry or confused about my dad's reaction.

During most summers when I was in high school, I worked at Leroy Percy State Park, located five miles west of Hollandale. It had a wonderful swimming pool and a large lake with piers and boats for fishing. After cutting the grass in the morning, I served as lifeguard when the pool opened in the afternoons. The pool attracted any number of beautiful young white damsels from around the Delta, many of whom I attempted to lure to the lodge to dance. Sometimes I was lucky and danced to a sparkling nickelodeon in that beautiful cypress lodge built during the Depression by the Works Progress Administration (WPA). I danced to love songs by Elvis Presley, Johnny Mathis, and others, but the whole world stopped spinning when Tony Bennett sang "Because of You" or when Teresa Brewer sang "A Tear Fell."

Blacks were not allowed to use the park or, for that matter, any public recreational facilities in the Delta. I once saw a carload of blacks drive into the park. I naturally thought they were lost, since it was unthinkable in the early 1950s that a black person would even imagine enjoying these wonderful facilities. But whether lost or not, their minds were quickly disabused of any such thought by a large white man who stopped them, his gun drawn from its holster. He told them to leave immediately or he would "blow their brains out." As angry as he was, I thought he might just do that very thing.

The blacks left hurriedly in a great cloud of dust, and I never saw any other attempt by a black to visit the park. During those days, it never occurred to me that it may not have been fair that blacks could not use the parks, swimming pools, libraries, or even the picture show, unless they crowded into the peanut gallery upstairs and entered through a separate door. The Jim Crow culture was so strong that it was not really possible for a young person to even recognize it just might be wrong.

I also worked in May's Cash Store, which sold everything from hammers to dresses and thimbles. It was managed by James's grandfather, Audie Turner. Later the store was bought by an Oklahoma-owned chain, C. R. Anthony Company. It was at Anthony's that I first met James. He and his sister, Susan, had moved to Hollandale in 1953 with their mother after their father drowned in a boating accident.

Desegregation Declared Unconstitutional

The 1956 presidential election was a disaster for the Democratic Party. Republican Dwight Eisenhower beat Democrat Adlai Stevenson by a wide margin. The loss spawned a fearsome new coalition that dominated Southern politics for decades. The coalition's cornerstone was the "Southern Manifesto," a document coauthored by Senator James Eastland and signed by ninety-six congressmen that boldly declared the U.S. Supreme Court decrees on integration "unconstitutional." The coalition caused a rift in Mississippi, with some leaders, such as Governor Coleman, remaining loyal to the Democratic Party and others calling for the creation of a new states' rights party. Since the Civil War, the Democratic Party had been the dominant political party in Mississippi.

Early in 1957 Governor Coleman made headlines by saying he thought it was "inevitable" that Mississippi would close its colleges if an African American were admitted by court order. He blamed Mississippi's racial problems on "professional agitators" who were getting the state's uneducated masses all riled up. At times he seemed schizophrenic in his policy statements. One day he was threatening to close the state's schools; the next day he was attacking political rivals such as John Bell Williams, who advocated the same thing. Coleman's vacillations jeopardized the effectiveness of the Sovereignty Commission and ultimately led to its takeover by extremists who didn't possess Coleman's respect for the law; but for the moment, the secret agency struggled to define its mission, making up the rules as it went along.

In its first year of operation, the commission bribed, cajoled, and outsmarted enough newspaper editors and reporters outside the South to strongly influence a significant amount of media coverage. It was what was happening beneath the surface that began to take on increasingly sinister overtones. Quietly, without fanfare or public recognition, the commission's investigative unit—former police chief Hicks and former FBI agent Van Landingham—organized a filing system based on the one used by the FBI.

In 1957 J. Edgar Hoover had ordered his agents to monitor the activities of Martin Luther King Jr. and the Southern Christian Leadership Conference (SCLC). At that time the bureau's top-secret domestic spy program, COINTELPRO, for Counterintelligence Program, had been in operation for little more than a year. The FBI didn't launch a formal investigation of King and the SCLC until 1962, but as early as January 1959, Hoover had ordered agents to break into the SCLC offices in Atlanta. Over the next five years, FBI agents broke into the offices of the civil rights organization at least twenty times, often to install electronic listening devices. When agents illegally obtained information, it was kept in a special filing system. For example, if an FBI agent broke into an individual's home and discovered something of interest, he forwarded the material to FBI headquarters under a code name for the COINTELPRO files. That way the information could be stored without giving any hint of the contents of the files, making it difficult for outside investigators to crack the system.[11]

Much of the Sovereignty Commission's efforts the first year were devoted to recruiting informants, compiling dossiers on African Americans and whites sympathetic to the enforcement of civil rights, and identifying blacks who'd registered to vote so that they could be intimidated and driven away from the polls. That first year, vouchers filed with the state auditor's office indicate that Hicks traveled more than two thousand miles. The vouchers also show that the commission put a priority on recruiting black informants, such as the Reverend H. H. Humes and Percy Green, both of whom agreed to tell interviewers for a television documentary about Mississippi that they believed in segregation. For their endorsements of racial separation, the commission paid Humes $150; Green received $35.

Politically, Mississippi entered a short-lived cooling-off period in 1957, as did the other states in the Federation for Constitutional Government. With no elections to excite the politicians, they found other outlets for their energies. Coleman signed a bill repealing the state's compulsory school attendance laws. In south Mississippi a grand jury called for statewide screening of all school and library books for the purpose of banning any books deemed critical of Mississippi Values.

James L. Dickerson:

Although Alex was nine years my senior, we became friends, at least during working hours at the store, with Alex playing the frequently challenging role of older brother. Together we learned to appreciate black culture, an experience that eluded our contemporaries. Typically, black families came into the store as a group, with mother and father and children all needing back-to school or back-to-work clothes. Most Saturdays, Alex and I fitted and sold clothing to dozens of black families. We learned the names and ages of the children and where the parents worked, and we learned to laugh with people we were forbidden to associate with outside the store.

In the 1950s and early 1960s, black store clerks in Hollandale didn't exist. The one exception was a diminutive black man named B. J. Jones, who did odd jobs at the Anthony's store. He was not allowed to wait on customers, but whenever the men's and women's shoe department became filled with people, he helped the white clerks by taking the customers—and their shoes—to the cash register to be "rung up" as Alex and I continued to fit shoes uninterrupted.

B. J. Jones was never referred to as "Mr." Jones. Instead, he was called "Shorty." Whenever I was in the store, I always referred to him as Shorty. I thought that was his name, because that was what everyone called him. Then one day, when I was around twelve, Jones was hired to build a patio at my house. I watched with great interest, especially impressed that he went to the trouble of raking a broom through the wet concrete so it would leave rough ridges that'd make it less likely that Mother would slip and fall in the rain.

"Shorty, how on earth did you learn to do that?" I asked.

Ignoring the question, he put the business end of the broom down and leaned into it. "Why you call me Shorty?"

Astonished, I replied, "Isn't that your name?"

"My name is B.J. I wish you wouldn't call me Shorty."

I learned that day that when it came to racial issues, things were seldom what they seemed. If a black person felt slighted in any way by a white, he or she seldom spoke up out of fear of reprisals. Of course, to a child, silence seemed like agreement. Jones continued to be called Shorty at the store, though he never asked anyone there to call him anything else. Whenever I called him B.J. in front of the others, he always smiled, an acknowledgment of our secret pact.

By the time that Alex and I went off to college, Anthony's broke new ground by hiring one of the first black salesclerks in the Delta. As you might imagine, even that small gesture was not without difficulty. My grandfather knew thousands of blacks in and around Hollandale, but he had no idea who would be right to become the town's first black salesclerk. To solve that problem, he went to the most prominent black in town, Professor Sanders, the respected principal of the black school. He was called "Professor" because whites couldn't stomach calling him "Mr." He recommended a young black woman, who accepted the job with great trepidation. My grandfather asked her to wait on both white and black customers but advised her to politely walk away if a white customer didn't seem to want her help.

The Commission Gets a New Director

Sovereignty Commission director Ney Gore resigned in 1957, leaving the agency adrift for several months until Representative Maurice Malone of George County agreed to serve as director. Within a week after Malone's appointment, commission investigator Zack Van Landingham met with Attorney General Joe Patterson and Governor Coleman to update them on the commission activities. Van Landingham explained the FBI-style filing system to them and expressed a need for a permanent and a temporary stenographer to help with the filing system. Two days later Van Landingham, who was eager to staff the commission with as many FBI personnel as possible, interviewed two stenographers, both former FBI employees, one of whom had worked in the New York office, after which he wrote: "I feel we would be fortunate in securing the services of either [woman]. Both of these ladies are not only competent stenographers but are well versed in the filing system which I am endeavoring to place in operation."

For the remainder of the year, the commission focused on identifying black preachers who were calling for school integration. Following a tip from an informant, Van Landingham traveled to Lucedale to investigate a man alleged to be an activist. Unable to find out much about the man, he met with the county sheriff, who promised to look into the matter and report back to the commission.

At the monthly meetings held in mid-October and mid-November, the investigations were discussed, but care was taken not to mention specifics in the board's minutes. In keeping with the system established by the FBI, reports were written that detailed the subjects of investigations, but no incriminating record was kept of the retaliatory actions that followed the investigations. Occasionally memos referenced favorable conclusions to investigations without spelling out specifics. In the case of the Lucedale preacher, Director Malone was told by the sheriff in February 1959 that he thought the man had "stopped preaching along this line." The memo is a good indication of how the commission outsourced intimidation to others—especially county sheriffs, highway patrolmen, and other law enforcement officers— putting only enough information into the files to keep a record of those targeted. You'd have to grow up in Mississippi to understand the meaning of the phrase "I'll talk to the sheriff about it—he'll take care of everything."

1959: The Commission Shadows the NAACP

The commission began the New Year by focusing on NAACP voter registration efforts. In April one of the agency's favorite black informants, a Cleveland educator, attended a Jackson NAACP meeting and provided the agency with a detailed report on what had happened at the gathering, along with the names of those in attendance.[12] He also notified the agency that NAACP executive secretary Roy Wilkins was scheduled to speak in Jackson on May 17. On that day Van Landingham and Attorney General Patterson drove to the Masonic Lodge where Wilkins was scheduled to speak.[13] When they arrived, they saw two city policemen directing traffic in front of the building. They flagged down one of the policemen and asked him to take down all the license tag numbers of the cars that stopped at the lodge. As they drove away, the chief of detectives ran after them until they stopped so he could talk to them. He seemed agitated.

"You know what some damn fools have done? They've gone and gotten out warrants for Roy Wilkins and Medgar Evers [head of the NAACP office in Mississippi]."

The chief asked Van Landingham and the state attorney general to follow him to police headquarters so that they could talk about the "damn fools" in the privacy of his office. It is doubtful that he was sympathetic to the NAACP, but as a law enforcement official he wanted to avoid racial violence if possible. Once they arrived at headquarters, he explained that a member of the Jackson Citizens' Council had sworn out the warrant calling for Wilkins's arrest. He identified Bill Simmons, who headed up the Citizens' Council, as one of the people behind the scheme. The chief was angry because he had thought he'd reached an agreement with a local judge and the county district attorney to withdraw the warrant, but since then the judge and district attorney had caved in to the Citizens' Council and proceeded as planned with the warrant.

Attorney General Patterson telephoned one of the leaders of the council, Dick King, and told him that it would be a grave mistake for the warrant to be served, because of the negative national publicity it would generate. King agreed with Patterson and said he would contact the others in an effort to stop the warrant. While the negotiations were taking place, Van Landingham drove back to the lodge and asked the deputy sheriff with the warrant to hold off serving it until after a definite decision was made. The deputy, who worked for the county sheriff and not the commission, said he couldn't do that. His orders were to serve the warrant as soon as Wilkins finished speaking. He intended to do that unless the county attorney ordered him not to proceed.

Van Landingham persuaded the deputy to accompany him to a telephone so that he could call the county district attorney. The deputy reluctantly went with him; however, calls to the county district attorney's office and home failed to locate him. Van Landingham pleaded for more time. The deputy refused, explaining that he had a job to do. Unsure what to do next, Van Landingham left the lodge and went to the courthouse, where members of the Citizens' Council were gathered, along with news reporters and photographers, all waiting for the arrival of Wilkins and Evers, presumably in handcuffs. He called one of the council members aside and tried to reason with him, but the man said he was only following orders and didn't have the authority to withdraw the warrant. The only person who could stop the warrants from being served was Simmons.

As this flurry of activity took place, Wilkins delivered his speech, totally oblivious to what was transpiring. Not knowing what else to do, Attorney General Patterson telephoned Governor Coleman, who was out of town to deliver a high school graduation address. Once the situation was explained to him, Coleman immediately left the graduation ceremony and hurried back to Jackson.

Before Wilkins finished his speech, a lengthy one as it turned out, Simmons agreed to withdraw the warrants, owing, no doubt, to the intervention of the governor. Wilkins left town that day oblivious to the swirling maelstrom that had accompanied his visit and threatened his personal freedom.

4

The Lynching That
Shocked the World

After spending the evening with relatives in Bogalusa, Louisiana, a young, white married couple—Jimmy Walters was twenty-two, and June was twenty-one—got into their aging 1949 Dodge and drove back to Mississippi, passing through Poplarville on their way back to their home in Petal. With them was their four-year-old daughter, Debbie Carol, a pretty little girl with bangs. It was a lonely, desolate drive, even during daylight hours. The pine forests squeezed up close to the highway, shutting out sunlight with a thick canopy of pine needles. But at close to midnight, when there were few cars out on the roadway and the cold February winds peppered sleet and rain mist against the windshield, it was a downright spooky drive, the sort of pulse-quickening experience you'd expect in a horror movie.

They were about seven miles outside of Lumberton, Mississippi, when the Dodge engine sputtered dead, a loud clank beneath the hood the only indication of the seriousness of the problem.[1] Since they were at the top of a hill overlooking Little Black Creek, Jimmy allowed the car to coast to the bottom of the hill. Once it came to a complete stop, he tried again and again to restart the engine. He looked under the hood and saw that the engine had locked up because of a thrown bearing. It was February 23, 1959, a good forty years before the availability of cell phones. Jimmy had two choices: he could stay with the car and wait for a passerby, or he could walk to Lumberton to get help. He couldn't see taking June and Debbie Carol out on the road with him, especially with June being two months pregnant, so he decided to leave them in the car while he went for help. He told June to roll up the windows and lock the doors and not open them for anyone she didn't know. With luck, he'd be back in an hour.

Jimmy had been gone only fifteen minutes when a Chevy pulled up alongside the stranded Dodge. There were five African Americans in the car. One of the men got out and shined a flashlight on the front and rear tires. Then he peered into the window on the driver's side and shone the flashlight inside, illuminating June, with Debbie stretched out on the seat with her head in her mother' lap. June trembled. She couldn't tell whether the man with the flashlight was white or black. She just hoped he wouldn't hurt them.

Suddenly, the flashlight went dark. Hurried footsteps. A car door slammed. The Chevy drove away, headed in the same direction that Jimmy had set out in for help. An hour and a half later, June was wondering what'd happened to Jimmy—hadn't he said he'd be back in about an hour?—when a car pulled up behind their Dodge. A black man got out and approached the driver's window. With his face pressed close to the window, he asked June if she needed help. June said she didn't. Thank you anyway. She expected her husband to return any minute. After a moment of silence, the man pressed a pistol against the glass so that she could see it. He told her to unlock the door. When she refused, he struck the glass vent several times with the pistol, smashing the glass. June screamed and covered Debbie's eyes with her hands to protect her from the flying glass. Debbie started crying, her voice small and whiney. As Debbie cried and June screamed, the man's rain-soaked arm snaked through the vent and reached down and unlocked the door.

June warned him that her husband would return any minute.

"You mean that white son of a bitch that's walkin' up the street?"[2] The man laughed and told her that he'd just escaped from prison and already had killed five people (this was never verified and was probably a scare tactic). Two more wouldn't make any difference. He reached into the car and pulled her scarf from her neck and looped it around her neck, making a noose. June pleaded with him not to hurt Debbie.

"You white trash bitch, I'm going to fuck you!"

June tried to pull away from him, she later explained to a journalist. He told her that if she gave him any trouble, he'd kill her and the little girl. Then he grabbed June's legs and dragged her from the car, not difficult since she was slender, weighing only one hundred pounds. When Debbie cried, he struck the child across the forehead with the pistol to shut her up. After that he walked them both back to his car and ordered them inside. He made June sit in the middle. As he drove off, he put his arm around her neck and pulled her over close to him.

He drove about one mile, then turned onto a logging road. He stopped the car and turned out the lights. He got out and told Debbie to climb out over her mother. Once she was out of the car, he took her hand and led her around to the rear of the car and left her there, warning her not to move. Then he walked back to the open door and told June to lie down on the front seat. She protested that she was pregnant. I've heard that before, he said. June did as she was told. Pull up your dress. She did, after which he ripped her panties off and forced his hand between her legs. Then he lowered himself onto her and raped her. When he was done, he got up and told her to take Debbie and start walking. If you look back, he warned, I'll kill both of you.

As mother and daughter started walking, it began to rain again. Mud splattered onto them from the dirt road. Their clothes were soaked. Once they reached the highway, they started walking north toward Lumberton, June dazed from her assault. Without realizing it, they wandered into the middle of the highway and were nearly hit by an eighteen-wheeler that braked and skidded over to the side of the road. The driver threw open the door and gazed down at the two of them, seeing right away that something was very wrong. June looked bewildered, and Debbie had a bleeding gash on her forehead.

"I've been raped by a nigger. Please help me to get to Lumberton to my husband."

The driver helped them into the truck. Within minutes they were in Lumberton, where they found Jimmy outside an all-night truck stop, talking to someone at a pay phone. The driver stopped the truck and helped them down out of the cab. Debbie ran screaming and crying over to her father, with June right behind her, collapsing in Jimmy's arms as Debbie explained that her mother had been attacked.

As Jimmy comforted June, the truck driver called the highway patrol. Lamar County sheriff C. H. Hickman arrived within minutes and rushed June to the hospital so she could be examined and given an antibiotic to combat any venereal disease that might be present. While she was at the hospital, nearly two dozen deputies and state troopers arrived to obtain a description of the assailant. June provided them with a detailed description of the man—African American, about five feet ten inches tall, around 160 pounds, around forty years of age—and a description of his car—broken door on the passenger side, torn seat, broken dome light.

Within twelve hours, Lumberton city marshal Hammond Slade received a tip that twenty-three-year-old U.S. Army veteran Mack Charles Parker was the man who'd raped June Walters. He and his deputies dragged Parker out of his mother's house and drove him to the jail, where he was charged with what they already had enough evidence to charge him with, drunken driving and possession of an expired driver's permit. Then they arranged a lineup and asked June to come to the jail to identify her assailant. With Jimmy at her side, June listened through a small window as five black men repeated the phrase "You white trash bitch, I'm going to fuck you!"

June didn't react until Parker spoke. When she heard him say the words, she collapsed, saying, "That's him."

Authorities then asked June to look at Parker.

"He looks like the one." When pressed, she refused to make a positive identification, explaining that it was a dark, moonless night. "I believe he's the one, but I can't be positive, because I was scared to death and there wasn't much light."

Parker was much younger and much smaller than the man she'd described to authorities after the rape. Authorities then showed her Parker's car. Again, she wasn't certain, though she agreed that it looked like the car she'd described.

Based on June's identification of his voice, Slade charged Parker with rape and kidnapping and transferred him that same day to the Hinds County jail in Jackson. Parker swore that he was innocent. He was subjected to polygraph tests at the jail and held for nearly two months before being transported to Poplarville, the county seat of Pearl River County, where the crime had been committed.

Parker's mother went to every white lawyer in Lumberton and the surrounding towns, but all refused to take her son's case.[3] Desperate to find him a lawyer, she approached a well-known black civil rights lawyer in Vicksburg, R. Jess Brown, who reluctantly took the case. Brown asked for a preliminary hearing but then withdrew his request when the county attorney told him it might be dangerous to transport Parker to Poplarville to attend the hearing. Not until an all-white grand jury indicted Parker on April 13 on charges of rape and two counts of kidnapping was the accused transported by highway patrolmen to the Pearl River County Jail.

When Parker was brought before Circuit Court Judge Sebe Dale on April 17, he pled not guilty on all counts. Brown made a number of motions. One that especially agitated courtroom onlookers was a motion that Dale should dismiss the charges against Parker because the grand jury had excluded blacks. He also asked for a change of venue. Dale rejected both motions and set a trial date of April 27. Brown should not have been surprised by Dale's hard line toward the defendant. An early supporter of the Sovereignty Commission, Dale was a member of the Citizens' Council. When it came to racial segregation—and the place of blacks in Mississippi society—no one had to guess his position on the issue.

Public reaction in Poplarville and the surrounding towns was intensely hostile to Parker. To their way of thinking, the rape threatened the social fabric of the community. It was not uncommon for white men to have sexual relations with black women, but it was strictly forbidden for white women to have relations with black men. White women were put on a pedestal by white males, but the prevailing sentiment was that if a white female had relations with a black male, she was off-limits to white males, even to her husband—rape or no rape, she was a "spoiled" woman and thus no longer worthy of pedestal status. For many whites the rape itself was bad enough, but the prospect of a black lawyer cross-examining June Walters on the witness stand about the sexual details of the rape was more than they could handle.

When the sheriff received an anonymous telephone call saying that people in nearby Hattiesburg were talking about making trouble in Poplarville, he passed the information along to Judge Dale and suggested that Governor Coleman be asked to send the national guard to keep order. Dale didn't think that was necessary, either because he didn't believe townspeople were capable of lynch law or because he didn't want the national guard to get in their way.

Lynch Mob Invades Poplarville Courthouse

Parker had been at the jail in Poplarville for only twelve days when a mob of nine or ten gun-packing and club-toting hooded men burst into the jail around midnight on April 25 and dragged him from the third-floor cell block.[4] "Help! Don't let them take me!" Parker cried out as four men, a man on each arm and leg, lifted him into the air and carried him to the stairway. The men all wore masks, gloves, and hats.

"Please don't kill me!" Parker pleaded.[5]

At the time, the jail was unattended by a jailer, so there was no one in the building to protect Parker from the mob. Several times, Parker pulled one of his arms free and grabbed the rail on the stairway, and each time his hand was kicked loose by one of the men. When they reached the outside door, Parker begged the men to turn him loose so that he could walk on his own. "Hell, no, you won't walk!" barked one of the men, who then whacked him across the head with a nightstick.

By the time they reached the street, Parker was bloodied about the face where he'd been beaten and his arms were scratched and bruised. He was struck on the head one last time and then tossed into the backseat of a car parked on the south side of the courthouse. Terrified, Parker screamed for help the entire time, his voice echoing up and down the streets. No one in the small town went to his aid. Everyone remained behind closed doors, windows darkened by pulled blinds and curtains.

Parker was taken in a procession of five cars to a bridge over the muddy, churning Pearl River. There he was shot twice in the chest with a .38-caliber pistol.[6] His body was weighted down with chains and then tossed over the railing into the river. The men stood on the bridge and watched as the body sank out of sight; then they returned to their cars and drove off into the night.

Within hours of the lynching, the highway patrol, Governor Coleman, the FBI, and the White House were notified. The next day, news reporters from across the nation descended on Poplarville.

Not until May 4 was Parker's body found, in a pile of driftwood on the Mississippi side of the Pearl River, about two and a half miles south of State Highway 26. The body was facing upstream, and only the right arm, shoulder, and head protruded from the driftwood. Sheriff's deputies loaded Parker's remains into a boat and transported them about a half mile to Richardson's Landing, where the corpse was unloaded so that it could be examined. The face on the body was so distorted that identification was impossible. Maggots covered the back and arms of the corpse. Not until later could Parker's identity be established through fingerprints. An autopsy disclosed that death occurred from a penetrating wound in the left auricle of the heart, an indication that the second shot had missed its mark.

Governor Coleman wasted no time requesting an FBI investigation. In a telegram to the governor, President Eisenhower said, "It is my earnest hope that there will be swift apprehension of the guilty persons. These agents will, of course, continue to provide full facilities to help in any way in this manner." Almost overnight Poplarville was flooded with more than forty FBI agents, who set up an office to conduct their investigation.

Soon Governor Coleman came under intense criticism for requesting help from the FBI.[7] Among his critics was state auditor Boyd Golding, who wrote a letter to the *Clarion-Ledger* challenging him to remove the federal agents: "I think the chief reason that the FBI is staying in Poplarville at so much expense to the taxpayers is that they are trying to make an example of Mississippi because we have refused to swallow integration." Defending Coleman and the FBI was Sovereignty Commission investigator Zack Van Landingham, a retired FBI agent: "Criticism of the FBI being brought into the Poplarville case is a political issue in an election year. An innocent person will have no trouble in establishing his innocence, if he cooperates with the agents."[8]

To everyone's surprise the FBI agents were soon recalled from Poplarville, and the U.S. Justice Department announced that it was withdrawing from the case, since the lynch mob had violated no federal laws. The case was turned over to state authorities. By that time the FBI had identified all the members of the lynch mob and turned the names over to Governor Coleman, who sat on the report for several months, taking no action.

Not until September did the governor provide the information to Pearl County prosecutor Bill Stewart and to District Attorney Vernon Broome, who agreed to present the case to a grand jury, though he decided against using the information compiled by the FBI. When Broome presented the case on November 2, 1959, he told jury members that they could call FBI agents in to testify if they wanted to, that was their right, and they could read the report if they wanted to. No one did. The next day the grand jury handed down the seventeen other indictments requested by Broome, but no one was indicted for Parker's lynching. In effect, the killers got away with murder.

Outraged, the Justice Department announced within a couple of days that it planned to take the case to a federal grand jury. Asked by reporters what federal laws had been broken, a Justice Department spokesman said the government would seek indictments on charges that Parker's killers violated a civil rights law prohibiting conspiracies to deprive people of their legal rights.

In December federal district judge Sidney Mize announced that he would empanel a federal grand jury on January 4, 1960, in Biloxi's new federal building. The grand jury that Mize selected included only one black man. Among the witnesses called was June Walters, who told the jurors the details of what'd happened the night of the rape. She confided that she was not absolutely certain Parker had been the man who'd raped her. She also said that he looked too young and had a voice that was higher than the rapist's voice. The jurors seemed especially interested in asking her about the details of the rape. One juror asked, "You mean you let that nigger fuck you?"[9]

June answered that she had no choice. Similar hostile questions sent her fleeing from the jury room in tears. When Jimmy was called to the stand, one juror asked, "You mean to tell me that after that nigger fucked your wife you still lived with her?" Jimmy avoided the question by saying that his family was under a lot of pressure and they had since moved to Bogalusa. To no one's surprise, after listening to thirty-two witnesses, the jury foreman returned no indictments to Judge Mize, explaining, "We were unable to arrive at any true bill." Judge Mize thanked the jurors for conducting themselves "fairly" and sent them home. There would be no justice for Mack Charles Parker.

Four years after the lynching, Judge Sebe Dale was speaking to a civics club in Connecticut on behalf of the Sovereignty Commission when someone in the audience asked him if he thought Parker's killers would ever be brought to justice.

Without thinking, the judge responded that there would be no need for that, since three of the killers had already died.

5

The Loose Ends
of Government

The 1959 gubernatorial campaign was unusually vicious, even by Mississippi standards. All three candidates—Lieutenant Governor Carroll Gartin, who had Coleman's support; District Attorney Charles Sullivan; and Jackson attorney Ross Barnett—had waged racist campaigns that focused on preserving segregation, though Sullivan, a resident of the majority-black Delta, was the least rabid of the three. There was no other major issue in the campaign, just a vague sense of madness. From the outset it was clear that the candidate who could spew the most venom and make the most promises about preserving Mississippi Values would win the election.

Barnett accused the current governor, J. P. Coleman, of adopting a defeatist attitude in his efforts to stop integration. He pledged that if he was elected governor, he would use the power of the office to stop anyone who got in his way. With his racially charged "Roll with Ross" campaign slogan, he won the contest hands down.

Shortly after the election Barnett turned up the heat by criticizing a federal government decision to reopen the Poplarville lynching case.[1] He told reporters that the federal government had no jurisdiction in the case and should allow local officials to conduct the investigation. The lynching already had been on everyone's mind all year: After one of the suspects was questioned by the FBI, he was hospitalized for what his doctor called a "nervous breakdown." A second suspect was sent to the hospital for treatment of a cerebral hemorrhage after FBI agents spent several hours grilling him on his whereabouts the day of the lynching. The local news media pumped the story and shifted the focus from the crime itself to the way the federal government was "abusing" the good citizens of Mississippi.

The rape itself was quickly forgotten once word got out that the victim, June Walters, was a native of New York—and thus not worthy of compassion.

Auditor Boyd Golding demanded that Coleman run the FBI out of Mississippi. Wrote Golding in a letter to Coleman: "I never thought I would live to witness the invitation of outsiders to come to the sovereign state of Mississippi to harass, browbeat, and torture people to the brink of death." Later, Golding told reporters that the FBI used "iron curtain tactics" to obtain information about the lynching.[2]

Coleman said that he thought race relations in Mississippi had reached a new low. Even though the legislature was set to convene in January under the leadership of governor-elect Ross Barnett, Coleman conferred with Representative Hilton Waits of Leland and called a special session of the legislature for that December to clean up what he perceived to be "loose ends" of government. Waits entered the picture because Speaker of the House Walter Sillers had been hospitalized while on a U.S. State Department mission to Germany and had designated Waits, a longtime friend and political ally, speaker pro tem of the House for the special session.[3]

James L. Dickerson:

I knew Hilton Waits quite well. His grandfather was my great-grandfather: Steve Turner, one of the authors of the Mississippi Constitution of 1890. As we say in the South, Uncle Hilton was family. I attended the special session because Hilton took me with him to serve as a page in the House of Representatives. It was an incredible experience for a fourteen-year-old. I had enjoyed Hilton's company at family gatherings for as long as I could remember, but I'd never seen him in a work environment. Hilton had served in the legislature since 1931 and had received national attention as the author of the sales tax, thus making Mississippi the first state to have that revenue-gathering option. He first outlined the tax in his master's thesis.

That August he was defeated for reelection by DeLoach Cope, a gentleman farmer from near Hollandale who'd served as a fighter pilot during World War II. For Uncle Hilton the special session marked the end of twenty-eight years of public service. Officially, at least. When the new legislature convened, the members quickly realized that none of them actually knew how to write legislation, so they invited Uncle Hilton to come back as a consultant. He was there all session, drafting almost every bill voted on.

What I liked most about serving as a page was not running through the House chamber passing out copies of legislation or delivering messages from one lawmaker to another, but rather exploring the capitol building in my off-hours. One day I ventured over to the Senate chamber while it was in recess. There were only three people in the chamber—Lieutenant Governor Carroll Gartin, who'd lost the governor's race; a man I didn't recognize; and Evelyn Gandy, a woman I did recognize since she'd just been elected state treasurer, the first woman in Mississippi history to be elected to a statewide office. I watched them for a while and then approached them and introduced myself. To their surprise, I asked for their autographs. Gartin signed his with a flourish. One of them, I'm not sure who, made a big deal out of the fact that I was the first person to ever ask for an autograph.

The following day I decided to ask Governor Coleman to sign a piece of paper asking my principal to excuse me from school so that I could serve as a page. I didn't need a written excuse—my principal already had given me permission to leave school to serve—but I thought it would be a cool thing to do, something I could use to win back the heart of my ex-girlfriend, a former state baton-twirling champion.

Outside the governor's office, I paced the corridor as well-dressed men in dark suits came and went through the door, sometimes with smiles on their faces, other times frowning. I wondered what was on the other side. If I opened the door, would I see the governor standing behind a podium, his hand reaching out to greet visitors? Or would the door open into a waiting room, like I was used to seeing at the doctor's office? I waited until the last man I'd watched enter the office finally exited and walked away, whistling.

The first thing I saw when I opened the door was a well-dressed woman with a ready smile, the kind of woman that Mother often had over for coffee. She asked if she could help me. I told her about my mission to meet the governor. She smiled the way older women always do right before they say no to something you've asked them to do, and she politely told me that was out of the question. She made it clear that the governor didn't meet with children.

Just outside the governor's office, I ran into Uncle Hilton, who asked what I was doing. When I told him my plan, he smiled and said, "Come with me."

I followed him back into the governor's office, with Uncle Hilton speaking to the secretary, who gave me a curious look and said, "Good morning, Mr. Waits."

"Is the governor in?" he asked, not even slowing down for an answer as he kept walking toward the door.

"Yes, sir," she said. "Just go right in."

But by the time she said it, we were already inside his office, where I encountered the governor, a man leaning back in his chair with his feet on his desk and his trousers a good six inches from the top of his socks. I noticed that he wore those thin, nylon socks preferred by men of a certain age. I knew all about socks because I sold a lot of them in my grandfather's store.

The governor gave me one of those "what in the hell are you doing in my office" looks, but Uncle Hilton ignored that and introduced me to the governor, prompting him to lean forward to shake my hand, his chair squeaking like a rusty door hinge.

Said Uncle Hilton, "The boy's got something he wants to ask you."

"Sure," said the governor.

I told him about my idea for a written excuse and held the crumpled paper out for him to inspect. He didn't. Instead, he looked at Uncle Hilton and said, "I don't have the legal authority to excuse him from school."

"He's a page. The principal already has excused him. He just wants it as a souvenir."

The governor shook his head. "Can't do it! That's a legislative matter."

"He's just a kid, Governor."

"Sorry. I just don't have the authority."

Uncle Hilton's face reddened, all the more noticeable since he was bald. I put the crumpled paper back into my pocket and backed away from the governor's desk, humiliated in my defeat. Uncle Hilton and the governor talked about something I didn't understand and then we left. Once we left the outer office, Uncle Hilton asked for my crumpled paper. I handed it to him and watched with pride as he signed my excuse. He said something derogatory about the governor—I don't remember exactly what—but he didn't curse him, since he didn't do that in front of children. I could tell that he was awfully put out by the governor.

Governor Coleman was in a foul mood all through the legislative session. With only a few weeks left in office (state law then prohibited governors from running for a second consecutive term), he was a lame-duck administrator, severely limited in what he could accomplish. Whatever it was that Coleman envisioned for the legislature that session, the final product was certainly less than anticipated. For the longest time no one could figure out why the session was held in the first place. The two most memorable actions taken by the lawmakers dealt with the Civil War and Miss America.

A bill was passed memorializing Walter Williams, who, as a former member of Quantrill's Raiders, had been the last surviving soldier of the Civil War. He'd died on December 19, 1959, in a Houston, Texas, hospital. Gone was America's last living link to the bloodiest war in the nation's history. The lawmakers observed a moment of silence for the last soldier, then, with a war whoop that could be heard all the way down the street, turned their attention to more important business—a date with Miss America.

A couple of months before the start of that session, Lynda Lee Mead had become Mississippi's second Miss America in as many years. The lawmakers were so in awe of her that they voted to invite her to address a joint session of the legislature. The way the lawmakers saw it, the judges for the Miss America contest had not only honored a native of Mississippi but also endorsed Mississippi Values, which is to say the lawmakers took it as a vote for segregation.

Thus with a tip of the hat to veterans of the Civil War—and a wink to a pretty woman whose victory seemed to represent all the values for which they fought—the legislature closed the door on the administration of Governor J. P. Coleman.

Mississippi's New Governor

January 10, 1960: Red-faced and bleary-eyed, Ross Barnett rushed down the stairway of the capitol on his way to the reviewing platform, where he was scheduled to be sworn in as Mississippi's fifty-second governor. In his haste he almost knocked over a startled teenager who had found himself in the governor-elect's path. Ross Barnett wasn't the kind of man to stand aside for anyone, not even a child.

In his inaugural speech, delivered in subfreezing weather, Barnett pledged to maintain segregation at all costs, and he castigated the "radical left-wing elements" of the national Democratic Party. He promised to do something about them as well. With his battle plan in place, he proceeded to launch a vicious attack against blacks and white liberals, most of whom he identified as Yankees.

James L. Dickerson:

I was the teen Ross Barnett forced against the wall on his way to the inauguration. With him were two beefy-looking men I assumed were his bodyguards. As they rushed past, I thought I detected the sweet scent of Old Spice.

For the life of me, I don't know why I was at Barnett's inauguration. Nor do I understand how I ended up on the platform. I remember it being a platform, though it may have simply been the capitol steps. A month or so after the event, I received a Mississippi magazine in the mail—I think it was the one published by the Game and Fish Commission—and there I was, big as life on the cover, standing in the crowd a few feet from the soon-to-be-sworn-in governor. In those days, I had a knack for being where I didn't belong, unlike today when I'm seldom where I belong.

I despised everything Ross Barnett stood for. I can't explain why, except to suggest that it was based on personal experience. By that age I'd never heard the word racist. It simply wasn't part of the vocabulary used by anyone

I knew. To me, Barnett was someone who advocated hurting people, and I disliked that about him. I was sympathetic to black concerns, not because I thought segregation was unconstitutional—that aspect of the issue was never mentioned in my school or church—but rather because I felt that hurting people of color was the wrong thing to do.

The previous summer, several months before I served as a page, I looked out my bedroom window one day and saw a black youth running out of the garage with my prized, big-wheel Yazoo lawn mower. Instinctively, I grabbed a pistol and a handful of ammo, not an unusual thing for a boy to do in the Delta in the 1950s, and chased after the youth, loading the pistol as I ran, scattering ammo along the way.

I chased after him, running down a nearby alley, my heart pounding. Once he saw the pistol, the black youth left the lawn mower behind and fled across the tracks. Later I told my mother about the incident, and she insisted that I report it to the police.

A week or so after the attempted theft, the police chief flagged me down on the sidewalk and asked me to accompany him to the jail to identify the supposed thief. Once we arrived at the jail, the police chief disappeared into the back as I waited in the outer office. When he emerged, it was with a sixteen-year-old boy. His face was swollen, where he'd been beaten, and his lip was split, still bleeding. Standing hunched over, his shoulders bowed, his spirit broken, he looked absolutely terrified. He wasn't much over five feet tall, but he had a stocky build. The police chief said, "This the boy?"

I looked at the black youth for a moment, startled by the depth of fear I saw in his eyes. I'd told the police chief that the person who tried to steal the lawn mower was tall and lanky, probably in his early twenties. I said, "No, sir—that's not the one."

"Son, he is the one. He's confessed."

"I don't care. He's not the one."

The police chief leaned over into my face, his threatening voice scaled down to a whisper. "You have to say this is the one. You don't understand. He's admitted stealing it. If he didn't steal your lawn mower, he stole a lawn mower from somebody else."

"No, sir. He's not the one."

"Shit," said the police chief, waving his hand. "Get on outta here."

I didn't get a ride home from the jail that day—I walked. But I left with a new understanding of how law and order worked in Mississippi.

Ross Hits the Ground Rolling

The new governor's first priority was to beef up the Sovereignty Commission. For the past eighteen months or so, it had foundered on indecision as Coleman limited its activities to spying and the manufacture of dossiers on blacks and liberal whites.

During his first week in office, Barnett met with leaders of the Citizens' Council, which by that time claimed a statewide membership of more than eighty thousand. He also traveled to Columbia, South Carolina, to attend a banquet for the Association of Citizens' Councils of South Carolina. Upon his return, he decided to allow the Sovereignty Commission to make sizable donations to the Jackson Citizens' Council.

Since the fiscal year ran from July 1 to June 30, Barnett waited until June 1960 to reorganize the commission.[4] To replace Representative Maurice Malone, he chose Albert Jones, a former Hinds County sheriff. For public relations director, he selected the man who had handled his publicity during the election campaign, Erle Johnston. He was well suited for the job. As publisher of the weekly *Scott County Times* in Forest, Mississippi, Johnston was on a first-name basis with most of the state's newspaper editors and publishers. Also hired were five investigators—Virgil Downing, Hugh Boren, Andrew Hopkins, Tom Scarbrough, and Robert Thomas—six secretaries, and a librarian.

Attending the first meeting, in addition to Governor Barnett, were Lieutenant Governor Paul B. Johnson, Attorney General Joe Patterson, Speaker of the House Walter Sillers, and several senators and representatives appointed to serve as commissioners. One of Barnett's first directives to the commission was for it to approve a request from William J. Simmons of the Citizens' Council for a twenty thousand dollar grant and a monthly payment of five thousand dollars to help support council activities. At the request of Senator James O. Eastland, the governor asked the commission to send prominent Mississippians out on the road to give speeches in support of segregation.

In July, Governor Barnett, leading a delegation largely made up of Citizens' Council members, went to Los Angeles to attend the Democratic National Convention. All summer, Senators Hubert Humphrey, Lyndon Johnson, and John F. Kennedy had campaigned for delegates, each man saying that only he could beat Republican Richard Nixon in the fall election. Barnett gave an impassioned states' rights speech at the convention that was carried on national television. He made it clear that Mississippi opposed the civil rights platform adopted by the delegates and would not support a candidate who endorsed it. Barnett was not surprised that Kennedy won the nomination, but like everyone else, he was surprised that Kennedy picked Johnson to be his vice president. Barnett returned to Jackson and complained about how "nauseating" the convention had made him feel. Griping that everyone was out "to get the Negro vote," he announced that he intended to support an unpledged electors' slate, which meant he was serving notice that he would not vote for the Democratic candidate.

Barnett's decision put Senator Eastland in a bind. If he didn't support the Democratic ticket, Eastland, once labeled the "nation's most dangerous demagogue" by *Time* magazine, knew he would be stripped of his chairmanship of the Senate Judiciary Committee, a position that the *New York Times* pointed out had enabled the senator to bottle up more than one hundred civil rights bills. At a televised press conference, Eastland announced that he would support the Kennedy-Johnson ticket but not the party platform, which he said was "out of step" with the American people.

Eastland hated everything that Kennedy stood for, but if the Democrat lost, Eastland would lose his power in the Senate. For that reason he wanted Kennedy to win, though he could admit that to only a handful of people. One of those he confided in was Armis Hawkins, a progressive Democrat who had lost the lieutenant governor's race to Paul B. Johnson the previous year.[5] Eastland asked him to run the

Democratic Party's presidential campaign for Kennedy, a request most Mississippians would have run away from, not wishing to go up against Barnett. Not Hawkins. He attacked Barnett's unpledged electors plan, and he told voters that Kennedy's opponent, Richard Nixon, "cares no more about Mississippi than he does for a swamp rat." Hawkins persuaded former president Harry Truman to deliver a speech at the Tupelo fairgrounds in support of Kennedy, an event that attracted ten thousand enthusiastic supporters.

When the ballots were counted on November 8, 1960, Mississippians, for the first time in history, went with an unpledged slate, as Governor Barnett had requested. But Hawkins came close to delivering the state to Kennedy, falling less than eight thousand votes short. Kennedy came in second with 108,362 votes; Nixon was third with 73,561 votes. Since it was a "winner take all" system, unpledged electors would be allowed to cast all eight of Mississippi's electoral votes.

Election reports were so close that evening that television commentators were speculating there was a possibility that Mississippi's eight unpledged votes could decide the next president. That scenario was avoided only when Illinois's twenty-seven votes went to Kennedy and gave him the victory.

Ross Barnett was horrified at the thought of having John Kennedy as the next president, but he took comfort in the fact that his unpledged electors scheme almost worked. Were it not for the miracle that occurred in the ballot boxes in Chicago, Barnett would have been in a position to handpick the next president of the United States.

Invasion of the Freedom Riders

By May 1961 busloads of civil rights activists calling themselves "Freedom Riders" poured into Mississippi from points outside the South with the goal of pressuring the federal government into enforcing Supreme Court rulings that affirmed the unconstitutionality of state laws requiring segregated seating on interstate buses.

Governor Barnett instructed the highway patrol to escort the Freedom Riders "nonstop" across the state, and Attorney General Joe Patterson told reporters the Freedom Riders would be arrested and jailed if they violated state segregation laws. Senator Eastland rushed to the floor of the Senate and proclaimed the Freedom Ride project "part of the Communist movement."

When the first Freedom Ride buses arrived in Mississippi, a journey organized by the Council of Federated Organizations (COFO), they were escorted to Jackson by nine highway patrol and national guard vehicles. Hundreds of national guard troops were stationed along the route. Once they arrived at the Jackson bus station, the Freedom Riders, both white and black, entered waiting rooms labeled WHITES ONLY and were arrested and taken off to jail. That scenario continued into the summer, with each busload of Freedom Riders attracting more and more attention from the national media. Among those arrested was the Reverend Robert Pierson, the son-in-law of New York governor Nelson Rockefeller. Another activist was Harold Ickes, whose father served as interior secretary during the Roosevelt administration. Ickes later found fame as deputy White House chief of staff in President Bill Clinton's administration. Pierson and Ickes were both targeted for dossiers by the Sovereignty Commission.

A page-one story in the *Jackson Daily News*, with a headline screaming, SOVIETS PLANNED "FREEDOM RIDES," reported that Mississippi authorities had learned that the Freedom Rides had been planned in Havana, Cuba, the previous winter by Soviet officials. Reported the newspaper: "The Highway Patrol said today it had learned that at least two 'students' who attended the Communist planning workshop have been convicted as 'freedom riders.'" The story was false and typical of the propaganda that the Sovereignty Commission planted in Mississippi newspapers.

Unknown to COFO, the commission had a spy in COFO's Jackson office (identified only as Operator 79) who provided the agency with copies of the applications submitted by the young people who'd volunteered to make the "Freedom Rides" to Mississippi.[6] The applications, which sometimes included photographs, provided the commission with a wealth of information.

One of the most celebrated Freedom Riders was a light-skinned, green-eyed African American woman from Chicago named Diane Nash. In the summer of 1961, while in Jackson teaching black children about nonviolent protest as preparation for their participation in Freedom Rides, she was arrested and charged with contributing to the delinquency of minors. It was a totally bogus charge, evidence of how police in Mississippi could arrest someone on just about any charge imaginable and the courts would back them up.

Nash was convicted and sentenced to two years in the state penitentiary at Parchman. She appealed the sentence and was released on bond; however, before the date set for her appeal motion the following May, she told the press that she could no longer cooperate with the "evil and unjust court system of Mississippi." She asked for a hearing in April so that she could withdraw her appeal and start serving her prison sentence.[7] You'd think that would make the judge dance with glee, but it didn't happen that way. When Nash, who was four months pregnant by then, entered the courtroom, she sat in the section reserved for whites and refused to budge, despite the judge's orders for her to move to the other side of the room that was reserved for "coloreds." As a result of her refusal to change seats, the judge cited her for contempt and sentenced her to ten days in jail. Each time she tried to comment about dropping her appeal, the judge cut her off, finally sending her off to jail without hearing her motion.

While she was in jail, someone gave the judge a copy of a statement she had issued to the press. In the statement, she said, "The only condition under which I will leave jail is that the unjust and untrue charge of contributing to delinquency is dropped." Her position left the judge with few options. He could send a pregnant woman off to Parchman Farm to serve two years of hard time, thus making a martyr out of her for the civil rights movement; toss out her conviction, suggesting that she indeed had been abused by the system; or simply suspend her sentence, leaving the conviction on her record. After she served time in jail on the contempt citation, she learned that the judge had decided her fate without a hearing. He suspended her two-year prison sentence without explanation, making it possible for her to leave Mississippi at her earliest convenience, an option she exercised without great deliberation.

In the fall of 1961, Thurgood Marshall, then a counsel for the NAACP, was nominated to the Second Circuit Court of Appeals. To get there, he had to pass through Eastland's Senate committee. Realizing that he could delay—but not block—the nomination, Eastland offered a horse trade to the president. According to author Robert Sherrill, who wrote a profile of Eastland for *The Nation*, Eastland made the offer to Attorney General Robert Kennedy after meeting him by chance in the corridor outside the committee room.

"Tell your brother that if he will give me Harold Cox, I will give him the nigger," Eastland reportedly told Kennedy, referring to Marshall.

William Harold Cox had attended college with Eastland, and the senator wanted to see him appointed to a federal judgeship. As a result of that horse trade, Marshall was confirmed for the appeals court and Cox, who in court once referred to a black civil rights defendant as a "chimpanzee," was confirmed as a U.S. district judge in the Southern District of Mississippi.

James L. Dickerson:

I remember when the Freedom Riders arrived in my hometown of Hollandale, though I don't recall whether it was the summer of 1963 or 1964. They stood on the street corners, handing out leaflets, passionately urging white residents to do the right thing insofar as black voter registration was concerned. One of my high school classmates, Charlie Sudduth, was fascinated with the students and walked with them as they made their rounds, from the corner in front of City Drugs, across the street to the Sunflower grocery store, offering leaflets to people who often as not slapped the papers out of their hands. It was not work for anyone with tender sensibilities.

One weekend, when I had returned home from Ole Miss (the University of Mississippi) with my friend and fellow Hollandale High School graduate Martin Kilpatrick, we ran into Charlie and drove around town, talking as we used to do in high school. Charlie was filled with enthusiasm about the Freedom Riders, proclaiming over and over again how brilliant they were and how knowledgeable they were about history and literature. He confessed that he'd handed out a few leaflets himself, though he acknowledged that he'd given them only to people he knew. Insofar as it is possible to be in love with a cause, Charlie was in love with the concept of Freedom Riders. He spoke about them with the same pride that our contemporaries talked about the Green Bay Packers or the St. Louis Cardinals.

Although supportive of Charlie, Martin and I were not comfortable with the concept of civil disobedience, since it was not taught in school or advocated by parents as an alternative code of conduct. I would change my mind in later years, primarily because of the "uncivil" disobedience exhibited by the KKK, but at that time I felt that civil disobedience was in the same legal swamp as, say, robbing a bank.

The following day my mother was approached by the chief of police—not the same chief of police that'd gotten angry at me for not making a false identification; this was a kinder, gentler chief of police—who told her that Martin, Charlie, and I had "been seen" talking together by a bad element in town and he feared for our safety. He meant the KKK, though he didn't say it outright. Charlie, it seems, had made someone's hit list because of his interest in the Freedom Riders. The police chief was afraid all three of us would be lynched.

When I learned of the police chief's warning, I telephoned Martin; we talked it over and decided to have what is now called an intervention. Martin picked me up in his aqua-colored Corvair, and we found Charlie and drove around town and tried to persuade him to keep a lower profile with the Freedom Riders. I don't recall Martin or myself being concerned about our own safety, probably because we were going to return to the rarefied air of Ole Miss and had serious doubts that any of the rednecks with lynching on their minds could make it more than twenty miles out of town in those beat-up trucks of theirs. We were, however, concerned about Charlie's safety. There was a rough element that lived in and around Hollandale, a flinty-faced, bleary-eyed collection of gum boot rednecks who perpetually had a chip on their shoulders.

Nothing ever came of Charlie's flirtation with the Freedom Riders. Martin and I returned to school, convinced that we'd saved Charlie's life, and the Freedom Riders simply disappeared from the town, leaving Charlie free to pursue new causes. In retrospect, I think Charlie would have gotten the best of whoever had it in for us. Charlie, who'd left Hollandale to attend a military school in south Mississippi, had an impressive arsenal of bowie knives and daggers—and a World War II German Lugar that I covet to this day. They would've had their hands full with him, no doubt about it.

Not so lucky were the Freedom Riders, many of them young women who'd been arrested in Jackson or the Delta and then bused off to Parchman Farm, where they were interned in cells on death row. In her book *Freedom's Daughters*, Lynne Olson writes a disturbing account of the arrests: "Ushered into different rooms, under the scrutiny of guards with cattle prods, both men and women were ordered to strip naked for thorough body searches. The women endured rough, painful vaginal searches by female guards, who used the same gloves dipped in Lysol over and over in their examinations."

One of the women interned at Parchman was Elizabeth Wyckoff, a white professor of classics from Vassar.[8] At one point during her imprisonment, she began telling her fellow prisoners stories about the Greek myths, an act that outraged one of the guards. She was told to stop. She didn't. As punishment, the guard removed the women's mattresses. The women responded by singing "The Star-Spangled Banner," which prompted the guards to take away their toothbrushes and towels. Still they sang. The guards retaliated by turning off the cooling fans, an act that brought the temperature inside their cells up into the one hundred–degree range. Still they sang. That night the guards blew cold air into the cells, causing the prisoners to shiver on their steel bunks.

The news media reported on Freedom Rider arrests, almost on a daily basis, but there was never any follow-up about what happened to them. If word had gotten out about their treatment at the prison, I am not sure if many whites would have cared, but I'd like to think that something would have been done by the handful of liberals in the state who weren't shy about pointing fingers at abusive situations.

Parchman was just up the road from my hometown. I had no idea that women were treated that way at the prison. Neither did Martin or Charlie. Our family had raised us to respect women—and we did. We would have been outraged if we had known that those things were happening to women there.

I had toured Parchman a few years earlier with my high school class. Female inmates weren't kept in cells but were housed in barracks segregated by gender and race, and I'll never forget the women's section. I walked though what amounted to a room about the size of a basketball court, with beds lined up in a row on either side of the aisle. The room was dim and smoky and had an odd smell to it. The women all froze in place when the door opened, some of them sitting on beds, others leaning against the wall. One of the women, leathery faced, with a smoking cigarette dangling from her lips, winked at me as I passed, and I figured she was probably there for killing a man or two, at the very least.

As we were leaving the prison, one of the guards, a grisly faced man with a potbelly, pulled me aside and whispered with tobacco-stained breath: "I hope you learned a lesson, son. Walk the line, straight and narrow, 'cause you don't never want to come back to this place, you hear?" I heard.

Decades later, when I learned of the treatment that the Freedom Rider women had received, I realized that they'd been put in cells to segregate them from the general prison population. I'd like to think that prison authorities segregated them to protect them, but it was probably done so that they couldn't organize the other women into a revolt. I'm sure that the toughest male guard there wouldn't have relished the thought of the woman with the dangling cigarette coming at him with a makeshift machete.

6

Hoddy Toddy: The Integration of Ole Miss

During the fall of 1960, as the top-ranked Ole Miss Rebels football team mowed down opponent after opponent in its quest for the national college championship, Mississippi played out a drama that was destined to define the University of Mississippi for decades to come. The drama began in the late 1950s as word circulated that blacks might try to integrate one of Mississippi's all-white universities.

The first serious attempt had occurred in 1955, when twenty-eight-year-old Clyde Kennard, a veteran of the U.S. Army and a recipient of the Korean Service Medal, applied for admission to Mississippi Southern College (now known as University of Southern Mississippi). Kennard's application was denied. He applied again in 1956. His application was denied. In 1959 he applied once again, only this time he threatened a federal lawsuit as a possible remedy for his rejections. In a letter to the *Hattiesburg American*, Kennard explained his reasons for wanting to attend the college: "Although I am an integrationist by choice, I am a segregationist by nature, and I think most Negroes are. We prefer to be alone, but experience has taught us that if we are ever to attain the goal of first class citizenship, we must do it through a closer association with the dominant [white] group."[1]

Before proceeding with the application, college president William McCain asked Kennard to meet with him so that they could discuss the matter face to face.[2] Prior to the meeting, McCain questioned his black maid about Kennard, since she was from the same community. She told him that Kennard was one of the most outstanding blacks in the community. All the other blacks looked up to him. McCain also contacted the Sovereignty Commission and asked for guidance; the commission's response was to send investigator Zack Van Landingham to attend the meeting, without disclosing his true identity. It was a trap. After Kennard left the meeting, he was arrested and charged with reckless driving and possession of five bottles of liquor, at that time a crime in "dry" Mississippi. Clearly he was framed, though it took decades of denials by state officials before the truth came to light.

With the help of the NAACP, Kennard beat the reckless driving and liquor rap and pressed on with his application for admission to the college. Annoyed that he had beaten the liquor charge, the Sovereignty Commission framed him for the theft of twenty-five dollars' worth of chicken feed, for which he was convicted and sentenced to seven years at Parchman Farm. Several years into his sentence, Kennard was diagnosed with colon cancer after complaining of stomach pains while working in the cotton fields. He was released from prison on humanitarian grounds and died six months later.

James Meredith Sets His Sights on Ole Miss

Hoddy toddy gosh almighty
Who in the hell are we . . . Hey!
Flim flam, bim bam
OLE MISS BY DAMN!
        —University of Mississippi football cheer

The day after John F. Kennedy's inauguration, James Meredith wrote to the registrar at the University of Mississippi to request an application for admission.[3] Five days later, on January 26, 1961, the university sent Meredith an application form, along with a letter expressing pleasure in his interest in Ole Miss. Since he lived in Jackson, where he attended the all-black Jackson State College, he went to see Medgar Evers, the director of the NAACP's Mississippi field office. Evers was well aware of what had happened to Clyde Kennard, and he urged Meredith to give his application more thought before proceeding. Once Evers saw that Meredith, a twenty-eight-year-old air force veteran, was determined to pursue the matter, he suggested that he contact Thurgood Marshall, then director of the NAACP Legal Defense Fund. In his letter to Marshall, Meredith said that he anticipated "encountering some type of difficulty."

On the advice of the NAACP, Meredith identified himself as an "American-Mississippi-Negro citizen" when he submitted his application to the University of Mississippi. Noting the university's requirement that prospective students submit the names of six Ole Miss graduates as references, Meredith pointed out that would be impossible for him, since "they are all white."

Not surprisingly, Meredith was denied admission. For months he corresponded with the university and attempted to negotiate his enrollment. Eventually the matter ended up with the Mississippi Board of Trustees for Institutions of Higher Learning, commonly referred to as the College Board, which also denied him admission to the university.

Meredith appealed the College Board's decision to the federal courts. In June 1962 the matter went before the Fifth Circuit Court of Appeals in New Orleans. Inside the courtroom the situation was unusually tense. At one end of the table were lawyers representing the Mississippi College Board, and at the other end of the table were NAACP lawyers representing James Meredith. The NAACP lawyers argued that the court should jail the state College Board for contempt and appoint its own board. At that point the court took a short recess, with each side retreating to private rooms.

The truth about what happened in those private rooms was not revealed for many years. According to College Board president Tom Tubb, who subsequently told his story to David Halberstam, a journalist with Mississippi connections: "We went in one of those conference rooms, and one of [Governor] Barnett's people came over to me and said, 'Tom, you're a lawyer and I'm not, and I don't hear so good. But I do understand that nigger woman from the NAACP to say that if we don't let Meredith in, then I'm going to jail and he's going to the University.'"

Tubb told him that he had heard correctly.

"Well, goddam," he said. "Vote me to admit the nigger."

After several months of legal wrangling, the U.S. Supreme Court assured Meredith's admittance on September 13, 1962, not by ruling in his favor on the merits of the case, but rather by refusing to hear an appeal to block him from entering the university.

Barnett was outraged by the court's decision. He'd promised white Mississippi that the "nigger" would never sully the Ole Miss campus, and he had no intention of giving up without a fight. Vowed Barnett: "Schools will not be closed if this can possibly be avoided, but they will not be integrated. . . . I interpose the rights of the sovereign state of Mississippi to enforce its laws and to regulate its own internal affairs without interference on the part of the federal government." Barnett's position was given a vote of confidence by most of the state's elected officials, including Senator Eastland and Lieutenant Governor Paul Johnson.

Barnett's defiance electrified white Mississippians. In effect, Barnett told the federal government that it would have to shoot its way into Mississippi if it wanted Meredith in the university. That was fine with most of the state's white citizens, who quietly went about the business of oiling their shotguns and stocking their pantries with groceries for the shoot-out they felt was inevitable. The entire state of Mississippi readied for a shooting war with the federal government. Barnett issued an executive order calling for the arrest of any federal official who attempted to prevent a state official from carrying out his duties. If there was going to be killing, he wanted it to be legal killing.

When Meredith arrived at the College Board offices in Jackson, he was escorted by Department of Justice attorney John Doar. There to greet them was Governor Barnett, who blocked their entry into the office by standing in the doorway. With a wink to the press corps, Barnett gave Doar his best tough-guy look and asked, "Which one of you gentlemen is James Meredith?"

Doar was not amused, but Meredith cracked a smile.

Barnett brushed Doar's court order aside and read a statement that said, in part, "I do, hereby, finally deny you admission to the University of Mississippi." Hearing that, Doar and Meredith turned and left the College Board offices, accompanied by several highway patrolmen. The following day they drove to the University of Mississippi campus at Oxford, under the protection of U.S. marshals, where Barnett and Lieutenant Governor Paul Johnson planned to block Meredith's entry into the university. Barnett, however, got cold feet at the last moment and holed up a safe distance away, leaving Johnson to face the marshals alone. Johnson was a wiry, hawk-faced man whose grimace was perpetually etched into his facial features. Like Barnett, he was born with that peculiar lack of grace familiar to fans of William Faulkner's hardscrabble Snopeses.

James McShane, the U.S. marshal accompanying Meredith, reached out to give Johnson a court order. Johnson grimaced and refused to take it, leaning back like someone was waving a snake in his face. McShane touched the papers against him and dropped them to the ground. Johnson, looking more like Barney Fife on steroids than a real threat, doubled up his fist and drew back his arm as if to strike someone. Seeing that, McShane doubled up his fists and stepped forward, swinging his arms at his side. When he spoke, his voice was forceful: "You understand that we have got to break through."

Johnson stood firm and told McShane that he would be responsible for any violence.

Faced with redneck belligerence, the federal government blinked.

Doar, McShane, Meredith, and the U.S. marshals turned away and left the campus. Once it was safe to do so, Governor Barnett arrived on campus and apologized for being late. He commended Johnson for "standing tall" for Mississippi. The Fifth Circuit Court of Appeals was not amused by the dramatic showdown. It already had issued a contempt order against Governor Barnett. Now it issued one against Lieutenant Governor Johnson.

President Kennedy was furious. Over the next several days, he and his brother, Attorney General Robert Kennedy, had a series of telephone conversations with Governor Barnett in an attempt to bring a peaceful resolution to the conflict. After days of tense conversations, Barnett and President Kennedy agreed that Meredith would be enrolled on September 27. Barnett was told that Meredith would be accompanied by about thirty armed U.S. marshals. In a conversation with Robert Kennedy, Barnett asked if it would be possible for all the marshals to draw their pistols.

"We'll have a big crowd here, and if we all turn away because of one gun, it would be embarrassing," said Barnett. "When you draw the guns, I will then tell the people. In other words, we will step aside and you can walk in."

It was a request that bordered on insanity.

"I don't think that will be very pleasant, Governor," said Robert Kennedy, trying to take the man seriously. "I think it is silly going through this whole facade of your standing there; our people drawing guns; your stepping aside; to me, it is dangerous and I think this has gone beyond the stage of politics, and you have a responsibility to the people of the state and to the people of the United States. This is a real disservice. . . ."

"I can't just walk back," muttered Barnett.

The Justice Department suggested that Meredith be secretly enrolled in Jackson while all the media attention was focused on the Oxford campus. Both President Kennedy and the governor agreed to that solution. Then, as word got out that thousands of armed men were arriving in Mississippi from neighboring states to support Barnett, the governor backed down from the agreement to enroll Meredith in Jackson. Hearing that, Robert Kennedy called Barnett and told him the president was going on national television that night to say that Barnett had gone back on his word.

"That won't do at all," said Barnett.

"You broke your word to him," insisted Kennedy.

"You don't mean the president is going to say that tonight?" said Barnett.

"Of course, he is. You broke your word."

The Kennedys returned to their original plan to enroll Meredith at the Oxford campus, accompanied by armed U.S. marshals. Barnett was advised to call out the national guard as a backup to the highway patrol.

At 2:30 P.M. on September 30, 1962, the day Meredith was scheduled to arrive on campus, President Kennedy and Barnett had another telephone conversation.[4] Said Barnett: "Mr. President, let me say this—they [those opposed to racial integration] are calling me and others from all over the state wanting to send 1,000, 500, and 200 [men to fight] and all such as that."

"I know," responded the president.

"We don't want such as that," said Barnett.

"I know, well we don't want to have, don't want to have people getting hurt or killed down there," said the president.

With Barnett emotionally exhausted, the conversation ended on an odd note, a clear indication of the governor's deteriorating mental state: "Appreciate your interest in our poultry program and all those things. Thank you so much."

Kennedy had an unsettling realization that he was playing chess with a lunatic.

Trucks packed with U.S. marshals pulled onto the Ole Miss campus at about 4 P.M. The marshals wore white helmets, and they were outfitted with tear gas guns, gas masks, and pistols. Not far behind were Deputy Attorney General Nicholas Katzenbach and other officials from the Justice Department, all flown into Oxford on an air force plane. Once they arrived, they were escorted to the campus by Mississippi highway patrolmen. As the convoy made its way along the two-mile route to the campus, rabble-rousers lined the route, heckling the marshals with jeers of "nigger lover."

Meredith arrived at the airport at 5:30 P.M. aboard a border patrol plane. He was escorted to the campus, where he was taken to Baxter Hall, a men's dormitory located on a hill that was one of the highest points on the campus. As crowds continued to form on the campus, Meredith settled into the dorm. That night, while Meredith slept, a full-scale riot erupted. Cars were overturned and set ablaze. Snipers fired out of the darkness at the marshals. Molotov cocktails exploded all over the campus, igniting small fires that sent waves of smoke drifting among the men's and women's dormitories. Roving mobs of men threw stones and chunks of concrete at the marshals. It was total war.

At 8:14 P.M., President Kennedy and Barnett spoke again. Kennedy wanted the patrolmen moved into place to aid the marshals who were engaged in a pitched battle. Barnett told the president that there were 150 highway patrolmen on their way to the scene. Kennedy said it was important to stop the shooting: "We don't want a lot of people killed just because they . . . evidently two or three guardsmen have been shot—our marshals and then, of course, that state trooper."

Barnett said he was coming under attack from Mississippians who accused him of giving up the fight. "I had to say 'No, I'm not giving up. I'm not giving up any fight. I'll never give up, I have courage and faith, and we will win this fight.' You understand, that's just [for] the Mississippi people."

Kennedy tried to be supportive. "Yeah, I don't think any of the Mississippi people or anyone else wants a lot of people killed." Kennedy had no way of knowing that radio stations all across Mississippi were giving play-by-play commentary on the riot as if it were a sporting event. All across the state, radios hummed with news about the riot. White male Mississippians began arming themselves and loading their trucks and cars with ammunition and supplies for a prolonged war. The stage was set for the first armed rebellion since the Civil War.

The fighting raged all night. But by sunrise order was restored and the campus was cleared of troublemakers. Tear gas fumes lingered like draped confetti across the campus. Two men died in the fighting. Paul Guihard was a thirty-one-year-old reporter with Agence France-Presse. Sent to Ole Miss from his bureau office in New York, he was on the campus for only a couple of hours when he was shot at close range and left to die. The second victim was Walter Ray Gunter, a twenty-three-year-old jukebox serviceman from Oxford who was shot in the forehead. As Meredith was escorted to the administration building to register for classes, he was overheard to remark, upon looking out across the battle-scarred campus: "This is not a happy occasion."

In the aftermath of the rioting, with many Mississippians demanding that Barnett close the university rather than open it to blacks, Ole Miss football coach John Vaught called his players together and urged them to help keep the university going: "We have got to band together. We have a purpose. We must keep our poise. We have to show the people of the United States just what we are down here. We're not a bunch of radicals. The only way is through our football."

The courage to win on the field that year was nothing when compared with the courage it took to simply survive as a football team. It was difficult to practice because the field was used by the army as a staging area for its helicopters. Instead, practices were held in Hemingway Stadium, where thousands of troops watched from the bleachers. Added to that pressure was the telephone call that Vaught received from Attorney General Robert Kennedy, urging him to do everything possible to calm the situation.

Later Vaught wrote: "When Ole Miss needed to survive and build a new image, as it sorely did in 1962, a great football team stepped forward. I always will rate the 1962 team as one of the most courageous in the history of the game . . . our football team tipped the scales . . . a university rode on their shoulder pads."

Ole Miss went on to win the Sugar Bowl that year, giving the football team its best record (10–0) in school history. Both the Associated Press's writers poll and the United Press International's coaches poll ranked the 1962 Ole Miss team number three in the nation behind Wisconsin and national champion Southern California.

Alex A. Alston Jr.:

When I was growing up in Mississippi in the 1950s, the plight of the Negro was the least of my concerns. All I knew was that I was having a glorious time. The caste system in place had represented the culture of my parents and ancestors for over seven generations. After serving in the Marine Corps, I looked forward to returning to Mississippi, entering the University of Mississippi School of Law, and practicing law in a state for which I had such fond memories. The memories I had, however, did not match what I experienced when I returned to enter Ole Miss law school in 1961.

Ole Miss history professor James Silver called it a "closed society," and that it was. It was a virtual police state that spied on its citizens. With the collaboration of the legislature, the politicians, the church, the professional class, and the mighty media, it could tolerate no deviation whatsoever from the orthodox system. The most modest notion of dissent was quickly and sometimes violently crushed.

Being the least educated and the poorest state in the nation, Mississippi had little to crow about, but on strolling onto the campus in 1961, I was genuinely surprised to find these facts to be largely irrelevant. Not that I particularly minded—the conversation most often would turn to beautiful women and superior football. Had not Ole Miss produced two Miss Americas in a row? Mary Ann Mobley in 1959 and Lynda Lee Mead in 1960. Mississippi was the beauty capital of the nation, with more Miss Americas than any other state. The Ole Miss Rebel football team had become national champions, and all of this, in the minds of the students, without allowing one black to sully the halls of any white institution of learning. To the students, that was sufficient proof of the superiority of the rigid caste system that was almost unanimously supported by white citizens.

On Saturday, September 29, 1962, I drove south to Jackson for the Ole Miss–Kentucky game at Memorial Stadium. All the radio stations blared "Dixie" and announcers chanted "segregation forever," frequently pausing to recite an ominous countdown to the final confrontation over Meredith's arrival at the school. Once I arrived at the stadium, I quickly realized that the spectators were on the verge of hysteria. At halftime, Governor Barnett shouted out his defiance to the federal government, saying "I love Mississippi! I love her people! I love her customs!" The students waved their rebel flags in approval.

Back on campus the pressure, consistency, and unanimity of this prevailing view made me think that perhaps my embryonic thoughts on equal justice for all might just be wrong. But that changed dramatically after entering law school at Ole Miss. On Sunday, September 30, I found myself in the middle of a vicious war of hate. I heard the sounds of war from my small apartment in "Vet Village." I ventured out to witness what Dr. Silver called "the most explosive federal-state clash since the Civil War." I saw tear gas being shot and bricks, stones, and bottles flying everywhere. I saw federal marshals falling and being taken to cover, cars and trucks being burned, and thousands of students and later hundreds of older-looking armed roughnecks in hysterical frenzy and cursing "niggers" and "Kennedy" with every screaming breath. Former general Edwin Walker stood by the monument in front of the Lyceum Circle, encouraging the frenetic rioters. I spent a good portion of that night asking any student I could recognize to take that bottle or brick out of his hand and to go back to his dormitory.

In walking across the campus to get to the law school on Monday morning, I found the ruined battlefield shocking, with cars and trucks still smoking and burning, with ammunition casings and debris of all kinds covering the grounds, and with the odor of tear gas still mingling in the air sufficiently to burn my eyes. I was surprised to see Ole Miss still standing and to learn that only 2 people had been killed and 160 marshals hurt, with 38 of that number having been shot. There has never been an accurate count of all the other casualties of this violent crisis.

I noted that all the entrances on campus were fully open, allowing hordes of racist thugs to storm in from all of the Southern states and even from a number of other states, such as California, all adorned with racist Confederate paraphernalia. Ironically, these entrances had been blocked for some time before this tragic event, allowing ingress and egress only to students and others having legitimate business on the campus.

My wife, Sarah Jane, had difficulty leaving the campus to teach in the little hamlet of Taylor, in order to support us in those law school days. We were fortunate to have the assistance of an African American woman, Elnora Jones, to help us take care of our young son, Trace, when Sarah Jane was at work and I was in school. Elnora loved our son very much and never missed a day of work during the three years we lived in Oxford, except for that fateful day of the riot. The war had spilled over into Oxford, with hundreds of hoodlums taking positions at the courthouse and at the intersection of Lamar Boulevard and University Avenue. In an attempt to reach our apartment, Elnora made every effort to get through town but was stopped by both the thugs and the soldiers. With tears in her eyes, she later explained to us how scared she was when she tried to break through at several entrances, before reluctantly returning to her home.

Needless to say, the University of Mississippi suffered mightily and continues to suffer from this atrocious debacle. Over fifty professors left, and much negative national attention was focused on Ole Miss. The distinguished history professor, Dr. James W. Silver, left the state. Before I graduated, the wonderful, witty, and highly respected dean of the law school, Robert Farley, was hounded out of Mississippi for daring to argue that James Meredith had a right to attend Ole Miss.

As I reflect on that terrible night, two vivid scenes come to mind. The first is the disturbing sneer of a wild-eyed student yelling "Kill the nigger," then pausing just long enough to catch his breath to scream "Kill Kennedy," all while rushing toward the marshals with a fluttering rebel flag. Of course, none of that surprised me. Wasn't that young man, brought up in small-town Mississippi, taught from birth that the Negro was inferior and that integration would destroy Mississippi's wonderful way of life? Didn't he see local sheriffs patrol the Ole Miss campus with baseball bats, pledged to defend Mississippi Values? Unless he had been rendered deaf by moonshine—or, as it was called in those days, "nigger pot"—he must have heard every elected official in the state encouraging resistance, against not just blacks but also the federal government. He would have been hard-pressed to find a single teacher, preacher, or businessman countering that position. The words "Do unto others as you would have them do unto you" would have fallen on deaf ears. In those days, it was the Citizens' Councils and the Mississippi Sovereignty Commission that stood tall, for the gospel of hate.

The second vivid scene that haunts me is the image of James Howard Meredith as he strolled across the campus, seemingly unaware of the chaos that surrounded him. His emotional makeup was so perplexing and otherworldly that it invites comparisons to two other figures that are associated with his hometown of Kosciusko. The first is a Polish soldier, Tadeusz Kosciuszko, for whom the town was named because of his selfless service during the American Revolution. The second is one of the wealthiest women in the world, Oprah Winfrey, who drew her first breath in Kosciusko. Like Tadeusz Kosciuszko, Meredith was a man of great courage, who took on not only the State of Mississippi but the entire United States of America. Like Oprah Winfrey, he used his talents to emerge from obscurity and plant his brand on American history. Winston Churchill had it right when he said, "Courage is the first of the human qualities because it is that quality which guarantees all others."

There is now a life-size bronze statue of James Meredith located on the campus at Ole Miss in which he is depicted striding toward a tall limestone archway, reenacting his historic step into the heart of segregation and forever bringing an end to the apartheid society then existing at that university. Above the archway, carved into the stone, is the word COURAGE. To me, this single word epitomizes my feelings about the character of James Meredith and should hopefully serve as a beacon of light radiating the everlasting truth that remarkable feats can be accomplished by the unremitting courage of a single person. Surprisingly, most major changes are made that very way.

A Second Black Student Enters Ole Miss

In June 1963, James Meredith was joined on campus by a second African American student, Cleve McDowell. Unlike Meredith, who entered the undergraduate program, McDowell enrolled in the law school. He arrived on campus with a team of U.S. marshals, but there were no incidents. There were still about 150 federal troops on the campus, and many of them maintained positions on the roofs of campus buildings, where they could be seen communicating with each other by two-way radio. It was an eerie sight, familiar to any student who spent Saturday afternoons holed up in the dorm watching World War II films.

A month before classes began, in an effort to gather incriminating information about McDowell, the Sovereignty Commission sent investigator Tom Scarbrough to McDowell's hometown of Drew, Mississippi.[5] To everyone's surprise, Scarbrough returned with a glowing report. "All of those to whom I talked in Drew, including all of the elected officials, stated they knew Cleve McDowell and his mother and father and had known the McDowell boy all of his life. All stated he had never been involved in any kind of meanness to their knowledge."

Notified of McDowell's peaceful enrollment, Attorney General Robert Kennedy wistfully commented, "I wish it could have happened that way the first time." No one was more surprised about McDowell's uneventful reception than James Meredith, who good-naturedly said, "Maybe it's just me they don't like."

Governor Barnett had the good sense to stay away from the campus during McDowell's enrollment, but he couldn't resist issuing a quarrelsome statement of protest. "The State of Mississippi cannot cope with the United States Army," he said. "We have done everything in our power to prevent the enrollment of Cleve McDowell in the university law school. His entry is in violation of the laws of the state."

By April 1963 Erle Johnston had replaced Albert Jones as the director of the Sovereignty Commission. On August 15, three days before James Meredith was scheduled to graduate from the University of Mississippi (since he was a transfer student, he needed only a year's worth of credit to graduate), Director Johnston received a midmorning telephone call from E. R. Jobe, the executive secretary of the state College Board. Jobe told Johnston that the College Board was going to have a meeting in thirty minutes to discuss a new development in the Meredith case. He asked Johnston to send a representative to the meeting. At issue were statements made earlier in the summer by Meredith, statements some members of the College Board considered "inflammatory." Board members wanted to know if they could use those statements to prevent Meredith from receiving his diploma. By a six-to-five vote, reason prevailed and the College Board adjourned without beating Meredith out of his diploma. Johnston was asked to tell the commission that the College Board had tried its best.

A week before his graduation, Meredith was asked by a reporter if he felt Mississippi had made gains in the direction of equal rights. "You can't make gains," he responded. "There's no in-between. Either a citizen has equal protection or he doesn't. If a man is innocent but unfairly sentenced to one hundred years in jail, you can't say it would represent a gain if he had been unfairly sentenced to only ten years."

On his last day of classes, Meredith wore a dark suit, white shirt, and red necktie. On his lapel was one of the NEVER, NEVER buttons that had greeted him when he arrived on campus—only Meredith wore his button upside down, an act of quiet defiance. As he explained in his memoir, "I am a Mississippian in all respects, even the bad ones."

Cleve McDowell, at twenty-one, was several years younger than Meredith. He optimistically told Charles Brown, a reporter with the *Memphis Press-Scimitar*, that he felt "just like any other student." Of course, he wasn't treated that way by the other students.

James L. Dickerson:

I began undergraduate classes at the University of Mississippi the same month that McDowell began classes at the law school. I was seldom in the vicinity of the law school, but the campus was arranged so that the student union, which contained the post office and the cafeteria, was the hub of student activity. For that reason I encountered McDowell on a daily basis, either coming in or going out of the student union, or in the student cafeteria. I always spoke to him, and he always returned my greetings, but speaking always seemed to be a distraction for him. There was always a faraway look in his eyes, a mixture of fear and bravado.

I don't blame McDowell for being afraid. About a month after he started classes, he learned that the U.S. marshals assigned to Meredith were going to be withdrawn. He went to Meredith's dorm room to discuss it with him and called the marshals' office from Meredith's telephone to request permission to carry a firearm. His request was denied. He did it anyway. A pocket-size .22 caliber pistol. I don't think he was as concerned about the other students as he was the Sovereignty Commission and the redneck hotheads who perpetually patrolled the back roads of the state with loaded guns and lord knows what else in the back of their trucks. He was tipped off about the commission's activities by his family, who told him about the investigator visiting Drew. He knew full well what had happened to Clyde Kennard after the commission had gotten involved in his case. He couldn't stop them from planting evidence, but he could protect himself if they came to kill him.

I never heard other students say anything derogatory to McDowell. They mostly looked away when he approached. The worst thing I ever saw was the way white students behaved when he showed up at the cafeteria. The building was constructed so that there were several different sections with tables. Whenever McDowell entered one of the sections with his food tray, all the white students rose en masse and relocated to another section, leaving him to eat alone in a room with a hundred or so empty tables.

The first time I saw that happen, I was seated in one of the other sections in a location where I could look into the adjacent section. The second time it happened, I was in the section he entered with his food tray. Everyone got up and left—except me. I stayed where I was. The other students glared at me, but McDowell nodded and smiled. Many years later I asked him if he remembered that day. He laughed and said, "So *you* were the one!"

That summer, while James Meredith and Cleve McDowell were fighting for their constitutional rights, I organized my first rock 'n' roll band. We named ourselves the Dynamics. We had a superb drummer named Howard Camp, who was really more of a jazz musician than a rocker, but he flat-out had a talent for doing magical things on this trap set. Our singer, Bill McKeithen, a pharmacy major from Philadelphia, Mississippi, was a Ricky Nelson clone. He sang in Nelson's shuffling vocal style and greatly resembled him in physical appearance. I don't recall our guitarist's name, but I do remember that he practiced in his dorm room at least eight hours a day. Our keyboard man was longtime Hollandale friend Martin Kilpatrick. I played sax. Rounding out the group was a trumpet player named Dalton Diamond of Memphis. We had a great deal of fun that summer and fall, mostly performing at fraternity and sorority dances. Outside of Kilpatrick, I got to know Diamond better than the others because, unlike the other instruments that usually went their separate ways musically, it was essential that Dalton and I synchronize our sax and trumpet parts. We played a lot of songs that required us to play our horns in unison, such as Bobby Bland's "Turn on Your Love Light."

That fall I pledged Kilpatrick's fraternity and encouraged Diamond to pledge as well. The active members were pleased to have three members of the Dynamics associated with the fraternity. At least I thought so. Not far into the fall semester, Diamond was dropped as a pledge. When I asked some of the active members why, they said it was because they'd heard that one or both of his parents were Jews.

I was astonished. *What's wrong with being a Jew?* I asked myself. We had Jews in my hometown. I had no idea that some people hated Jews. To this day I don't know for certain if Diamond is a Jew. If he is, he would never have shared that information with other students. Certainly it never came up in our conversations. At that time, Jews were targeted for bombing, just as blacks were targeted for lynching.

They thought he might be a Jew, and that was enough. Shortly after they told me their reasons for dropping him, I was eating dinner in the fraternity house dining room when the subject arose. I got so angry that I jumped to my feet and slammed a chard of cornbread into my stew, splattering several of the active members seated at the table. I stormed out of the room, as angry as I was when I saw that beaten and battered black teen in my hometown jail. When I returned the next day, I was informed that the fraternity had accepted the resignation I'd never offered. I would have "de-pledged" anyway, but the incident was a valuable lesson not only in religious intolerance but also about the paucity of free speech in a closed society. Diamond left Ole Miss shortly after that to attend Tulane University in New Orleans. He subsequently received a medical degree and distinguished himself as a brigadier general in charge of the U.S. Army Medical Corps.

That August, James Meredith became the first African American to receive a degree from the University of Mississippi. The excitement over that milestone was short-lived, however, because the following month Cleve McDowell was arrested by the county sheriff and taken off to jail and subsequently dragged before the student council after a pistol fell from his pocket in full view of other students.[6]

Because of the firearm violation, McDowell was expelled from school. There wasn't much celebration on campus when he left. The university was once again all- white, but when McDowell left, something important was taken from the students. They weren't sure exactly what, but they felt it. There were no parades proclaiming victory. When one of the white students who had seen McDowell drop the pistol on the steps of the law school was asked about it by a reporter, he was sympathetic to McDowell's plight. "I just wish I hadn't been there," said the student.

On Friday, November 22, 1963, the Ole Miss campus was relatively quiet. The Ole Miss Rebels had the weekend off to prepare for the season finale the following week against the Mississippi State Bulldogs. With Ole Miss ranked number three in the nation and Mississippi State ranked thirteenth, everyone was expecting fireworks.

It had been two months since Cleve McDowell had been expelled. Ole Miss was again a segregated institution. Life went on somehow, with emphasis again shifting to issues such as football and weekend parties. Politics and social issues seemed far removed from the reality of getting an education. I continued to perform with the Dynamics at frat parties, most of which ended up being drunken orgies.

That November afternoon the sky was deep blue. I was in one of the older dorms, where I had a single room—the better to be a rock 'n' roller. The temperature was in the fifties, crisp and cold for Mississippi. That day I was aware of a general increase in noise outside my window. It started out slow and then sort of exploded, prompting students to subject themselves to icy blasts of air as they opened their windows to peer out into the street. Car horns echoed across the campus. Pickup trucks, convertibles, souped-up Corvettes—all sped up and down the narrow streets as students hung out the car windows, their arms outstretched. Rebel yells filled the air.

Suddenly, I heard screams amid the car horns.

"He's dead!" someone screamed. "The son of a bitch is dead!"

I peered out the window. A large rebel flag the size of a bedsheet was unfurled from a dormitory window. Bug-eyed students, their faces flushed with excitement, rushed out into the street, arms waving.

"Kennedy's been shot!"

Someone began a cheer. "Hoddy toddy, God a'mighty, who in the hell are we?" went the cheer, then ended with, "Ole Miss, by damn!"

As students at Ole Miss danced in the streets—and as an entire nation was paralyzed by shock—news of the assassination of President John F. Kennedy filtered out across the country. I was devastated by the news. President Kennedy was my hero.

7

The Assassination
of Medgar Evers

We preach freedom around the world, and we mean it, and we
cherish our freedom here at home, but are we to say to the world
and, much more importantly, to each other that this is a land of
the free except for the Negroes; that we have no second-class
citizens except Negroes; that we have no class or caste system, no
ghettos, no master race except with respect to Negroes? Now the
time has come for this nation to fulfill its promise.

—President John F. Kennedy

On June 11, 1963, President Kennedy delivered a speech on race to a
national television audience. It was what many historians consider the
defining moment of his presidency. Medgar and Myrlie Evers watched
the speech with a renewed sense of optimism. Perhaps there was
hope, after all.

The following night, on June 12, 1963, Medgar pulled into the
driveway of his Jackson home, just after midnight.[1] Inside the house,
his wife, Myrlie, and two of their three children were watching television, struggling to stay awake at that late hour.

At the age of thirty-seven, Evers was not so much a rising star of the civil rights movement as he was its dependable, high-profile disciple, someone who had come up through the ranks, a thoughtful, hard worker who in 1954 had been named Mississippi's first NAACP field officer. Wearing a white shirt, Evers got out of his blue Oldsmobile and gathered up an armload of papers and a bundle of NAACP T-shirts printed with the slogan JIM CROW MUST GO. Earlier in the evening, he had attended a rally at a church, where he had a private meeting with Tougaloo College chaplain Edwin King, a white Methodist minister from Vicksburg who had become an early convert to the civil rights movement.[2]

As Evers slammed the car door shut, a gunshot shattered the night stillness. A .30-06 slug cut through the night air, penetrated his right shoulder blade, and then ripped through his body and crashed into a window of the house, landing finally with a thud on the kitchen counter. Leaving a trail of blood, Evers crawled up the driveway to the back door of the house, before collapsing facedown, still clutching his car keys. That is what Myrlie saw when she threw open the back door.[3] What she heard were her children's horrified screams as they gathered around him, screaming, "Please, Daddy, please get up!" On the way to the hospital, Evers regained consciousness and tried to sit up. Unfortunately, the damage done to his chest by the .30-06 slug was too massive and he died fifty minutes after arriving at the hospital.

Police found a 1917 .30-06 Enfield rifle, equipped with a telescopic sight, hidden in a honeysuckle patch behind a tree across the street from Evers's house. The large-caliber rifle, which could be purchased by mail for less than twenty dollars, was popular with gun collectors and big-game hunters across the South. The killer—or killers—had vanished after murdering Evers with the same caliber weapon that the civil rights leader had used while fighting with the U.S. Army in Europe during World War II, the killer perhaps seeing that as some sort of twisted justice.

As the leader of the Mississippi NAACP, Evers was one of the Sovereignty Commission's primary targets. Considering the high level of surveillance the commission maintained on Evers, it is hard to believe that one of its investigators was not there to witness the assassination. As far back as December 1961, then–commission director Albert Jones had personally participated in surveillance activities against Evers. On one occasion, upon seeing a white woman enter a Lynch Street address after Evers already had entered the building, Jones and one of his investigators crept up to the window and peered inside, hoping to witness a sexual encounter. As they peeked through the blinds, they saw Evers in conversation with Hazel Brannon Smith, the editor of the Lexington and Durant newspapers. If they could catch him intimately involved with a white woman, it would give them all the ammunition they'd need to run him out of town. As it turned out, they got nothing except sore knees.

News of Evers's murder rippled not just across Mississippi but throughout the country, confirming the worst fears that people had about Mississippi—that it was a backward, barbaric swamp inhabited primarily by murderous psychopaths who'd just as soon kill you as look at you, an assessment that headlines seemed to confirm on a regular basis.

The hatred against Evers in Mississippi had soared a few weeks before his death, when he was given seventeen minutes of airtime on television station WLBT to respond to comments made by Jackson mayor Allen Thompson. WLBT did not want to give Evers the airtime but relented after the television station was ordered to do so by the Federal Communications Commission under its fairness doctrine. The response of white viewers was predictable. They wanted Evers off the air—immediately. One caller angrily said, "You don't have to put these black jungle bunnies on TV." Another caller said, "I'd just like to call in and tell you that I think that's very horrible, this nigra [sic] on TV with all his lies. . . ."

With Evers's death, many white Mississippians retreated to the delusional comfort that he somehow got what he deserved, reasoning that even if they themselves didn't condone murder, there were situations in which it was understandable.

Evers didn't go down easy. At his funeral more than five thousand supporters, most of whom were black, walked behind his casket as it slowly made its way through the streets of Jackson. The funeral procession moved in silence for a while, the kind of hard silence that gnaws away at the reins of anger, slowly, moment by moment, loosening the hold on emotion, so that there came a point when the marchers couldn't be held back any longer, could no longer deny their emotions, finally channeling their anger into soaring hymns and inspirational freedom songs, which violated police demands for silence.

That was when the nightsticks started swinging. It wasn't in the police training manual, but every white man in Mississippi who ever wore a police uniform understood the unwritten rule that if you told a black man to do something and he didn't do it, there was nothing else to do but to beat him half to death, or else the entire social structure would collapse, or so they believed. Acting on that principle, the Jackson police waded into the funeral marchers, first beating them and then arresting as many of the mourners as they could get their hands on, chasing them through the streets and, in some instances, into buildings where they'd fled in search of protection. Edwin King, the minister whose farewell handshake with Evers had been his last, was among those dragged from a building and taken to a makeshift prison at the fairgrounds.

King offered to treat a wounded man with his handkerchief.

A police officer demanded to know what he thought he was doing.

"What I was doing was obvious," King later wrote. "But I tried to reason with the officer. Although my clothes were torn, I still wore part of my clerical collar and looked like some sort of ragged priest. 'I want to wipe off his wound, and chase the flies out of the blood, away from his head.'"

"The policeman looked at me. He raised his rifle in the air, holding the butt end ready. 'You nigger-loving son of a bitch. What the hell you think this is, a damn hospital? I know you ain't no damn doctor. Shit, you ain't no preacher either. You touch his head, and you get one just like it.'"[4]

King paused, not so much fearing death as fearing the pain that he knew would precede death, and it was during that hesitation that he was jerked to his feet, taken to the other side of the room, and ordered to stand in line with the other prisoners.

So it went in Mississippi, if you were bold enough to sing during a funeral procession for a fallen hero.

To Catch a Killer

By the end of June 1963, the FBI had a suspect in the murder. Fingerprints lifted from the rifle matched those of a forty-two-year-old ex-marine from Greenwood, a rabid segregationist named Byron De La Beckwith, the same man who had offered his skills as a marksman to the Sovereignty Commission. He was taken into custody by FBI agents at his lawyer's office in Greenwood and transported to Jackson, where he was lodged in the city jail. Upon learning of his arrest, the *Clarion-Ledger* offered the following headline: CALIFORNIAN IS CHARGED WITH MURDER OF EVERS—a reference to the fact that the suspect had not been born in Mississippi; it was a tactic that the newspaper often used in news stories to deflect criticism from the state.

Despite being born in California, Beckwith had deep Mississippi roots. His father, Byron De La Beckwith V, had married Susie Yerger, who came from a well-connected Mississippi family in Greenwood, a city of eighteen thousand located at the eastern edge of the Mississippi Delta, where the Tallahatchie and Yalobusha rivers meet to form the Yazoo River. Other than the rivers, Greenwood has no notable geographical characteristic that would set it off from other Delta towns. It is an island of flowered greenery in a sea of black, gumbo mud, surrounded by miles of stark cotton fields that have made the city one of the largest cotton markets in the country.

When Beckwith was five, his father died in a sanatorium and left the family deeply in debt, prompting Susie to take her fatherless son to Greenwood, where she could get emotional and financial support from her family. Six years later Susie died of cancer, leaving her son, who by then was called "Delay," to be raised by his two bachelor uncles. There came a time in his upbringing when his uncles thought it best to send him off to school. They chose the Webb School, a prep school in Bell Buckle, Tennessee, that had been founded in 1870 by William Webb, an educator who went on to become a U.S. senator. Preceding Beckwith at the school was Ingram Stainbeck, the first governor of Hawaii, and former Mississippi governor Fielding L. Wright. Another illustrious alumnus was Vermont Royster, the conservative Pulitzer Prize–winning editor of the *Wall Street Journal*, who probably attended classes with Beckwith at the school.

Unfortunately Beckwith found the school more intellectually challenging than he could handle, and he was withdrawn by his uncles, who sent him to a less demanding military school for a time before calling him back to Greenwood to attend the local high school. By most accounts he was a loner, a socially awkward teen who demonstrated all the negative characteristics often associated with a boy who is raised without the guidance of a birth father or suitable male role model. When he wasn't in school, he retreated to the woods around Greenwood, where he hunted and developed an obsession with firearms.

After high school graduation Beckwith enrolled at Mississippi State College, now known as Mississippi State University, where he lasted only a few months. Academics were never his strong point. With absolutely no educational or financial prospects, he found himself at a crossroads, just as the United States itself was at a crossroads with the bombing of Pearl Harbor. Less than a month after the attack, Beckwith enlisted in the U.S. Marine Corps, where he found himself in the company of other men who appreciated the history and attributes of firearms. When the time came for the United States to challenge Japanese control of the Pacific, by attacking Japanese forces on Tarawa Atoll in 1943, Beckwith was in the first wave of troops that fought in that bloody battle. While manning a machine gun, he took a bullet in the leg and spent the next four months in a hospital.

After leaving the hospital, Beckwith was sent to recuperate in Memphis, where he met and married a U.S. Navy Wave named Mary Louise Williams. After their discharge from the armed forces, they went to Greenwood, where they started a family with the 1946 birth of their only child, Byron De La Beckwith VII. He attempted to make a living as a thirty-five-dollar-a-week clerk with Chicago and Southern Airlines, but it wasn't enough to support his family, so for the remainder of the 1940s and into the 1950s, he held numerous sales jobs with locally owned and operated companies that sold everything from candy to cigarettes, each new job an attempt to increase his meager income.

James L. Dickerson:

I was born in Greenwood, not because my family lived there—Mother and Father lived in Greenville—but because Mother wanted to give birth in a hospital where she could be near her sister, my aunt Marcie, a registered nurse who lived in Greenwood. After I was born in 1945, we returned to Greenville, where my family lived until I was three, at which time we moved to Greenwood, where my father operated a department store named May's, which had an entire wing of army surplus goods left over from World War II.

To the best of my knowledge, I never met Byron De La Beckwith, though I almost certainly encountered him from time to time in my father's store, which would have been difficult for Beckwith to stay away from, since it was the only source in that area for the type of military gear with which Beckwith had an obsession. It is also likely that his son and I played on the same school playground, though I was a year older. The year I was born, there were two other people living in Greenwood who went on to achieve fame—mystery writer Mickey Spillane, who lived there with his first wife, Mary Ann Pearce, and Bobbie Gentry, whose 1967 number-one hit "Ode to Billie Joe" made music history.

Another contemporary I never met at the time but surely must have encountered on the streets was movie actor Morgan Freeman, whose childhood experiences in Greenwood overlapped my own. In 2003, I met Freeman for dinner at his upscale Clarksdale restaurant, Madidi, to talk about our shared experiences in Greenwood. Although there is a seven-year difference in our ages, we watched the same parades (and there were plenty of those), shopped in the same stores, and attended the same movie theater, the Paramount, though he was forced to sit in the balcony, since it was during the days of segregation and blacks were forbidden to sit in public areas with whites. As we talked, it became apparent that we were attracted to similar films, mostly westerns and war films staring Gary Cooper, Roy Rogers, John Wayne, and Jimmy Stewart.

I asked Freeman if he'd heard anything about Byron De La Beckwith while he was growing up. He hadn't. As a child he was insulated from the harsher realities of racism.

Suddenly, Freeman drew a line with his finger across the starchy white tablecloth, denoting the way the railroad intersected the city.

"Where did you live?" he asked.

I pointed to one side of the tracks.

"Ah," he intoned, picking up the salt and pepper shakers. "You lived here"—and he placed the salt shaker on one side of the tracks—"and I lived here"—and he placed the pepper shaker in the part of town where he lived.

"I don't remember anything about racial problems," he said. "What I remember is being diagnosed as malnourished by a doctor. I didn't know I wasn't getting the right food. There seemed to be enough food on the table for everyone to eat."

As we talked, a class of high school students from Charleston, the small town outside of Greenwood where Freeman now makes his home, came into the restaurant with one of their teachers. It was a mixed crowd—boys, girls, whites, blacks. When the time came to be seated, they paired off in mixed groups. Black boys and white girls sitting together in a restaurant. Laughing, looking slightly nervous about being in a restaurant with tablecloths. They were obviously there as part of a school function. But what?

Seemingly from nowhere, one of the teachers appeared at our table. She apologized for interrupting our conversation, but she wanted to know if Freeman would be kind enough to pose with the students for a group picture. Freeman smiled and said that he'd be happy to. When he returned to the table, he lowered his voice. "Isn't that something?" he said, speaking in a whisper so that the students wouldn't overhear. "They've come to my restaurant to learn the proper etiquette for eating. Things have really changed since I grew up."

What I was most curious about was why a movie actor of international acclaim, someone who could live anywhere in the world, would choose to return to the Mississippi Delta to live out the rest of his years. The answer was simple: because it felt like home. I couldn't resist asking the obvious: "How did you go through everything that everyone else went through but turn out so differently?"

The answer arrived with the speed of a tennis serve. "How did you do that and turn out the way you did?"

Greenwood offered a full cultural menu. You could pick what you wanted. Byron De La Beckwith looked at that menu and sought nourishment in racial hatred. Morgan Freeman looked at the menu and found emotional nourishment, despite the fact that his actual menu left him malnourished. I looked at the same menu and found racial tolerance. After we moved to Greenwood, I quickly befriended a black man named Ben who worked in my father's store. He was the only African American sales clerk in the entire city. My father, who was from a part of Virginia that had no African Americans, had no idea that there was anything wrong with hiring a black sales clerk. Ben, who was probably in his early fifties, worked in the army surplus wing, where he spent hours explaining to me the uses of various military items. He waited on white customers as well as black customers, but he was good at sensing which white customers did not want to be waited on by a black man. When that happened, he asked my father or one of the white clerks to wait on them. One of the highlights of my day was that he met me at school each day at three o'clock and walked me back to the store so that I could stay with my father until my mother got home from work. I don't recall ever being aware of racial hatred while I lived in Greenwood, though it obviously was festering in the hearts of some. I never heard blacks called niggers. I never heard women called bitches. And I never heard men of any color called sons of bitches.

I had always felt safe in Greenwood. For me it was an idyllic place, where I could walk to school and explore the neighborhood at dusk in search of fireflies without fear of anything bad ever happening to me. That sense of well-being ended rather suddenly on July 29, 1953, the date of my cousin's fourth birthday. Mother and Aunt Marcie planned a party for Janet at the city park near our home, but I really didn't want to go to a party with a bunch of four-year-olds, so I asked my father if he'd take me fishing. We'd gone fishing a couple of weeks before at Third Bridge Lake, and I was eager to return. Father told me that I could invite my best friend, Richard, to go with us.

Since Richard's father had just purchased a new outboard motor he hadn't yet tried out, they decided to make it a father-son affair. We drove to the lake in Father's car, a two-seat roadster with a rumble seat that was perfect for a couple of seven-year-old boys.

The lake was a thirty-minute drive from Greenwood, on the other side of Sidon, a small Delta crossroads town. Once we turned off the main highway, we drove past a row of shotgun shacks to a dirt road that wound several miles through cotton fields and swampy forests before it dead-ended at the lake. Before Father got out of the car, he did something I'd never seen him do: he tucked the car keys behind the sun visor.

We fished on the bank of the lake for a long time, using roaches and crickets for bait, but the fish were not biting that day, so we didn't catch a single one. Finally, when it became obvious that we would be taking home no bluegill bream or bass to fry up for supper, we decided to rent a boat and go for a ride, using Mr. Cooper's new outboard. Two types of boats were available for rent—sixteen-foot military surplus boats that rode deep in the water and had plenty of room to walk around in and fourteen-foot, lightweight skiffs that barely skimmed the surface of the water. We chose the skiff because it was the only boat that would take the outboard motor.

The boat had a seat at the stern, where the outboard was attached, and Mr. Cooper and Richard shared a seat there. Midway up the boat was a seat on which I sat with my father. The third seat was at the bow. It was a wooden boat, and every time we moved our feet, it clanked with dull thuds, sending sound waves out across the water.

The son of the woman who owned the boats, an eight-year-old who was just a year older than I, helped us get into the boat and then untied it so that it could drift away from the dock. Mr. Cooper had a hard time cranking the motor. It had one of those hand cranks, and he pulled it over and over again, right elbow pumping, with no results. Each time he pulled the crank, he adjusted the gasoline flow. Still the motor wouldn't start.

We drifted quietly out into deep water. It was a hot, humid day, with the temperature in the high nineties, and the water was still, with hardly a ripple in sight. Father and I, our backs to Mr. Cooper and Richard, started talking about something and paid no attention to the troubles with the motor. Suddenly, the motor started with a sputtering roar and the boat lurched forward. We turned and looked back at Mr. Cooper, who was frantic because the motor had started at full throttle and he didn't know what to do about it. We turned back to the front of the boat and saw the bow dip beneath the surface of the lake, allowing water to pour over the front seat. The boat was sinking.

We panicked and sprang to our feet, all four of us. I felt my father's strong arms slip around me as he grabbed me and leaped into the water. Mr. Cooper and Richard followed immediately afterward. Even though the boat was made of wood and should have floated, it sank out of sight beneath the muddy water.

With my father's arms wrapped around me, I fell into what felt like a velvet tunnel, a soundless, motionless cocoon that enveloped me like something in a dream. You would think there would be a lot of screaming and thrashing in a situation like that, but no one uttered a sound. The lake was stone-cold silent.

Watching from the dock was the eight-year-old boy, now frightened out of his mind. He jumped into a boat and paddled in our direction. Father held me close against him in the water, keeping the two of us afloat. The rescue boat reached Mr. Cooper and Richard first. As the young boy helped Richard into the boat, my father and I treaded water, about thirty feet away, neither of us saying a word. I had water in my nose from when we first jumped into the lake and I had trouble breathing. I gasped for breath.

Abruptly, without warning, I was airborne, hurtling nearly thirty feet through the air toward Mr. Cooper, a sensation so unlike anything else that I'd ever experienced that I can remember it to this day. Still in the water himself, Mr. Cooper scooped me up and lifted me up to the boat. When I looked back to find Father, he was gone.

The young boy paddled us back to the dock. Mr. Cooper ran to the house with the young boy to get help. But the boy's mother said that she was there alone and could not swim. Neither could Mr. Cooper or Richard or I. The only one who could swim was Father. Mr. Cooper called the sheriff's office and asked them to send help.

I stood on the edge of the dock, shivering, helpless, more scared than I'd ever been in my life. "Daddy!" I called out, peering down into the water. "Daddy, where are you?"

Mr. Cooper returned, and we all stood on the dock and stared out at the lake. Not a ripple or bubble in sight. The greenish water seemed heavy and lifeless, like a huge stained carpet. We waited for the sheriff's deputies. When they arrived, we pointed to where Father had disappeared. The heavyset deputies all stared helplessly at the water. Incredibly, none of them could swim either. After a while Mr. Cooper walked away from me to have a private conversation with the deputies. When he returned, he said, "Let's go find your mother, son."

We walked back to the car and got inside. When Mr. Cooper realized he did not have a key to the car, he asked if I knew if Father kept a second key hidden anywhere. I pointed to the sun visor, and within minutes we were on our way back to town, the rancid, Delta dust behind us, billowing high into the treetops.

Mr. Cooper knew about Janet's birthday party, so he went directly to the park and parked the car near where the party was taking place. As we got out of the car, I saw my mother's head rise above the children and look our way. She saw Mr. Cooper and Richard and me—but not my father. There was a sudden look of panic on her face.

Only a few steps from the picnic table, Mr. Cooper stopped and grabbed me by the shoulders, leaning over to whisper in my ear, "You go tell her, son."

I broke into a run, my arms outstretched to my mother. I cried out, my voice cracked and forlorn, "Mama, Daddy's dead! Daddy's dead!"

Mother took me in her arms and held me tight, looking back at Mr. Cooper. She could tell by his face that it was true. The other women, including Aunt Marcie, gathered around, and together they approached Mr. Cooper and asked what'd happened.

I watched as he told them, their bodies slowly deflated by the bad news, their faces a tangled knot of emotion.

By the time they drove back out to the lake, an ambulance had arrived. There were about a half dozen police cars there. Grim-faced men stood on the dock as a boatload of deputies paddled about in the water, dragging the lake bottom with a metal rod that contained several rows of metal hooks.

They were there only a few minutes when one of the men in the boat screamed out, "Got him!" My heart sank. They found my father only twenty feet from the dock. Mother pulled me, facefirst, into her dress and held me there while the deputies removed my father's body from the water and placed it on a stretcher on the dock. As they tried to resuscitate him, Mother held my face so that I could not watch. Finally, one of the deputies, his hat in his hand, came over to her and said, "I'm sorry, ma'am."

By late afternoon the house had filled with people. Aunt Marcie, who had the face of a saint, held my three-year-old sister, Susan, and talked to her, speaking in soft, measured tones. Susan did not understand what was going on. She was pleased to be getting so much attention. Mother was in the bedroom with the other women.

"Please, just leave me alone!" she cried out.

Finally, everyone did as she asked and left the room.

I quietly made my way back to the bedroom. The sun was just setting, and there was still light coming in the windows. Mother lay facedown across the bed, sobbing, crying out with pain, saying nothing that made any sense to me. An electric fan blew the white, lacey curtains out away from the window. I pressed my back against the wall and quietly edged my way into the room in an attempt to get closer to her.

I'd never seen my mother cry in such torrents. It frightened me to see her in that condition. I felt totally isolated. How would we ever get by without a daddy? I wanted to say something to her, but I was too afraid. I stood there, alone though she was in the room, still smelling of lake water even though I'd changed clothes, feeling smaller and smaller, finally disappearing into the darkness that eventually overtook the room.

For me, Greenwood was the City of Death. Years later, when Beckwith did his foul deed, it confirmed that impression, creating in my mind an image of Beckwith rising out of the swamp, like some sort of hideous Hollywood monster, wearing a hockey mask and clutching a chain saw, a traitor to the tranquility that once resided in Greenwood.

Beckwith's New Obsession

For Byron De La Beckwith, the stresses of making a living were overtaken by the distress he felt over the U.S. Supreme Court's desegregation decision. Now he had a new obsession—the black struggle for equal rights. Somehow he calculated that the freedoms achieved by blacks would be taken away from him. A successful salesman, in the sense that he could relate to others in a folksy manner and make them think that he had what they not only wanted to buy but needed to buy, he added racist spiels to his usual sales pitches for candy, tobacco, and fertilizer. He became an early member of the Greenwood Citizens' Council and worked tirelessly on its behalf, sometimes alternating from concerned citizen to raging psychopath. It was when he read about the Memphis gathering, and then later stories about the creation of the Mississippi Sovereignty Commission, that he sent Governor Coleman the letter offering his skills as a marksman.

In 1955 the Citizens' Council moved its headquarters to Greenwood, a decision that fed Beckwith's obsession. That same year, interestingly enough, one of Beckwith's cousins on his mother's side of the family, Wirt Yerger Jr., spearheaded a movement to reestablish the Republican Party in Mississippi. As you might expect, the fledgling Mississippi Republican Party was not the GOP of Abraham Lincoln but rather more like the intolerant party of Richard Nixon. Yerger, who subsequently has been described as the father of the modern Republican Party in Mississippi, was a delegate to the 1956 Republican Convention, which saw Dwight D. Eisenhower renominated for a second term with Richard Nixon as his vice president. Later, Yerger would be angered by Eisenhower's decision to send the 101st Airborne Division to Little Rock, Arkansas, to protect black children; he would charge Eisenhower with "joining hands with the NAACP" in a scheme to destroy the U.S. Constitution. Like Yerger, Beckwith despised President Eisenhower, and he divided his time between railing about Eisenhower and attacking integration in general. As with any other obsession, his racial hatred deplored a vacuum and fed his obsession for firearms, to the point where he sometimes traveled with as many as thirty or forty pistols, rifles, and shotguns in the car with him, sometimes out in full view, riding beside him on the front seat, and other times hidden in suitcases.

As Beckwith's obsessions spiraled out of control, his marriage to Mary Louise, or "Willie" as Beckwith called her, disintegrated to the point where they fought constantly, sometimes violently.[5] Neighbors said she was as mean and racist as her husband and was known to fire off a few rounds at him on occasion.

By the early 1960s it appeared that Beckwith's street corner rants, during which he handed out literature and preached the gospel of hate, were beginning to pay off. Greenwood underwent a radical transformation, taking on the personality of Beckwith himself, as normally polite discourse between the races boiled over into a level of fear and loathing unknown in the city's history. Mayor C. E. Sampson blamed the city's problems on communism and issued a statement to that effect that was read by Senator James O. Eastland on the floor of the Senate.[6]

In August 1962 two representatives of the Student Nonviolent Coordinating Committee (SNCC) lead a parade of about two dozen blacks who marched through the cobblestone streets to the county courthouse, where they attempted to register to vote.[7] Several were disqualified and rejected by the clerk. The Sovereignty Commission listed some of the reasons in a report: "Ida Mae claims she could not read or write, which disqualified her. . . . Aaron had tried twice previously and failed both examinations. He is mentally incapacitated. . . . Ida Emma was caught cheating and disqualified by the clerk."

The registration attempt attracted a camera crew from CBS Chicago and several wire service reporters, all of whom witnessed a violence-free parade and registration. Once the news media left town, however, one of the SNCC leaders was pulled from his car by several white men and given a good beating. The following year, four voter registration workers in Greenwood were fired on with a shotgun by white men in a light-colored station wagon.[8] None of the workers were hit by the pellets, but two received cuts from the broken glass. In a front-page editorial, the *Greenwood Commonwealth* deplored the racial incidents: "Those who think guns will bring any kind of solution

. . . can't think past the end of their noses. They aren't doing their neighbors any favors."

By the time Medgar Evers was shot in his driveway, Beckwith had observed firsthand a constant stream of senseless racial violence in his hometown.[9] He and his wife had been divorced, remarried, divorced, and married again—and, according to the *New York Times*, he had been treated by a psychiatrist at the University of Mississippi Medical Center for undisclosed problems.

Beckwith was a deeply troubled soul who mistook dark obsession for righteousness.

8

Philadelphia Burning

Not far into the second month of his administration in 1964, Governor Paul B. Johnson received a letter from State Representative Betty Jane Long of Meridian requesting an investigation of Michael and Rita Schwerner, a white couple from New York who ran the Congress of Racial Equality (CORE) office in Meridian.[1] The governor referred the letter to Sovereignty Commission director Erle Johnston, who assigned an investigator to the case.

The investigator compiled a dossier on the couple, along with reports of their daily activities and their schedules, and passed it along to Representative Long in a series of reports. Included in the report was a description of the 1963 station wagon the couple drove and the vehicle's Hinds County license number—H25 503. It's not known what Long did with those reports—she later served on the commission from 1968 to 1972, so she obviously considered herself a guardian of Mississippi Values—but it seems safe to say that the information fell into the wrong hands, whether it was intentional or not.

As surveillance of the Schwerners intensified, the commission sent an undercover agent—identified only as "Investigator 51"—to Selma, Alabama, to make an arms purchase.[2] It is one of the most chilling episodes in the commission's history. In a report to the governor on the agent's activities, Johnston wrote:

> We authorized the investigator to buy two .38-caliber pistols and bring them back to the Sovereignty Commission. These revolvers are being sold by the dealer for only $11 each and are very similar to the pistols which were shipped into Walthall County by a dealer in California. These pistols are now in a cabinet in the Sovereignty Commission office. The dealer had on hand about 1,500 rifles and several cases of weapons still unopened.

In his report the investigator said that after he picked out the pistols, the dealer took out a notepad and asked the investigator for his name. "I gave the name as Douglas Graves, Route 1, Brandon, Mississippi," the investigator said, indicating he had lied. As the dealer finished his paperwork, the investigator cased the room. He noted in his report, "This area is just behind [the dealer's] house, and any forced entry could easily be seen from the house." He seemed to suggest that it would be difficult for a commission operative to break into the store without being seen.

Schwerner, Goodman, and Chaney

On Sunday, June 21, 1964, Michael Schwerner, along with two other civil rights workers, Andrew Goodman of New York and James Chaney of Meridian, set out from Meridian to investigate the burning of the Mount Zion Methodist Church in the eastern part of Neshoba County, not far from Philadelphia, the county seat.[3] Schwerner and Chaney had been under surveillance by the Sovereignty Commission for several months. Goodman had arrived in Meridian the night before from Oxford, Ohio, where he had undergone training for the Mississippi Summer Project, a voter registration effort organized by CORE, the Student Nonviolent Coordinating Committee (SNCC), the Southern Christian Leadership Conference (SCLC), and the NAACP.

As they passed through Philadelphia, with Chaney at the wheel, they were stopped for speeding by Deputy Sheriff Cecil Price. After he pulled them over, Price asked Chaney, who was black, and Schwerner and Goodman, who were white, what they were doing in Neshoba County. They said they had come to investigate a church burning. Price gave Chaney a ticket for speeding and told them he was going to have to take them in for questioning about the church burning.

As they were talking, one of the station wagon's tires went flat. Price radioed for backup from the highway patrol and was helping the men change the tire when two patrolmen arrived.[4] With the tire changed, the highway patrolmen escorted the deputy sheriff and the men in the station wagon to the Neshoba County jail. Price told the men that they could make a telephone call, but for reasons that remain a mystery, they chose not to do so, a mistake that sealed their fate. The three prisoners were fed a big country dinner, held until 10:30 that night, and then released after they paid a twenty dollar bond set by the justice of the peace. As they were leaving, Price asked them where they were headed. They said they were returning to Meridian. Price stood outside the courthouse and watched them drive onto Highway 45 and head toward Meridian.

When the three men failed to return to Meridian that night, their families and friends notified authorities. By the next morning word had spread throughout Philadelphia that something bad had happened to the men after their release. For local residents, it was a "perfect storm" of circumstance for disaster. Chaney was black, reason enough to be on the Klan's hit list. Schwerner and Goodman were white, but they were also "Jesus killing" Jews from the North, more than enough to land them on a hit list.

Buford Posey, a white Neshoba County resident who had been under surveillance by the Sovereignty Commission for voicing pro-NAACP opinions, received two telephone calls the next morning, one from the jailer's wife and the other from his daughter. Both women expressed concern that something had happened to the missing men.

Posey notified the FBI of his concerns and said that he thought the county sheriff, Lawrence Rainey, was a member of the Klan.

On Tuesday, June 23, an anonymous caller notified the FBI of the whereabouts of the station wagon the men had been driving. With little trouble, FBI agents located the vehicle on a narrow country road near the Bogue Chitto swamp. It had been doused with gasoline and burned. There was no sign of the civil rights workers. As news of the discovery made headlines across the nation, Attorney General Robert Kennedy ordered an FBI investigation and President Lyndon Johnson sent two hundred sailors from the naval base in Meridian to assist in the search for the missing men.

Ex-CIA Chief Visits Commission

On Wednesday, June 24, the day after the missing car was found, former CIA director Allen Dulles walked into the offices of the Sovereignty Commission for a meeting with Erle Johnston. Dulles had been sent by President Johnson to compile a report on the activities of two organizations under general investigation: the White Knights of the Ku Klux Klan of Mississippi and the Americans for the Preservation of the White Race.

Commission director Johnston downplayed KKK involvement.[5] Instead he blamed the Communist Party, citing evidence that he had linked "Communist front organizations with racial agitators." Dulles was not impressed. He returned to Washington and met with the president, after which he issued a statement saying that Mississippi had a "very real" law enforcement problem.

Johnston was stunned by Dulles's comments. Dulles was not technically a member of the government, but he was a representative of the president and one of the nation's top former spies. Why would a man of Dulles's reputation be interested in the Mississippi Klan? Wasn't that an encroachment into states' rights? Johnston asked.

Because of the inquiry, Johnston felt the need to send a memo to the governor explaining his meeting with Dulles. "They asked me if it were true that the APWR [Americans for the Preservation of the

White Race] was responsible for five deaths in southwest Mississippi," he said. "I informed them that the Sovereignty Commission had a few files on both of these organizations and some of their literature, but we had no cause for any concern or policies toward these groups so long as the groups and their members observed Governor Johnson's policies of law and order. I told him that we had no knowledge of any connection between APWR as an organization and any violence in southwest Mississippi."

On the day after Johnston's meeting with Dulles, the parents of Goodman and Schwerner went on national television in New York to talk about their missing sons. Chaney's mother joined them from Mississippi via a telephone hookup. Americans were outraged by the inability of Mississippi law enforcement officials to locate the missing civil rights workers, but for the Sovereignty Commission it was business as usual that week. On June 26, Johnston sent a memo to the highway patrol requesting an escort for a paid commission informant who was traveling back to Mississippi from Oxford, Ohio, where he had participated undercover in a CORE training program for civil rights workers. The informant was identified only as a black male.

Johnston informed the highway patrol that the CORE informant would be traveling in a 1957 green-and-beige Cadillac. He said the informant would be accompanied by his wife and a white male. "It is very important that you understand that the white male does not know about the informant's connection with the Sovereignty Commission," Johnston said. "Subject has been advised that if the car is stopped for any traffic violation, etc., that whatever fines are imposed be paid without question."[6]

When the informant arrived in Jackson, he reported that John Doar, the despised U.S. Justice Department official who had assisted James Meredith at Ole Miss, was a guest speaker at the training session.[7] He detailed some of the group's activities, then told Johnston what he wanted to hear. "The white girls have been going around with the negro boys and negro girls going with the white boys. I have seen these integrated couples going into the dorms together for extended periods of time."

While FBI agents, sailors from the naval base, and CORE volunteers searched through the unfriendly Neshoba County countryside for the missing civil rights workers, the Sovereignty Commission was providing a CORE informant with safe passage through the state. CORE was at the top of the commission's hit list.

James L. Dickerson:

I was attending the University of Mississippi when the news broke about the missing civil rights workers in Philadelphia. The student newspaper, the *Daily Mississippian*, kept students informed with page-one stories written by Associated Press reporters. From the day the civil rights workers were reported missing, it seemed that there was a new story every day exploring some new facet of the case.

Late one night that summer, I went into what I think was the only coin-operated Laundromat in Oxford. It was located in a small strip mall, a dingy, poorly lit hole-in-the-wall that reeked of laundry detergent and damp concrete. There were about a half dozen plastic chairs to sit in while your clothes washed and dried—thirty minutes to wash, forty-five minutes to dry. I usually took a book to read while I waited.

On this particular day, I was occupied with a Faulkner novel when a gruff-looking man with Mark Twain hair and thick, bushy gray eyebrows about the density of a squirrel's tail entered the Laundromat and started checking the machines in an official capacity. I looked up and saw that he was staring at me—and at my book—a pronounced frown breaking his forehead into hundreds of tiny wrinkles. I continued reading, trying my best not to make eye contact with him.

Without saying a word, he left the room and got into the cab of a truck that was parked in front of the Laundromat. A few minutes later he reentered the Laundromat, walked up to me, and shoved a book in front of me, sort of grunting but saying nothing. I put my book aside and took his book to examine. The title was *The Formation of the Negro* by L. G. Lynch.

"That's me," he said, proudly popping his finger against the book.

"Oh," I said, impressed that I was in the company of an author. I had never met an author. I was impressed until I started thumbing through the book and saw some of the most racist writing I'd ever encountered.

Lynch didn't wait for me to ask questions about the book. With his voice sputtering like a lawn mower, he started telling me about it while I continued to flip the pages. "That book tells nothing but the truth. The Negro is nothing more than a high form of the ape. They're no more human than dogs are."

I was speechless. I'd been around racists my entire life, but that odd fellow with fiery eyes was in a category all to himself. Luckily, my dryer buzzer went off. I handed him his book and hurried over to the dryer.

"I got an extra copy in the truck I can sell you," he shouted after me.

I told him the truth: I didn't have enough money on me to purchase the book. I saw no point in arguing with him about his comments or his book. It was late at night, and he looked like something the dogs had dragged out of the swamp. Sometimes it's better to just walk away, which is what I did as quickly as I could gather up my clothes.

Forty-four years later I came across the name of L. G. Lynch while I was doing research in the Sovereignty Commission archives. In a memo to his boss, one of the investigators reported on Lynch's book. "This author has a very unusual theory regarding the Negro race. He says the negro is a high form of ape, much less a low form of man." He went on to say that while he had not personally read the book, he had looked through a copy owned by a Canton justice of the peace.

As disturbing as L. G. Lynch was to me, he was just another brick in the wall.

The Bodies Are Found

With the investigation into the disappearance of the missing civil rights workers entering its eighth day, Sovereignty Commission investigator Andrew Hopkins returned to Neshoba County on June 29 to continue surveillance of the FBI. Hopkins met with Sheriff Lawrence Rainey and Deputy Sheriff Cecil Price. Rainey told Hopkins that he, Price, and Hale Singletary, an investigator with the Mississippi Fire

Marshal's Office, were at the burned church when they received word that the station wagon driven by the civil rights workers had been found. Together, they rushed over to the swamp, where they found twelve FBI agents at the crime scene. Hopkins reported that when the sheriff first arrived on the scene, he was told by an FBI agent not to approach the car, but that he later was given permission by FBI agent John Proctor. Hopkins said in his report that when the sheriff asked who had found the car, Agent Proctor told him that it had been reported to his office in Meridian but he could not disclose the person's identity.[8]

From the details provided in his report, it was obvious that Hopkins knew as much about the crime as the FBI:

> The results of my investigation indicate that the automobile was parked and burned on the log road between 11:00 a.m. and 1:30 p.m., Monday, June 22. I reached this conclusion because a witness was working on a log truck within 200 feet of the spot where the car burned. . . . The condition of the car, the washed out tire and footprints indicated that the car and terrain was rained on after the car was burned. I was in the Philadelphia area at this time and the only rain in this area between 11:00 A.M. Monday and Tuesday afternoon when the car was found, occurred between 1:30 P.M. and 3:00 P.M. Monday, June 22.

Sheriff Rainey told Hopkins he resented the way the FBI had treated his wife. She was in the hospital convalescing after surgery, he said, when she was questioned by FBI agents about his whereabouts on the evening the civil rights workers disappeared. Hopkins noted that Sheriff Rainey himself was a suspect in the disappearance of the three civil rights workers. Wrote Hopkins: "The sheriff stated that near the end of the interview, an agent said to him: 'Now come on sheriff and tell us what you did with those people.' One agent asked the sheriff if he was a member of the KKK and, of course, the sheriff denied being a member of the Klan as he has repeatedly denied it to me since the beginning of this investigation." Sheriff Rainey told Hopkins that at one point during his questioning, an FBI agent pointed his finger at him and said, "Don't you defy the federal government!"

Hopkins attempted to find out from the FBI who had reported the location of the station wagon, but agents refused to share that information with him. Sheriff Rainey told him that he expected to be arrested at any time. For that reason, the sheriff confided, he had called Attorney General Joe Patterson to inquire about the procedure for making bail in the event he was arrested. Reported Hopkins: "Sheriff Rainey and his deputy, Cecil Price, and Richard Willis, a night policeman of Philadelphia, are the prime suspects in this case as Deputy Price and Richard Willis were the last two persons to have seen the missing individuals."

As the FBI dug for more information about the missing civil rights workers, Hopkins continued his surveillance of the FBI. He noted that they had set up headquarters in Room 18 at the Delphia Motel in Philadelphia, "where they have a radio and straight-line telephones installed." On July 1, he observed the FBI installing a radio antenna on top of the city water tower "in an effort to contact Meridian direct by radio and to better receive communications from their mobile units."

About one month later, on August 4, based on a paid informant's tip, the FBI discovered the bodies of the civil rights workers buried deep within an earthen dam just outside Philadelphia. When U.S. attorney general Nicholas Katzenbach asked to be informed of the identity of the informant, the FBI balked, taking the position that they could not share that information since it would result in the source's death.[9]

When Hopkins heard the news that the bodies had been found, he rushed back to Neshoba County and spoke to Mrs. Frankie Chisolm, an office deputy who had heard rumors that the FBI planned to arrest Deputy Price and charge him with the murders. Mrs. Chisolm told Hopkins that Sheriff Rainey was vacationing in Biloxi with his wife and two sons when the bodies were discovered but was expected to arrive back in town later that night. After talking to Mrs. Chisolm, Hopkins drove out to the crime scene, a distance of about six miles from the courthouse. Not far from the dam, Hopkins encountered a roadblock manned by two Mississippi highway patrolmen. They told him the bodies had been removed and were on the way to University Hospital in Jackson, where an autopsy would be performed.

Hopkins was considerably more interested in finding out who had tipped off the FBI about the location of the bodies than he was in identifying their killers. He was told that the FBI had offered Deputy Sheriff Price one million dollars for evidence that would solve the case. Noted Hopkins in his report: "The agents told Price that he could 'leave Mississippi with that kind of money and buy a cattle ranch in Wyoming.'"

Hopkins was convinced that the FBI informant was an eyewitness to the killings, since "the bodies were found in the section where very little searching had been done." Apart from learning the identity of the informant, the thing that most interested Hopkins was whether the FBI knew the caliber of the gun that was used to shoot the men. His source informed him that there was one bullet in Schwerner's body, one bullet in Goodman's body, and three bullets in Chaney's body, but the caliber of the bullets or whether they were all fired from the same gun was still unknown. Hopkins shared the results of his information with the highway patrol, but not with the FBI, since "they already have most of it."

The next morning, when Hopkins returned to the crime scene, he encountered Sheriff Rainey and Deputy Price, who were inspecting the area with a coroner's jury. Rainey told him the FBI had made "threats" to encourage him to tell them what he knew about the crime. By "threats," he explained that they'd told him they had information linking him to a bootlegging operation. If that information were turned over to the IRS, the agents allegedly told him, he would owe several thousand dollars in back taxes. If he would cooperate with them, the agents promised to keep quiet about the bootlegging.

Hopkins remained in Philadelphia through August 6 and then returned to Jackson. In his report he said that the FBI informant would be in "danger" if his identity were ever revealed. "Several people, including trouble-makers, have expressed their dissatisfaction that someone informed to the FBI and have made remarks that they would hate to be in his shoes when people find out who he is."

The FBI is an investigative agency, not a prosecutorial one, so when it uncovers evidence of a crime, it turns the information over to the prosecuting authority that has jurisdiction over the case—local, state, or federal. In this case, however, the agency did not turn the evidence over to the local district attorney, because two county officials were thought to be involved and the agency had no confidence that the case would be prosecuted. Neither did the agency turn the evidence over to Governor Johnson or Attorney General Patterson. The last time they'd shared evidence with Mississippi state officials—in the Poplarville lynching case—no effort was made to pursue prosecution. Because they didn't trust Mississippi officials to prosecute the case, the FBI turned the evidence over to the U.S. Justice Department so that the men implicated in the crime could be prosecuted in federal court. Since murder is not a federal crime, the Justice Department decided to prosecute the suspects on civil rights violations.

Alex A. Alston Jr.:

The month of June 1964 was a very busy time for me. The law firm I joined had an extremely heavy work load. I had been practicing law for only a few months, and the firm had no hesitation in laying a huge amount of work on me. I was required to do what the firm called "community work," and to that end I was asked to become scoutmaster of a local Boy Scout troop. My wife had just delivered our second baby, Alyce, earlier that month. The overwhelming legal work, chasing fifty Boy Scouts around, and trying to keep my family intact—all on a starting associate's salary of five hundred dollars a month—were quite challenging.

I paid little attention to the murder of the three civil rights workers in Philadelphia, which had occurred earlier in the month. Other priorities were overwhelming me. The local newspaper was telling us that it was probably a Communist plot to make Mississippi look bad, and the editorials suggested that the three were probably in the Bahamas drinking Bahama Mamas and laughing at all the commotion. Like nearly everyone, I kept silent. There was no talk about these murders in the law firm or in my circle of friends, other than admonitions not to get involved. The sinister plot to embarrass the state would soon be exposed.

But I surprised even myself when I broke that silence. At ten o'clock every morning, all fourteen members of the firm went downstairs to the Belmont Café for a coffee break. This was not just routine; it was a required ritual. Although legal matters were discussed, nothing was mentioned about the murders. The head of the firm, whom the younger members called "the Big Cheese," W. Calvin Wells III, always sat at the end of the table and often would steer the coffee conversation. One morning after it had been reported in the newspaper that someone had broken the conspiracy of silence and told the FBI where the bodies of these three civil rights workers were buried, the Big Cheese surprisingly stated that he "could not believe a white man in this state could have possibly ratted on those people and told the FBI."

Without thinking, and almost in shock, I exclaimed, "My God, Mr. Wells, I can't believe that any person would not have told. This is murder." Silence! All coffee cups stayed at half-mast. Slowly and silently the cups were eased into their saucers and each of the lawyers around the table arose from their seats and went to their offices without a word to me. I remember that the only lawyer left seated with me was my young friend and associate Walker Watters.

I looked at him and said, "What now?" because I did not know whether I would be fired or what would happen. Walker simply patted me on my shoulder and said, "It will be okay." As far as I can remember, it was okay. The firm kept piling the work on me, and I stayed with the firm until it dissolved four years later and I started my own firm.

The FBI Makes Arrests

On the morning of December 4, 1964, Mrs. Chisolm turned on her radio and heard that the FBI was making arrests in the murder case involving the civil rights workers. Her worst suspicions were soon confirmed. Her boss, Sheriff Lawrence Rainey, and his chief deputy,

Cecil Price, had been arrested, along with nineteen other citizens of Philadelphia and Meridian, including Olen Burrage, the thirty-four-year-old truck company manager that the Sovereignty Commission suspected of being the informant, and Edgar Ray Killen, a thirty-nine-year-old preacher who lived in Union. Mrs. Chisolm wasted no time in calling commission investigator Andrew Hopkins, who rushed to Neshoba County as soon as he got the news.

When Hopkins arrived, he learned that all twenty-one men had been brought before a federal commissioner in Meridian, charged with violating the civil rights of the murdered men, and then transported to the naval base in Meridian, where they were not being allowed visitors. In a report to the governor dated December 8, 1964, Hopkins listed the names of the men who were arrested. With unusual candor, he admitted that several individuals he considered suspects were not among them, while others he had never suspected were. "[The FBI] theory seems to be that some of those involved observed the civil rights workers when they left Meridian and then notified others in the Philadelphia area who were in on the plot," he wrote in his report. "They evidently believe that these subjects were followed out of Philadelphia for several miles where they were stopped by several carloads of white men who blocked the highway (four cars). From that point, the FBI evidently believes that the victims were taken to a deserted spot in rural Neshoba County where they were executed." Hopkins concluded that Schwerner was the real target of the killers; Chaney and Goodman were just in the wrong place at the wrong time.[10]

Four days later U.S. Commissioner Esther Carter shocked the country by dropping charges against most of the men. (The commissioner's office is no longer in existence, but at that time U.S. commissioners performed most of the duties now assigned to federal magistrates.) Carter, a grandmotherly white woman in her sixties, was not a lawyer and had requested that a law clerk sit at her side during the proceedings. Federal prosecutors were stunned by her decision. On the heels of that disappointment, a second commissioner in Biloxi released another defendant. The two remaining defendants were held in jails in Mississippi and in Louisiana for a while longer, and then charges against them also were dropped.

More than a month after federal prosecutors were dealt a stunning defeat in the Neshoba County murder case, they were successful in obtaining indictments from a federal grand jury in Jackson on eighteen of the twenty-one men originally charged. The trial would be held in the courtroom of Judge Harold Cox, the race-baiting jurist Senator Eastland had won in a trade for Supreme Court justice Thurgood Marshall. Eastland was confident that Cox would do the right thing and stand tall for Mississippi Values. Cox didn't disappoint. His first judicial act in the Neshoba County murder case was to dismiss all the felony indictments. He ruled the defendants could be charged with only misdemeanors.

The Sovereignty Commission sent investigator Andrew Hopkins back to Neshoba County to gather more information. In his report Hopkins gave a detailed description of the murders, details, he said, that were obtained from a reliable source.

> I was informed that the civil rights workers were shot and killed in the following order. Michael Schwerner was shot one time and killed and was the first victim. Andrew Goodman was the second victim and was also shot one time and killed. James Chaney, the colored member of this group, is alleged to have broke [sic] from the group of men that were holding them captive. Shortly after he made the break, he was shot several times by several different people but was struck by only three bullets each of which was alleged to have been fired from a different firearm.[11]

Hopkins said similar information was contained in confessions allegedly given to the FBI by two of the defendants. After the FBI arrested one of the men, Hopkins explained, he was taken to a local motel and forced to sit in a chair for ten hours without water and had limited access to the bathroom. "I was further informed that on at least two occasions, the FBI gave this subject substantial sums of money for his confession or cooperation and offered him more money if he would go to Dallas, Texas, and remain there until the trial."

Hopkins concluded with the ominous admission that "the defense attorneys already have this information and probably will handle it in the manner it should be handled."

Justice on the Rebound

The Justice Department appealed Judge Cox's decision to the United States Supreme Court—and won, receiving a favorable decision in March 1966. While the case was on appeal, many people assumed the issued was closed. Mississippi judges had circled their wagons. The consensus was that it would take more than the power of the federal government to break through the state's legal barricades.

If Governor Johnson thought the Neshoba County case was closed, he must have been shocked to receive a sixteen-page letter later that month from Roy Moore, agent in charge of the Jackson FBI bureau. The letter, stamped SECRET, provided the governor with the names of known KKK members in Mississippi. Not only did the letter identify Sheriff Rainey and two of his deputies, Cecil Price and Hop Barnett, as members of the Neshoba County Klavern of the White Knights of the Ku Klux Klan of Mississippi, but it also listed the names of sheriffs, constables, and highway patrolmen all across the state. In addition, the FBI letter listed the leadership of the statewide organizations of the United Klans of America, the Mississippi Ku Klux Klan, and the White Knights. Also included was a county-by-county breakdown, with the names of each Klan member listed in alphabetical order. The FBI was particularly interested in Klan involvement among law enforcement officers. Earlier in the summer, the Klan had held a large rally at Delta City, a small community not far from Greenville, to swear in twenty-nine new members. Twenty-seven of the new members attended the ceremony. The two who did not were employees of the Mississippi Highway Patrol.

Justice in Mississippi was put on hold for almost a year before the U.S. Supreme Court overruled Judge Cox in March. Defense attorneys filed a motion to throw out the indictments on the grounds that the grand jury had been chosen improperly. To everyone's surprise, the Justice Department agreed. Judge Cox promptly dismissed the indictments, allowing the defendants to think they had gotten off scot-free.

Only later did it become obvious that the Justice Department had agreed with the defense motion in order to reorganize its case. It dropped several defendants from the case and added KKK "imperial wizard" Sam Holloway Bowers Jr. and former Neshoba County sheriff Hop Barnett. In February 1967 prosecutors went before a new grand jury in Jackson and secured indictments on the original conspiracy charges.

On October 19, 1967, eighteen defendants went on trial in Judge Harold Cox's courtroom on charges of conspiracy to deprive Goodman, Chaney, and Schwerner of their civil rights. The prosecution was led by John Doar, who had battled with Mississippi over the integration of Ole Miss. It was an important case for Doar. Not only would it be the first time the Civil Rights Division had ever tried a case in Mississippi, but it was also Doar's *last* case as a federal prosecutor. He had announced plans to retire from the Justice Department at the conclusion of the trial.

Facing off against Doar were *all* of the practicing attorneys in Neshoba County. All twelve of them. With eighteen defendants and twelve attorneys, the defense table had the look of a rather large family reunion picnic. Some of the men, such as Sheriff Rainey, had their cheeks bulging with chewing tobacco. The defendants and their attorneys seemed confident. They laughed and joked with each other. They reacted warmly with the spectators. They seemed impatient to get the whole thing over with, so they could go home and resume their lives.

Doar presented his evidence in a methodical manner to the all-white jury of seven women and five men. He traced the movements of the civil rights workers from the time they left Meridian to when they arrived in Philadelphia and were arrested and jailed. One of the government witnesses was the Reverend Charles Johnson, who had worked with Michael Schwerner in Meridian that summer. When he was cross-examined by one of the defense attorneys, he was asked if it were true that he and Schwerner had tried to get young blacks to agree to rape white women in the city. Saying the question was "highly improper," Cox asked for an explanation. The defense attorney responded that he asked the question because he had been slipped a note from one of the defendants instructing him to ask it. Cox looked agitated. "Who is the author of that question?" he demanded.

The courtroom grew very quiet as the judge waited for an answer.

Finally, the defense attorney identified the defendant.

With the jury still in the courtroom, Cox eyed the defendants. Speaking sternly, he said, "I am not going to allow a farce to be made of this trial. And everybody might as well get that through their heads, including every one of these defendants." As the judge's words deflated the defense team, the courtroom got so quiet, according to observers, that you could have heard a pin drop.

One of Doar's key witnesses was James Jordan, who had been named in the original indictments. After he agreed to become a government witness, he and his family were relocated to Georgia for their protection. When Jordan was delivered to the courthouse earlier that day by five FBI agents, with guns drawn, he showed signs of tension. Before he could be called to the stand, he collapsed and was removed from the courthouse on a stretcher. That made defense attorneys think that they had won the case. To everyone's surprise, Jordan returned to the courthouse the next day surrounded by FBI agents. When he was called to the witness stand, he told the jury that he had been in the group that had abducted and killed the civil rights workers—and he told about burying their bodies.

Another key witness was Carlton Miller, a forty-three-year-old Meridian police officer and Klansman who became an informant in the summer of 1964. Memos to FBI director J. Edgar Hoover from the Jackson FBI office as early as September 1964 indicate that the agency had checked him out and was confident of his credibility.[12]

At the trial Miller testified that he had gone to school in Neshoba County with Edgar Ray Killen, a distant relative. He was recruited by Killen in 1964 to become a member of the White Knights of the Ku

Klux Klan. It was shortly after that, he testified, that Killen talked to him about the Philadelphia murders: "He told me that he wanted to talk to me and he and I went back to my back room and we sat on the bed, and we were discussing the civil rights workers. Mr. Killen told me that they had been shot, that they were dead, and that they were buried in a dam about fifteen feet deep."[13]

In his closing argument Doar assured the jury that the federal government had no intention of "invading Philadelphia or Neshoba County." He praised the courage of the three informants who had testified for the government. They were essential in cracking the case. "Midnight murder in the rural area of Neshoba County provides few witnesses," he said. He pointed his finger at Deputy Sheriff Cecil Price and said he had abused the power of his office and was responsible for the conspiracy.

After deliberating for one day, the jurors returned to the courtroom and reported that they were deadlocked. Judge Cox instructed the jury to resume their deliberations. He made it clear he wanted a verdict. The following day the jury returned with verdicts. The jury foreman handed a sealed envelope to the court clerk, who tore it open and began reading: "We, the jury, find the defendant Cecil Ray Price not guilty."

There was a gasp in the courtroom. Then the jury foreman continued speaking. "I'm sorry, Your Honor, may I start over?"

Cox nodded.

"We, the jury, find the defendant Cecil Ray Price *guilty* of the charges contained in the indictment. . . ."

Guilty verdicts against six additional defendants were announced. Named were Jimmy Arledge, Jimmy Snowden, Sam Bowers, Alton Wayne Roberts, Billy Wayne Posey, and Horace Doyle Barnette. Eight defendants were acquitted, including Sheriff Lawrence Rainey. The jury was unable to reach a verdict on three of the defendants, including Edgar Ray Killen, the Baptist preacher who was accused of masterminding the plot, and former sheriff Hop Barnett.

Cox allowed the defendants who were acquitted to leave the courtroom while he explained the bond procedures to those who had been found guilty. He then released everyone on bond except Price and Roberts, whom he told to approach the bench. Cox told them that it was his intention to deny them bond over the weekend because of inflammatory comments they had made in the courtroom and outside in the hallway. Said Cox: "I'm not going to let any wild men loose on a civilized society."

At the sentencing hearing on December 29, Judge Cox gave Roberts and Bowers ten years each; Posey and Price six years each; and Barnette, Snowden, and Arledge three years each. Cox later explained his sentences this way: "They killed one nigger, one Jew, and a white man. I gave them all what I thought they deserved."

The Justice Department was happy to get the convictions, but the trial left many questions unanswered. Where were the guns used in the murders? Why did informants not disclose the location of the guns? Or did they? Why did the state not press murder charges after the men were convicted in federal court? What involvement did the Sovereignty Commission have in the murders?

The defendants immediately filed an appeal and went home to their families, released on bond while their appeals were prepared. Cecil Price was still deputy sheriff. Lawrence Rainey was still sheriff. Life quickly returned to normal in Neshoba County.

Murders! What Murders?

In 1969 the Fifth Circuit Court of Appeals denied a new trial application from the men convicted of violating the civil rights of Schwerner, Goodman, and Chaney. It was going on five years since the murders, and the convicted men were still free. Their lawyers appealed to the U.S. Supreme Court, but in 1970 the High Court refused to revisit the case. Sam Bowers, Cecil Price, and the other conspirators were taken off to prison.

Mississippi could have prosecuted the men for murder but declined to do so. The crime with which they were charged—violating the civil rights of the murdered men—was a federal law, not a state violation. The murders themselves were inconsequential to the

State of Mississippi. Periodically, Mississippi officials were asked by reporters if the men were ever going to be tried by the state for murder. Over the years official reaction ranged from "We're looking into that" to a final admission that it was too late because "those files were lost a long time ago."

FBI agent Jim Ingram, who was in charge of the civil rights desk in the Jackson office, later was haunted by the fact that the three murdered men had been offered a telephone call by their jailers but had declined to take advantage of the offer. In an interview with the authors, he explained: "I don't know what their thinking was. [Some people] thought they were not in harm's way in Neshoba County and would return to Lauderdale County. But they should have made that phone call. A lot of lessons were learned from that day. After that, any civil rights workers who came to Mississippi knew, if they were arrested, to immediately make that phone call."

9

Charles Moore and Henry Dee

Racial violence occurred with alarming regularity all across Mississippi in the 1960s, but looking at Pike County alone, the horrific acts of savagery are astounding. Roy Littlejohn, staff attorney for the United States Commission on Civil Rights, in hearings held in Jackson in 1965, reported a dismal record for Pike County, a southern Mississippi jurisdiction that has a common border with Louisiana. According to Littlejohn, terrorist activity during 1964 included the bombing of fourteen black homes, a Masonic meeting hall, and a church, and arson attacks that destroyed or damaged four other churches.

Earlier, a firebomb was thrown at NAACP leader Curtis Bryant, and on two different nights numerous crosses were burned throughout the county. Littlejohn continued his report by noting that on one night in June, three black homes were bombed, "two local Negroes were abducted and beaten, and three northern white men were assaulted, while the third was held at gunpoint."

Littlejohn noted that violence had reached a peak during the first three weeks in September, when seven black homes were bombed, one church was destroyed by fire, and three Council of Federated Organizations workers were assaulted. Similar acts of brutality could be cited in counties all across the state in 1964. Mississippians didn't need a lawyer from the Commission on Civil Rights to tell them that. All they had to do was stick their head out the front door and listen. Night screams were as common as summer thunderstorms.

"What's that I hear outside?"

"A bobcat maybe? Panthers scream, don't they?"

"No, I don't think it's a cat. I think somebody got a hold of a nigger."

"Pass the cornbread, please."

Meadville's Mean Streak

Charles Eddie Moore and Henry Hezekiah Dee, both black nineteen-year-olds, were typical teens for the 1960s. There wasn't much to do in Meadville (population 594), except to walk around town to see what everyone else was doing, which was usually not very much. Meadville was the county seat of Franklin County, which had been named after Benjamin Franklin. In the mid-1960s there were only about six thousand people in the entire county. In many ways, it was identical to nearby Pike County, a hotbed of so much racial violence.

Meadville didn't have much to distinguish itself. Even today, the town's promotional Web site doesn't list any historical developments since the mid-1800s, which was apparently the town's golden era.[1] At that time it had three inns and taverns, a post office, a telegraph office, lawyers' offices, and a tailor shop. Time stood still.

By 1964 Meadville had lost the inns and telegraph office but had picked up a weekly newspaper, a barber shop, and a gas station or two, and not much else. Meadville has a Main Street that also doubles as U.S. 84, a two-lane highway that runs through the middle of town on its way to Natchez, a roadway so dismissive of the town that it has a marked intolerance for stoplights. On the surface the town in 1964 was very much like the fictional Mayberry in the *Andy Griffith Show,* a television show popular with those residents who could afford a television antenna tall enough to capture broadcasts from Jackson or Monroe, Louisiana. Unlike Mayberry, however, there was a dark, mean streak that ran through Meadville. Like the scrub pine towns in Pike County, only about forty miles away, Meadville was rife with racial intolerance and violence. There were stories about black prisoners being beaten at the jail. Stories about black homes coming under gunfire at the midnight hour. Some stories that couldn't be told in mixed company.

Moore and Dee knew all that as they walked along Highway 84 on May 2, 1964, occasionally pausing to stick out a thumb in the hopes of catching a ride. When they saw two white men in a white Volkswagen approach, they dropped their hands, not wishing to flag them for a ride. The car stopped anyway. James Ford Seale, a twenty-nine-year-old truck driver and member of the Klan, got out and falsely identified himself as an agent with the Internal Revenue Service. He told the teens to get into the backseat because he needed to talk to them. Once they were in the car, he drove out of town on Highway 84 in the direction of Natchez. The teens were skeptical. He wasn't dressed like a federal agent. With his greasy black hair slicked back away from his forehead, he looked more like a stereotypical 1950s greaser. Apprehensive about where he was taking them, Moore and Dee asked him to stop the car so that they could get out. He refused. Instead he pulled out a walkie-talkie and called the Klansmen in the pickup truck that drove behind them. By 1964 terrorism standards, these guys were high-tech.

Not far out of Meadville, Seale pulled off into a deserted area of the Homochitto National Forest, a 189,000-acre wildlife preserve located about thirty miles from Natchez.[2] They remained in the car until the pickup pulled up and stopped. Then Seale and the other man got out of the car, with Seale pointing a sawed-off shotgun at the teens until the other men got out of the truck. The frightened teens were led over to the edge of a clearing, where their wrists were bound with duct tape and they were tied to a tree.

The men accused the teens of being Black Muslims who had come to Mississippi to cause trouble. The teens said they didn't know what they were talking about—they weren't Black Muslims. The men demanded to know who was coordinating the civil rights activity around Meadville. Again, the teens said they didn't know. It was at that point that the men picked up branches and started beating the teens, striking them thirty to forty times each until they were a bloody pulp.[3]

Throughout the beating, which lasted about thirty minutes, Seale and the others asked them where the guns were hidden. Finally, reacting the way torture victims usually react when asked for information, one of the teens "confessed" and swore that the guns were hidden in Roxie Colored First Baptist Church. At that point the beatings stopped. One of the men, Charles Marcus Edwards, thinking that neither of the teens would be turned loose, asked Dee if he was "right" with the Lord.[4]

Seale and another Klansmen left with the teens, with the understanding that Edwards and another man would get the sheriff so they could search the church identified by the teens as a hiding place for illegal guns. When Edwards and the deputies arrived at the church, they told the Reverend Clyde Briggs they'd received a tip that the church was going to be bombed and needed to search the building to make sure a bomb had not already been planted there. The pastor, under duress, gave them permission to search the church, but they turned up nothing illegal and left.

Meanwhile, Seale and another Klansman took the bloodied teens to a farm outside Meadville. When they learned that no guns were found at the church, they stuffed them into the trunk of a red Ford that was summoned from another Klansman in Natchez. If guns had been found, they could have turned the teens over to the sheriff for prosecution. Once they realized that they couldn't release the teens, they decided they could be used to lure the biggest prize of them all—Martin Luther King Jr.—to Franklin County, where the Klan was strong and capable of pulling off an assassination.

Still alive, the teens were driven nearly one hundred miles to Palmyra Island, an old channel of the Mississippi River near Tallulah, Louisiana, not far from Vicksburg, Mississippi. For years it was known as Davis Island because of its association with the president of the Confederate States of America, Jefferson Davis, and his brother, Joseph Davis, both of whom had plantations there.[5] During the Civil War the pear-shaped body of land, which was about twelve miles long and twenty-eight miles in circumference, was made into a paradise for over six hundred freedmen who established their own government. Giving the former slaves their freedom resulted in record-breaking cotton production; one of them, Benjamin T. Montgomery, raised a cotton crop one year that took all the prizes at the Cincinnati Exposition. Davis Island may have been a paradise for blacks 150 years ago, but by the 1960s it was such a rough place that blacks would more quickly call it "hell's punch bowl."

Moore and Dee were dumped out of the Ford at Parker's Landing.[6] The original plan was for the men to finish the teens off, put them into a boat, take them out into the Mississippi River, and dump their bodies into the deep water. However, the only way to kill them without bloodying their hands was to shoot them, and Seale worried that would leave a trail of blood into the boat. Instead, they tied Jeep engine parts to Dee with a heavy chain and wrapped baling wire around his feet, with Moore watching the entire time. Then they attached several metal wheels and a railroad rail to Moore, also wrapping baling wire around his feet. Once they were done with that, they loaded Dee into the boat and paddled out into deep water, where they rolled him over the side. Then they went back and got Moore, took him out onto the river, and rolled him into the water. One can only imagine the fear and terror the teens felt as they sank to the bottom of the muddy river, unable to see beyond a few inches from their faces, first trying to hold their breath, then gasping for air as the inevitable rush of water flooded their lungs.

The killers watched until the air bubbles stopped. Then they returned to the landing and drove back to Meadville. Later Seale told the other Klansmen that he was afraid the bodies would surface and the FBI would find his fingerprints on the duct tape. They told him not to worry about it—those bodies would never surface, weighted down the way they were. Still, Seale worried. Killing blacks wasn't as easy as it had been in his father's day. He trusted his fellow Klansmen, not just because they were "running buddies" but also because of the blood oath that all Klansmen take never to betray another member. He trusted the deputies who had gone to Rev. Briggs's church with Edwards. He trusted his white neighbors, because in Franklin County white was right. The only person, outside of his tight group, who could link any of them to the murders was Rev. Briggs.

The Bodies Surface

On July 12, more than ten weeks after the murders, a man and a woman were fishing in the old river shunt when the woman's hook snagged on something.[7] When she pulled it out of the water, she saw that it was a human vertebra. The couple contacted the sheriff, who promptly notified the FBI. By the time FBI agents arrived on the scene, they were confident that they had found the bodies of the three men abducted in Philadelphia. At that point they had no reason to suspect that Moore and Dee also had been murdered. Not until they pulled two rotting, headless torsos from the water were they able to identify Moore and Dee from the items found in their pockets. Unfortunately, investigators had no motive, no time line, and no suspects in the murders.

The murders made the newspapers, creating a stir not just in the river towns along the river, Vicksburg and Natchez, but also in sleepy Meadville, where the two youths were last seen alive. People started talking. Was Meadville going to become another Philadelphia and Poplarville? Would federal agents invade their little town the way they'd done in Philadelphia?

Among those giving thought to the matter was the Reverend Clyde Briggs, helped along by the gunshot that tore through his house on the night after the bodies were found, an obvious warning for him to keep his mouth shut.[8] That wasn't the first trouble he'd had since the teens disappeared. On May 24, three weeks after their disappearance, two carloads of white men yelled at him as he walked along the highway. When he didn't obey their command to stop, one of the men jumped out of the car and confronted him, telling him that he'd better pay attention the next time they told him to do something.

Not long after the murders, a Klansman named Ernest Gilbert approached FBI agents and told them he had information that would be helpful. He said that Seale's brother, Jack, and another Klansman had bragged about killing the teens. He said that James Seale had voiced concern about his fingerprints being on the duct tape used in the crime. Once Gilbert gave the agents specific information, such as a description of the weights used to drown the teens, the FBI called in navy divers to search the river floor. What they discovered—a human skull and ribs with steel rails attached—verified Gilbert's story.

On November 6, 1964, James Seale and Charles Edwards, the only Klansmen that authorities felt they had enough evidence against, were arrested by the FBI and sheriff's deputies and charged with killing Moore and Dee. They were transported to Jackson for questioning and then returned to Meadville. On the drive back, FBI agent Leonard Wolf talked to Seale about the crime.

"We know you did it. You know you did it. The Lord above knows you did it."

"Yes, but I'm not going to admit it. You are going to have to prove it."

Each man was released on a five thousand dollar bond, and a hearing was set for January 11, 1965. Meanwhile, the FBI turned the evidence over to District Attorney Lenox Forman in Natchez, who promised to present it to the grand jury.[9]

James Seale was not concerned that he would be charged with killing two young African Americans. No white man in Mississippi had ever been successfully prosecuted for killing an African American involved in civil rights work. He knew the local district attorney would not prosecute him regardless of the evidence. He scoffed at the notion that he would be arrested. He knew that a decade ago, in 1955, the Reverend George Lee had half of his face blown off in Belzoni for helping fellow blacks register to vote. There wasn't even an investigation of his death, and when the sheriff was confronted with the fact that lead pellets were taken from his head and face, he simply said they were probably tooth fillings. In Brookhaven another black activist, Lamar Smith, was shot in broad daylight on the courthouse lawn for voter registration activities. Although any number of persons witnessed this blatant murder, and the sheriff saw a white man leave the scene covered in blood, there was no prosecution and the killer again walked free.

Two years later Herbert Lee was killed by a white Mississippi state representative, E. H. Hurst, in Liberty, Mississippi. Again, there was no prosecution. A black witness to this shooting, Louis Allen, was beaten after he talked to the FBI. He made plans to get out of Liberty and Amite County and take his family to Milwaukee, where his brother lived, but he never made it. He was killed before he could get out of town. No one was ever arrested for his murder either. The next year Corporal Roman Duckworth Jr. was killed by police in Taylorsville, Mississippi, for failure to move to the back of the bus. There was no arrest or prosecution.

Indeed, killing blacks was not viewed as a crime by many white Mississippians. For many it was viewed as a patriotic act, an expression of Mississippi Values.

Two months before the murders of Moore and Dee, Clinton Walker, who was an excellent employee of International Paper Company for fourteen years, was returning home from work when he was brutally murdered by being shot in the back.[10] He was married, had children, and lived near Natchez. As usual the state turned a blind eye and no one was arrested. In addition to horrible killings such as these, the hundreds of beatings and brutal whippings of blacks suspected of civil rights activities in Mississippi are too numerous to enumerate. Many of these were carried out around Natchez by hooded men at about the same time that Moore and Dee were murdered. The Sovereignty Commission reported that James Seale and his brother, Jack, were suspects of some of these beatings and whippings. Again, the State of Mississippi turned a blind eye and there were no arrests.

On July 23, 1964, a little over two and a half months after he masterminded the despicable murders of Moore and Dee, Seale wrote a scathing letter to the local *Franklin Advocate*, revealing his racist thoughts and perhaps reflecting the minds of most white Mississippians at that time. He encouraged the readers to defy the Civil Rights Act, which he said was "a giant step to a communist dictatorship in America." He wrote that the Civil Rights Act would not give "the nigger" what he wants, that what he wants is to "sleep in the white hotel or motel, swim in the white pool, or go to the white church, or go to the white school. In short, they want to marry your white daughter, or live with her, the only thing they know." He concluded by stating that "the time has come for Christian people of this nation to fight what a few men in Congress or the Senate decided on under pressure from the niggers and communists." Surely such a letter would not have been written by someone who was apprehensive of being prosecuted for the murders of two young blacks he'd committed some two months before.

As it turned out, Seale's confidence in the strength of Mississippi Values was well founded. The January 11 hearing never took place because District Attorney Lenox Forman dropped all charges against Seale and Edwards. An FBI memo dated the day after the hearing was scheduled to take place indicated that Forman had discussed the case with Franklin County sheriff Wayne Hutto, Assistant Attorney General Garland Lyle, and Charles Snodgrass, a highway patrolman with strong ties to the Sovereignty Commission, and had concluded that the case was "greatly prejudiced" against the defendants because the men had told local residents that they'd been "brutally mistreated" by investigators and denied medication by the highway patrol.[11] According to the memo, Forman had said that if the case was presented on January 11, he would have no choice but to dismiss the charges. He told the FBI that if more evidence was obtained, he would reconsider presenting the case to a grand jury.

On April 6, 1965, the Sovereignty Commission reported that a group of "outside agitators" were arriving in Fayette, Mississippi, and dispatched its investigator, Andrew Hopkins, to the scene. Not surprisingly, the investigator saw Klansman James Seale brazenly marching around with an armed guard. Fortunately, there were no shootings and no arrests that day.

James Seale Lives the Good Life

On January 14, 1966, James Seale impudently appeared before the House Committee on Un-American Activities, clinching a cigar in his teeth and looking every bit the backwoods roughneck. Over forty times Seale refused to answer questions, citing the Fifth Amendment.

Five months after the hearings, a black man named Ben Chester White, who had never been involved in any civil rights activity or even attempted to vote, was killed by the Klan in Natchez, probably by the members of the Cottonmouth Moccasin Gang, whose rite of admission was the "killing of a nigger." The members of the gang who committed this atrocious killing were well known in the community. The following year, on February 27, Wharlest Jackson of Natchez was killed after being promoted to a "white" job at Armstrong Rubber Company. Jackson, the treasurer of the NAACP in Natchez, had been offered a job previously reserved for whites. He hesitated to take the job because word was out that the Klan would kill any black who accepted one of these positions, but Jackson needed the seventeen cents an hour raise in order to feed his wife and five children. Jackson's vehicle was blown to smithereens by a time-delayed bomb after he punched out at work and climbed into the cab of his pickup truck. No one was ever arrested for his murder.

The years rocked merrily along for James Ford Seale. The state closed its files on the Dee/Moore case. The news media all but abandoned any interest in Seale. He had reason to believe that he was immune to prosecution.

Seale's rocky background didn't keep him from flying crop duster airplanes all over Louisiana and Mississippi. By the 1970s he'd found work as a police officer in Vidalia, Louisiana, a small town across the Mississippi River from Natchez, serving as a city policeman while continuing to dust cotton and ferry people about in his airplane.

For a while Seale lived on Peach Street in Vidalia. On November 18, 1970, he was involved in a deadly air disaster not far from Vidalia, when his airplane collided with another airplane, causing the deaths of five people. Somehow Seale survived. Two years later he was piloting a crop duster that crashed near Vidalia in a soybean field, where he suffered a broken wrist, cuts, and bruises. In 1975, Seale arrested a former Vidalia city judge for driving while intoxicated, and he was convicted largely on the testimony of Seale. By the 1980s, Seale had moved back to Franklin County, Mississippi, where he lived in obscurity, most people outside the community thinking that he was probably dead.

Cold Case Reaches Boiling Point

In July 2004, David Ridgen, a producer with Canadian Broadcasting Corporation (CBC), a public television and radio network that is similar to PBS in the United States, was in the CBC viewing room watching a forty-year-old documentary titled *Summer in Mississippi*, a film about the murders of civil rights workers Schwerner, Goodman, and Chaney. He was stopped cold by a sequence showing a body being pulled from a river, accompanied by a narration explaining that law enforcement officials, searching for the three missing civil rights workers, had found "the wrong body." Intrigued by how any body pulled from a river could be a "wrong body," he researched the story until he learned that it was the body of Charles Eddie Moore.

Ridgen was no stranger to Mississippi. A graduate of Queens University in Kingston, Ontario, a St. Lawrence River city known for its racial tolerance, the award-winning producer had traveled to the state in summer 2004 to undertake a documentary, *Return to Mississippi*, about the murders of Schwerner, Goodman, and Chaney. Prior to that he'd produced several documentaries, including *Canadian Images of Vietnam*, the first documentary about Canadian involvement in the Vietnam War.

Convinced that there was still a story to be told, Ridgen searched for a living relative of Moore or Dee, someone around whom he could build a documentary. After almost a year's search, he found Charles Moore's brother, Thomas, living in Colorado Springs, Colorado, and asked if he would be willing to participate in a documentary that would involve him returning to Mississippi to confront Meadville residents about his brother's murder. What Ridgen didn't know was that Moore had written a letter in 1998 to District Attorney Ronnie Harper asking him to look into his brother's death. Harper agreed to do so, attracting some media attention, including an investigative report published by the *Clarion-Ledger* that the murders had taken place on federal land, thus opening the door to a possible prosecution by federal authorities. Nothing ever developed from that, however, and Harper lost interest in pursuing the matter after the FBI told him that the agency was unwilling to cooperate with him.[12]

After that disappointment, Thomas, a U.S. Army veteran who'd served in Vietnam, readily agreed to cooperate with the CBC documentary, thus beginning a journey that would have a profound impact on a murder case that had been not only forgotten but also relegated to a protected status by Mississippi law enforcement officials, state and federal prosecutors, the FBI, and the news media.

Prior to going to Mississippi, Ridgen telephoned Donna Ladd, editor of the state's only progressive newspaper, the *Jackson Free Press*, to inquire about the newspaper's coverage of an upcoming trial in which he had an interest because of his film *Return to Mississippi*.[13] Ladd told him she wasn't sure how passionate the newspaper would be about the Killen trial, since the newspaper wanted to pursue a "cold case" murder involving two bodies found in 1964 in the Mississippi River. Ridgen excitedly told her that that was the same story he planned to tackle for a new documentary. Would the *Jackson Free Press* be interested in working with him to get the case reopened?

There was only one possible answer—yes. A Mississippi native, Ladd had returned to the state in 2001 to start up a newspaper with her partner, author Todd Stauffer; this was a major departure from her previous job as editor of the *Colorado Springs Independent*. She was passionate about righting the wrongs of the past in her home state, so there was no question about her commitment to the project.

The more they talked, the more convinced Ridgen became that the best angle would be to focus on Ladd and her team's efforts to find enough evidence for prosecutions in the case.

When Ridgen and Moore arrived in Mississippi, they linked up with Ladd and *Jackson Free Press* photographer Kate Medley and struck out for Meadville, with no idea where the story would lead them. What they found was a town in which whites suggested that scratching old wounds would be of benefit to no one—and blacks who didn't seem especially eager to get involved, for whatever reason. First on their list was seeking an interview with Charles Marcus Edwards, who was known to still live in Meadville. With the camera rolling and Moore scrunched down on the floor of the van, Ridgen drove up to Edwards's house and asked him for an interview about his involvement in the murders. Edwards kept his composure, but he firmly asked Ridgen to leave his property.

At that point their plan was to continue to try to talk to Edwards while interviewing other residents to gather material for the documentary. Everything up to that point had pretty much gone as expected. It was during a trip to Natchez that they learned something that left them breathless. Wrote Ladd: "While in Natchez, we learned . . . that the other primary suspect, James Ford Seale, is also still alive and lives in Roxie, near the intersection of Highways 84/98 and 33 in a Winnebago-type trailer on land believed to belong to his brother."[14]

Ridgen and Moore drove to Roxie and stopped at a BP station, where Moore engaged a black man in a conversation that produced dramatic results. To their surprise the man pointed off into the distance, identifying the trailer where Seale lived. They got back onto the highway and drove a short distance and then pulled over and spotted Seale helping his wife unload items from their car. Moore yelled out to him from a safe distance that he wanted to talk to him, but Seale ignored him and went into his house. They debated driving up to his house, as they had done with Edwards, but decided that approach was too risky.

Instead they continued to delicately stalk Edwards, finally catching him walking with his wife from his car toward a church in which he served as a deacon. This time Moore got out of the van and approached Edwards with an envelope that contained FBI reports mentioning Edwards's involvement in the murders. Not far away was Ridgen, wearing sunglasses with a hidden camera attached. Unaware that he was being photographed, Edwards took the envelope, almost as a reflex response, and then handed it back to Moore. Standing only a few feet from one of his brother's suspected killers, Moore calmly offered the envelope once again, stating the importance of the material inside. This time Edwards took the envelope and went into the church, but not before stating emphatically that he had nothing to do with the murder of Charles Moore.

Encouraged by the revelations about Seale's whereabouts, they telephoned U.S. Attorney Dunn Lampton and asked about the status of the case. Lampton admitted that he knew nothing about the case, but he set up an appointment for Moore to meet with him. Once he got off the telephone, Lampton called FBI headquarters in Washington for a briefing on the case. By the time their meeting took place, Lampton had gathered enough information about the case to assure Moore that it would be reopened for investigation.

During their meeting, which was captured on film, Lampton's interest increased dramatically once he learned that Thomas Moore and he had served in the same army brigade in Vietnam. Although they'd never met, it was a bond that gave added emotional appeal to Moore's search for justice. After the meeting Moore told Ladd, "He respected my rank as a command sergeant major. He knows the authority and power my commission invested in me. It's kind of like old soldiers taking care of each other. He's a fine gentleman."[15]

One week after Moore's meeting with Lampton, Ladd published a story in the *Jackson Free Press* that told about Moore's return to Mississippi and the dramatic discovery that James Ford Seale was still alive. The first notable response from Meadville came from Mary Lou Webb, editor of the *Franklin Advocate*, who wrote an editorial attacking the reopening of the case. "The editor sees no new evidence—no reason—to put a new generation through painful memories." Incredibly, information surfaced from the Sovereignty Commission files revealing that Webb's late husband, David Webb, was publicity director for Americans for the Preservation of the White Race in 1964 while serving as editor of the newspaper.[16] Webb's outing as a leader in a racist organization whose stated purpose was "to unite and organize the white man" offered yet another example of the twisted priorities of the Mississippi news media.

But times change, and new hope rises from the ashes. As a result of the media performing their historical watchdog role, under the guidance of Donna Ladd and David Ridgen, on January 24, 2007, the federal government filed an indictment against James Ford Seale relating to the murders of Dee and Moore, some forty-two years, eight months, and twenty-two days after the brutal murders. The indictment charged Seale with two counts of kidnapping and one count of conspiracy. On January 25, 2007, Seale, dressed in prison orange and bound in shackles, appeared before United States magistrate Linda Anderson and pleaded not guilty. Anderson denied bond, stating, "Neither the weight of the crime nor its circumstances have been diminished by the passage of time."

PART II

Complete Breakdown

10

Mississippi's Legal Jungle

For many Mississippians the question was not "Have you have taken your children to church this week?" but rather "Have you bombed a church this week?" In 1964 more than fifty black churches were burned or bombed in Mississippi. That year in McComb every black church was burned or bombed, earning Pike County's principal city the title of "Bombing Capital of the World."

It is safe to say that none of those cases, if prosecuted at all, was heard before a black juror. Segregation was the filter through which justice was dispensed. The judge, bailiff, stenographer, clerk, and, of course, jury were all white. Even in capital cases, when an African American's very life was in peril, there was no "jury of his peers." If he looked at the jury, he'd see twelve white men, often eager to impose the death penalty.

Blacks did appear on juries to some extent during Reconstruction, but that ended with the Constitution of 1890, which provided that all potential jurors must be "qualified electors"—that is, the juror must be able to read and properly interpret any portion of the Mississippi Constitution and prove by receipts that he'd paid poll taxes for the past two years.[1] In 1896 the Mississippi legislature further restricted jury service to qualified electors of "sound judgment and fine character." That subjective requirement provided white officials with the means to ban all blacks from jury service.

That scheme to prevent blacks from serving on juries was dealt a blow in 1947, when the U.S. Supreme Court handed down its decision in *Patton v. Mississippi*.[2] Eddie Patton, a black man, had been indicted in Lauderdale County by an all-white grand jury on a charge of murder and was promptly convicted by an all-white petit jury and sentenced to death by electrocution. Lauderdale County had a population that was 35 percent black, but it had not had a black juror for more than thirty years. On appeal, the Mississippi Supreme Court said that was perfectly all right, and although it acknowledged that these numbers were correct, it found there was not an arbitrary, systematic exclusion of African Americans.[3] The Mississippi Supreme Court, with a straight face, made the same argument that was made back when the constitution was enacted in 1890: that on its face there was no discrimination against African Americans, since all qualified electors could serve. The catch here was that the legislation was rigged so it was almost impossible for a black to be a so-called qualified elector, thus disqualifying him from becoming a juror.

After looking at the population figures of Lauderdale County, the Mississippi Supreme Court, with gallows logic, reasoned that the ratio of white to black "qualified electors" in Lauderdale County was 400 to 1, so there was only a chance of 1 in 400 that an African American would appear on a venire of one hundred jurors. The Mississippi Court then reasoned that if the sheriff had brought in an African American, he would have had to discriminate against white jurors, not against African Americans, for how could he be expected to bring in "one-fourth of one Negro"?

The NAACP financed an appeal to the U.S. Supreme Court that scolded the Mississippi Court by reminding it that "sixty-seven years ago this Court held that state exclusion of Negroes from grand and petit juries solely because of their race denied Negro defendants in criminal cases the equal protection of the laws required by the Fourteenth Amendment." On the uncontradicted proof that for thirty years or more no African American had served, the State of Mississippi was

Methodist Church, Carrollton, Mississippi, in 1906. Father of Alex A. Alston Jr. third from right in front row, barefoot with hands in pocket. Grandmother in black in front of door, directly in front of bearded man. ALEX A. ALSTON JR.

Black workers in Leland, Mississippi, receive typhoid shots during the Mississippi River flood of 1927. AUDIE TURNER

James L. Dickerson with Sallie Mae Elle in Greenville.
JUANITA DICKERSON

Five Mississippi sheriffs and one deputy sheriff preparing for anticipated violence prior to James Meredith's registration at the University of Mississippi in 1962.   CHARLES MOORE/ BLACK STAR

Deputy U.S. attorney general Nicholas Katzenback, left, and U.S. marshal James McShane on the Ole Miss campus for the registration of James Meredith.   MISSISSIPPI VALLEY COLLECTION, UNIVERSITY OF MEMPHIS

James Meredith during graduation ceremonies at the University of Mississippi in 1963.   MISSISSIPPI VALLEY COLLECTION, UNIVERSITY OF MEMPHIS

FBI missing persons poster showing, from left to right, Michael Schwerner, James Chaney, and Andrew Goodman.   FBI PHOTO

FBI agent Joseph Sullivan, who supervised the investigation of the Schwerner, Chaney, and Goodman murders.   FBI PHOTO

Jim Ingram, the agent in charge of the FBI's civil rights desk in Jackson, looking over evidence seized at the home of a Klansman.   COURTESY JIM INGRAM

Newly elected Mississippi governor Paul B. Johnson, right, with former Mississippi governor Hugh White during the 1964 inaugural parade.
JIMMY WARD, COURTESY MISSISSIPPI VALLEY COLLECTION, UNIVERSITY OF MEMPHIS

Body of Martin Luther King Jr. viewed by mourners in 1968.   MISSISSIPPI VALLEY COLLECTION, UNIVERSITY OF MEMPHIS

Mississippi Ku Klux Klan member.   STEVE GARDNER

Ku Klux Klan cross burning in Lee County, Mississippi, 1978.   STEVE GARDNER

Ku Klux Klan march in Tupelo, Mississippi, 1978.   STEVE GARDNER

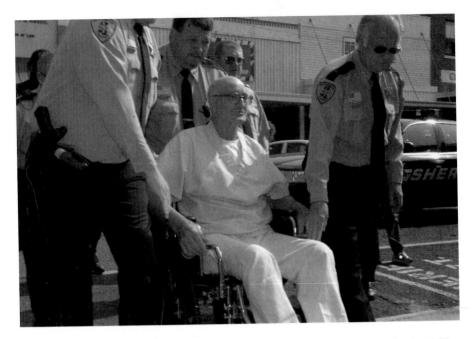

Edgar Ray Killen, surrounded by deputies, entering courthouse for sentencing in 2005.
KATE MEDLEY/*JACKSON FREE PRESS*

James Ford Seale led into van after being denied bond in 2007.   MATT SALDANA/*JACKSON FREE PRESS*

Jim Ingram at his home with a cold case file in 2008.
JAMES L. DICKERSON

compelled to show that there was no purposeful discrimination. Accordingly, the U.S. Supreme Court in 1947 reversed the decision. But it took more than scolding by the Supreme Court to stop the jury system in Mississippi from remaining all white.

For the next twenty years Mississippi courts still got around this ruling by upholding convictions whenever local authorities merely denied discrimination. In 1957 an African American by the name of J. C. Cameron was indicted for rape in Lincoln County, where no blacks had served on juries for more than thirty years.[4] A local lawyer, Emmette P. Allen, was appointed to defend the accused. Allen vigorously defended him, moving to quash the indictment by reason of the "systematic intentional and invariable practice . . . to exclude Negroes from jury lists, jury boxes and jury service."[5]

All members of the board of supervisors testified that the jury list had been made up solely on the basis of the qualifications for jury service and not on the basis of race. The Mississippi Supreme Court held that the motion to quash was filed late and the trial judge was warranted in "accepting as true the testimony offered by the state" to show that there was no discrimination in the names submitted for jury service. It was not until 1965 that the Mississippi Supreme Court finally instructed the lower courts that this would no longer work and "token summoning of Negroes for jury service does not comply with equal protection."[6] But even these rulings of the U.S. Supreme Court and the Mississippi Supreme Court did little to change the complexion of the jury panels. The judicial system continued to purposely exclude blacks. The new tool used by lawyers was peremptory challenges, allotted in both civil and criminal cases.

An explanation may be in order. A party to a suit may challenge as many jurors as desired "for cause," that is, if there is a sufficiently close relationship to one of the parties that could cause the juror not to be fair and impartial, such as kinship. In the other pocket, the lawyer has a magic wand that allows him or her to dismiss any juror for any reason, by means of a peremptory challenge. This tool, to ensure a fair and impartial trial, has been around for lawyers for many centuries; however, there is some limitation in Mississippi on the number of these strikes. For example, in a capital case, the parties are limited to twelve peremptory strikes; but in ordinary felony cases, the number is six. Historically, the lawyer could dismiss any juror for any reason as long as it was related to the lawyer's view concerning the outcome of the case. In 1986, however, the U.S. Supreme Court limited this practice by holding that racially discriminatory use of peremptory challenges violates the Equal Protection Clause of the Constitution.

In the celebrated case of *Batson v. Kentucky*, an African American man was indicted on charges of second-degree burglary and receipt of stolen goods.[7] After a number of jurors were excused "for cause," the prosecutor then used his peremptory challenges to strike all four black persons on the trial panel, thus leaving an all-white jury for the trial. The U.S. Supreme Court addressed this issue directly in *Batson*, and held that a lawyer ordinarily is entitled to exercise peremptory challenges for any reason, as long as that reason is related to his or her view concerning the outcome of the case, but the Equal Protection Clause of the Constitution forbids lawyers to challenge potential jurors solely on account of their race.

Mississippi courts fell in line with *Batson*, requiring the prosecution to provide nonracial reasons for using its peremptory strikes to remove blacks from a jury panel if: the defendant is a member of a cognizable racial group; the prosecution exercised a peremptory challenge to remove a member of the defendant's race; and these facts and others raise an inference that the prosecution used this practice to exclude blacks.[8]

It took Mississippi a long and laborious time to get to the point of actually allowing women to serve on juries. As late as 1968, Mississippi still barred women from jury service, as journalist Bill Minor reminds us. The Senate was debating a bill on the juror statutes to change them in some insignificant way, but whatever change they had in mind would in no way alter the fact that only male citizens were eligible to serve. Unobtrusively, a female senator, Jean Muirhead, stood up and quickly walked to the clerk's desk and handed the clerk a handwritten amendment, according to Minor. All the amendment did was strike the word *male* in the first line of the bill, which had previously read that "all male citizens over the age of 21" were entitled to serve as qualified jurors. Before members knew what had happened, the Senate had adopted the amendment. When some of the mossbacks realized that women now could serve, they almost exploded. It was too late—the motion for reconsideration failed, and the momentum swept through the House. There were no more impediments to women serving on juries. Wrote Minor: "Although she [Muirhead] was a hero, certainly to many, she was defeated for reelection. Yes, by a male who, incidentally, was barely literate."

Mississippi was also slow to grant women voting rights. The Nineteenth Amendment to the U.S. Constitution provided that citizens may not be denied the right to vote on account of sex. The amendment, which became law when it was ratified by three-fourths of the states in 1920, caused a serious uproar in Mississippi, and it was not until 1984 that the amendment was finally ratified by the state. Women could vote prior to that, of course, but it was still the state's position that it was opposed to women voting, and it displayed that opposition by refusing to ratify the amendment.

Alex A. Alston Jr.:

As if the previous horrific confrontation on the campus of Ole Miss and the arbitrary killings and shootings were not enough, 1964 was getting really hot. I joined Wells, Thomas & Wells, at that time the largest and perhaps the most prestigious law firm in the state.

The conspiracy of Mississippi lawyers and judges to keep blacks off the jury knew no limits and continued well into the late 1960s. I recall in Hinds County going to circuit court to try cases and the judge, or more often the opposing lawyer, would ask, "Alex, you, of course, will follow the rule that we will knock off the jigs that may appear and that it will not count against your peremptory strikes." Although I was not familiar with this so-called common law rule, I did go along with it and can attest to its enforcement well into the late 1960s. If a potential black juror happened to sneak through the legalistic maze carefully constructed to restrict him from even showing up on the venire, he was summarily dismissed through another layer of legal chicanery that lasted until the beginning of the next decade.

One of my first assignments at Wells, Thomas & Wells was to study the Civil Rights Act of 1964 so we could advise clients on how to avoid its provisions. Sometimes it is difficult for nonlawyers to understand how lawyers can represent killers, rapists, and other nefarious characters, but part of being a lawyer is accepting that everyone is entitled to legal representation. So it was with the Mississippi businesses that hired legal guns to find loopholes in civil rights legislation. Title II of the act was especially onerous to some of our clients in the restaurant business, since it required any place of public accommodation to fully serve, without discrimination or segregation, all persons without, as the act stated, regard to "race, color, religious, or national origin."

This was unthinkable. The color line dictated that whites just could not sit down in the same restaurant where a black also was seated, and it would be a sacrilege for a white to eat with a black. Of course, it was all right for a white to stand with blacks. Whites have always stood with blacks at the grocery store or the bank, walked together in the department stores, and stood at the same drugstore counters. It is only "when the Negro 'sets' that the fur begins to fly," as Harry Golden, a Jewish newspaper reporter in the 1940s who spoke out against racial segregation, facetiously put it. We actually thought this just might be a good idea and considered installing stand-up tables or providing some other type of mechanical device to hold the food while eating without the opportunity to sit. This innovative "vertical black" idea was considered but rejected.

As lawyers we looked for loopholes, and the one we found was private clubs. Private clubs could be exempted. Why not turn our client, the Belmont Café, the site of our first morning ritual, into a private club? The Belmont was located adjacent to the bottom floor of the Lamar Life Building, a particularly handsome building, built around 1924, in which our offices were located on several floors. At that time it was Jackson's only bona fide skyscraper, the architecture being a pleasing combination of distinctive lines and a crenellated clock tower. The building resembled a scaled-down version of the Woolworth Building in New York City.

In order to convert the Belmont Café to a private club, I drew up the bylaws, charter, membership certificates, and cards (preventing transfer) and installed a one-way mirror for the entry guard. The Belmont Café was changed overnight into the Belmont Club. This worked okay for a couple of months until the owners, Mr. and Mrs. Sylvester, had to turn down busloads of hungry customers because of my firm rule that customers could not be admitted without proper membership cards. Not long after that, the Belmont Club closed its doors, another casualty of Mississippi's fight to preserve segregation.

Even as late as 1965, as a young lawyer in Jackson, I was admonished by circuit court judge M. M. McGowen for using a courtesy title in addressing a black witness. At a break in the trial, he told me that only "nigger lovers" or "civil rights agitators" used courtesy titles in his court. On another occasion, I appeared before Judge Leon Hendrick representing a gracious black woman, Ester Mikell Hill, in a wrongful death action in which her son was killed by falling off a defective scaffold. After a hard-fought trial, the all-white jury awarded Mrs. Hill fifty thousand dollars, a very tidy sum in 1965 for the death of a young black man. When the verdict was returned in open court, she was overcome with joy and excitement. She ran over to me, picked me up, and, with tears running down her face, kissed me on the cheek.

Needless to say, that caused quite a scene in the courtroom.

Traditionally, all the lawyers and court personnel gathered around Judge Hendrick's dais before a case was called. After the incident with Mrs. Hill, whenever I was present in his court, Judge Hendrick, without exception, would address me in his deep, gruff voice, "Alex, those niggers still picking you up and kissing you in public?" to the shrieks of laughter from the surrounding crowd of lawyers and their assistants.

Mississippi's Lynch Law

The Mississippi Supreme Court's disgusting reference to the sheriff hauling "one-fourth of one Negro" to court could very well have been literally possible. Although the number of lynching victims in Mississippi had decreased somewhat since the Depression years, from 1930 to 1939 there were fifty reported black lynchings in Mississippi.[9]

Mutilation was commonplace in the first half of the twentieth century, where the lynchers and spectators gathered souvenirs—body parts from the lynched person—to display as curiosities in service stations and general stores or to use as personal items, such as watch fobs.[10]

Lynch law was supported by the press, which seemed to take pleasure in reporting all the grisly details. Any Mississippi politician who proposed a modest restriction on lynching was severely punished at the polls. More than two hundred antilynching bills were introduced in the United States Congress in the first part of the twentieth century, including bills supported by Senator Hubert Humphrey and President Harry Truman; all were blocked by Southern senators.

Although no antilynching bill was ever passed, finally, on June 14, 2005, the U.S. Senate passed a resolution apologizing for not enacting antilynching legislation. Nearly 150 years after the end of the civil war, and forty-one years after the passage of the Civil Rights Act, eighty-five members of the Senate apologized. Fifteen members—all Republicans, including Mississippi's Trent Lott—did not.

Of course, lynching was the South's ultimate form of social control. Reports tabulate nearly six hundred lynchings in Mississippi between 1880 and 1940. Many of the trials of black defendants were not much better than a lynching. Rapid indictments and trials were arranged. Usually inadequately represented by counsel, the defendants were quickly sentenced to death after an all-white jury imposed the guilty verdict. The speed of these convictions was mind-boggling. Even when a black defendant pleaded not guilty, many proceedings took less than one hour, and cases of only four to six hours were common.[11]

Lynchings were often publicly acclaimed and favorably announced by the press. In some cases the date of the lynching was advertised in advance, and special trains were engaged to transport large crowds for these celebrated acts of racial violence, with many putting on their "Sunday best" for these spectacles.

Alex A. Alston Jr.:

The unyielding battle to preserve segregation spawned some fascinating litigation. Another case in which my firm was deeply involved was the case
brought by former general Edwin Walker against the Associated Press concerning the James Meredith debacle at Ole Miss. In this suit General Walker,
who was once relieved of command for suggesting that President Truman was
a Communist, claimed he was defamed by an AP article stating that he had
"led a charge of students against federal marshals" and that he had "assumed
control of the crowd."

My senior partner, Earl T. Thomas, vigorously represented the AP as lead
trial lawyer. Libel suits were rampant in 1964, the Kluckers (as Klansmen were
sometimes called) and their ilk knowing that jurors hated the national media
and would award any amount in damages if the case was allowed to go to the
jury. General Walker had long espoused right-wing propaganda. He publicly
stated that he was standing beside Governor Ross Barnett to protect segregation and to do everything possible to prevent the enrollment of Meredith. He
considered Meredith's entry into the University of Mississippi a disgrace to
the nation, part of a conspiracy by the anti-Christ conspirators on the Supreme
Court.

The lawsuit was filed in Fort Worth, Texas, and members of my firm were
dispatched to Ole Miss to find students who could testify that they had seen
General Walker lead a charge against the marshals and assume control of the
crowd. Sure enough, a number of male students had witnessed that very thing
and were asked to travel to Fort Worth for the trial. My partners, Bob Gillespie
and Jack Brand, gathered this rather rowdy crowd together and took them to
Fort Worth. It was difficult enough getting this rambunctious group to Fort
Worth, but keeping these young students together to be available to be called
as witnesses at any moment was a real problem. Some wanted to go home,
others wanted to get out of the hotel and party, and still others wanted to get
to Dallas and Houston. There was also a problem that if they got out of the
hotel, agents of General Walker would get to them, discourage them from
testifying, and send them home or to some other place, making them unavail-
able to testify.

Earl Thomas ordered that these witnesses stay in the hotel but with permission to enjoy all the amenities there. My partners entertained them, offering them all the liquor they could drink, "girly magazines," evening trips to strip joints and the like, and this worked fairly well. Later, after the trial was over, one of the notorious student witnesses, Travis Buckley, presented a bill for his expenses that would choke a cow. The bill included not only enormous charges from the hotel bar but also ridiculous charges for flimsy negligees he had purchased in the hotel store for a number of girlfriends. When confronted with this preposterous bill, Buckley simply stated that Mr. Thomas had told him he could have anything he wanted as long as he stayed in the hotel. The Associated Press paid the bill, and Travis "Cannonball" Buckley ultimately became a celebrated lawyer for the Ku Klux Klan, his most famous case being the defense of Klan imperial wizard Sam Bowers in the 1966 murder of Vernon Dahmer, the trial taking place some thirty-two years later in 1998. Justice was finally rendered for Bowers's culpability in the murder, and he received a life sentence.

As expected, the jury's hatred for the national media manifested itself in a verdict in favor of General Walker—in the sum of $800,000. The Associated Press promptly appealed to the U.S. Supreme Court, which rendered its historic opinion on June 12, 1967, overturning the verdict of the jury and extending the requirement of a finding of actual malice on all "public figures."[12] The Court had previously held, in *New York Times v. Sullivan*, that this standard was required for all "public officials," but now, to the jubilation of all media, the same standard was required for "public figures."

Mississippi Outlaws Waterboarding

Forcing confessions in Mississippi was not uncommon. In 1928 a black man named Hines Loftin was seized one night in Smith County, a rope hung around his neck and his hands tied behind his back. He was pushed before a mob of several dozen people, some of them with guns, who demanded he confess to a murder. Loftin finally confessed, but there was no lynching, since he was promptly brought to court and the confession was entered into evidence. A jury quickly found Loftin guilty, and he was sentenced to be hanged.[13]

At the other end of the state, in DeSoto County, Oscar Perkins, a black man, was arrested for the alleged murder of a white store owner. On the way from his place of arrest to the jail, he was hanged by his neck from a tree and a fire was built under him to make him confess. After getting to the jail, authorities laid Perkins on a bed and measured him for a coffin with a string after hitting him with a pistol. Perkins was convicted, the court finding the confession freely and voluntarily given, and he was sentenced to be hanged.

To obtain confessions, although whippings and beatings were common, a special technique, known as the "water cure" was "a species of torture well known to the bench and bar of the country."[14] With the defendant tied or held securely down, water was poured from a dipper into the nose of the accused to strangle him, thus causing pain and horror for the purpose of forcing a confession.[15] In one case in Sunflower County, an eighteen-year-old African American was accused of stealing jewelry from a store and murdering the shopkeeper. He was taken to a store, placed in front of the deceased victim with his hands tied behind him, and made to lie on the floor on his back while some of the white mob stood on his feet and a very heavy man stood on him, with one foot on his chest and his other foot on his neck. While in that position, the water cure was administered to force a confession. It was successful, but the posse later found out that the information given to them about the whereabouts of the stolen jewelry was entirely wrong; the confession had been blurted out by the accused only in order to stop further torture.[16] It is an amazing torture device that has a phenomenal success rate of 100 percent in obtaining confessions.

In the 1920s the Mississippi Supreme Court made it clear that the water cure was torture and that confessions made as a result were inadmissible. No one would accuse the Mississippi court during this time of being "liberal," or bent on coddling criminals. It is ironic that during the war in Iraq, some eight decades later, the U.S. government was especially fond of this method—calling it "waterboarding"—as an acceptable means of extracting confessions or other information from those deemed a threat to our security. Shortly after taking office in 2009, President Barack Obama put an end to interrogation techniques such as waterboarding, saying, "America doesn't torture."

Alex A. Alston Jr.:

In my first year out of law school, I was sent to Philadelphia, Mississippi, to defend Time, Inc., the publisher of *Life* magazine. The town had become notorious for the brutal 1964 murders of civil rights activists Andrew Goodman, James Chaney, and Michael Schwerner. It was a hotbed of Klan activity, and anyone representing the media was despicable in the eyes of local residents. It was not a pleasant experience to walk up those courthouse steps, trying to dodge the volleys of spit and listening to the screams of "nigger lover" and "Communist" from the rowdy crowd.

The genesis of this dispute arose from an article in *Life* magazine showing photographs of law enforcement officers looking for the bodies of the three activists. Another photograph showed nine young men, including the plaintiff in this action, Charles Breckenridge, standing on a bridge above a swamp, laughing and jeering. Part of the caption stated, "They guffawed when one hooted, 'We throw two or three niggers in every year, to feed the fish.'"

Breckenridge, taking offense at this article and photograph, filed a libel action against Time, Inc.[17] The local Mississippi circuit court judge for this district, Judge O. H. Barnett, cousin to Ross Barnett, had a reputation as an ardent segregationist whose grand juror charges sounded as if they were written by the imperial wizard of the Klan.

Sheriff Lawrence Rainey, a known Klan member who later was charged with having a leading role in the abduction of Goodman, Chaney, and Schwerner and who eventually was convicted in federal court for violating the civil rights of the victims, was praised by Judge Barnett as "the most courageous man in America."[18]

Philadelphia was swarming with reporters and FBI agents desperately searching for these three missing civil rights workers. Sheriff Rainey was critical of these meddling outsiders, and the locals were becoming more hostile, especially toward the national media. We knew that Time, Inc., must do everything possible to keep this lawsuit from being decided by a local jury. Although the photograph and reporting were surely true, the outcome in favor of the plaintiff (the poor, local, barefoot boy on the bridge talking about throwing "niggers in to feed the fish") was a foregone conclusion.

After numerous conferences with our New York cocounsel, the decision was made to move to dismiss the action on the grounds that the local Neshoba County Circuit Court did not have jurisdiction because Time, Inc., was not "doing business" in the state of Mississippi. Some explanation may be due here. You see, a court cannot proceed with a case unless it has what lawyers call *in personam* jurisdiction, that is, personal jurisdiction over the defendant. In other words a resident of Neshoba County could not haul off and sue a resident of the state of Maine unless that resident of Maine was caught in Mississippi, committed a tort in Mississippi, entered into a contract in Mississippi, or was otherwise "doing business" in Mississippi. This not only is the law but also is fair and equitable, requiring a plaintiff to sue a defendant where the defendant is located and "can be found," and not requiring a defendant to come all the way to another state and present his or her defense before strangers.

But what about *Time* and *Life* magazines? Surely they pierced the "cotton curtain" and were read by citizens across the state of Mississippi. For all of these reasons we approached the court with some trepidation, first to get past the mob on the courthouse steps whose hostility to anyone representing the media was vicious, and second to approach the hostility of the infamous segregationist, Judge Barnett.

Amazingly, the arguments were proceeding fairly smoothly until the one witness we had from New York, John R. Hallenbeck, a vice president of Time, Inc., who was sent down to testify on the issue of whether Time was doing business in Mississippi, was served with a subpoena in open court by Laurel G. Weir, the plaintiff's wily Philadelphia attorney. Weir logically argued to the court that even if the court believed that Time, Inc., was not "doing business" in Mississippi, Time was now "caught" in Mississippi since it had been served with process there and, therefore, was subject to the jurisdiction of the court under the law. I was devastated. Time had been "caught" in Mississippi by my advice to bring a vice president down.

In my despondency, I was saved by my brilliant partner, Earl Thomas, who immediately cited the Mississippi case of *Arnett v. Carol C. and Fred R. Smith, Inc.* to Judge Barnett, this case having established that a witness in attendance in a court outside his own jurisdiction is immune from being served subpoenas while testifying in that court as a witness. Judge Barnett could not get around that controlling authority, quashed the service of process, and held that the attempted service was invalid. Then, immediately after the hearing, and to the surprise of everyone, Judge Barnett dismissed the case, sustaining our motion. The case was immediately appealed to the Mississippi Supreme Court, where it was affirmed on November 1, 1965.[19]

For some inexplicable reason, during these hellacious days, both state and federal courts in Mississippi went a long way in protecting the media from monstrous damage suits by requiring heightened sensitivity to the First Amendment.

White Women, Black Men

In the first sixty years of the twentieth century, racial lines grew tighter as the Mississippi courts and legislature continued to restrict African Americans in order to ensure complete segregation. The Mississippi Constitution of 1890 already prohibited the marriage of a white person "with a Negro or mulatto or person who has one-eighth or more of Negro blood." In 1906 the prohibition was expanded to include "Asians or persons with one-eighth 'Mongolian' blood" and made it a crime for anyone to print or circulate written material promoting the acceptance of interracial marriage.

By 1930 interracial marriage had been declared a felony. The politicians did everything possible to incite passions against interracial relationships. The "unthinkable" horror of a white woman having sex with a black man justified the most barbarous forms of violence and made the injunction against "amalgamation" the first law of white supremacy. Young black men were taught early on not to smile or even look at a white woman. The slightest breach of this uncompromising code could never go unpunished.

Of course, the "unthinkable" can happen, and it did happen in 1930 in Kemper County, where a married white couple named Frank and Luella Williamson lived about three-quarters of a mile from the Lauderdale County line in Kemper County. He farmed and she stayed home, taking care of the house, their three precious children, and her chickens. In late 1930 Luella gave birth to a fourth child, a healthy baby boy who was given the auspicious name of James Walton Williamson.

Right from the beginning, it was obvious that something was terribly wrong. The baby's complexion was not black but was overly dark. The entire area was excited by the birth. The local doctor came by with a committee of citizens and told Luella that the baby had to be "put over" and that it would be impossible for the baby to stay in the home with her three white children. The local committee visited Luella's husband, Frank, who courageously defended his wife. Luella's parents had serious problems over the possible race of their grandson and informed Luella that there was talk all over the county about the baby. Luella's father was convinced the baby was black.

An African American man, Ervin Pruitt, who lived about two miles from the Williamsons, had worked for Frank for about a month. Pruitt had been seen going into the house once. On another occasion a neighbor had come to the Williamson home to buy "homebrew" and saw Pruitt on the front porch with Luella and her children. The neighbor, when leaving, expressed some doubt about leaving Luella with Pruitt in the absence of her husband, but Luella convinced her it was okay because Pruitt had just stopped by so she could show him some chickens he was going to buy.

The entire neighborhood was becoming more excited, and there was serious talk of mob action against Pruitt, who already had been threatened for "having this baby by a white lady." In late February 1931 the baby boy became seriously ill. While Luella's mother and father were talking with Frank outside, they heard Luella scream. They rushed back into the house and found the baby suffering intensely with his mouth, tongue, throat, and lips badly burned. The baby died while on the way to the hospital in Meridian, about forty miles away. The authorities were convinced the baby had been poisoned but couldn't figure out exactly what to do. They came up with the idea of arresting both Frank Williamson and Ervin Pruitt on a charge of petit larceny in the theft of some cottonseed. Luella also was placed in jail at the same time. A short time later Frank was released, but Pruitt was indicted for the murder of Luella's baby and placed on trial in the Circuit Court of Lauderdale County, Mississippi.[20]

Pruitt was brought into the courtroom in shackles, but even with his head down, he was still able to glance over to see the twelve stolid white men selected to determine his fate. The state put on evidence that the baby was poisoned, and then the courtroom went silent as Luella Williamson walked to the witness chair as the prosecution's star witness. She showed no hesitation in pointing her finger directly at Pruitt and testifying that Pruitt was the father of her mulatto baby boy. Luella further testified that the day her father and mother were at her home, Pruitt came into her house, threatened her with a gun, and told her he would kill her and her family if she didn't give the stuff he handed her in a blue wrapper to the baby. Luella said the substance was a white powder that Pruitt had told her was strychnine. The prosecutor claimed that Pruitt was making eyes at her while she was testifying.[21] Pruitt did not testify, his attorney knowing that in circumstances of this kind it is utterly futile and perhaps fatal for a black man to testify in contradiction to the testimony of a white woman.

After hearing the evidence, the jury found Ervin Pruitt guilty, and the court sentenced him to be hanged. The case was appealed to the Mississippi Supreme Court, where the verdict was affirmed. The court summarily denied each of the trial errors argued by Pruitt's attorney. First, the court said no expert was needed to tell whether a baby had a mixture of black blood and that any layman in Mississippi is competent to so testify. Next, the court said that Luella's testimony as an accomplice was proper to incriminate Pruitt and that the testimony was not so unreasonable and improbable as to make the jury verdict a palpable miscarriage of justice.

The court refused to take race into consideration, the defense arguing that since Pruitt was a black man and Luella was a white woman, Pruitt was actually convicted not of murder but rather of the abominable crime of "miscegenation." In justifying its opinion the Mississippi Supreme Court accused Pruitt of being the "mastermind" and said that Luella had been "subjected to his lecherous embraces" and "had gone the limits of degradation with him." The court thought it important, in finding credibility in Luella's testimony, that she confessed to not only "infidelity to her husband" but also "infidelity to her race." Finding no error, the court set April 15, 1932, as the date for Pruitt's execution.

Two justices dissented, stating that the conviction was based solely on the testimony of an accomplice, Luella, and that her testimony was "so unreasonable and improbable (as) to be unbelievable." Pruitt was hanged as ordered.

Alex A. Alston Jr.:

All of this is not to say that there were no courageous lawyers in Mississippi during those apartheid days. I recall that shortly after I became a lawyer, I was working with my senior partner, Earl T. Thomas, who that year happened to be president of the Mississippi Bar. He was getting pressure from lawyers and bar associations across the United States for the dismal failure of the Mississippi lawyers to represent and protect blacks in their constitutional rights.

Thomas had seen and heard enough. He called together the nineteen commissioners of the bar, kept them in session all day, and impressed upon them that the attorneys of this state through the Mississippi bar must provide criminal defendants with lawyers and that the defendants must be represented zealously to the full extent of the law "regardless of higher or lower state, whether rich or poor, resident or nonresident, or any race, color, creed or national origin."[22]

To that end the Mississippi bar, under the leadership of Earl Thomas, passed a resolution dated July 15, 1964, recognizing the duty of all members of the Mississippi bar to be faithful to their duties and oath and to represent all persons regardless of race and provide a fair and impartial trial with competent counsel. The action of the bar met with mixed success, but some were relieved to see that at least the bar of the State of Mississippi recognized its responsibilities. Thomas was criticized by the local media and on several occasions was called a "pinko Communist" for merely reminding the Mississippi attorneys of their obligations as lawyers.

The barbarous manner in which blacks were treated in the Mississippi courts until well into the twentieth century is shocking and disgusting. Where were the Atticus Finches? Atticus Finch was the fictional character in Harper Lee's novel *To Kill a Mockingbird* who during this same period in history zealously represented a one-armed black man charged with the rape of a white woman. Against massive white hostility, Finch not only represented his defendant to the fullest extent of the law but also held back an unruly mob that was making every effort to lynch the defendant. Unfortunately such heroes were few and far between.

There were almost no black lawyers. Even when appointed to represent an indigent black, white lawyers risked retribution and social ostracism. Michael de L. Landon, in his 1979 history of the Mississippi bar, wrote that there were only three black attorneys residing in the state in the early sixties. He recognized that "Mississippi attorneys who took on 'outside agitators' or 'uppity' blacks as clients were apt to come under intolerable pressure from their friends, neighbors, and other clients. In the late 1950s and 1960s, many of the lawyers of this state were members of the Citizens Council."[23] Unfortunately many attorneys were actually sympathetic to the terrorist Klan organizations.

To fill a void of attorneys needed to represent black defendants and civil rights workers, various organizations were formed and established offices in Jackson, including the Lawyers' Constitutional Defense Committee, the Lawyers Committee for Civil Rights Under Law, and the NAACP. The NAACP's Legal Defense Fund and brave lawyers from across the United States rallied to this need. The need was exacerbated in the 1960s by the voter registration drives and the brutal and often violent resistance of local authorities.

Getting local white lawyers to buck the hostility of the local citizenry to assist these groups was almost impossible. Even if a local lawyer could be obtained, frequently that lawyer could not be relied upon to raise all pertinent constitutional defenses. I recall the local hostility to these out-of-state attorneys, often called "nigger lovers," "pinko Communists," or "outside agitators."

One must admit that the conduct of the lawyers in Mississippi in protecting the rights of African Americans caught in the throes of the law is dismal. Their failure to file motions to protect the constitutional rights of their defendants is abysmal. But that problem pales with the problem of getting an attorney in the first place. The Fifth Circuit Court of Appeals noted that those white lawyers in Mississippi who would represent blacks in cases opposing whites, especially in murder or rape cases, must be "courageous and unselfish" and that even to raise such a constitutional issue as "exclusion of Negroes from juries," Mississippi lawyers did so "at the risk of personal sacrifice which may extend to loss of practice and social ostracism."[24]

Lawyers Under Fire

William "Bill" Higgs grew up in Greenville, attended the University of Mississippi, and finished at Harvard Law School. When he returned to Mississippi in 1958, at the age of twenty-two, he was willing to lend a hand in African American efforts to assert their basic rights as American citizens.

Not surprisingly, Higgs attracted the attention of the Sovereignty Commission, the depth of the agency's surveillance not apparent until the files were made public in 1996, revealing more than 340 documents related to his activities. In the agency's eyes, there was little distinction between civil rights "agitators" and the lawyers who defended them. Higgs is a great example of one who paid dearly for being, as racist Mississippians called him, a "traitor to his race."

Although Higgs had the audacity to assist in the legal machinations in the enrollment of James Meredith at the University of Mississippi, his greatest "sin" in the eyes of Mississippi probably was filing a lawsuit in federal court to stop the Sovereignty Commission from donating taxpayer dollars to the Citizens' Council.

Just after New Year's 1963, within a few hours after he had asked the federal court to order the enrollment of another black at the University of Mississippi, Higgs was arrested and charged with the delinquency of a minor, a runaway boy he had befriended. He left Mississippi after his life was threatened, and he was convicted *in absentia* and disbarred from practicing law in Mississippi. Higgs later obtained from the young man, with whom he was charged with inappropriate conduct, an affidavit that the entire time he knew Higgs there was nothing unnatural in their relationship.[25] Higgs never returned, knowing he would end up in prison. The exiled Higgs ultimately relocated to Acapulco, Mexico, where both he and his mother died in 1988, five days apart. They were buried in Mexico in unmarked graves.

An example of a true heroic Mississippi lawyer that can stand by the idealized fictional Atticus Finch is John A. Clark of DeKalb, Kemper County, Mississippi. He was appointed by the circuit judge to represent three black men in the trial for the murder of Richard Stewart, a sixty-year-old white planter. Although he was jerked around and not given time to prepare for trial, Clark did, nevertheless, take on the case without pay.[26]

When the defendants were arraigned, Clark was ill and asked to be excused as defense counsel. The request was denied. This was a major turning point in the case since if Clark had been excused as defense counsel, the three defendants almost certainly would have been hanged. Throughout the trial Clark's reasoning was that the defendants were probably guilty because of the assurances from the sheriff that the confessions were truly voluntary. He began to have doubts, however, after hearing the defendants testify of their brutal beatings and one defendant's story of being hanged (the rope marks were still visible at the trial), before finally belching out a confession. After the trial was over, Clark drove to Meridian, where the defendants were languishing in jail, and talked to them again. They convinced him that they were innocent and had made the confessions, as they said, to stop "the law" from the barbaric and brutal beatings.

Clark mustered the strength and courage to appeal the case to the Mississippi Supreme Court. He vigorously briefed and orally argued the case but to no avail. The Mississippi Supreme Court affirmed the conviction, whereupon the case was appealed to the U.S. Supreme Court, where it was reversed. The High Court adopted, almost verbatim, the dissent in the Mississippi Supreme Court and scolded the court for tolerating the rack and torture chamber.

No doubt Clark had significant questions about this appeal. He was fifty years old and not in good health. Serious emotions had been aroused, and the appeal would be exceedingly unpopular and personally expensive. Although Clark was a state senator (having served for fifteen years), a Democratic committeeman, and a Senate floor leader, he probably knew that the appeal would be the end of his political career. His close friend Judge Marvin W. Reily had advised Clark not to make the appeal, since he would be "wasting his time on a losing cause." Reily was right about his future. After experiencing intense personal abuse, Clark lost his seat in the Senate in 1935 and suffered a physical and mental collapse. He retired from the law in 1938 and died the following year.

The first sixty years of the twentieth century presents a wretched picture of the Mississippi judiciary. The courts proclaimed they were conducting their judicial system under a rule of law without distinction of class or race. This high-minded proclamation was far from the truth, since the courts, including attorneys as officers of the court, operated under another code—to protect the Mississippi way of life, which demanded complete and absolute segregation of the races. Whenever these two codes conflicted, apartheid prevailed. The controlling white population tolerated no deviation and would quickly and decisively punish any attorney who evidenced any inclination to deviate from this absolute code of complete segregation, white supremacy, and solidarity.

Alex A. Alston Jr.:

I believe it was in about 1971 when I found myself president of a group we then called the Jackson Junior Bar Association. Every member of the Mississippi bar under a certain age was automatically a member. One of my duties was to arrange a place to have our monthly meetings. It occurred to me that my lawyer friends who were black, such as Reuben Anderson and Fred Banks, had never been invited and could not participate in our meetings because of segregation policies in the places we met.

Without asking anyone, I called Primos Café, the Heidelburg Hotel, and other places where we held our meetings, and I was specifically told they would not allow blacks to eat in their establishments. I continued my search for a location, again not bringing this before the board or asking for any authority, since I did not want this to become an issue. There simply was no place that would admit an African American. I then thought of the young manager at my tennis club. The club had a large dining area that would be adequate, and although it was a short distance from downtown, I thought I would give it a try.

I called the manager and had a frank discussion with him, telling him it would bring the tennis club substantial sums for a major function every month, but we had several blacks whom we wanted to join us. He assured me that we could make the arrangements and that it would be quite all right.

Sure enough, I made the arrangements, sent out the notices, and called my black friends and asked them to attend. The meeting went well, but I was expecting to hear a loud and vociferous protest for my unilateral action; however, there was not one word of protest. Only one member came to me after that meeting and said, "Alex, I don't remember us voting on whether to admit those Negroes."

My only response was, "Well, I don't remember anyone voting on you to become a member." That ended it. I heard nothing further.

11

Mississippi Gestapo

As pastor of Harmony Baptist Church, Dennis Hale felt far removed from the racial violence that was sweeping across Mississippi like a raging wildfire. He watched over a small congregation in a rural community about five miles from Picayune. You'd be hard-pressed to find more than a handful of blacks in the sandy, pine-scented communities in that part of the state. But Hale and his wife, who didn't like what was happening to blacks, felt compelled to speak out on the issue of equal rights.

Out of conviction, Hale wrote a letter to Senator James O. Eastland in 1963 that expressed his views.[1] Then he resumed his pastoral duties, forgetting about the letter. One day, two investigators with the Mississippi Sovereignty Commission, Andrew Hopkins and Tom Scarbrough, showed up unannounced at Hale's house. They flashed their badges and informed the startled couple that someone had been signing their names to scandalous letters and sending them to members of Congress. Hale confessed that he had written letters to Senator Eastland and others protesting the treatment that blacks received in the state, but he said there was nothing scandalous in the letters.

The investigators asked to see copies. Hale refused, citing his First Amendment rights. They asked if he felt that his church should be integrated.

"That would be a matter for the members of the church to decide."[2]

They asked how he'd feel about blacks going to his church.

"Everyone should have the right to attend the church of his choice according to his religious convictions and baptism."

They asked if he thought the schools should be integrated.

"Everyone should go to the school of his choice."

The visit became confrontational. When the investigators asked the couple if they wanted their children to marry "niggers," the Alabama-born Hale, who at six feet two inches towered over the investigators, became angry and asked them to leave his house. The Hales were perplexed by the incident. They had no way of knowing that Senator Eastland worked closely with the Sovereignty Commission and provided them with information on a regular basis. "I was writing a letter to influence my senator to support civil rights legislation in Congress," Hale later explained to a reporter. "I did not think it was right for him to send somebody out to try to intimidate me."[3]

The investigators confided in Judge J. E. Stockstill, a member of the commission, and asked for advice on how to handle the situation. He suggested that they obtain copies of the letters and show them to the deacons and members of the congregation.

Today it is incredible to think that a state agency would use intimidation against citizens who argued for racial equality, but that was standard procedure for the Mississippi Sovereignty Commission. On other occasions the commission used the type of spy techniques and psychological warfare later adapted by the CIA and other government agencies at the federal level to deal with terrorists, only instead of targeting terrorists, the agency went after ordinary citizens who supported the Constitution.

Target Ole Miss

After Ole Miss was desegregated, the Sovereignty Commission stepped up its covert activities on college campuses and recruited students to spy on other students. Special attention was given to the University of Mississippi, which the governor felt was at greatest risk of becoming a willing participant in desegregation.

Sometimes the commission sent its own investigators. Other times, the governor sent investigators from other agencies to compile reports for the commission. In 1964 Rex Armistead, an investigator with the highway patrol, went to the University of Mississippi at the request of Governor Paul B. Johnson to conduct covert surveillance of television news commentator Howard K. Smith, who had been invited to speak to students at Fulton Chapel, the main campus auditorium. Armistead shadowed Smith's every move once he arrived in Oxford, following him to a private home, where he met with Professors James Silver and Russell Barrett, and then to Fulton Chapel, noting his precise times of movement. Armistead observed no "subversive" activities by the newsman.

While keeping an eye on Smith, Armistead witnessed an incident that occurred when five blacks showed up at the auditorium to hear Smith's speech. "At the alcove inside the main door, one of the Negroes was stopped by a student . . . [who] advised him that he was not wanted there and that this was a meeting for white people and [he] was asked to leave," reported Armistead.

> The Negro attempted to walk over to the student, at which time the student grabbed him and carried him outside and proceeded to give him a good whipping. Chief Tatum [head of campus security] immediately grabbed the white student and without attempting to find the cause of the disturbance, began to beat the student across the ears and face and then pushed him down a flight of stairs where other campus police were waiting. At this time Chief Tatum advised the student that he was under arrest and was to be placed in the county jail.

When the student was transported to the jail, the county sheriff refused to incarcerate him. Instead he took the student home with him and allowed him to spend the night. Armistead said there was general agreement among law enforcement officers that Chief Tatum should be removed from office. "By doing so, eighty percent of the campus trouble would be dissolved," he said. "[He] listens only to [the professors] and to the other liberals. On the campus he refuses to cooperate with any law enforcement agency other than that of the federal government."

Prior to Armistead's visit, the Sovereignty Commission had already targeted James Silver, a professor in the history department, and Russell Barrett, a political science professor, because of their statements to newspapers that exonerated the marshals for their actions during the Ole Miss riot.[4] Noted the investigator about their testimony before the grand jury investigating the riot: "The grand jury felt it was the responsibility of the university professors to teach what their position required that they teach and certainly not to take the position of siding with anyone concerning a controversy, much less a racial matter which everyone in this state is very much concerned about." The Sovereignty Commission found Ole Miss fertile ground for the cultivation of informants. One group of students, which named itself the Knights of the Great Forest, spied on professors and turned in the names of those they thought supported racial integration.

Howard K. Smith was not the only national television personality to come under scrutiny. The popular NBC television show *Bonanza*, staring Lorne Greene, Michael Landon, and Dan Blocker, was targeted after *Jet* magazine published a story about a black actress who was scheduled to appear in an upcoming episode. In an effort to block the program, commission director Erle Johnston enlisted the help of Dumas Milner, a Jackson Chevrolet dealer. At Johnston's request, Milner wrote a letter to General Motors to put pressure on the sponsor of the show, and another to television station WLBT, the NBC affiliate in Jackson, to block the filming of the episode with a black woman. Wrote Dumas: "We have been advised that this show has not been filmed as of this date. If this is true, I am sure Chevrolet would like to prevent it because the show is very popular as it is now and I think there is more to be lost than gained by adding this [black] girl to the show."[5] Both the television station and the automaker refused to bow to the request.

As the governor and the commission pondered the best way to deal with the university campuses—especially Ole Miss, considered the most liberal campus in the state—a new crisis arose: Robert Kennedy, the newly elected United States senator from New York, announced that he would accept an invitation from the Ole Miss law school to visit the university in March 1966 to address the students.

The Ole Miss newspaper, the *Mississippian*, was critical of the decision to invite the senator, saying that his visit was a matter of "great concern." Mary Cain, editor of the *Summit Sun* and president of the Women for Constitutional Government (WCG), condemned the former attorney general's visit. At her request the WCG passed a resolution stating that the organization "can neither forgive nor forget" the role Kennedy played in the desegregation of Ole Miss. To the disappointment of some, Governor Johnson, who as lieutenant governor had physically blocked James Meredith's entry into the university, said he would "stay out of it" this time.

In the days leading up to the senator's visit, the campus buzzed with gossip. There were rumors of a potential riot. Professors paused during their lectures to comment on the visit. Newspapers quoted right-wing activists and Klan leaders as promising a strong presence on the campus. It had been four years since Meredith's enrollment, and, except for a few panty raids that got out of hand, most of the students had never witnessed anything close to a full-blown riot.

When Kennedy arrived on campus with his wife, Ethel, it was nothing like what he had expected. The campus was calm and disarmingly charming. There were no mass demonstrations. He spoke in the coliseum, a new basketball and concert arena that still smelled of fresh paint, to a carefully screened audience. Nonstudents were prohibited from entering the building.

James L. Dickerson:

About an hour or so before I went to the coliseum to hear Kennedy speak, the janitor of my dorm—I had a private room in one of the smaller, older dorms—stopped by my room to pick up trash. Over the months, we'd become friends, frequently talking about things happening on the campus as he went about his chores. He was a stoutly built black man of medium height, probably in his midforties. He knew that Kennedy was scheduled to speak that day. "You going?" he asked, tossing the comment over his shoulder as he worked. Seeing me nod in the affirmative, he said, "Wish I could go."

"Aren't you entitled to go—as a university employee?"

"No, no. They wouldn't do that. I asked my boss. He said I couldn't go."

I felt bad that he couldn't go to hear Kennedy. The school administration probably banned university employees out of fear that some of the white employees might be Klansmen. Some of them sure looked as if they could be, judging by their demeanor and the smug, often hostile way they interacted with students.

I arrived at the coliseum just a few minutes before the program began and had to sit farther away from the platform than I would have liked. Robert Kennedy, wearing a pin-striped suit with a white handkerchief tucked into his top front pocket, received a polite round of applause when he walked onto the stage, flanked by a solemn procession of university officials and student leaders. To my surprise he seemed shy and hesitant in front of the student audience. He paced the stage with his hands behind his back, radiating bursts of nervous energy.

Kennedy began by saying he was told by friends in New York that his visit to Ole Miss would be like a fox stepping into a chicken coop. That's not the way it turned out, he told the students. Instead he felt more like "a chicken in a fox coop."

The students laughed, and Kennedy made new friends.

During a question-and-answer session following his speech, a student asked who he felt was responsible for the 1962 riot. Kennedy declined to place blame on any one individual, but he discussed his telephone conversation with Governor Ross Barnett, the one in which Barnett had asked if it would be possible for the marshals to draw their guns. "I thought maybe he could just step aside when he saw the marshals," Kennedy said.

When I returned to my dorm, I was surprised to find the janitor leaning against the wall next to my door. I looked at my watch. "You're working late."

"I've been off the clock for a while. I wanted to hear all about it, while it's still fresh in your thinking."

At the time I didn't fully appreciate his interest in Kennedy. In later years, when I had occasion to enter black homes in the Delta as a newspaper reporter, I learned that I could always count on seeing certain images in the houses: An image of Jesus Christ. An image of Martin Luther King Jr. And an image of either John or Robert Kennedy.

"What would you like to know?"

He asked about the speech, and I repeated everything that Kennedy had said. He nodded a few times during the telling and left with a broad smile on his face.

Not too enthusiastic about Kennedy's speech was Ross Barnett. The next day he issued a statement attacking Kennedy's "twisted" and "willful" misrepresentation of the facts. "It ill becomes a man . . . who was responsible for using 30,000 troops and spent approximately six million dollars to put one unqualified student in Ole Miss to return to the scene of this crime and discuss any phase of this infamous affair," Barnett said, spewing venom. To him, Kennedy was a "very sick and dangerous American."

Enforcing Racial Purity

There were a number of issues at play during the racial turmoil of the 1950s and 1960s, but at the heart of the conflict was fear of interracial sex involving white women. Not even Senator James O. Eastland was immune to obsessive thoughts about the issue.

One day Eastland was driving through Spartanburg, South Carolina, on his way back to Washington, D.C., when he stopped to chat with one of the commanders in the South Carolina Highway Patrol. Eastland learned that a car containing two black men and a white woman had been stopped for speeding in South Carolina. That meant only one thing to him—the defilement of a white woman.

When Eastland reached Washington, he was so worked up that he telephoned the Mississippi Highway Patrol to give a description of the car and its tag number, since he thought it might be headed for Mississippi.[6] He said he didn't have the white woman's name, but he did have the names and addresses of the black men. It is not known if the car traveled into Mississippi or, if it did, what happened to the woman and the two men.

When the Sovereignty Commission received word in 1964 that a white woman in Grenada, Mississippi, had given birth to a baby of suspicious racial origins, investigator Tom Scarbrough was sent to the small town to conduct an investigation.[7] After touching base with his initial source, who informed him that the thirty-eight-year-old woman had been having an affair with a thirty-one-year-old motel employee who was black, Scarbrough met with the local sheriff, who expressed relief at seeing the investigator in town, since he wasn't sure what to do about the situation. In his report Scarbrough wrote that the sheriff had told him that people in Grenada were disturbed about the rumors, all the more so since the husband and wife were from respected families.

Scarbrough decided the easiest way to solve the dilemma would be for the sheriff to examine the baby to determine if it had a black father. The sheriff agreed. He called the woman and talked her into stopping by his office. Under questioning by Scarbrough, the woman, who was in a legal dispute with her ex-husband over custody of their two sons, denied having an affair with a black man but admitted to having an affair with a white man who worked at the motel. Scarbrough told her that the sheriff was sympathetic to her situation and would do his best to squelch the rumors if it turned out the child was not black. He suggested that she grant the sheriff permission to examine her baby. The woman told him she had no objection to that.

After arranging a time for a home visit the following day, the woman left and Scarbrough went to the motel to interview the black man rumored to be the father. He asked him point-blank if he had ever had sex with the white woman.

"No, sir," answered the black man.

The next morning the sheriff went to view the baby. When he returned to his office, Scarbrough was waiting for him. He said he had seen the baby but wasn't sure about the child's parentage. He asked Scarbrough if he would mind taking a look at the baby. The two men returned to the anxious woman's apartment.

"We both looked at the baby again and I was looking at the child's fingernails and the end of its fingers very closely when she remarked, 'I know what you're thinking, but that baby is not part Negro. Its father is an Italian,'" Scarbrough said in his report. "After viewing the child I had a weak feeling in the pit of my stomach and the sheriff expressed he felt likewise. We both agreed we were not qualified to say it was a part Negro child, but we could say it was not 100 percent Caucasian."

Scarbrough returned to the motel and shared his conclusions with the black man's employer. "[The employer] stated there was nothing left for him to do except to dismiss [the black man] from his employ," he said in the report. "What disposition will be made of [the black man] is yet to be seen." He noted that the white motel owners had a lot of trust and confidence in their black employee and "in all probability would not believe anything against him. This I found to be pretty well the opinion of all people to whom I talked."

The Sovereignty Commission ended the year by notifying the State Board of Health that a white woman who had been working with Council of Federated Organizations workers in McComb was a carrier of venereal disease. "Subject is said to wear black stockings to conceal sores," Erle Johnston said in the report. "She reportedly has been afraid she will be picked up by a public health officer. . . . We notified Dr. Blakey of the state board of health. Dr. Blakey said they would pick up the subject for an examination and notify the Sovereignty Commission if the tests were positive. . . . Any further steps regarding above subject will be determined after a report from the state health department."

Three years later Scarbrough was sent to Carroll County, a picturesque rural area off the beaten path between Greenwood and Grenada to investigate the activities of a white woman who had been seen in the company of black men. There were few blacks in the county, and most of the whites were farmers who had worked the same sparse hillsides for generations. When he arrived, Scarbrough found a community that was in an uproar over Janet Maedke, a twenty-seven-year-old white woman from Wisconsin who, accompanied by several black activists, had arrived in Carrollton, the county seat, to integrate the town's main cafe.[8] They were prevented from entering the cafe by the sheriff, who stood by and watched as the cafe owner went outside and started a fight. The window of Maedke's car was shattered during the altercation, the broken glass peppering her arm.

Maedke and the black civil rights activists left town, followed by the cafe owner and another man, who pursued them on the highway at high speed and fired shots at them. Driving at speeds that exceeded one hundred miles per hour, Maedke and her black companions escaped their pursuers and made it to a place of safety. When they stopped and examined the car, they found that one bullet had shattered a taillight and a second bullet had penetrated the trunk of the car. After five days of hiding, Maedke wrote to a friend expressing her fear, disgust, and determination to continue with their efforts. She said she had not slept for days. She kept a rifle on the dashboard of her car and a shotgun on the backseat. She was convinced someone was going to kill her.

The case was turned over to the Sovereignty Commission, after Maedke contacted Wisconsin governor Warren Knowles and asked for his help.[9] Knowles called the U.S. Justice Department and spoke to John Doar, the assistant attorney general in the Civil Rights Division who had been involved with the Meredith case at Ole Miss. In a follow-up letter, Doar gave the governor a full report on the incident and told him that Maedke should report it to the proper law enforcement officials. Copies of Maedke's letter to her friend and Doar's letter to the governor of Wisconsin somehow ended up in the Sovereignty Commission files.

Following Doar's advice, Maedke pressed assault charges against the cafe owner, but when the matter went to trial, a jury composed of four blacks and two whites acquitted him. In his report, Scarbrough said the sheriff told him that Maedke was a "typical looking, white beatnik" who associated with "no one but a low class of Negroes." At the trial, according to Scarbrough's report, Maedke "was dressed in a very slouchy manner and was sitting among her usual crowd of Negroes." He said the sheriff saw one of the black men reach over and pat her on her knees and thighs during the trial. "Miss Maedke and her Negro companions had successfully integrated other places in Vaiden [a nearby town], before this incident," said Scarbrough. "It appears that they went to Carrollton for the purpose of making trouble."

The Vietnam War

By 1967 the Mississippi Sovereignty Commission had added a new weapon to its intimidation arsenal: eighty-two draft boards, one for each county in the state. The boards were composed of presidential appointees who had the life-and-death power to decide who was drafted into the armed forces.

Draft boards were often used as a weapon to punish citizens who favored civil rights and opposed the war. In one instance commission director Erle Johnston received a letter from a frantic mother who said her white teenage daughter was having an affair with a man she thought might be part black. Johnston assigned the case to an investigator and instructed him to determine the man's racial heritage. Then, anticipating the worst, he proposed a solution. "If subject is at least twenty-two years old, it is possible we could arrange that he be drafted."

Mississippi draft boards were composed entirely of white males. When the Sovereignty Commission requested that targeted individuals be drafted, they were sent induction notices, no questions asked. Next to lynching, it was the preferred method of removing male civil rights troublemakers from the state.

Some draft board members also held membership in the Ku Klux Klan. When Rick Abraham, director of the Mississippi Draft Information Service, pointed out to the State Headquarters for Selective Service that the chairman of the Washington County draft board was a member of the Klan, state officials responded that there was nothing illegal about that. Recalled Abraham: "They likened the situation to a Catholic being able to make an unbiased classification of a Jewish registrant."[10]

As the FBI expanded its secret COINTELPRO program to include antiwar activists, the commission and the highway patrol gave the Mississippi antiwar movement equal status with the civil rights movement. In the eyes of racist Mississippians, it was just as radical to advocate peace as it was to advocate racial equality. Commission investigators were authorized to pursue either group. They were limited in what they could do to punish antiwar activists from outside the state, but against native-son activists they could exercise the ultimate weapon: they could have them sent to Vietnam.

The Meredith Nightmare

Less than three months after Robert Kennedy's 1966 visit to Ole Miss, James Meredith organized a voting rights march that began in Memphis on June 5 and continued down the interstate to Jackson, a distance of about two hundred miles. Just outside Memphis, about one mile south of Hernando, Meredith and a group of marchers walked past a white man standing beside the highway. The moment was captured by newspaper photographers stationed across the road. Just over the hill was a carload of FBI agents. About two hundred yards past them was the county sheriff. After Meredith passed, the man called out, an ominous tone to his voice, "Which one of you is James Meredith?"

Hearing those words, the group scattered, everyone running for cover. There just was something in the man's voice that sounded like trouble. As they dived for cover, there were three blasts from a 16-gauge automatic shotgun.

Bam! Bam! Bam!

Meredith was the only one struck by the buckshot.

The shooter, later identified as Memphian Aubrey Norvell, made no attempt to escape. After Meredith fell to the ground, wounded and bleeding, Norvell stood his ground, looking awkwardly out of place as he waited for the police to arrive.

Meredith was rushed to a Memphis hospital, where it was determined that his wounds were not serious, though they were troublesome enough to prevent him from rejoining the march.[11] The nation reacted with outrage. Civil rights leaders Martin Luther King Jr. and rising star Stokely Carmichael rushed to Mississippi to lead the march on to Jackson. Amid the uproar, the Mississippi Sovereignty Commission dispatched investigators to the scene. In a report labeled CONFIDENTIAL—NOT FOR THE FILES, Tom Scarbrough detailed his investigation of the incident. It was his gut feeling that the shooting had been planned by civil rights activists to draw attention to the march.

Scarbrough arrived at the sheriff's office and found the lawman talking to one of Norvell's two attorneys. He called the sheriff aside for a private conversation and asked if he thought either of the lawyers was interested in "bringing the truth to light." The sheriff said he already had talked to one of the lawyers about the possibility that Norvell had been hired to shoot Meredith. It was the lawyer's view, according to the sheriff, that if it was a shooting for hire, the lawyer would get "far more out of it in a monetary way than he could possibly get out of defending Norvell."

Scarbrough told the sheriff that he was certain the courts would be lenient with Norvell if he provided the names of the people who hired him. He asked the sheriff to pass that message along to the lawyers.

"I asked him if he would talk to [one of the lawyers] on his own and advise him that he would give him a sizable sum of money to get the truth out of Norvell concerning the shooting." Scarbrough suggested that the sheriff start with an offer of five thousand dollars, an amount that Scarbrough would personally guarantee if it could be established that the shooting had been planned in advance. In his report to the Sovereignty Commission, he explained: "I further told the sheriff that the proposition I was making him was on my own and did not involve the state in any shape, form or fashion, but he could rest assured in making the proposition to [the lawyer] that the money would be available when proof is shown that Norvell was hired to do the shooting."

Scarbrough's offer was illegal and would have been interpreted by most courts as a bribe, and his statement to the sheriff that he was acting alone in making the offer was an outright lie. In a memo dated June 14, commission director Erle Johnston advised the governor that he had authorized Scarbrough to offer the money to Norvell.[12] "I know of no other investigator better qualified by judgment and temperament to handle such an assignment and assure there will be no repercussion against the Sovereignty Commission." It was yet another example of how the commission used carefully written reports to divert attention from its true mission.

Norvell was in serious trouble: caught red-handed at the scene of the crime with the gun in his hand, he was photographed by newsmen on the scene. However, if he told the court that he was hired by a civil rights organization, he could pocket a sizable amount of money, plus receive a guarantee of leniency. If he told the court he acted alone, he would receive no money and go directly to jail.

Norvell stuck to his story that he acted alone. He may have been a forty-year-old unemployed white man who gunned down a black man in cold blood in full view of the entire world, but, by God, he was no liar and certainly had no intention of taking tainted money from the government. Instead of playing along with the Sovereignty Commission, he pleaded guilty to the shooting and received a five-year sentence.

Joining the marchers on June 8 was Martin Luther King Jr., who stayed a short time before returning to Memphis. As the marchers passed through Batesville, Scarbrough noticed that everyone was in a holiday mood. "One thing I noticed was the whites were singing those freedom songs to the Negro rhythms just as well as the Negroes themselves were singing, and a great number of the marchers were dancing or slapping their hands," he said. "It must be a great temptation to the local Negroes to fall in line with them because the marchers appeared to be having such a jubilee time."

When the marchers arrived in Canton, just outside Jackson, they were teargassed by police when they attempted to camp on school grounds; but the next day they made it all the way to the capitol building, where they held a massive rally. It was at this historic gathering that black activist Stokely Carmichael first urged the use of *black power*, a phrase that would have an explosive impact on the civil rights movement as the decade progressed. Thanks to Carmichael, Mississippi once again was on the cutting edge.

The Commission Cracks Under the Strain

As early as 1966, cracks were forming in the wall. Faced with the realization that it was Mississippi versus the rest of the world, Governor Johnson instructed Sovereignty Commission director Erle Johnston to search the agency's files for possible incriminatory information. In a memo to investigators, Johnston said: "It is necessary that we remove from the files any reports of investigators which might in any way be construed to mean that the Sovereignty Commission has interfered in any way with voter registration drives or demonstrations." All future reports, he said, should refer to the targets of investigations as "subversives" and not put undue emphasis on their race.

In a memo to the governor, Johnston notified him that "the files we considered incriminatory have been pulled and are now on the big table in the large office. We await your further instructions." There is no record of how many files were destroyed, or of what was in the files. There are hints, however. At that time the commission augmented its staff of three investigators with a network of private detective agencies, most of which had ties to the FBI. It's not clear what spooked Governor Johnson, but it may have had something to do with the Neshoba County civil rights murders. Whatever the reason, the governor sent Johnston a curt memo: "Please do not engage or employ any outside investigating agencies until further notice." In his reply to the governor, Johnston said he would suspend use of private agencies until further notice, but he defended the use of the agencies by pointing out that one of the commission's investigators, Virgil Downing, had died two weeks earlier, and a second, Andrew Hopkins, had been out sick for more than six weeks. Johnston also mentioned, for the first time, that one of his top secret agents—code named "Operator X"—was being handled by Day Detectives, a private investigative agency. He assumed the governor would want him to continue to use the agency for that purpose.

As the trial date for the Neshoba County civil rights case approached, Johnston seemed preoccupied and less willing to launch major new initiatives. In 1967, after seven years on the job, he was feeling the pressure. It wasn't easy putting in a full day running a top-secret spy agency and then commuting forty-five miles to Forest to put out a weekly newspaper, the *Scott County Times*. Physically, he was wearing down. He wasn't alone, either. Hopkins, his chief investigator, had frequent health problems and took extended leaves of absence. Then he was involved in a minor traffic accident while he was out on assignment. Soon Hopkins stopped coming to work. By the fall of 1966, Sovereignty Commission members were asking questions. They instructed Johnston to send Hopkins a letter asking for the names of his doctors and written permission from him for commission members to contact the doctors. The investigator was now being investigated. "I assured the committee you would be happy to cooperate with them," Johnston said to Hopkins. "As I told members of the Commission, I certainly hope that you soon become fully recuperated and can get back on the job."

Hopkins chose to resign.

Early in 1968, with the inauguration of a new governor, John Bell Williams, Johnston began showing signs of emotional stress. Obviously frustrated about his future with the agency, Johnston leaked to the press the contents of a report he had prepared for the new governor. For the most part it was self-serving and filled with outright falsehoods. Reporter Mike Smith, one of Johnston's contacts at the *Jackson Daily News*, described the report, under the headline SOVEREIGNTY COMMISSION "PREVENTATIVE MEDICINE," as the "never-before-revealed story" of how the commission had "solved countless racial irritations."

Johnston was depicted as a racial moderate who had worked hard to avert racial violence in the state. It was Dixie doublespeak. None of it was true.

That spring Erle Johnston collapsed while at work. He was rushed to a hospital, where doctors treated him for a heart attack. Later, doctors discovered it was not a heart attack but a reaction to stress. Johnston stayed out several weeks, calling his ailment "combat fatigue." When he returned to work, he sent word to the governor that he wanted out of the commission. He was asked to stay on until a replacement could be found. In late August, Governor Williams notified Johnston that he had found a replacement for him. The new director would be Webb Burke, a career FBI man with strong Mississippi connections.

Johnston didn't have much notice. Four days after Burke's appointment was announced, the new director reported for work. Johnston knew him by reputation but had never met him. He spent the day with Burke, showing him the filing system and going over reports with him, after which he packed up and went home to Scott County, where he lived in relative obscurity until his death in 1995. Governor Williams didn't say much about Johnston's departure, other than that he was leaving for health reasons. About Burke, he said: "[His] past experience in the law enforcement field should eminently qualify him for this sensitive but important position within our state government."

In January 1972, Mississippi got a new governor—William L. "Bill" Waller, the man who twice unsuccessfully prosecuted Byron De La Beckwith for the murder of Medgar Evers (see chapter 15). Most political observers considered his election victory a surprise. During the campaign Waller had surprised everyone by promising to appoint blacks to high-ranking positions in his administration. He was criticized for making overtures to black voters, who by 1971 made up nearly 30 percent of the electorate, but disenfranchised blacks had become a natural constituency for him after the Beckwith trials. Beckwith walked, but blacks knew Waller had tried, and that was important to them.

After he took office as governor, Waller didn't make any changes in the Sovereignty Commission. Webb Burke was left in charge, and his entire staff remained intact. Of course, the commission got new members on its board by virtue of the election. Joining the board for the first time was the new lieutenant governor, William Winter. The commission was allowed to go about its business as usual.

Abolishing the Commission

Governor Waller endured the Sovereignty Commission for almost a year and a half, and then in the spring of 1973, without warning, he pulled the plug on the secret agency. The legislature had passed a two-year appropriation bill for the commission, as it had done without question since 1956, but when the bill arrived on Waller's desk, he vetoed it. That meant the commission would cease to exist on July 1, the date its current funding expired. In a brief veto message, Waller said the work done by the commission would be transferred to the highway patrol. "The Sovereignty Commission," he said, "performs no real indispensable services to the people of this state." The legislature was stunned by the veto but did not override it.

Director Burke, who was not consulted about abolishing the agency, was caught off guard. Contacted by reporters, Burke said: "I definitely don't think we've been utilized as a negative force. . . . We've been accused of a lot of things we're not guilty of."

When the commission's offices were closed, its secret files were transferred to a storage warehouse accessible to the Mississippi Highway Patrol, an agency that the FBI once had found to be infiltrated by Klansmen. The situation remained in limbo until late 1977, when two bills that would formally transfer ownership of the Sovereignty Commission files to the highway patrol were prefiled for the upcoming legislative session.

When the legislature convened in January, the bills spurred a passionate debate over what to do about the commission. Technically the agency could be revived any time the governor signed a new appropriation by the legislature. Everyone seemed to agree that the commission should be abolished. Disagreement arose over what to do with the files. The bills were killed in committee. No one wanted the files officially turned over to the highway patrol, although everyone knew that the agency already had made copies of any files it wanted to keep. Many legislators wanted to destroy the files; others said they should be preserved. Among those wanting to see the files preserved were the state's black legislators. Said Horace Buckley, "I thought all the book burning and manuscript burning ended in the 12th century." Another black lawmaker, Doug Anderson, said, "If there is evil in those files, we should keep them to learn a lesson." Former lieutenant governor William Winter also went on record as being opposed to the destruction of the files. Interviewed in 1996 by the authors of this book, Winter said he had not changed his mind about preserving the files. "My concern is the same as that expressed by [others] that however the records are handled, they should be handled with sensitivity to the innocent individuals who may be included in the files.[13]

By the time the dust settled from the 1977 session, the legislature had voted to abolish the commission and to preserve the files. But there was a catch—the files were ordered sealed for fifty years and delivered to the Mississippi Department of Archives and History. Sitting in the legislature when the vote was taken was Representative George Rogers, who had seen the Sovereignty Commission come full cycle. "I voted to seal those records," said Rogers. "I knew there was a lot of junk in there, investigative reports that could damage people's reputations. The press wanted to make them public. I voted to seal them, not because I didn't want people to know, but because I was concerned about what was in the files."[14]

James L. Dickerson:

In the summer of 1996, I met with former governor Bill Waller in his Jackson law office to talk about the Sovereignty Commission. He was affable but clearly uncomfortable talking about his decision to kill the agency: "My opinion [of the commission] was based from the outside and seeing them operate. I vetoed their appropriations because it was a joke. Certain politicians would use [director] Burke to go out and get information secretly [that] they could use in their campaign or for fund-raising. But as a state agency it had very limited activity and very indefinite goals and assignments."[15]

Waller said he was not surprised that the legislature had not overridden his veto. "There were maybe a half dozen ultraconservative legislators who wanted to keep it around as a personal tool," he explained. "People have a way of getting even with a governor, and sometimes after a veto they don't say anything—they just lay in ambush. But I never got any response [to the veto]. I got overridden on several of my vetoes but not on that one."

Waller downplayed the significance of the commission. "They were strictly an ideological censor group . . . a conservative watchdog censorship group on the Keystone Cops level. They didn't really have any operations. They were more of a censors group. They were trying to find out who was on the liberal side of an issue and then making a record in their files."

The only question I asked him that seemed to catch him off guard was whether he knew the commission had opened a bank account that would allow it to handle money from private sources, without it going through the state auditor's office.

The former governor's face sank into a frown.

"Why, no," he said, his voice lowering almost to a whisper. "Did they really?"

The Fight to Open the Secret Files

Shortly after the legislature voted to seal the files, Representative Rogers resigned from the legislature to work for the Intelligence Community, an arm of the CIA that coordinates intelligence from all government agencies. Rogers, a Rhodes scholar, was driven out of office by the racist Citizens' Council.

Not long after the files were closed to the public, the American Civil Liberties Union (ACLU) filed suit in federal court to have the files opened. The lawsuit ended up in the courtroom of the infamous Judge Harold Cox, who promptly dismissed the case. The ACLU appealed, and the lawsuit was reinstated by the appeals court. Explained David Ingebretsen, director of the Mississippi office of the ACLU:

We agreed to take the case . . . to give victims a chance to sue for damages and to see what actions were taken by the government to promote segregation. Our position was that the files should be opened. The state was opposed to opening any files at all. There is damaging information about state officials. Damaging information about prominent individuals. Damaging information on people who had relatively clean records [on the surface].[16]

On July 27, 1989, Judge William Barbour ruled that the Sovereignty Commission files must be opened to the public. In his ruling he said:

This court finds that the state of Mississippi acted directly through its state Sovereignty Commission and through conspiracy with private individuals to deprive the plaintiffs of rights protected by the Constitution to free speech and association, to personal privacy, and to lawful search and seizure, and statutes of the United States. . . . Deprivations were accomplished through unlawful investigations and through intentional actions designed to harass and stigmatize individuals and organizations engaged in speech and conduct protected by the United States Constitution. The targets of Commission activity were designated by members and agents of the Commission. There is no record that a search warrant or any other judicial sanction of Commission acts was either sought or received. The avowed intent of the Commission and its co-conspirators was to chill or preclude the plaintiffs from speech, assembly, association, and the petition of government.

Barbour's decision did not mean the long ordeal was over. The state could appeal the decision and keep the matter in the courts almost indefinitely. At that time the governor was Ray Mabus, who was well into the second year of his term. As state auditor he had attracted considerable attention in his efforts to ferret out corruption in government. He had entered Ole Miss well after the trauma of the riots and, like many other Dixie Baby Boomers, had found that entire era of segregation an embarrassment and a moral travesty. After Barbour's decision was made public, Mabus announced that he was opposed to appealing the decision. The governor's office would not stand in the way of those who wanted to open the files.

With the State of Mississippi terminating its fight against making the contents of the files public, all that remained was agreeing on a procedure for opening the files. To the surprise of Ingebretsen, and nearly everyone else associated with the case, two of the plaintiffs, the Reverend Edwin King and civil rights organizer John Salter, filed an appeal with the Fifth Circuit Court of Appeals asking that Barbour's order be overturned. Ingebretsen was stunned by the appeal. "I think [King] is very sincere in what he is doing [but] . . . I think he's very wrong here." The appeal meant that two of the primary critics of the commission had become, almost overnight, its only remaining defenders.

In January 1995 Salter notified the Fifth U.S. Circuit Court of Appeals that he wanted to withdraw from the fight to keep the commission's files closed to all but the victims. That left King as the only stumbling block. Many of his friends were mystified by his behavior in light of his long-standing involvement in the civil rights movement. On June 11, 1996, the appeals court upheld Judge Barbour's decision to open the commission files. It bothered King that people would attack him for his stand on keeping the files closed unless opened by individual victims. Responding to allegations that he was an informant for the commission, King declined to either confirm or deny the allegations, citing his conviction that to do so would violate his rights. "If some people see that as evidence as to why I am doing this, they will have to interpret it that way. . . . My primary responsibility is to the victims, especially the ones I don't even know. Whatever happens to me happens."[17]

To the surprise of no one, King appealed to the U.S. Supreme Court. Mississippi watched and waited as summer faded into fall. Finally, as tempers frayed among those waiting for justice, the Supreme Court announced its decision: on November 18, 1996, the High Court said it would not hear the case, thus affirming the lower court's decision that the files should be opened.

The twenty-year battle to reveal the secrets of the Sovereignty Commission was finally over, and hopefully so was the nightmare. There was, however, skepticism about the integrity of the files, fears that state and federal officials had too many opportunities to remove incriminating information. In its heyday, commission members had bragged of files on over 120,000 individuals and several thousand organizations. Now state officials said the files contained information on only 87,000 individuals and only a few hundred organizations.

When the files were removed from the commission office in 1973 and stored in a warehouse where the Mississippi Highway Patrol and other law enforcement agencies had access to them, there was no record of who maintained them and no trace of who removed particular files. "On the night they came to move the files [to the Mississippi Department of Archives in 1977], the files were loaded into two trucks," said Ingebretsen, who learned of the incident from various sources. "One truck went to the archives. No one knows where the other one went."

Dealing with the Mississippi Sovereignty Commission files has been a painful experience for everyone involved, but former Mississippi governor William Winter felt it would offer all Americans an opportunity for some much-needed soul-searching. "In addition to the obvious lesson—that we must never again succumb as a society to the hysterics that overwhelmed us in the 1950s and 1960s—I guess the main lesson is that the way to respond to actions of government, legislative or judicial, is not to do it as we did [then]. The second lesson is that government needs to be as open as it can be, that any sort of clandestine effort [toward] influencing public policy and private attitudes is counterproductive. Government needs to be open."

12

Praise the Lord, but Don't Seat the Blacks

The Mississippi Delta was in a tizzy over rumors that blacks might show up at white churches to worship. Some white churches hired armed guards to keep them out. Other white churches considered allowing them to attend services. One Delta congregation, a Presbyterian church with deep cultural roots, was split right down the middle. Half of the deacons voted no; the other half voted yes. After a contentious meeting to resolve the stalemate, one of the church elders hurriedly left the meeting to deliver the news to his mother, a firm believer in old-time segregation.

"Well, what did you decide?" she demanded.

"We decided to let them attend services."

"You know I'm very much opposed to that!"

"I know, Mother—but think about it this way. What would Jesus do?"

"I know good and well what He'd do," she huffed. "He'd say, let 'em in!" She paused a moment, pondering the implications, then added, "But He'd be *wrong!*"

So it went all across Mississippi.

At 9:15 in the morning, April 28, 1960, Sovereignty Commission investigator Zack Van Landingham received a telephone call from Bill Simmons of the Jackson Citizens' Council, who told him he'd heard that the NAACP had asked members across the state to integrate white churches on a specific date.[1] The tip had originated in the Delta town of Clarksdale, but Simmons told the Jackson police about the plan in the event that blacks decided to attend white churches in the capital city. The implications were clear: force would be used to stop blacks from worshiping in white churches.

Van Landingham telephoned a source in Clarksdale, who confirmed that there was a movement afoot in that city for black residents to show up at white churches to praise the Lord. The investigator was told that the Citizens' Council had arranged for policemen to be stationed in front of all the local churches. Wrote Van Landingham in a memo:

> They would ostensibly be directing traffic. . . . All the ushers in the churches had been informed in order that they might prevent any negroes from entering the church. The ushers had also been requested to watch strange white people who entered the church, especially if they appeared to have anything like a camera in their possession, for it was believed such individuals might be there for the purpose of taking pictures of any such attempts made to integrate by the negroes.

Van Landingham telephoned contacts in surrounding Delta communities, including Cleveland, Greenwood, and Itta Bena, in an effort to get to the bottom of the great worship conspiracy. The Cleveland contact said he'd heard some talk about integrating the white churches but nothing definite. One contact told Van Landingham he was certain that "responsible negroes in Greenwood were told to put a stop to any such meeting" to plan strategies for integrating churches in that city. Van Landingham turned his attention to Jackson. The chief of detectives told him that he had no idea whether the NAACP had issued a directive to integrate Jackson churches, but he assured the investigator that the major white churches always had policemen directing traffic.

Van Landingham spent five days tracking down leads about the great worship conspiracy and then filed a report, noting that the target date had come and gone with no efforts made to integrate the churches. As a postscript he added that Clarksdale civic leaders had installed a permanent program to protect white churchgoers from blacks who might want to attend white churches. The good white people of Mississippi were ready to do whatever it took to protect the House of the Lord.

If the South is the Bible Belt of the nation, Mississippi is its buckle. It has the largest number of churches per capita in the nation, boasting more than 5,433. A recent survey recorded that a scant 7 percent of all Mississippians reported no religious affiliation, the lowest percentage recorded in any state. A 1989 poll showed that the state's capital, Jackson, had the most Bible readers of any place in the country—and if recent trends are any indication, Mississippi is even more religious today, not less.

Today, Southern Baptists dominate the landscape, with well over one-half of the churches and more than 34 percent of the state's population; the United Methodists come in a distant second, with about 9 percent of the population; Catholics account for about 3.7 percent; and Presbyterians and Episcopalians claim less than 1 percent each. Surveys show large increases in membership among the black churches and white conservative churches including the Church of Christ, the Seventh-Day Adventist Church, and Pentecostal churches such as the Church of God Prophecy and Pentecostal Church of God.[2]

Alex A. Alston Jr.:

I have vivid memories of the small Methodist church I attended as a youth in Hollandale. When the church held a revival, the school dismissed us for the daytime services. This was no time to play hooky, because the teacher would take the name of anyone absent, and the pleasure of escaping the service was not worth the punishment. Saving the soul was a big thing. One of the high-lights would be to see someone saved who we knew had been saved several times before. I wondered how many times it took to get really saved.

It was not difficult to get saved. These revivalist preachers were really good. With their long hair flowing and their free-and-easy style, they were persuasive and confident as they stoked the horrible flames of hell and dam-nation that would befall the unsaved as compared with the heavenly bliss and eternal pleasure of the saved. "With every head bowed, every eye closed," the evangelist would embrace us, assuring us that we were all forgiven of our sins and that we could live forever in eternal love and bliss if we would then and there accept the Lord Jesus Christ as our personal savior. The revivalist would cry and wring his hands in despair, and toward the end of the sermon the choir would burst forth leading the congregation in "Just As I Am" over and over again, emphasizing the last stanza: "O Lamb of God, I come, I come." This was powerful indeed, causing many a wretched soul to walk down the aisle with tears streaming down his or her cheeks, to be born again and be saved from a life of sin and damnation.[3]

Sometimes my friend Kathryn Dean and I would get tickled at something the evangelist, in his enthusiasm, would say. We did everything possible to muffle our snickering, but it was all but impossible. The human body is amaz-ing—when something really amusing is experienced, it feels compelled to express that emotion by laughter. If the body is restrained from that psycho-logical response, it nearly goes into convulsions, especially when a friend nearby is experiencing the same thing. Once Kathryn and I got so tickled that in an attempt to control her giggling she wet her pants. Kathryn survived that embarrassing trauma by my walking close behind her, with her holding the Sunday school lesson book over the front of her dress. But none of this stopped our giggling.

The grown-ups put a great deal of pressure on us to attend the revival meetings. One of my friends, whose father had never been to a church meet-ing, finally, after several days of begging, persuaded him to come. The son was very proud to have his father sitting beside him on the first night of the revival. In our church there were certain times when one would stand and other times when one would remain seated. My friend's dad got confused and stood when everyone else was seated. Obviously embarrassed, he let out a loud and explosive expletive and ran out of the church, never to return.

I went to church with my family every Sunday and, quite frankly, remember almost nothing about it except the wonderful invasion of the wasps every spring and summer. No matter how hard the men of the church stopped up every crack and sprayed enough DDT to kill a herd of cattle, several large red wasps found their way into the sanctuary during preaching time. The big red wasps were especially skilled; they could perform amazing aerial acrobatics and would gracefully fly through the air with amazing speed. Sometimes they would suddenly dive straight into the bouffant hairdo of a prominent church lady. After the furious waving of hands and frantic slapping by the church matron's dutiful husband, the wasp always would escape and begin circling the room again in search of its next victim. Surely it cannot be true, but I have a vivid memory of seeing a grin on the wasp's face after making a successful attack.

At times I was required to sing in the choir. I'm using these words loosely because I could not sing or carry a tune under any circumstances. The choir director nevertheless asked me to stand in the choir, admonishing me sternly not to sing but only to move my lips. She even made me come to choir practice when there was nothing for me to practice except moving my lips—I already had plenty of practice at that, so my teachers said.

Despite the attacking wasps, the childhood giggling, and the occasional obscenities, I do remember Brother Rush Glen Miller's sermons on brotherly love, and later, while a student at Millsaps College, I would occasionally attend the unforgettable sermons of Dr. W. B. Selah at Galloway Memorial Methodist Church, the largest Methodist congregation in the state, to be spellbound by his heartwarming portrayals of the love of God to all men and the Christian imperative that we love one another, regardless of race, creed, or color. As a child in Sunday school, I sang:

Jesus loves the little children
All the children of the world,
Red and yellow, black and white,
They are precious in His sight,
Jesus loves the little children of the world.

The Golden Rule was taught as the fundamental concept of religious life, and the parable of the good Samaritan was a favorite in many sermons.

Mississippi Churches Reject Golden Rule

Where was this "brotherly love" in the 1950s and 1960s in Mississippi? With more churches per capita than any other state, one might imagine that some of the shining luster of the Golden Rule might escape the walls of the state's numerous ecclesiastical edifices and permeate the state with brotherly love. But this was not the case. The state had become violently obsessed with race, a virtual police state, and a fearful place for any African American. Unfortunately most (but not all) Mississippi clergymen either supported white supremacy and made peace with the status quo or they left the state.

As the civil rights campaign intensified, the Mississippi churches rejected the position of their national conventions or assemblies and quickly condemned any movement toward integration of the races. White churches across the state passed resolutions warning that social equality had always led to what racists call "miscegenation" and the dreaded state of "amalgamation," and must be resisted at all costs.

The First Baptist Church of Summit passed a resolution proclaiming that "the Word of God endorses the idea of segregation" and that "integration of the races would open an era of bloodshed, immorality, and crime unmatched in the history of our nation."[4] In Jackson, at Galloway Memorial Methodist Church, the board passed a resolution in 1961 leaving admittance to the judgment of the ushers and greeters.[5] Later, in 1963, the board passed yet another resolution declaring that "we prefer to remain an all-white congregation" and "we earnestly hope that the perpetuation of that tradition will never be impaired." Other Methodist churches across the state, including the First Methodist Church of Lexington, passed resolutions condemning the position taken by their council of bishops. The First Methodist Church of Clarksdale resolved that they were irrevocably opposed to integration. The Mendenhall Baptist Church passed a resolution, which no doubt articulated the viewpoint held by most Southern Baptists, that "condemned any teaching . . . that is biased toward social equality" and called on religious leaders "to keep the races pure."[6] At Galloway a paddy wagon was sent over by the police department, and uniformed policemen were on hand with their billy clubs, ever ready to subdue any would-be worshipper of color at a signal from the usher.

Scenes such as this were commonplace. Surely some whites must have had some misgivings about turning away worshippers because of the color of their skin. If so, most of them responded with silence. The white church as a whole agreed with the politicians. The ministers were willing to preach "brotherly love," but when it came down to a conflict between God and white supremacy, the latter prevailed.

Many of the churches, especially the Baptist churches, maintained that they had no business in becoming involved in political and social matters, especially if the matters involved race relations. It is ironic that these arguments did not preclude these churches from being involved in other social issues such as drinking and gambling, which the churches were very much against. Regardless of the intensity of the violence against blacks, the church piously regarded this as a social issue that was of no concern to white churches.

To keep African Americans in their place, the state of Mississippi had a long history of lynching. The grisly details of many of these lynchings are shocking, even to the most callous soul. Bodies were not just hanged but also, as previously mentioned, torn apart, mutilated, burned, decapitated, and disfigured, often with ears, eyes, and fingers taken as souvenirs.

Again, where was the church? Surely one would expect the benevolent hand of the church to be reaching out to condemn this abominable and revolting wrong. Here, again, the most religious state in the union "held back" and failed to lend its prophetic voice against racial violence. During the turmoil of the 1960s, the churches continued to remain silent. Even when blacks were lynched and murdered, the churches remained silent, acting as if they'd bonded together to become the collective Antichrist.

Delta Democrat-Times editor Hodding Carter summarized the situation as follows: "By the end of 1958, it can be safely said, virtually the only Mississippi ministers who still expressed any viewpoint on segregation were those who supported its continuation."[7] Congregations continued to fire ministers who preached integration. In October 1964 Chester A. Molpus of the First Baptist Church of Belzoni resigned to avoid a vote to oust him, after his church banned integrationist preaching and officially barred blacks.[8]

Presbyterian minister Preston Stevenson alienated his congregation by proposing a local ministerial association that would include blacks. He was fired as City Hall chaplain and became aggravated when the church began planning an annex to establish a private school for white students in order to avoid desegregation. Stevenson was written off as a nuisance who did not appreciate the Delta way of life. He finally escaped Mississippi and sought exile in Bristol, Virginia.

In Madison County in 1956, a white Baptist preacher named Thomas E. Johnson worked among the rural blacks, started a Sunday school, and distributed free clothing to the poor. For these actions his children were tormented and ostracized. His eldest child required psychiatric treatment. After his house was hit by a barrage of eggs and stones, he took his neighbor to court. The neighbor was acquitted, and Johnson was charged and convicted of perjury in the case. Although his conviction was finally overturned, he paid a high price for merely attempting to express some brotherly love to the poor.

Rabbi Charles Martinband led a courageous fight for racial justice in Hattiesburg.[9] The Citizens' Council targeted him in 1958, and, when he was away on a trip, the council warned the temple to fire him or face the consequences. The congregation stood firm, but by 1963 he realized he must leave, and he did so a few months later.

Throughout the 1950s and 1960s, the Citizens' Council turned up the pressure on white ministers who preached the social gospel. The council strenuously objected when Ole Miss chaplain Will Campbell invited the Reverend Alvin Kershaw to speak at the university. Kershaw was an Episcopal rector from Ohio who became famous for winning $32,000 on a popular television show, *The $64,000 Question*. When asked what he was going to do with the money, he said he wanted to give some of his winnings to the NAACP, since he believed "the core of religious faith is love of God and neighbor." Under pressure from the Citizens' Council, Campbell was forced to rescind the invitation. Rev. Campbell got in further trouble when he invited Carl Rowan, a young black journalist, to his home when he was gathering material for a book. Campbell was finally hounded out of Mississippi and took a job with the National Council of Churches.

Scores of other ministers were forced to leave the state. On January 3, 1963, twenty-eight young native Mississippi ministers published a statement titled "Born of Conviction," in which they asked for a free and open pulpit and full support of the public schools, which Mississippians were abandoning because of fears that they would be racially integrated. Hostility to the statement was so strong that most of these young ministers left the state.

Malicious false rumors were circulated about some of these ministers. Segregationists swore it was true that Jerry Furr, associate pastor at Galloway Memorial Methodist Church and one of those who left, was given a new automobile by the NAACP. Even after this and many other rumors proved false, these young ministers still were harassed and a large number of them were hounded out of the state. Many others who attempted to express their social conscience followed in their wake. Between 1959 and 1964, seventy-nine ministers transferred out of the Mississippi Methodist Conference. When these were added to the ministers lost from the other Mississippi denominations, the number would run into the hundreds, a tragic and irreparable loss to such a state steeped in economic and spiritual poverty.

The Reverend Keith Tonkel was one of the white Methodist ministers to sign the "Born of Conviction" statement. Although most of the young ministers were forced or elected to leave the state, Tonkel planted his feet squarely in the center of the turmoil and, regardless of the consequences, preached the brotherhood of man. Tonkel joined Wells United Methodist Church as pastor in 1969, a small, aging, and dwindling congregation in the inner city. He immediately welcomed rich, poor, white, and black and set the church on a course of racial reconciliation. Soon he had an integrated congregation of over five hundred. Tonkel is now a much-sought-after speaker across the nation, and he has received numerous honors.[10] Perhaps the most remarkable honor came in 2007, the year of his seventieth birthday, when the once-race-haunted State of Mississippi presented him with a unanimous Senate resolution commending him for his lifetime of humanitarian and civic leadership.

One of the tragic losses to this state and to the ministry of the church was that of Dr. W. B. Selah, longtime minister of Galloway Memorial Methodist Church in Jackson. Dr. Selah could not remain silent and in January 1963 made a strong and eloquent statement to the Associated Press that appeared on the front page of the *Clarion-Ledger*:

> We must seek for all men, black and white, the same justice, the same rights, and the same opportunities that we seek for ourselves. Nothing less than this is Christian Love. To discriminate against a man because of his color . . . is contrary to the will of God. Forced segregation is wrong. . . . There can be no color bar in a Christian church. . . . Race prejudice is a denial of Christian brotherhood.

In June 1963, during his nineteenth year as pastor at Galloway, Dr. Selah's young associate, Jerry Furr, right before the Sunday sermon, told Dr. Selah that five blacks had been turned away from worship by ushers at the door.[11] Dr. Selah abbreviated his sermon that morning and stated that he loved this congregation but could not serve a church where people were turned away from worship. He had to either take back all that he had been preaching for nineteen years or leave. He had the integrity to leave.

Shocking incidents continued at Galloway, one of which occurred on Easter Sunday 1964, when two Methodist bishops, one black, were barred from worship.[12] This continued Sunday after Sunday until January 1966, when the board at Galloway finally voted to admit all persons regardless of race.

It was not safe in the 1960s to show friendship toward a minister associated with "outside agitators" such as the National Council of

Churches. In the summer of 1964 the Albert Heffner family of McComb made that mistake.[13] On a trip to Greenville, the Heffners bought a large can of tamales from Doe's Eat Place, a tamale and steak restaurant that *Esquire* magazine once named one of the top eateries in America. They took the tamales back to McComb and invited a minister to help them eat the delicious morsels. The minister, who was representing the National Council of Churches in their civil rights work, asked if he could bring several of his friends. As it turned out, the friends were a racially mixed group of civil rights activists. Albert Heffner, a prominent insurance agent in McComb, who had recently won a prestigious community service award, readily agreed. He was a gregarious and likable soul, and everybody knew him as Red. He and his wife, Malva, had two daughters, one of whom was the reigning Miss Mississippi. Sharing his valuable tamales was a generous thing to do, but what a horrible mistake it turned out to be! After his guests arrived, cars began circling his house, and his phone began ringing off the hook with anonymous threats. Within days his lease for his insurance office was canceled, and his business vanished. His family was threatened, and life became untenable for him in McComb. Soon he and his family were hounded out of town, fleeing first to Jackson and then to Washington, D.C.

When faced with the overwhelming power of a state determined to maintain racial segregation at all costs, most white ministers and priests in Mississippi looked the other way when they were asked to extend a helping hand to black citizens. Rather than be branded a "nigger lover" or a "Communist," labels that in all probability would cause the loss of their churches and their income, not to mention social ostracism, they chose to deny the most basic tenets of Christian doctrine.

Alex A. Alston Jr.:
Closer to home, on the night of November 19, 1967, my wife and I were returning to our residence from a movie and were shocked to witness a horrible explosion on the corner of Poplar Boulevard and St. Mary Street in the Bel-

haven area of Jackson, in which we lived. I drove quickly over and saw my friend Dr. T. W. Lewis running into the house in an attempt to save the occupants. The owner of the house, Bob Kochtitzky, his wife, and a house guest barely escaped the force of the blast, which blew through the downstairs. The Kochtitzkys' infant son was miraculously saved from serious injury by the headboard of his crib, which shielded him from the debris that sprayed the room.

But why was Bob Kochtitzky, a seminary-trained layman, targeted? He had made the "mistake" of using his house as a meeting place for Layman's Overseas Service, a benevolent organization placing laymen for short-term service in Third World countries. Meetings in his home for this organization were occasionally attended by members of the black community. As recently as late 1967, that could not be tolerated, and he was targeted for destruction. The local newspaper printed a picture of the Kochtitzkys' house but did not editorialize against the bombing and violence. Bob's pastor at Galloway Memorial Methodist Church acknowledged his own reluctance to speak out and quoted Abraham Lincoln, "To sin by silence when they should protest makes cowards of men."

The two major newspapers in the state, the *Clarion-Ledger* and the *Jackson Daily News*, sputtered racism with every headline and literally became the mouthpiece for the Citizens' Council. The television media were little better. In fact the NBC affiliate in Jackson, WLBT, lost its license for repeated acts of racial injustice and discrimination in its programming. Because the decision to grant a new license was expected to take a long time, an interim license was awarded to Communications Improvement, Inc. (CII), a nonprofit biracial organization that operated the station from 1971 to 1980.

The CII board was headed by Kenneth L. Dean, a Baptist minister and former director of the Mississippi Council for Human Relations. One of the first policy changes concerned religious broadcasting. For years WLBT had broadcast the Sunday morning service from First Presbyterian Church, a large and influential church in Jackson. One of the changes that CII made was to pull that Sunday morning plug on First Presbyterian and suggest that this time slot be allocated among various churches in Jackson, including black churches, other Protestant churches, and the synagogue.

The leadership of First Presbyterian was incensed. Letters of protest flooded CII and the FCC. The pastor of First Presbyterian demanded a hearing before the board of directors of CII. As attorney for the CII board, I readily consented. At the meeting, Dr. Donald P. Patterson, pastor of First Presbyterian, stood up with authority and vigor, making his plea to the board to allow the church to continue using WLBT to broadcast its Sunday morning services.

Dr. Patterson eloquently started his presentation by beginning almost every sentence with the phrase "the Lord told me that you should know . . ." He stated with assurance, "the Lord told me that you should know that your action has caused great spiritual harm to numbers of people that have listened to the services every Sunday and received enormous spiritual blessings"; "the Lord told me that you should know that many of your directors are from states other than Mississippi and are not aware of our way of life"; "the Lord has told me"; and so on. The room became absolutely silent. I felt extremely anxious because normally the board would turn to its young, green attorney for a proper response, yet I was unsure how I would respond to the Lord.

Blessedly, the intrepid Baptist minister and president of the board, Ken Dean, stood up with equal authority and spoke with assurance, likewise invoking the Lord with every breath, "Brother Patterson, the Lord has told me that you should know," etc., etc., etc. The meeting adjourned with everyone feeling good about the outcome, but in the end First Presbyterian did not get to keep its time slot. Although I recall no further problems for CII concerning religious broadcasting, I did learn one valuable lesson—only the Lord can respond to the Lord when one claims the Lord is speaking through him.

"The Preacher Is Our Most Deadly Enemy"

The Citizens' Council quickly targeted moderate ministers and anyone who associated with them.[14] One council publication bluntly put it, "The preacher is our most deadly enemy." To combat the moderate views that might be expressed, the council enlisted the support of prominent segregationist ministers such as Dr. G. T. Gillespie Sr., president emeritus of Belhaven College, whose pamphlet entitled *A Christian View of Segregation* was widely distributed by the Citizens' Council.

Millsaps College, the state's most moderate institution, was attacked with vigor. When Ernst Borinski, a refugee from Nazi Germany and a professor of sociology at Tougaloo College, spoke at Millsaps and stated that "racial segregation violates Christian premises," the council went berserk and used this statement in every way possible to inflame public opinion.[15] Millsaps College kept its integrity throughout these turbulent times through a strong and fearless faculty led by a courageous, moderate Mississippi native and Methodist minister, President Homer Ellis Finger Jr., who forever will be remembered as protecting the sanctity of academic freedom. The school voluntarily opened its doors to African Americans in the spring of 1965.

Amazingly, for about twenty years an interracial cooperative venture called Providence Farms operated peacefully in northern Holmes County near the small town of Tchula. When its existence was discovered, the Citizens' Council launched an intensive investigation. It could not allow such a peaceful racial cooperative to exist in the very heart of the state. In 1955 a teenage white girl reported that some black boys from Providence rode by while she was waiting for a bus and whistled at her. In September 1955 a large, angry crowd of about a thousand Holmes County citizens met at Tchula High School to hear taped "confessions" of these young blacks. These citizens, incited by members of the Citizens' Council, concluded that the staff of Providence must leave the state. That direct threat, constant harassment, and the cutting of telephone lines finally convinced the few white staff members to get out while they could.

One courageous minister, the Reverend Marsh Calloway, pastor of the Durant Presbyterian Church, took the floor during the meeting and passionately attempted to make the crowd understand that their actions were both un-American and un-Christian.[16] Perhaps the understatement of the evening was a loud voice over the deafening boos saying, "This ain't no Christian meeting, Brother." Mr. Calloway continued his work as pastor of Durant Presbyterian Church but found only his wife left in the pews to hear his well-prepared sermons. It was just another ministerial casualty in Mississippi's war against race and reason during these tumultuous years.

The Baptist Church continued its staunch policy of not allowing blacks to worship in their white institutions.[17] But the Baptists were little different from the less populous Methodists and Presbyterians. In 1967, seven thousand Methodist laymen signed a petition urging Bishop Edward J. Pendergrass to do all that was possible to oppose integration.

The campaign waged against religious moderates was bitter and vituperative. The headlines in Citizens' Council publications are a good indication of the racial texture of that era's war of words:

DOES CHURCH FAVOR MONGRELIZATION?

ARE SOME CHURCH LEADERS BETRAYING THEIR COUNTRY?

METHODIST PATRIOTS EXPOSE PINKS

WAKE UP! OR BE AWAKENED BY THE
SQUALLS OF A MULATTO GRANDCHILD

The Reverend W. J. Cunningham remembers that when he became pastor of Galloway Memorial Methodist Church in 1963, a sizable arrangement of Citizens' Council literature was on display in the church, and copies were freely distributed.

Black Churches Slow to Respond

The church was and is the most important and effective public institution in the black community. From slavery onward the church was the one place that African Americans could call their very own. No white dictated what they said or sang in the confines of their own church. The black ministers could preach their own distinctive doctrine, and the congregation could set its own agenda. The importance of religion and the religious networks established by these churches is reflected in Mississippi's history and by the careers of many of the leaders who emerged during the civil rights era.

With some notable exceptions, the black churches in Mississippi seemed slow to exert influence in the early days of the civil rights struggle. This is understandable because some black ministers were actually on the payroll of whites. The Delta Council, an organization of leading Delta white planters, paid a black newspaper, edited by the Reverend H. H. Humes, to publish editorials encouraging sharecroppers to accept their second-class status. Humes actually spied at post offices to see if the sharecroppers received union information, and yet he was one of the most prominent black ministers in the state.

Many black ministers in those days were very cautious because often their livelihood depended on their white segregationist employer, and many were actually afraid their church would be burned if it was used in civil rights activities. They had every right to believe that their churches would be burned, because that is exactly what happened. Although the exact number of burned or bombed black churches during the civil rights era never has been fully documented, various tabulations are available. The high priest of white Christian militancy, Sam Holloway Bowers Jr., who was elected in 1964 as imperial wizard of the White Knights of the Ku Klux Klan of Mississippi, is alleged to have orchestrated seventy-five bombings of black churches in his four-year reign of terror.[18]

The testimony before the United States Commission on Civil Rights, held in Jackson, Mississippi, in 1965, informs us that for a period in 1964 in Pike County alone, a black Masonic lodge and two churches were destroyed by fire and three others were seriously damaged; in Adams County at least four black churches were burned in June through August 1964, and one was burned in September 1963; in Neshoba County in April 1964, the Mount Zion Methodist Church was burned; in Madison County three churches were burned in August and September 1964; and in Tippah County in November 1964, Antioch Baptist Church was burned.

Black churches were crucial to the culture of the black community in Mississippi. The blacks owned these churches, and most often it was the only thing a black Mississippian owned. Yet the state, its citizens, its lawyers, and the white religious leaders sat back in almost unanimous silence and let these monuments to God go up in flames. Martin Luther King Jr. tells us that the ultimate tragedy is most often not the work or cruelty of bad people but the silence of the good. The silence of the whites in Mississippi leading up to and during the civil rights crisis was deafening. These acts of terror against the black religious community in Mississippi constitute perhaps the most atrocious attack on an American religious institution in the twentieth century.

After these bombings and burnings, Joe T. Odle, editor of the Mississippi *Baptist Record*, was a strong force in persuading the Southern Baptist Convention's executive committee to receive donations to help rebuild some of the burned black churches. In September 1964 the effort became a cooperative enterprise, with various Mississippi denominations working under the title the Baptist Committee of Concern. The committee rebuilt forty-two of the fifty-four black churches destroyed during 1964 and 1965. It avoided the issue of segregation in its appeal, and the Mississippi Baptist Convention justified its activities as a contribution to evangelism.[19]

Baptist institutions were thrown into a serious dilemma by Title VI of the Civil Rights Act of 1964, which required denominational colleges to sign desegregation compliance pledges or forfeit federal grants and loans for the schools and their students. Although William Carey College, located in Hattiesburg, complied, the three remaining Baptist colleges preferred to forfeit federal loans for buildings and deny any loan to even the most impoverished student in order to keep their institutions white. Although the colleges had previously accepted these loans, college trustees stated that they could not depart from this lifelong commitment of separation of church and state.

In 1966 this issue dominated the Mississippi Baptist Convention, which finally rejected a resolution that would allow acceptance of federal funds. It took until 1969 for all of the Mississippi Baptist colleges and hospitals to ultimately sign the compliance pledge and adopt an open admission policy so a needy student or patient could have access to these funds. Perhaps because the argument was not made in the name of equal rights and justice, and only after some of the colleges tried and failed to replace federal funds with private contributions, the colleges finally relented to the glaring truth that their students desperately needed these funds.

The Klan Targets Beth Israel Congregation

For most of the state's history, Mississippi Jews have kept a low profile. They have excelled in law, medicine, and business, and they have contributed their money and their time for the betterment of their communities; but for the most part they have avoided running for public office and refrained from taking public stands on controversial issues. All that changed in 1954 when Canadian-born rabbi Perry Nussbaum came to Mississippi to serve at the Beth Israel Congregation in Jackson. At the age of forty-six, after living in Australia, Texas, Kansas, New Jersey, Massachusetts, and New York, Nussbaum was hopeful of finding a permanent mission in Jackson, a place to finally call home in his quest for *tikkun olam*, greater justice.

What he found was a congregation that was unlike any others he had ever known. Members quickly let him know that they didn't want a lot of ritual added to their worship ceremonies, nor did they want him to do anything to draw attention to the Jewish community. The best way for a Jew to be successful in Mississippi, they explained to Nussbaum, was to do nothing to draw attention to the congregation. Many Mississippi Protestants felt a deep kinship to Jews because of Judaism's historic links to Christianity, and Jewish leaders wanted to do nothing to diminish that fragile bond.

A low profile was not at all what Nussbaum envisioned for his congregation. It was unacceptable to him for Jackson Jews to accept segregation and do nothing to assist African Americans who were fighting for their rights. Against the wishes of his congregation, he began interfaith services and worked with black religious leaders. When the Freedom Riders started showing up in Jackson, he ministered to them in jail, wrote comforting letters to their parents, and welcomed them into his home when they were released. Individual members of the congregation pleaded with him to stop. He refused.

On September 18, 1967, a bomb destroyed most of Beth Israel's newly built synagogue. Two months later Rabbi Nussbaum's home was bombed, sending the rabbi and his wife, Areme, running out onto the lawn with glass fragments in their hair. Immediately after the home was bombed, FBI agents rushed to the scene.[20] Among them was Agent Jim Ingram, who was in charge of the FBI's Violent Crimes Division in Jackson. While he was at the home interviewing Nussbaum, a delegation of white clergy showed up and offered their encouragement. Recalls Ingram:

> He yelled at them. If he could have used profanity, he'd have done it. He made it clear to them that they were responsible for what was happening because they had not assisted in any way. They were still staunch segregationists themselves. They were fearful of leading any type of demonstration to show that the churches had turned around and were not going to put up with this violence. . . . They did not stay very long. They left right after that. Later, there was a small demonstration, a march going to the synagogue, and a few of the white clergy came forward.

No one was ever prosecuted for the bombings, but the FBI knew who was responsible—the order had gone out from Klan leader Sam Bowers. There was just never enough evidence for a prosecution. Since Nussbaum had received other threats, the FBI told him that he might want to leave the state for a while. At that point his life was not worth much in Mississippi. Rabbi Nussbaum and his wife did leave town, but they came back after a brief absence and lived in Jackson for another six years, before retiring and moving to California.

"People in the community wanted to help," said Ingram. "But they were confused. They could not go to the mayor. They could not go to the sheriff. They could not go to other businesspeople and say, 'Enough's enough—Mississippi is being embarrassed.' No one said, 'Why don't we stand up and ask for justice?' It just didn't happen. When the FBI talked to these people individually, they wanted to turn things around."

13

All the News
That's Fit to Print—
for White Mississippians

In the late 1800s several white men, one of whom was married to a black woman, an extreme rarity in Mississippi at that time, turned in the names of a number of prominent white citizens thought to be members of the Ku Klux Klan.[1] All were promptly arrested by U.S. marshals and taken before a federal court judge, who questioned them about Klan activity in and around Jackson. Unlike today, when the Klan is afforded civil liberties, Klan membership at that time was outlawed because the KKK was rightly considered by Mississippians to be a terrorist organization.

One of the prisoners, a Confederate veteran named T. M. Scanlan, became an immediate folk hero among whites when he refused to answer questions about the Klan. He didn't stand on the Fifth Amendment; he stood in defiance.

"He stood firm, refusing to give the court the names of the members of the Klan or divulge any of its secret work," reported R. H. Henry, editor of the *Newton (Mississippi) Ledger*. "He was ordered to jail, where he remained three months, when he was released by order of the court, but never gave away any of the secrets of the Klan." About the Klan, Henry wrote: "The negroes and their carpet-bag friends were mortally afraid of the Ku Klux Klan, which has been organized to bring peace and order out of chaos in the South, and to make negroes and their associates behave themselves."

White Mississippians were so outraged by Scanlan's treatment that they urged Henry to relocate to Jackson and merge his newspaper with an existing Jackson newspaper, the *Clarion*, to create a single newspaper powerful enough to protect the interests of white citizens. Thus out of that cauldron of racial hate and fear was born the *Clarion-Ledger*, which has remained Mississippi's highest-circulation newspaper for more than one hundred years.[2]

In the beginning it was racial prejudice and irrational white fear, not free speech, that motivated Mississippi newspapers. Newsprint was viewed as a means of controlling the social and political aspirations of black citizens, a vehicle for maintaining apartheid; however, racism was only one of the media's characteristics. Of equal importance was the media's continuing opposition to the liberal principles that defined the Revolution.

Henry remained at the helm of the *Clarion-Ledger* until 1920, when two brothers, Tom and Robert Hederman, bought the newspaper and continued its white supremacist legacy of espousing a protectionist attitude toward the state's white residents, regardless of economic or social standing. White was right. Black was not. That's the way it was.

In 1954 the Hederman brothers purchased the *Clarion-Ledger*'s chief rival, the *Jackson Daily News*, which was published and owned by Major Frederick Sullens, one of the newsmen who'd been displaced by Henry's acquisition of the *Clarion*. The two newspapers operated independently, except on Sundays, when they published a combined edition that featured editorials from both newspapers. When Sullens died in 1957, he anointed his managing editor, Jimmy Ward, as his successor.[3] A World War II bomber pilot who flew fifty combat missions, Ward had a background in journalism that was more as a photographer than a reporter. On the day of the announcement of Ward's promotion, it was also disclosed that he would be taking over Sullens's page-one column, which Ward renamed "Covering the Crossroads." As editor, Ward made all the news decisions, wrote the editorials, and served as the spokesman for the newspaper. However, he used the column as comic relief from the serious news stories that appeared in the newspaper each day. In the beginning, "Crossroads" was a collection of humorous observations, jokes, and ironies of ordinary life, written in the folksy style of Will Rogers. It was so distinct in its approach that it attracted the attention of radio commentator Paul Harvey, who frequently quoted the columns on his nationally syndicated radio program, identifying their author as "Jackson Jimmy." But as the years went by, the humor in the columns became darker, less playful, as Ward became a national spokesman for segregation and reflected the do-or-die racial madness of the white majority in the South.

Greenville: A Liberal Oasis

As the Hederman family consolidated power in Jackson, painting the city with brush strokes that gave the newspapers a reputation as the most right-wing in the nation, Delta planters, who had a more liberal perspective, fought back by recruiting a newspaperman from Hammond, Louisiana, named Hodding Carter.

With the financial support of leading citizens, Carter moved to Greenville in 1936 with his wife, Betty, and founded the *Delta Star*. There was already a newspaper in Greenville, the *Democrat-Times*, but Carter hired a strong staff—one reporter was Shelby Foote, who later achieved fame as an award-winning Civil War historian—and made an effort to distinguish the *Delta Star* from the competition by writing editorials that resonated with the Delta's moderate white leadership and its African American majority.

Before the first year was up, he wrote a page-one editorial that shocked white readers and delighted black readers. When a black man was lynched after being charged with the murder of a white storekeeper in tiny Duck Hill, Carter wrote, "In Washington, Congress debates a federal anti-lynching bill extreme in its encroachment on state's rights. To the vindicators of that encroachment Mississippi has now contributed a mighty bludgeon. . . . Is there justice in Mississippi? Then, punish the Duck Hill mobsters."

Before white readers could catch their breath, he followed up by publishing a photograph of African American Olympic medal winner Jesse Owens, who had come to the all-black Delta town of Mound Bayou to help celebrate its fiftieth anniversary. As a result of the criticism that flooded into the newspaper, Carter thought for a while that he might be lynched. Few newspapers in the nation published photographs of African Americans, much less newspapers in the South. Carter responded by writing an editorial that defended his decision. "Jesse Owens is a remarkable athlete," he wrote. "And so we printed his picture. We'll print it again when we feel like doing so."

Within two years of starting up the *Delta Star*, Carter bought out the *Democrat-Times*, renaming his newspaper the *Delta Democrat-Times*. If critics thought that he would pull back from controversial positions once he owned the only newspaper in town, they were wrong, for he was passionate about his fellow Southerners living up to the promise of the U.S. Constitution. As a result of his editorials—and his willingness to name names and publish photographs, if necessary—it became extremely tough in Greenville for officials to publicly espouse racist views.

In 1945 Carter's views took a surprising twist when he began writing about the discrimination faced by Japanese American soldiers in the U.S. Army and the Japanese American internment camps located across the river in Arkansas. This time he reached beyond the city limits of Greenville and showed national leadership by criticizing polices that allowed Japanese-born Americans to be rounded up and placed in internment camps. Carter was awarded a Pulitzer Prize in 1946 and cited for editorials "on the subject of racial, religious, and economic tolerance," with special note of an editorial with the headline Go for Broke, written about Japanese American soldiers during World War II. Later Carter often said that winning the award was one of the happiest moments in his life, not so much for the prestige as for the validation of his editorial stands on controversial issues.

James L. Dickerson:

My family was always devoted to the *Delta Democrat-Times*, even before I was born. My maternal uncle, Rex Turner, started delivering the *Delta Democrat-Times* in 1941, at the age of fourteen. An electronic genius—he later would become one of the first ham radio operators to bounce a signal off the moon—he built a radio from scratch and attached it to his bicycle so that he could listen to music while he delivered newspapers. An enterprising reporter for the newspaper spotted him one day and interviewed him for a feature article, providing my uncle with his first brush with celebrity.

My grandfather religiously subscribed to the *Delta Democrat-Times*, which arrived late in the afternoon, and the *Commercial Appeal*, which arrived early in the morning. By the time I was old enough to read, both newspapers had won Pulitzer Prizes for their support of basic human rights. As a youth I did not always understand the issues that Hodding Carter wrote about on the editorial page, but I understood enough to know that his thinking ran counter to the opinions of many people in my community (by then I lived in Hollandale)—and for some inexplicable reason I was drawn to Carter, impressed by both the clarity of his thinking and the fearlessness of his actions, even when it meant him hiding in the bushes outside his home with a loaded shotgun to intercept marauding night riders.

Hodding Carter was one of my first heroes, along with my grandfather, the latter of whom taught me to shoot so straight that I was banned from the shooting booths of the carnivals that rolled into town each fall. The only time I was ever disappointed in Carter's *Delta Democrat-Times* was when the newspaper got word that I owned the only set of groundhogs in the entire state of Mississippi. A photographer called and asked if he could come over the next day and photograph my groundhogs. Within minutes after putting the telephone receiver down, I was off to get a new shirt for my photo session—and, at the insistence of my mother, a haircut, topped off with the barber's infamous Rose Hair Tonic, which was about 70 percent alcohol. I told all my friends that my picture was going to be in the newspaper, and I hardly slept at all that night.

The next day, when the photographer arrived, he was accompanied by the Hollandale High School homecoming queen, a beautiful blonde with a ready smile. As my spirits deflated faster than a marble rolling off a kitchen table, he explained that he thought a beauty queen would make a better picture than I would. I accepted his decision with good grace—he promised to spell my name right—but there are no words to express the embarrassment I felt, not just because I had told my friends what turned out to be a lie, but also because while working in my grandfather's store, I'd recently sold the homecoming queen a Wonderbra—the designation 36-C still etched indelibly into my memory—and I could not look at her posing with my groundhogs without wondering if she was wearing it, thoughts that made my face blazing red.

There came a time when Hodding Carter handed off the editorship of the newspaper to his eldest son, Hodding Carter III, a summa cum laude graduate of Princeton who served two years in the Marine Corps before joining the staff of his father's newspaper. He was first a reporter, then managing editor, and, finally, in 1960, editor, when his father retired after penning some twenty books and leading the newspaper—and his community—through some of the roughest years of social unrest imaginable. Long before Hodding III became editor, however, he wrote award-winning editorials for the newspaper, editorials that I read in high school and then later as a student at the University of Mississippi.

My first byline in the *Delta Democrat-Times* was a freelance book review written for book editor Ben Wasson, an elderly gentleman who was William Faulkner's first editor and literary agent. For one of my subsequent reviews, I provided the newspaper with a real "scoop" by solving the mystery of where Faulkner found the name *Snopes* for some of his most downtrodden characters (it is an anagram for peons).[4]

I began working full-time for the *Delta Democrat-Times* in 1977, around the time Hodding III left the newspaper to accept a position as a State Department spokesman in the Jimmy Carter administration. Taking over from Hodding III was his younger brother, Philip, who lived in New Orleans, where he published a weekly newspaper. He commuted to Greenville on a weekly basis, and I often got the feeling that he would have rather been in New Orleans. One weekend Philip flew back to New Orleans to take care of business there and did not return the following Monday. To my surprise I was asked if I would like to write editorials until he returned.

My first editorial was about lawyers.[5] I figured I couldn't go wrong there. My second editorial called for the complete overhaul of the food stamp program. I was troubled that an individual in need of food stamps would have to pay for a portion of the stamps. For example, to receive one hundred dollars in stamps, people might be required to pay seventy-five dollars. I thought that was absurd. I suggested they simply be given the twenty-five dollars in stamps for which they were eligible.

I don't recall how many editorials I wrote, but one day Betty Carter, the most elegantly gracious lady you would ever want to meet, and one of my favorite people, took me aside and told me that she thought I was a little too liberal to be writing editorials for the *Delta Democrat-Times*. I wasn't offended. I figured it was too good to be true, anyway. I resumed writing feature articles, one of which was a series about death and dying. As I was working on the series, she took me aside, once again, and told me she had a story to tell me, but I would have to promise not to use her name. That was an easy promise to make. After all, she was the boss. She proceeded to tell me about an out-of-body experience she'd had in 1938.[6]

She was pregnant with twins but miscarried. She lost more blood than she should have and went into shock, prompting a call for blood in the community. Despite the best efforts of the doctors, she started slipping away.

"At some point, I found myself floating up near the ceiling," she said. "I looked down and there I was in the bed. There were three doctors and several nurses standing around the bed. 'It's 107,' I heard one of the nurses say, and I thought, well, I'm dying—but then I thought to myself, I can't die, because there are things I need to see about. The next thing I knew I was back on the bed inside my body."

With her story attributed to an unnamed source, the account of her experience ran on the front page, without anyone ever knowing the truth, until now.

A Failure to Communicate

Throughout the 1950s, 1960s, and 1970s, the Hederman media block, consisting of the *Clarion-Ledger* and the *Jackson Daily News*, along with several weekly newspapers, stood solidly behind the Sovereignty Commission. Jackson television stations WJTV, which was partially owned by the Hedermans, and WLBT parroted the state's newspapers, which meant that they totally ignored black viewpoints. Unlike the newspapers, they could not cloak their racism in journalistic tradition. For example, it was—and still is—newspaper style to refer to people on second reference by their last name. That style created problems for television stations, which relied heavily on on-air interviews and news readers. Television reporters were forbidden to refer to African Americans with courtesy titles such as Mr., Mrs., or Miss; they had to refer to them by their first name or not at all. Added burdens were policies of the television stations not to broadcast any programming that included people of color.

Early one morning in 1960, Thurgood Marshall, then a civil rights attorney, was being interviewed on the nationally televised *Today Show*, which was broadcast on WLBT, when suddenly, in the middle of the black attorney's comments, television viewers saw their screens go blank. A logo that read CABLE DIFFICULTY appeared on the screen. Moments later, when the Marshall interview was concluded, the *Today Show* returned to the air.

Suspicious of the blackout, Hodding Carter III, who by then was in charge of the *Delta Democrat-Times*'s editorial operations, called the NBC network and asked if there had been any transmission difficulties. They replied that there had been none. Some time later, Fred Beard, the station manager, attended a Citizens' Council meeting at which he complained about how the networks had become mouthpieces for black propaganda. Then, to wild applause, Beard boastfully confessed that he himself had pulled the plug on the Thurgood Marshall interview. Carter later played an important role in the television station making the transition from all-white ownership and personnel to a racially integrated management group. That could happen with television stations because they are regulated by the FCC. Not so for newspapers, since they possess stronger constitutional protections against government control.

Throughout the civil rights era, Mississippi newspapers consistently failed to live up to their responsibilities as constitutionally protected institutions by secretly working with the Sovereignty Commission, the Citizens' Councils, and racist white elected officials to deny black residents the full range of their constitutional rights.

Of course, Mississippi's corruption of the media was not confined to the Magnolia State. Commission director Erle Johnston once called a friendly editor at a newspaper in Pipestone, Minnesota, and asked him to run an editorial he had written about Mississippi. The editorial, which was decidedly anti–John F. Kennedy, bore the headline MISSISSIPPI IS BEING WATCHED. It began:

> The eyes of the nation will be watching Mississippi on November 8 because results of the election may indicate a new viewpoint on segregation. . . . A Kennedy victory in Mississippi would indicate that segregation in that state is no longer a concern because Kennedy says he will integrate life in Mississippi at all levels.

The editor balked, explaining that his newspaper didn't run editorials. Johnston asked if he would run off about a dozen fake newspapers with the editorial for use in Mississippi. The editor agreed, and Johnston distributed the fake newspapers, advertising the editorial as one written by a "Minnesota" editor.

Johnston considered the news media a crucial ingredient in the state's fight against civil rights and antiwar activists. He attended state and national press association meetings whenever possible, working the attending journalists as if he were a candidate at a political event, and he made an effort to maintain his friendships with other journalists. Those friendships paid off on a regular basis.

When a television station in Seattle contacted the Associated Press office in Jackson to verify information submitted to the station by the Sovereignty Commission, Jim Saggus, the AP bureau chief, met with Johnston and examined commission files on the subject in question and verified the information. In a memo to the governor, Johnston bragged that Saggus had been able to verify "every bit of the information we had furnished."

Johnston, who continued to publish his newspaper, the *Scott County Times*, while he served on the commission, was proud of the way he manipulated the media. He once submitted a package deal for radio station WBBM in Chicago, a CBS affiliate. The station had contacted him about airing a program that presented Mississippi's point of view on the racial issue. Johnston thought it would be a good idea if the governor himself went to Chicago to be interviewed. He also invited reporters Kenneth Toler of the *Commercial Appeal* and William Chaze of the *Clarion-Ledger*. The group flew to Chicago aboard the governor's DC-3 to participate in a two-hour television program. Later Johnston reported that they received twenty-one calls on the air and had a backlog of 733 calls that could not be taken. "We believe the program was very successful in . . . explaining some of the fallacies about the state that have been reported in news media."

Johnston once asked a *Jackson Daily News* reporter to write a story about how Charles Evers, the brother of murdered civil rights leader Medgar Evers, had deserted his child and forced the child's mother to apply for welfare. When the reporter turned the story in, however, Jimmy Ward balked at running it without proof the child was really Evers's. In a memo Johnston said he had been told by Ward that attorneys for the newspaper had advised against publishing the story without documentation. Wrote Johnston: "We are working now to obtain the necessary proof and will resubmit it to Mr. Ward." The commission subsequently obtained a birth certificate on the child and other documents and turned them over to the reporter. Years later, when Evers was shown a copy of Johnston's memo, he said they didn't know what they were talking about. "I've got seven daughters from five different mothers and I've always admitted that—and I've always taken care of them. I don't think a man should be ashamed of his children. They [the commission] should be the ones who are ashamed."[7]

In 1967, during the gubernatorial race, which pitted William Winter against John Bell Williams in the runoff race for the Democratic place on the ballot (Williams won and later defeated the Republican candidate), Governor Paul B. Johnson ordered the Sovereignty Commission to cease providing the media with copies of his reports until after the election. That decision angered Tom Hederman, editor of the *Clarion-Ledger*, who asked his city editor, Charles Smith, to find out why the newspaper no longer received the secret reports. When Smith called the commission office, Johnston explained that the governor had asked that only he receive the reports, at least until after the election. In a memo, Johnston explained that it was the Sovereignty Commission's intention not to get involved in politics. He told Smith that if Tom Hederman wanted back on the mailing list, he would have to ask the governor.

The records don't indicate if Hederman made that request, but they do indicate that Johnston had a much cozier relationship with the *Clarion-Ledger* than previously had been revealed. In a routine letter addressed to the Houston Council on Human Relations, Johnston disclosed that one of the clippings he had enclosed from the *Clarion-Ledger* was, in fact, written by him.

The *Jackson Daily News* and the *Clarion-Ledger* knowingly printed stories authored by members of the commission on a regular basis, but sometimes the commission's cloak-and-dagger operations flimflammed the newspapers into printing stories that they did not know originated with the commission. One such instance occurred in 1966, when the *Jackson Daily News* reprinted an editorial it had picked up from the *Lemmon Tribune* in South Dakota. The editorial actually was written by commission director Johnston, who smugly noted in a memo that the same editorial had been printed by a total of twenty-seven newspapers around the country. He scored that success by sending the editorial to a friend at the US Press Association, a Washington-based editorial service that distributed editorials to over three thousand newspapers. When the editorials were published, editors were not told who actually wrote them, nor were they told that Johnston had paid the service a small sum to deceive its clients.[8]

Sometimes the Sovereignty Commission's influence was based on more than the good-old-boy network. Percy Greene, the black commission informant mentioned earlier, was editor of the *Jackson Advocate*, and he was regularly paid to run stories provided to him by the commission. Greene was a good catch for Johnston, and he often bragged about it in his memos. In one editorial published by the *Jackson Advocate*, Johnston wrote, "The greatest need for the Negro in Jackson, in Mississippi and in the rest of the South is more and more 'Uncle Toms.'" Johnston must have had a good laugh over that one. No doubt he provided copies to newspapers around the country, using it to point out how blacks in Mississippi really felt about integration.

Editors at the *Clarion-Ledger* and *Jackson Daily News* were not simply passive receptacles for propaganda stories supplied by the commission; they sometimes went to the commission in search of story ideas. Once Jimmy Ward asked Johnston if he had information on any "professional agitators" who had worked in other states before coming to Mississippi. Ward had a story idea in mind. Johnston was happy to oblige, providing Ward with a confidential dossier on a white female activist from Berkeley, California, who had been arrested for civil rights activity in Alabama before participating in the James Meredith march earlier in the year. Johnston also gave Ward a photograph but asked that the commission not be identified as the source of the information. After the story was published, Johnston referred to the incident in a memo, bragging that the story had resulted in the woman leaving the state.

James L. Dickerson:

My first contact with *Jackson Daily News* editor Jimmy Ward came in 1960, when, at the age of fifteen, I wrote to him about a school project involving his predecessor, Major Frederick Sullens. My family didn't subscribe to the *Jackson Daily News*, but my best friend delivered the newspaper in the afternoons on his motor scooter and I often rode shotgun, using the downtime to read the newspaper. As a teenager I was a prolific reader, poring over the *Jackson Daily News*, the *Commercial Appeal*, the *Delta Democrat-Times*, and the weekly *Deer*

Creek Pilot, in addition to subscribing to magazines such as *Look*, *Life*, *Sports Afield*, *Field & Stream*, and the U.S. State Department–authorized *Soviet Life*, all which I paid for with the money I earned at my grandfather's store. The same year that I wrote to Ward, I wrote a letter to the state agency charged with environmental controls, the Game and Fish Commission, and asked why the state allowed the city of Hollandale to dump untreated sewage into Deer Creek, the waterway that wound through town. W. H. Turcotte, chief of the game division, responded with a letter explaining that the state's pollution laws exempted municipalities from control in the disposal of domestic sewage. He ended his letter on an optimistic note: "Eventually all cities should be required to properly treat their wastes." I was quite the junior activist as a fifteen-year-old.

Three years later, during my first semester at the University of Mississippi, I wrote a term paper that shocked my political science professor by revealing that not only did my hometown's water supply fail health department standards that year, but it had never passed minimum quality standards, not in the history of testing. Residents were never told that, which was why, year after year, they suffered stomach ailments. When I showed the report to Mayor J. W. Fore, a kindly man who later possibly saved my life by tipping me off about Klan activity against me, he released the longest sigh I'd ever heard and told me that Hollandale was far too poor to have clean drinking water.

Fast-forward to spring 1979, when after working for several Southern newspapers, I wrote to Jimmy Ward again, this time to ask about job opportunities at the *Jackson Daily News*. He said there were none, but he invited me to stop by the newsroom to talk to him the next time I was in Mississippi (I was living in Florida at the time). By then he'd been diagnosed with throat cancer and had a gaunt appearance and a hoarse voice that rattled whenever he spoke. I was shocked when I met him, not only because of the health issues but also because he looked nothing like I'd expected. He was friendly, smiled broadly, and, despite serious illness, had a twinkle in his eye. To his surprise, I showed him the letter he'd sent me nineteen years ago in response to my letter. He sat bolt upright in his chair and smiled and said he'd be in touch. During the time it took me to drive back to Florida, he had called his relatives in Hollandale to ask about me—and he was told the truth, that I was pro–civil rights and very much against the Vietnam War, and I grew up asking a lot of questions. I no sooner arrived in Florida than I received a telephone call from Mississippi's highest-profile segregationist offering me a job.

My first position at the *Jackson Daily News* was as education reporter, but that lasted only a couple of months. To my surprise I was asked to write editorials. At that time Ward wrote the lead editorials, with an even older gentleman providing the secondary editorials. My first editorial was published under the headline SOUTH TOWARD HOME FOR WILLIE MORRIS. The editorial was written in response to a story that Morris, considered by many to be second only to Hodding Carter III as the state's leading "integrationist," would be guest lecturer at the University of Mississippi. I had met Morris a couple of years prior to that and considered him a friend. "While New York is, without a doubt, the place to be to talk about the latest literary harvest, Mississippi continues to be the place where those literary seeds first take root. So, come on home, Willie." When I wrote the editorial, I was pretty sure that Ward would nix it, but he didn't. Instead he brought the editorial and dropped it on my desk, giving me a literal thumbs-up before uttering a phrase I would hear each time he returned an editorial to my desk, "How's it going, Hoss?"

Within weeks I made editorial page editor, with full control of the editorials, the op-ed page, the columnists, and the cartoons. By that time Ward no longer had control of the news pages. The publishers had assigned that responsibility to the managing editor, Bob Gordon. My philosophy for the editorial page was simply to move it from the far right to the center, where I felt it could exert the most leadership. That doesn't mean I compromised on the issues. I highlighted issues on which a centrist position would get the most traction. There was no editorial board. I never discussed the editorials with anyone before I wrote them. Each day I gave them to Ward for his approval and he never failed to return them to my desk, always handing them off with a thumbs-up. Never once did he veto an editorial I wrote. Never once did he change a single word. One day, however, he sent me a memo that suggested an editorial on a specific subject. It read:

> The TV set glowed with the noise and the face of Fonda—so did the wires hum the same tune in connection with the recent Fonda/Hayden anti-oil event. I think the *Daily News* carried one graph (the

last one in the story), quoting an oil industry spokesman who was supposed to present the view opposite that at the rally. See if you can do an editorial pointing out activists often get more media attention because they are noisy.

The editorial was titled GETTING OURSELVES WORKED INTO A FRENZY. It began with a Marshall McLuhan reference and made the point that the medium is the message: "Television, with its enormous power to shape public opinion, has made electronic-picture slaves of us all."

As the months and years went by, I wrote editorials attacking the Reverend Donald Wildmon's "moral" crusade against television, calling him a "crusading ayatollah" (Wildmon was best known for his efforts to censor television); editorials supporting legal efforts to punish sexual harassment; editorials in favor of black ownership of land; editorials advocating equal rights for female athletes in Jackson; editorials calling for education reform; and editorials attacking corruption on the college board. I also wrote editorials calling for the consolidation of the smaller, academically weaker black colleges as a means of promoting integration, and I was criticized by some black leaders for doing that, but other than that, criticism of the editorial pages by African Americans was rare. One of the innovations I added to the op-ed page was a "man in the street" feature, which required a reporter and a photographer to stop people on the street to ask their opinion about the issues of the day. The result was a collection of photographs of white and black respondents; it was the first time that photographs of blacks had ever been presented in a positive light in the editorial pages. As a result I got more hate mail and death threats for that than for anything else I had ever done at the newspaper.

Another "first" for the editorial pages was my addition of a weekly political column written by the reporter who covered the legislature, David Hampton (he is now editorial director of the *Clarion-Ledger*). For all these years Hampton has thought that his benefactor was Bob Gordon, primarily because Gordon had told him that was the case. That wasn't the way it happened at all. I personally asked Ward to allow the column, and he approved with the understanding that it would be my responsibility if Hampton ever stepped too far over the line to the left or right. He never did.

One of the oddest things that happened at the *Jackson Daily News* while I was there was the discovery in 1980 that the assistant news editor, the person who edited national news stories, was the leader of a neo-Nazi faction organizing in Jackson.[9] The story came to light after a reporter infiltrated the National Socialist White People's Party, more commonly called the Nazi Party, and recognized its leader as being his colleague James "Beer Can" Quinn, a mild-mannered man with fuzzy hair and a beer gut. Quinn agreed to talk to him with the understanding that his identity not be disclosed. In the article Quinn was quoted as saying that he feared that the white man would soon become an endangered species. He added, "When I see a person with blonde hair and blue eyes, who I know to be Aryan, a true Nordic, I want to go up and just touch their hair. I feel insufficient because I am not as ideal in blood as I would want to be."

When Bob Gordon learned the identity of the Nazi Party's leader, he overrode the reporter's promise and fired Quinn on the spot, causing the reporter to resign in protest. Quinn's response to the firing was to say, "I love my people. I love my race. If they find that to be a crime, then that's their belief. And I have mine." He appealed to the ACLU for help but he was turned down on the grounds that there is no statute concerning protection of political beliefs in the private sector. One of his friends and coworkers, who asked not to be identified, said that Quinn was a card-carrying Nazi, literally. He actually had a card in his wallet that identified him as a Nazi. Said the friend:——

Two or three days [after his firing], I looked out the window of my apartment and saw him walking up the steps, carrying a six-pack of beer, just like old times. We shook hands and were glad to see each other. We sat in my living room, drank beer and just bullshitted like always. Then he got very serious. "I want you to know that I'll never forget how you came up to me in the break room that day and in front of everybody sat down and talked to me like always. Everybody ran out on me but you and I won't ever forget that." Then he said something that stunned me. "I want you to know that when we come to power, I'm going to see to it that you have a high position in the government."

Before I left the *Daily News* to accept a position as an editorial writer at the *Commercial Appeal*, my editorials won first place in the annual Associated Press competition. I was told that it was the first time in the newspaper's history that it'd won an award for editorials. Ward was quite pleased.

I never understood why Jimmy Ward took such a liking to me. I was for civil rights, and he led the opposition against civil rights. I was an early opponent of the Vietnam War, and he flew combat missions in Vietnam as a member of the Mississippi Air National Guard. The day I left the newspaper, he posted in the newsroom a copy of the letter of reference he'd sent to the *Commercial Appeal*. In part, it read: "I have been associated with the *Jackson Daily News* since 1938 and editor for over 24 years. Please consider this the highest recommendation I have ever prepared for a departing employee and co-worker." He attributed our relationship to "mutual respect and confidence."

Several years ago I received a letter from Lloyd Gray, editor of the *Northeast Mississippi Daily Journal*, who commented, "We never could figure out how you got away with what you did." The short answer is that at his core, Jimmy Ward was a decent human being who made mistakes about his positions on racial issues and lived long enough to regret them. The longer answer is that he was under siege by Robert Hederman's brilliant son, Rea, who joined the *Clarion-Ledger* as executive editor and worked tirelessly to improve that newspaper. Ward's solution to that threat was to hire the most liberal Mississippian he could find and turn him loose to shift the newspaper's editorial position. I just happened to be in the right place at the right time. Frustrated by the *Clarion-Ledger*'s limited editorial options, Rea Hederman left Mississippi to purchase the respected *New York Review of Books*, which he has led with distinction. Two years before Ward's death, the *Jackson Daily News* and the *Clarion-Ledger* were sold to the Gannett Company, which shut down the *Jackson Daily News* in 1989, forever stilling its scrappy voice.

Voices of Reason

All in all, the 1950s, 1960s, and 1970s were a disgraceful period for the U.S. media. Newspapers around the country routinely printed stories about the civil rights movement or the antiwar movement without verifying their accuracy or even their authorship. Television was just a bad, accepting news stories from government sources without ever questioning them or broadcasting opposing viewpoints. It wasn't just a Mississippi problem; it was a national disgrace.

In some respects Mississippi was ahead of the curve. Most are aware of the tremendous contributions made by Hodding Carter and Hodding Carter III during the civil rights era, but fewer know of those of Hazel Brannon Smith, editor of the *Lexington Advertiser* and the Durant *News*, and Ira Harkey, editor of the *Pascagoula Chronicle*. Both editors were awarded Pulitzer Prizes for editorials that supported civil rights and criticized the political leadership for suppressing those rights. Harkey was always fond of pointing out that he won his Pulitzer on the same day that William Faulkner won his Pulitzer for his final novel, *The Reivers*.

These days it is sometimes difficult to even imagine the strength of character and moral courage that it took for a handful of newspaper editors in Mississippi to stand up for a wide range of racially charged constitutional issues such as school desegregation, voting rights, and the right for all residents, regardless of color, to enter public buildings or dine in restaurants open to the public.

Looking back on those days now is a little like watching *Lonesome Dove* and wondering if life was ever remotely like that. Yet the bad old days of the civil rights era really existed. For his opinions in favor of James Meredith entering the University of Mississippi—and his positions against Governor Ross Barnett, whose authority "to withhold citizenship from half our people" he questioned—Harkey received death threats and social alienation, and he endured boycotts against his newspaper that resulted in loss of readership and revenues.[10] Still, Harkey stood firm for what he knew in his heart was the right thing to do. In an editorial he wrote, "For eight years, since the 1954 Supreme Court ruling that cast out the separate-but-equal doctrine, our state has heard nothing but violent talk from its leaders. Only one or two politicians, almost no religious leaders and less than a half-handful of newspapers tried to warn of the calamity that was being prepared."

Unlike Harkey and the Hodding Carters, Hazel Brannon Smith never once advocated racial integration—instead, she wrote, "We know that it is to the best interest of both races that segregation be maintained in theory and fact"—but she was a relentless foe of the Sovereignty Commission and the Citizens' Council for the simple reason that their hateful actions violated her concept of "Southern decency." Her reputation as an editorial powerhouse began with a signed opinion piece that criticized the local sheriff for shooting a black man in the leg after he didn't "get goin'" in response to an order from the official. Smith wrote that the sheriff had "violated every concept of justice, decency and right in the treatment of some people" in the county, adding, "He has shown us without question that he is not fit to occupy that high office."

When the sheriff sued her for $57,500 in libel damages, Smith responded in print: "We don't know whether to be flattered at being sued for so much—or surprised that the sheriff places the value of his reputation at so little." In another editorial she wrote, "There are some sheriffs in office in Mississippi now who have lied to every man, woman and child in their counties—but they have no more remorse than an egg sucking dog." The sheriff was awarded $10,000, but he thought that was not enough, so he appealed and the Mississippi Supreme Court reversed the lower court judgment and took away the $10,000. In a follow-up editorial Smith wrote: "I am a firm believer in our Southern traditions and racial segregation, but not at the expense of justice and truth." Comments like that led to her being targeted by the Sovereignty Commission, which compiled more than 150 papers about her. The commission did everything it could to drive her out of the state, but she stood firm, responding in editorials with such headlines as State Gestapo Rule, Personal and Press Freedom Are at Stake.

On the surface she was a maze of contradictions. As tough as she was at the typewriter on issues about which she felt a passion, in person she was a gentle soul, and an attractive women with a child-friendly face and delicate features. At the 1940 Democratic National Convention in Chicago, which she attended as a delegate, legendary

New York journalist Damon Runyon was so smitten by her that he wrote a story that called her the "prettiest delegate" at the convention.[11]

In 1962, Hodding Carter nominated Smith for the Pulitzer Prize for editorial writing.[12] It didn't stick. The following year, Hodding III nominated her. This time the Pulitzer committee listened and awarded her the prize in 1964, the first woman to be cited for editorial writing. The week after her victory, she wrote a column that read:

> Yesterday people may have fled in terror before the flaming cross carried by a hooded knight. Today a loaded shotgun by the bed is standard equipment in most every Mississippi hut and hamlet— and the hoodlum who comes to terrorize is more apt to get his hood blown off—and with it his head.[13]

Standing up for one's rights seems so . . . well, ho-hum these days. Everyone does it, or so it seems. But that wasn't the case back then, when standing up resulted in what amounted to a baptism of fire. The Carters, the Smiths, the Harkeys of the state—all were ready and willing to stand tall.

14

Inside the FBI: The Truth About Mississippi

Maybe we didn't know the FBI as well as we thought we did.

The FBI of today bears little resemblance to the FBI of the 1950s and 1960s, when FBI director J. Edgar Hoover operated the agency with a near-obsessive devotion to three concepts from which he never wavered.

First was his belief that the FBI was defined by the integrity of the agents who worked in the field. He was fond of telling agents, "One man didn't build the FBI, but one man can tear it down."[1] During his tenure, agents, present and former, were expected to follow a high moral code of conduct that always reflected well on the agency. In Hoover's mind there was no category called "ex-agent." Agents were expected to maintain the same code of conduct whether active or retired. It was unheard of for a former agent to work for an organization that stood in opposition to the U.S. Constitution.

Second was his belief in the FBI National Academy's overt mission to foster cooperation between state and local law enforcement and the FBI and a belief in its covert mission to monitor state and local law enforcement for early signs of subversive activity. By 1956 more than three thousand local and state lawmen had participated in training at the academy. It was Hoover's pet project, and he allowed only his most trusted agents to serve in important posts at the academy.

Third was Hoover's determination to carry out a top-secret directive from President Roosevelt to investigate Communist activities throughout the country, prompting the FBI to declare war on the Communist Party. In time that "war" spilled over into the South. During the 1950s and 1960s, what united the Sovereignty Commission, the Citizens' Councils, and the KKK was their strident insistence that the civil rights movement was somehow affiliated with the Russian Communist Party.

Supporters of the civil rights movement felt it was absurd to link the movement to communism. As it turns out, there was a Communist connection to the Southern civil rights movement, at least in the early years. That did not become obvious until the turn of the millennium, when Glenda Elizabeth Gilmore, a Yale University history professor, traveled to Russia to research the Communist Party's involvement with the American civil rights movement. According to Gilmore the Communist Party set up two Southern districts from which to operate: District 17 included Alabama, Tennessee, Georgia, Mississippi, and Florida, with headquarters in Birmingham; and District 16, which included Virginia, North Carolina and South Carolina, with headquarters in Charlotte.[2]

In her book *Defying Dixie: The Radical Roots of Civil Rights*, Gilmore reveals that Southern civil rights leaders traveled regularly to Russia to study and experience life under a Communist system. Some liked what they saw; others did not. The central core of civil rights activists who went to Russia included well-known figures such as NAACP secretary James Weldon Johnson, and lesser-known people such as the first American-born black Communist, Lovett Fort-Whiteman.

Understanding this tenuous connection is important because it explains, but does not justify, Hoover's obsession with monitoring Martin Luther King Jr. and the civil rights movement. Hoover had evidence that some movement members were going to the Soviet Union, but he had no informants at the other end to report what was taking place among the Americans and the Soviets. That "evidence" proved to be dangerous in Hoover's hands. He assumed the worst, which as it turned out was a gross overinterpretation of the facts. In retrospect it explains how otherwise moral people could be corrupted by Hoover into becoming racists because they mistakenly believed that civil rights activists were fronting for the Communist Party.

Incredibly, Mississippi was the only Southern state in which the Communist Party was reluctant to recruit new members. In other words, despite the vitriolic railings of the Sovereignty Commission, the Citizens' Councils, and the KKK, and the intense scrutiny of the FBI, the Mississippi civil rights movement was barren of Communist influence. It never existed. It was a factor only in Hoover's paranoid mind.

From the beginning it was obvious that the Mississippi Sovereignty Commission was walking in lockstep with J. Edgar Hoover. The agency's mission mirrored the FBI's mission against communism, though it did so in a more public manner. There is no "smoking gun" document that officially affiliates Hoover with the Mississippi Sovereignty Commission, but there is overwhelming circumstantial evidence that he was not an innocent bystander to the work done by the Mississippi spy agency. From the time the commission was established on May 2, 1956, until it was disbanded in 1973, it was staffed by ex-FBI agents and at the end of its existence it was under the direction of an ex-FBI agent with whom Hoover had a close association.

As Hoover waged a secret war against civil rights, using Mississippi as a test-tube specimen, the CIA chose a Mississippi-born man, Frank Wisner, to be in charge of its covert actions against communism.[3] Reflecting the conservative myopia of his Mississippi and Virginia upbringing, Wisner transformed the agency from one of intelligence gathering to one of activism by undertaking a program of skullduggery that included sabotage, economic warfare, subversion, assistance to terrorist groups, and direct action, most of which were illegal in the countries in which they took place. Former CIA chief Richard Helms once described Wisner as a man who burned with "a zeal and intensity which imposed, unquestionably, an abnormal strain" on him. In 1958, Wisner suffered a nervous breakdown, diagnosed as manic depression, which resulted in him receiving a series of electro-shock therapy treatments. Seven years after the treatments began, he blew his brains out with a shotgun.

Mississippi was at the epicenter of secret government experimentation during that era. Just off the coast of Mississippi, the U.S. Army maintained a top-secret facility to raise yellow fever mosquitoes for use as biological weapons. Not far from the authors' hometown in the Delta, there was a secret satellite tracking station that was surrounded by barbed wire and dire warnings of what would happen to trespassers. Seemingly, the feds were everywhere.

The FBI and the CIA had supreme confidence in Mississippians as recruits for covert activity. They were not encumbered by the same devotion to equal rights that characterized recruits in other parts of the country. On a per capita basis, there were probably more recruits from Mississippi in the 1950s and 1960s than from any other state, providing the state with a reputation as "spook central." Even today it is difficult to travel through the Delta without bumping into retired secret agents, many of whom have transformed themselves into gentlemen farmers.

Major FBI Players Inside the Sovereignty Commission

FBI special agent Zack Van Landingham received a ground-floor appointment to the commission in 1956, when he was hired as an investigator. His first assignment was to organize the commission's filing system, using the FBI model as a guide. At the time, the FBI was undertaking its secret COINTELPRO domestic surveillance program. The filing system for COINTELPRO, which was devised to conceal illegally obtained information about American citizens, allowed the agency to keep a double set of books. For example, if an FBI agent obtained information without a court order, he forwarded it to FBI headquarters under a code name. That way the information could be filed using the code name without giving any apparent indication of the file's contents. If individuals named in the file suspected they had been spied on and succeeded in obtaining a court order to search the files, the search would come up empty unless they had knowledge of the code name used to conceal the information gathered about them. It was that type of no-fault filing system Van Landingham set up for the commission.

Van Landingham investigated a wide variety of cases, but he seemed obsessed with the perceived threat of subversion, as was Hoover. In his mind the NAACP was a Communist threat that had to be stopped dead in its tracks, despite never finding a single Communist in Mississippi. One of his targets was Carl Braden, a former reporter for *Newsweek* and the *Chicago Tribune* who, along with his wife, Anne, helped a black family in Louisville, Kentucky, purchase a home in a white neighborhood in 1954, an act of generosity that earned him a fifteen-year prison sentence, which was overturned after he served eight months in prison.[4] Shortly before he showed up in Clarksdale to work on behalf of the NAACP, Braden refused to cooperate with the House Un-American Activities Committee, for which he received a nine-month prison sentence. At a hearing before the Mississippi General Legislative Investigating Committee, whose purpose it was to probe alleged Communist activities in the state, Van Landingham testified that Braden's organization, the Southern Conference Educational Fund, a racially integrated group whose goal was to end segregation, was un-American.

The following year Van Landingham swung to the other end of the political spectrum when he was sent to Clarksdale to investigate Paul Clark, a descendent of the town's founding family. In his report he stated that a House of Representatives member from that district told him Clark was a "crackpot and very radical." He continued: "He said that Clark is a segregationist but that he also hates the Jews.

They won't let him join the Citizens Council at Clarksdale because they are unable to control his actions and believe that he would give the Citizens' Council a black eye."[5] Van Landingham said he couldn't confirm that Clark was the head of a neo-Fascist organization, as a New Hampshire newspaper apparently had reported.

In Van Landingham's eyes, racial equality was a creation of Communists and Nazis who wanted to destroy Mississippi Values.

John D. Sullivan was a retired FBI agent who worked in the 1960s for the Mississippi Sovereignty Commission, the Citizens' Council, and segregationist senator James O. Eastland. A native of Vicksburg, he established a detective agency named Delta Investigative Bureau, with an office in Vicksburg, about an hour's drive from Jackson.

Sullivan started working for the commission in 1958 as an independent contractor, but he asked to be hired full-time in 1965, after a U.S. Supreme Court ruling that he felt opened "the floodgates for the movement of more Communists and Communist sympathizers into Mississippi."[6] According to commission director Erle Johnston, who sent a memo to the governor about his conversation with Sullivan, the former FBI agent argued that the commission should develop "a broader and more comprehensive program for investigating subversives and filing information." If such policy were adopted, reported Johnston, Sullivan would give up his lucrative private agency and work full-time for the state.

When the governor expressed a feeling that the state could not afford to pay Sullivan a salary high enough to compensate for him closing down his agency, Sullivan agreed to continue working as an independent contractor. He was especially interested in Tougaloo College, an all-black institution just north of Jackson. The Sovereignty Commission had a highly placed informant at the college, and Sullivan urged Johnston not to disclose his identity under any circumstances: "A good informant is a jewel to be highly prized and protected because if nothing else to remain true to the promise you no doubt made to him, plus the fact that when you expose him you are closing the door on further information." He urged Johnston never to use information from the informant in a court of law: "Remember the FBI has been forced to bring their files in many cases."[7]

Sullivan also advised the commission on surveillance techniques. In a 1964 report, he wrote that highway patrol personnel should be trained in the use of surveillance equipment such as tape recorders and cameras, adding, "Also, they should be able to disguise their talk over radio so if a person is listening he won't be able to know for sure he is being surveilled."[8]

In the summer of 1967, Sullivan went fishing on a lake near Vicksburg and then returned to his home, where later in the day he was found dead in his bedroom. Authorities ruled his death a suicide.

In the weeks that followed, commission director Johnston spoke to Sullivan's widow about purchasing her husband's files and books for the Sovereignty Commission. She told him that she would think about it, but when he didn't hear back from her, he wrote her a letter that expressed his continuing interest in the files and books. When she didn't respond to his letter, he sent investigator Andrew Hopkins to Vicksburg to discuss the matter with her. Since she was at work when he arrived, Hopkins went to the police station and telephoned her from there. In his report Hopkins stated that Mrs. Sullivan said she'd decided not to dispose of the materials in that manner. Instead, she explained to Hopkins, she burned all of his files because of the confidential nature of the information in them. As far as the books were concerned, she stated that most of them had been loaned out to people who had not returned them.

FBI special agent Webb Burke played a larger role in the Mississippi Sovereignty Commission than any other agent.[9] Born in Hattiesburg, Mississippi, the son of a U.S. Postal Service superintendent, Burke entered the University of Mississippi in 1923 and impressed his professors as a country boy whose outgoing personality and athletic prowess compensated for his lack of academic performance.

Burke lettered in three sports at Ole Miss—football, basketball, and baseball—and garnered a reputation as a campus hero. He was the captain of the football team in 1926, and the following year he was presented the highest athletic award given at the university, the Norris Trophy. Burke ended up spending six years at Ole Miss, graduating in 1929 with a law degree. He moved to Jackson, where he signed on as a pitcher with the Jackson Senators, a minor league baseball franchise. He pitched thirteen games, winning twelve of them, but then abruptly quit and moved to Memphis, where he settled into his first full-time job as a football coach at Southwestern (now Rhodes College).

Burke did everything right at Southwestern, except win football games. After a losing season his contract was not extended and he was forced to look for employment elsewhere. He quickly landed a coaching position at Jonesboro High School in Arkansas, just across the Mississippi River from Memphis. That job lasted only three years, after which Burke was hired as an assistant coach at the University of Mississippi, where he stayed for five years before being asked to leave.

After three unsuccessful coaching jobs, Burke decided that his future was not in college sports and applied for a position as an FBI special agent. In November 1937, Burke was interviewed by FBI agent J. E. Clegg, who reported that Burke had coarse features, answered general questions vaguely, and was not likely to develop as an agent. He impressed Clegg as being "a boxer or hardened athlete," someone who was "slow of speech and gave the impression of being below the average mentally." According to the FBI interviewer, Burke "was questioned very thoroughly on matters which the ordinary educated man would know and most of his answers were very poor. In answer to questions, he stated that the population of New York City is 'slightly over two hundred million' and the population of the United States is 'approximately two billion.'"

Burke was not offered a job, but it is unclear whether he voluntarily withdrew his application or was formally turned down (his FBI personnel files does not address that issue). Shortly after Burke learned that he would not be given an FBI appointment, Mississippi governor Hugh White approached T. B. Birdsong, a former Ole Miss professor, and offered him the state's top law enforcement job, commissioner of the Mississippi Highway Patrol. Birdsong accepted the appointment only on the condition that Webb Burke would be appointed his assistant, a job that also carried the title of Highway Patrol Chief. It was an odd stipulation that was not challenged by the governor.

In 1940, less than two years into that job, Burke reapplied for a job with the FBI, only this time he attached considerable political clout to his application. Listed as references were Governor Hugh White, a congressman who had declined to be a reference for his 1937 application but this time around enthusiastically recommended him for the job, a U.S. senator, the mayor of Oxford, and his boss, Commissioner Birdsong, all of whom provided Burke with splendid references.

Burke underwent a second background check by an agent who had attended Ole Miss with him. Indeed the two men had been members of Beta Theta Pi social fraternity. Most of the people interviewed spoke highly of Burke; however, when a former high school classmate of Burke's was interviewed, he said that he did not think of Burke as the smooth type, but if the bureau wanted someone to "go out and get 'em," Burke was the man for the job. Said the report: "He [the classmate] is of the opinion that Webb Burke is the type of man who could not conduct an unbiased investigation, allowing his personal feelings to sway his judgment. He said he has no personal dislike toward him and he wanted to express it frankly."

A little over four months after Burke reapplied with the FBI, he was sworn in as a $3,200-a-year special agent, swearing to "support and defend the Constitution of the United States against all enemies, foreign and domestic; that I will bear true faith and allegiance to the same; that I take this obligation freely, without any mental reservation or purpose of evasion." Because of his police training at the highway patrol, Burke was assigned as a firearms instructor at the FBI academy at Quantico, Virginia, where he was responsible for training new agents, bureau officials, supervisors, and members of the Washington field office. Henry S. Sloan, the special agent in charge of the academy, soon named Burke acting director in his absence.

By June 24, 1960, Burke had moved on to the FBI's Newark, New Jersey, office, where he was the agent-in-charge. On that date he met

with J. Edgar Hoover in his office to receive an award to commemo-
rate his twenty years of service with the agency. Hoover presented
him with a personal letter that read:

> The record you have maintained has been an exceptional one and
> you have taken command of your heavy responsibilities with con-
> fidence and have inspired respect in others as to your ability and
> leadership. Your years of service have played an integral part in
> the achievement of the Bureau and you have made valuable con-
> tributions to the esteem with which the FBI is held.

After accepting the award and the letter, Burke notified Hoover
of his desire to retire from the agency. A few days later Burke sent
Hoover a letter explaining his decision: "As I indicated to you, the
Bureau has been my life for the last twenty years and certainly it was
not without a great deal of serious thought that I reached the decision
to apply for retirement, and for the specific reason that I mentioned
to you." He added, "I most certainly want to reassure you of my complete loyalty to you and to the Bureau. I stand ready to be of assistance
at any time."

On July 6, 1960, Hoover wrote him back, saying, "You have served
the Bureau in numerous positions of responsibility with a loyalty and
devotion which have been admirable. Your contributions have been
noteworthy, and I want to take this opportunity to express my thanks.
I am grateful for your kind remarks and your offer to be of assistance
in the future."

Eight years later Burke accepted the position as director of the
Mississippi Sovereignty Commission, where he remained until the
commission was disbanded in 1973, one year after the death of FBI
director J. Edgar Hoover. He stayed in close contact with the bureau,
receiving a letter from the new FBI director, Clarence Kelley, in January 1977 informing him of an upcoming visit to Jackson. The contents
of the letter are not known, since it was redacted from his personnel
file, along with hundreds of other documents. We do have Burke's
handwritten response, addressed "Dear Clarence," in which he asked
to meet with him while he was in town. Burke wrote, "I know quite

well that times have been rough and don't you ever forget that I stand ready to ask anyone to give the proper aid and assistance to you as director to the FBI that we know."

Webb Burke died of natural causes on June 19, 1987, at the age of eighty-one. Upon his death his wife wrote to acting FBI director John Otto to request permission to attach an FBI emblem to her husband's tombstone. Approval was granted.

J. Edgar Hoover Visits Jackson

Ten days after former CIA director Allen Dulles traveled to Mississippi in June 1964 to meet with Governor Paul B. Johnson, President Lyndon Johnson had a fateful conversation with FBI director J. Edgar Hoover. Asked the president, "How many people can you bring in there? . . . I think you ought to put fifty, a hundred people after this Klan. . . . Their very presence may save us a division of soldiers. . . . I read a dozen of your reports here last night, here till one o'clock, on Communists, and they can't open their mouth without your knowing what they're saying."

"Very true," said Hoover.

"Now I don't want these Klansmen to open their mouth without your knowing what they're saying. . . . We ought to have intelligence on that state because that's gonna be the most dangerous thing we have this year."

Within hours after the president's conversation with Hoover, Lyndon Johnson signed the Civil Rights Act of 1964. By then Hoover was already making plans for a visit to Mississippi to address the concerns that Governor Johnson had made to Dulles. According to Frank Barber, a longtime political operative who was on the governor's staff, Johnson had requested two favors of the president. The first was for the FBI to open an office in Jackson. The second was for the FBI to accept more Mississippians into the FBI Academy.[10]

Hoover was not enthusiastic about the trip, not just because he resented Dulles's involvement in what he considered a domestic matter—indeed, Hoover considered the CIA a continuing threat to his control of domestic surveillance—but because he felt he had the situation under control in Jackson. While in Jackson, Hoover met with the governor, Attorney General Joe Patterson, highway patrol commissioner T. B. Birdsong, *Jackson Daily News* editor Jimmy Ward, and *Clarion-Ledger* editor Tom Hederman, on the top floor of the First Federal Building. Prior to that Hoover had talked privately with Birdsong on the drive in from the airport.

When Hoover returned to Washington, he sent a letter to Birdsong thanking him for his hospitality. Birdsong responded with a letter that expressed approval of a "close association" with the bureau and concluded with assurances of "our abiding friendship and desire to cooperate with your department."

Hoover's visit to Jackson and the governor's request for more FBI involvement came as a surprise to Sovereignty Commission director Erle Johnston, who seemed confused by the state publicly embracing the FBI. Memos and correspondence of that time make it clear that the governor had no knowledge of the extent to which former FBI agents worked with the commission. Likewise, Johnston, who was fully aware of the extent with which the commission worked with the FBI, was not aware of governor Johnson's past history as a detective in the New Orleans police department. Barber once described the governor as a "cops and robbers" kind of guy, and it is clear that he was infatuated with the G-man image associated with the FBI.

Once the new FBI office opened and agents began working the state in large numbers, agents learned that the highway patrol was a weak link in law enforcement, primarily because the department was infiltrated by Klansmen. When the FBI asked to interview patrolmen suspected of being Klan members, the department stonewalled the agency and refused to authorize the interviews. FBI agent Jim Ingram, who was in charge of violent crimes associated with civil rights cases, went to Birdsong to talk with him about the problem. He asked how the FBI could resolve the cases if Birdsong didn't allow the troopers to be interviewed. Birdsong relented and the troopers cooperated with the FBI. Recalls Ingram: "The troopers didn't mind it. They could tell their story, instead of being hung out to dry and indicted without their side of the story being told."[11]

Later in the year, after a series of bombings in McComb, Erle Johnston wrote a memo to Governor Johnson in which he said the FBI had asked the Sovereignty Commission to share the information in its files. Johnston was disturbed by the request. Noting the highway patrol's decision to cooperate with the FBI, Johnston wrote, "We would like to know from you whether the Sovereignty Commission also should cooperate with the FBI and, if so, to what extent."

Unknown to Johnston, Special Agent Roy Moore, head of the new FBI field office in Jackson, had provided the governor with a list of law enforcement officials in the state who were suspected of membership in the Ku Klux Klan. The list included names of highway patrol officers, game wardens, city marshals, town constables, and county sheriffs. Said Moore, "If you intend taking any action against the above-named individuals, their Klan membership should be established by separate investigation as this Bureau would be unable to produce any individuals to testify at any necessary hearings."

Governor Johnson passed the letter on to Commissioner Birdsong, who replied to the agent in a letter dated August 24. "I deeply appreciate this information," said Birdsong. "Steps have now been taken to eliminate this situation, *in part*."

Once Klansmen had been purged from the highway patrol, the FBI made an unusual request. It asked that a highway patrolman be assigned to each agent. "That worked out well because when we went out to interview Klansmen and other suspects, you had not only the federal government, but also the state—and the sheriffs got the message," recalls Ingram. "We had sheriffs that also were members of the Klan. When we arrived with highway patrolmen, they began to look at their situation also. We started naming names. The highway patrol came out in full force, too. The highway patrol can play rough."

By September, Johnston had figured out that the governor had forged a working relationship with the new FBI bureau office in Jackson. In a cryptic September memo, Johnston notified the governor that the FBI had cleared his upcoming speech in Pontotoc: "They agree with us that the Justice Department should publicize its findings in all those cases where there is no evidence to justify charges."

Was Johnson unaware that the FBI had two presences in Jackson? One public and focused on solving civil rights crimes—and the other secret and focused on assisting the Sovereignty Commission in its efforts to maintain segregation? In the immediate wake of Hoover's visit, there is no indication from the correspondence between the commission and the governor that the latter had any knowledge of the depth of the FBI's involvement with the commission. However, it may be surmised that Johnson subsequently was educated about the matter from someone on his staff, because by late October, Johnston had dictated a revealing memo for the file:

> The Sovereignty Commission has been ordered by the Governor's office not to reveal any information in the Commission's office to the Federal Bureau of Investigation except on specific cases. Even on specific cases, they must be cleared with the Governor's office before any information is revealed. The investigator staff of the Sovereignty Commission has been so notified of this policy.

FBI Agents Not Associated with the Commission

Joseph Sullivan was the FBI agent who was sent to Mississippi in 1964 to supervise the investigation of the murders of Michael Schwerner, James Chaney, and Andrew Goodman, the civil rights activists killed near Philadelphia. (He was not related to John D. Sullivan, the former agent who worked for the Sovereignty Commission.) Before the investigation was concluded, Sullivan oversaw more than 250 FBI agents who were assigned to the case. Based in the New Jersey bureau, he was a legendary agent who was involved in some of the major cases of the 1960s and 1970s.

Only months prior to being sent to Mississippi, he was instrumental in protecting President Lyndon Johnson from a bomb threat in Florida. In that instance he went to Jacksonville, Florida, and learned that the bombers planned to assassinate the president while he traveled by train. Sullivan figured out which bridge had been targeted and crawled along the bridge in the dead of night until he found the bomb. As he removed the explosive, other FBI agents flagged down the presidential train as it neared the bridge, allowing Sullivan enough time to complete his work. He was also instrumental in solving a Gambino crime family truck theft operation in New York City, and he played a role in identifying James Earl Ray as the assassin in the 1968 murder of Martin Luther King.

Joseph Sullivan died on August 2, 2002, after fighting cancer for quite some time. Leave it to a fiction writer to approximate the truth about the man. Wrote novelist Tom Clancy, "Joe Sullivan has been the defender of our rights. He has held the most valuable of public trusts. He has been the guardian of our constitution."

Jim Ingram's introduction to Mississippi Values was a fiery one.[12] As a young FBI agent working in the New York office, Ingram received a telephone call in 1964 from a friend and fellow agent, John Proctor, who recently had been assigned to the Meridian, Mississippi, office. Proctor wanted him to come to Mississippi. J. Edgar Hoover was sending agents by the dozens to Mississippi to investigate the case involving the missing civil rights workers in Philadelphia. After speaking to Proctor, the Oklahoma-born Ingram asked Hoover for permission to go to Mississippi.

Recalls Ingram: "Of course, many of the New York agents said, 'Ingram, you're crazy!' I was not from Mississippi, I was from Oklahoma, and they said, 'You don't want to go to Mississippi. You're going to work seven days a week. You're going to get threats. You're going to be surrounded by rednecks. You're going to have to deal with snakes in your car. That's the worst place you could ever go.' After hearing all that, I talked to Proctor again and he said, 'Oh, it's not so bad.'"

Ingram and Proctor were part of the team that worked under agent Joseph Sullivan. To Ingram and many other agents, Sullivan was "one of the premier investigators in the world. He was brilliant, and he knew how to organize. He was single, no children, so he had all the time, twenty-four hours a day, to devote to Mississippi."

Ingram quickly learned that he had his hands full investigating the Philadelphia case. He notes that there's a different atmosphere in Neshoba County today than there was in those days.

> No one cared whether Schwerner lived or died. Goodman just happened to be in Mississippi for a few days. The Klan was after "Goatee" [Schwerner], as they called him. Goatee was targeted for death. It was just a matter of time. The agents had a most difficult time with the townspeople and the officials. We are taught to do the investigation, gather the facts and present them to the U.S. Attorney and then step out. It was a different situation in Mississippi because we were gathering facts that the state should have gathered and we were then presenting these facts to the authorities and they were turning their backs and saying, "Not enough evidence." The FBI had no jurisdiction whatsoever, but when the president orders the director of the FBI, no matter what the cost, no matter what it takes, "I want these cases solved," that's a pretty good instruction from the most powerful person in the world, so we did. That's what irritated so many of the citizens of Mississippi. Their lawyers told them, "You don't have to talk to the FBI. You can tell them to leave your property," and they were correct. But it was clear that the U.S. government was going to follow all the rules and all the non-rules to get the Schwerner, Goodman, and Chaney case into court—and we were very happy with the outcome.

Of course, the Philadelphia case never would have been solved without informants. Ingram and the other agents accomplished that in various ways, but the most brilliant means was worthy of a psychological warfare expert. The agents would watch a Klan suspect's home until he left, and then they'd knock on the door and ask his wife if he was there. She'd say, no—he's gone to work. The agents then would ask, "Would you mind too much if we came in for a cup of coffee?" Invariably, they'd be invited into the house, which more often than not would be just a notch or two above a shanty. After they were seated at the kitchen table, sipping coffee, making small talk about the weather, an agent, his voice sterner, would inform the suspect's wife that the FBI knew about her husband's involvement with the Klan. They'd let her know in no uncertain terms that he was headed for jail. Once the shock of that set in, the agents would offer to "help" her husband stay out of jail. *We don't want him to go to jail any more than you do.* As soon as the hook was set, they'd offer to help the family with financial support. One line was "We can pay your husband more to help us than he's making now at that job of his." If the suspect's wife said she'd be afraid he'd be killed if he informed on the Klan, the answer was always "We won't let that happen." If you work at it, with a little imagination you can hear those wives talking to their husbands when they got home after work.

"What'd the Klan ever do for you?"

"We need the money, honey."

"I'll tell you one thing, if you don't take that free money, I'm taking the kids and going home to Mama."

Not surprisingly, it worked. Not every time, but enough. Women were key to breaking the cases. In the end breaking the cases was all about informants. Ingram recalls that the FBI had informants all over the state. Every Klan member had an agent assigned to him or her. "When Martin Luther King Jr. was assassinated in Memphis, I was in Jackson and got a call from Memphis asking me to get all my agents going. We had every agent in Mississippi knocking on doors." The plan he devised was to have his agents "eyeball" their Klan subjects so that they could verify their whereabouts. "If they were working the night shift, they had to go there and see him. Then we would go down the list and say these are the ones that we know could not have been in Memphis and these are the ones we couldn't find."

One of the people who immediately came to mind as a possible suspect in King's murder was J. B. Stoner, the Georgia segregationist who was the longtime chairman of the National States' Rights Party, the political arm of the KKK. But as it turned out, Stoner was speaking in Meridian at the time of the murder. Recalls Ingram: "Our agents were across the street in a building with the lights off monitoring what was going on. All of a sudden they heard cheering and clapping. The people in the audience had just gotten word on the radio that King had been assassinated. They ended up jumping out in the streets. At least the agents knew where J. B. Stoner was that night."

One of the untold stories about the FBI's "invasion" of Mississippi was that not all the agents were of the same mind. Not all of the FBI agents ordered to Mississippi showed up. Ingram recalls that some resigned from the FBI rather than go to Mississippi.

> They called and talked to agents already here and they said, "Don't come here." I had agents call me from New York and I said, "It's exactly the way you've heard it. You'll work six and a half days a week. You'll have Sunday morning to go to church and do your laundry, but you'll have to be at work at one o'clock Sunday afternoon. You'll not only work six and a half days a week, you'll work fourteen or fifteen hours a day. You won't be sleeping much. You'll be traveling and staying at some of the worst places you've ever stayed in your life." That's why we had agents coming in, going out. Some of the agents showed up, but their wives wouldn't come.

Along with investigating violent cases, the FBI was asked to look into violations of the Civil Rights Act of 1964 that dealt with public accommodations. Basically the law said that restaurants and hotels could not discriminate against African Americans by preventing them from eating in the same room with whites or by having a "white only" restroom inside the business and a "colored" restroom outside the building. Recalls Ingram: "We had a squad that did nothing but check accommodations. It was called the 'crapper squad.' They had to go out and check facilities around the state that had separate facilities. I'm telling you, there were a lot of agents who didn't want to work that squad."

Prior to the civil rights murders in Philadelphia, the FBI office in Memphis handled all the cases from Memphis to Jackson, and the FBI office in New Orleans handled the cases from Jackson to the coast. Once Hoover opened the office in Jackson, agents had to travel the length and width of the state, a distance of four hundred miles from Memphis to the Gulf Coast. When Ingram arrived in Mississippi, agents started working cases all over the state, an escalation of federal authority that many citizens had a difficult time accepting. At that time, Ingram recalls, the Citizens' Council ran things north of Jackson and the Klan ran things to the south. Recalls Ingram: "The council members in the Delta were the respected people there. They didn't want to say they were in the Klan, but they held the same views. If violence came from others, well, that was all right with them."

Ingram was transferred out of Mississippi in 1970 and assigned to the Washington, D.C., office, where he became an inspector and traveled the world on behalf of the FBI, serving in South America, Mexico, and Canada, before finally returning to Washington to serve as deputy assistant director at the bureau. Before retiring he headed up the New York and Chicago bureaus, the two largest offices in the country.

Ingram's career took many surprising turns during the thirty-plus years he worked for the FBI, but none were as surprising as his decision to live out his retirement in Mississippi. "I came back to Mississippi because I fell in love with it. Mississippi is filled with tremendous people. There is a lot of talent here." Three of his sons enrolled at Ole Miss; two of them became lawyers and set up practices in Jackson.

Once Ingram returned to Mississippi, one thing led to another and he ended up heading up the Mississippi Highway Patrol from 1992 to 2000, the very agency that had caused him so much grief in the 1960s. After he retired from the patrol, he thought his career in law enforcement was over, but in 2005 his life took another dramatic turn when the FBI asked him to return to work to help with investigations on cold-case murders from the civil rights era.

John Proctor, an FBI agent stationed in Meridian during the 1960s, is credited with breaking the case involving Schwerner, Chaney, and Goodman. Born in Reform, Alabama, he spent ten years keeping Soviet diplomats under surveillance at the United Nations, before being assigned to Mississippi, where he was responsible for investigating civil rights violations, Indian reservation crimes, and interstate auto theft.

Proctor is the tough-talking prototype for the character played by Gene Hackman in the 1988 movie *Mississippi Burning.* Proctor worked closely with Joseph Sullivan, the FBI's ace major-case inspector, to solve the Philadelphia murders.

One day Proctor got word that a Mississippi store owner had bragged he was going to beat the hell out of any FBI agent who entered his store. Proctor went to the business and called the owner to the front of the store, causing the customers and clerks to stop what they were doing to watch. Once the owner stepped into view, Proctor said, "You stated last night that if an FBI agent came in here, you were going to beat the hell out of him. Well, sir, I'm an FBI agent. I'm not armed. And I'm waiting for you to try to beat hell [sic] out of me."

The shaken owner mumbled that it was all a misunderstanding.

Proctor said, "I think in the future it would be better if you didn't make threats."

Then, without another word, he turned and left.

When Proctor retired from the FBI in 1978, he opened a detective agency in Meridian. Interviewed several years before his death, Proctor refused to discuss the Philadelphia case, saying, "I'm not a hero. I did my job."

Surprising Conclusions

The undercover agent who went to Selma, Alabama, at the end of May 1964, just three weeks before the murder of Schwerner, Goodman, and Chaney in Philadelphia, to purchase two .38-caliber revolvers for the Sovereignty Commission, was Jerry Harrison, owner of Harrison Detective Agency, which had offices in the King Edward Hotel in Jackson.[13] In July, Harrison contacted commission investigator Andrew Hopkins again, this time with the claim that the Justice Department had sent its own operative, code named "Savage," to Alabama to purchase guns for a local group.

It was Harrison's belief that the Justice Department was involved in a conspiracy to arm "troublemakers." In his report to the commission, Hopkins admitted that it was a "pretty wild story" but not one that he discounted. What troubled him was that he knew of no law enforcement officials who purchased firearms from the federal government. The gist of Hopkins's report was that if the Justice Department wasn't purchasing firearms for state law enforcement officers, whom were the weapons for?

Since it is highly unlikely that federal prosecutors or active FBI agents were purchasing illegal weapons to pass on to "troublemakers," it is reasonable to conclude that Harrison's source was correct about the weapons but incorrect about the agency that was passing the weapons on to these so-called troublemakers.

The mystery deepened ten days after Hopkins reported Harrison's information, when the bodies of Schwerner, Goodman, and Chaney were uncovered beneath the earthen dam. At the autopsy one bullet was removed from the left lung of Michael Schwerner. One bullet was removed from "near the chest" of Andrew Goodman. And three bullets were removed from the body of James Chaney. Ballistic experts concluded that all five of the bullets were fired from the same type weapon—a .38-caliber pistol. The five bullets were identified as "reloads," indicating they had been hand-loaded and not purchased in a store.

The fact that .38-caliber weapons were used in the killing, the same caliber weapons purchased by the Sovereignty Commission—combined with Harrison's information that a government agency was purchasing firearms for "troublemakers"—opens the door to the likely possibility that someone affiliated with the commission passed the firearms on to the KKK for use in the murders. It was no secret that the commission was staffed by ex-FBI agents, and it would not have been unreasonable for a Klansman to think the weapons were being furnished by the FBI itself, causing them to inadvertently supply misleading information to Harrison. Supporting that theory is the fact that the pistols mysteriously disappeared from the commission offices and were not listed in subsequent agency inventories—and the fact that the murder weapons were never found by authorities.

Interviewed five years before his death, retired FBI agent Joseph Sullivan, who liked to describe himself as a "country boy" from a Wisconsin mining town, said that he was very much aware of the Sovereignty Commission. "I was aware that they had money. I always suspected the White Knights were funded in some fashion by the commission. In the years that followed, I wish we'd done some probing in that area. The problem was that we had nothing that would allow us to subpoena [commission] documents."[14]

Sullivan said he knew the commission was watching his agents, but not to the extent later revealed in the commission's secret files. Nor was he aware of the private banking account used by the commission. Asked if he thought that New Orleans mobster Carlos Marcello, a notorious racist and Klan supporter, could have contributed money to a secret bank account maintained by the commission, he answered in the affirmative. "It would have been part of the price of doing business."

Webb Burke's name also arose during the interview. Burke did not become commission director until 1968, four years after the Philadelphia murders, but Sullivan was aware of his activities with the commission. "As far as I know Burke wasn't fraternizing with the Jackson agents, and that always surprised me. He was always a real gung ho FBI type and I would have expected him to [have had more contact with local FBI agents]. There is no indication that our confidence was betrayed in any way [by Burke], whatever else may have gone on."

There is no one who had a more intimate knowledge of the Philadelphia murders and the personalities of the individuals involved than FBI agent Joseph Sullivan. If he suspected that the commission was giving support to the KKK, as he stated in an interview with the authors, that suspicion is reason enough to give serious consideration to the possibility that the commission supplied the Klan with the weapons used in the murders. Asked if he thought that the commission could have been involved with the murders, Sullivan did not think the question was out of line: "If you can tie Sam Bowers in any way to the state [you would have the link]. Bowers must have had some people working with him. There may be a whole area of conspiracies there."[15]

Former FBI agent Jim Ingram confirmed Sullivan's interest in the commission. "He was very concerned over what the commission had been doing over the years. Were they funding the Klan? That was one of his questions. Were they providing the Klan with weapons? Were they providing the Klan other means? Were they shielding Klan members in their church-burning activities? He wanted to get into their finances. Joe and I talked about that after I was transferred out of Mississippi. We spent hours together restructuring the MIBURN case. [MIBURN is the code name that the FBI gave to the civil rights investigations in Mississippi.] The Sovereignty Commission was one of the things that he always felt he should have gotten into."

After Sullivan left Mississippi, he spoke to Roy Moore, the agent in charge of the Jackson office, regarding his concerns about the commission, but Moore told him that he had his hands full with other cases and didn't have time to pursue the commission. Moore, who had once worked for Burke and considered him a friend, told Sullivan that Burke had assured him "everything is on the up and up" at the commission.

In 1968, the year Burke was appointed director of the commission, Mississippi Highway Patrol head T. B. Birdsong, Burke's mentor and sponsor for a job with the FBI, was in his final year of service. Of the three top law enforcement agencies in the state—the FBI, the highway patrol, and the office of the attorney general—Burke had personal relationships with individuals in two, and in the third, Attorney General Joe Patterson was an actual member of the Sovereignty Commission.

Moore, who remained in charge of the Mississippi office until 1971 and then again from 1973 to 1974, never looked back at the Sovereignty Commission, allowing the commission to close its doors without ever coming under needed investigative scrutiny by the FBI, despite agent Joseph Sullivan's concerns. There is no hard evidence that Moore and Birdsong actively conspired with Burke, based on their friendships, to protect the commission from a criminal investigation, but there is enough circumstantial evidence to make the case that during the 1950s and 1960s, Hoover's FBI worked both sides of the fence by using active agents to investigate civil rights crimes and retired agents to support Mississippi's losing battle to fight imaginary communism in the state and to maintain segregation for as long as possible.

Of course, the lingering question is whether sensitive information provided to the FBI by trusting civil rights informants was ever passed along by Moore to the Sovereignty Commission and its investigators in contact with the KKK. Agent Sullivan didn't think so, but with Moore's passing in 2008, that question can be answered only by full disclosure by the FBI, at the highest levels, of the agency's secret relationship with the commission. A president of the United States committed to civil rights has the power to make that happen.

PART III

Justice Delayed

15

Byron De La Beckwith: Ordeal by Trial and Error

Byron De La Beckwith had an answer for everything. Police told him they had a .30-06 Enfield rifle with a telescopic sight that had his fingerprints on it. It's probably mine, he said—it was stolen recently. Police also told him they had witnesses who had seen him in Jackson the night of Medgar Evers's murder. No way, he countered—and gave them the names of two Greenwood police officers he said had seen him that night in Greenwood.

As Charles Evers, the slain leader's brother, took over management of the NAACP field office, Beckwith pleaded not guilty and the murder trial went forward in 1964 under the direction of District Attorney Bill Waller. Since serving as district attorney was a part-time job at best, Waller, a graduate of the Ole Miss law school, continued to maintain his private law accounts with his partner, John Fox, a practice that was neither uncommon nor illegal among elected officials in Mississippi at the time.

Waller was no liberal; nor was he pleased about the agitation being stirred up in Mississippi over the rights of blacks. He was comfortable with Mississippi just the way it was. But Waller was more than that would suggest—he was a man of passion and justice. A horrible crime had been committed in his judicial district. That didn't sit well with him. In addition to Waller's forthright recognition of his obligation as district attorney to perform his sworn duty regardless of threats and intimidation, he was committed to do all within his power to see that the perpetrator of Evers's murder was brought to justice. But saying that and doing it were two different things. Evers was assassinated on June 12, 1963, and the trial was not until the beginning of 1964. Of course, the jury would be composed of white males. Strange as it may seem now, up to that time no white in the state had ever been convicted of killing a black. Under the Mississippi system, white supremacy and solidarity prevailed at all costs. One of Evers's friends remarked that a white man would get more time for shooting a rabbit out of season than for killing an African American.

Waller had almost no encouragement and little help from white citizens, except that provided by his able partner, Fox, the son of an illustrious law professor at Ole Miss who had intellectually terrorized law students for decades. This was also a time of trial by ambush, with almost no way to discover the opposing side's case. Witnesses were reticent to appear for fear of being branded a "nigger lover" or a "Communist."

Beckwith was represented by some of the best and most well-connected criminal defense attorneys in Mississippi, Hardy Lott and Stanny Sanders from Greenwood and E. H. Cunningham Jr. of Jackson, a law partner of Governor Ross Barnett. The Citizens' Council eagerly raised substantial sums to pay for this well-fortified defense. Before his arrest on Saturday night, June 22, 1963, Beckwith went home, put on his spiffy clothes, and obtained his favorite picture of himself to distribute to the media before he was incarcerated. He went to jail and to the trial as if he were a great emperor returning to Rome. Municipal judge James L. Spencer refused bail, which meant that Beckwith had to remain in jail. It didn't seem to bother him. He acted more like a celebrity than a prisoner.

Waller had heard that the defense might raise an insanity plea, and he asked the court for a preemptive mental evaluation at the Mississippi State Hospital at Whitfield, a mental health treatment facility in Rankin County. Judge Leon Hendrick agreed, and Beckwith was sent to Whitfield. Instead of appealing that decision to the Supreme Court, Beckwith's attorneys filed a writ of *habeas corpus* before Judge O. H. Barnett, the segregationist Rankin County circuit judge and Governor Ross Barnett's cousin. Judge Barnett readily set aside Judge Hendrick's order and directed Sheriff Jonathan H. Edwards to take custody of Beckwith in the Rankin County jail.

Beckwith now was like the storybook character Br'er Rabbit, who pleaded with his captors not to throw him into a briar patch. Beckwith's jailhouse doors were never closed. He entertained scores of associates, kept his guns and books, made frequent excursions from the jail for personal reasons, and conducted himself more like a hero than a felon. Eventually, however, Waller was able to get his appeal heard in the Supreme Court, which ordered Beckwith back to the Hinds County jail on November 25, 1963.[1]

Two months later the trial began. On the first day of the trial, there was not a vacant seat in the courtroom. Emotions were boiling over, and the racial situation in Jackson was tense. Waller recalls the trial as "not just a high profile murder case, it was a national and international event."[2] The major wire services and the *New York Times* published daily summaries. The two Jackson newspapers continued to stir the pot. Two days after Evers was murdered, the *Clarion-Ledger* stated that "desperately ruthless forces may have used [Evers] as a sacrificial offering to rekindle the flames of unrest here and to spur the drive for 'victory' elsewhere."

In examining the transcript of the first trial, any attorney would be overwhelmed by the herculean effort that Waller and John Fox exerted in preparing and prosecuting the case.[3] But perhaps the most interesting portion of this trial, as it is in many trials, was the selection of the jury. The importance of this portion of the trial cannot be overstated, because it is the jury selected through this process that determines the outcome of any case. Waller was savvy enough to know that many white Mississippians felt it was not a crime to kill an African American, especially if the black was, like Evers, advocating equal justice for all. Waller went straight to the jugular, and one of his first questions to the jury was: *"Do you believe it is a crime for a white man to kill a 'nigger'?"*[4]

In order to finally pick a jury, it took Waller several days to winnow through the panel to find enough white men who thought that killing a black man just might be a crime. Early on in his *voir dire*, he stressed to the jury, "I'm one of you," and "I don't enjoy what I'm doing," but "I think it's my duty."[5]

Waller turned a deaf ear to the murmurs of anger from a large audience of African Americans in the courtroom, because he knew what he had to do and felt he was performing his sworn duty to do everything possible to obtain a conviction. He certainly was not sympathetic to the defendant, but for Waller to have any chance of obtaining a conviction, it was essential to let the jury know that he was no flaming liberal.

To prove his case, Waller put on almost sixty witnesses and introduced more than fifty pieces of documentary evidence. He proved Beckwith's motive, ability, and capacity to commit the crime; the planning of the murder; the rifle that was used; the rifle scope that bore Beckwith's fingerprint; the cut over Beckwith's right eye, which was consistent with the recoil of the rifle causing the scope to contact and make a semicircle over his eye. Waller brought out evidence of Beckwith's car having been seen near the murder scene. Beckwith had written dozens of letters before his arrest and during his incarceration expressing his rabid racist beliefs.[6] The year of the murder, Waller identified one letter to the National Rifle Association: "Gentlemen: For the next 15 years we here in Mississippi are going to have a lot of shooting to protect our wives, children and ourselves from bad niggers." Waller then brought out an earlier letter by Beckwith that had appeared in a Jackson newspaper on April 16, 1957: "I believe in segregation like I believe in God. I shall oppose any person, place or thing that opposes segregation. I shall . . . bend every effort to rid the U.S. of the integrationists, whoever and wherever they may be." On cross-examination he readily agreed that he wrote the letter and confirmed that he held those beliefs.

The president of the Citizens' Council, Robert Patterson, described Beckwith as "a gentleman and a law-abiding citizen." Spectators at the trial were outraged at white witnesses who implicated Beckwith, voicing surprise that one white person would testify against another white person.

Regardless of the evidence, Beckwith was not really worried, and throughout the trial he looked very relaxed, dressed in his dapper suits, winking and nodding at the bailiffs and clerks. He had every reason to feel relaxed. The jury, of course, was all white, and he was aware of the fact that no white man had ever been convicted in Mississippi for killing a black person. The defense team hardly bothered to refute the substantial evidence that Waller put forward, but they did produce two surprise witnesses, both Greenwood policemen, who testified that they had seen Beckwith at a filling station in Greenwood at about the time Evers was murdered.

On the last day of the trial, in an obvious attempt to express approval, a smiling Governor Barnett strode into the courtroom, shook Beckwith's hand firmly, and chatted with him for a few minutes. Also, General Edwin Walker, who was quite prominent in the Meredith riot at Ole Miss, expressed his allegiance to Beckwith by paying a brief visit to him that afternoon.

On Thursday, February 6, 1964, the jury heard the judge's instructions and listened to the oral arguments. The defense concluded its argument by having attorney Stanny Sanders send the jurors off with these final words: "I do not believe you will return a verdict of guilty to satisfy the Attorney General of the United States and the liberal national media." At 12:30 P.M. on that same day, the jury retired to the jury room to begin deliberations. The twelve men argued for seven hours that night and for four hours the next morning.

On the morning of February 7, on the trial's twelfth day, the jury reported they were hopelessly deadlocked. The judge had no choice but to declare a mistrial. At the time there were a number of different accounts as to the division of the jury.[7] One account had the jury dividing seven to five for acquittal, another six to six. Waller stated sometime later that he'd learned the division on the panel was seven for a guilty verdict and five for acquittal. Of course, the mistrial did not set Beckwith free, since he remained under indictment. Bond was denied, and he was sent back to jail by Judge Hendrick to await the second trial, to begin on April 16, 1964.

The Second Trial

As Waller prepared for the second trial, investigators with the Sovereignty Commission secretly intervened on Beckwith's behalf. Records show that commission investigator Andrew Hopkins obtained a list of prospective jurors and investigated their backgrounds. That information, which contained comments such as "believed to be Jewish" or "fair and impartial" scrawled out beside individual names by the investigator, was provided to Beckwith's lawyers.[8]

On April 6, 1964, Waller began jury selection. One of the prospective jurors was a member of the Citizens' Council, which had held a fund-raiser for Beckwith to help with his legal expenses. Another prospective juror was a distant cousin of Hopkins. The full extent to which the Sovereignty Commission intervened—whether individual jurors were contacted or information was relayed to them—is unknown, but the results of Hopkins's work were certainly favorable to Beckwith: for a second time an all-male, all-white jury was chosen to hear the case.

After two days of *voir dire*, the state began calling its witnesses. The witnesses were virtually the same as in the first trial, except the defense came up with a surprise witness who claimed he owned a white Valiant similar to Beckwith's and that his car was near Evers's house on the night of the murder.

After a ten-day trial, on April 16, 1964, the jury began deliberations. After ten hours, the jury foreman announced to Judge Hendrick that the jury could not agree. Judge Hendrick again declared a mistrial. This time Beckwith was released on a ten-thousand-dollar bond. Now free on bond, Beckwith arrived in Greenwood in grand style. Chauffeuring him was the sympathetic sheriff of Hinds County, Fred Pickett, leading a sizable motorcade, with balloons flying, horns honking, and people crowding the streets screaming "Welcome Home" to their favorite son. On the outskirts of town was a large sign: WEL-COME HOME, DELAY. Beckwith told reporters that all that had brought tears to his eyes.

Waller was disappointed that he did not obtain a conviction. But he had performed his duty in prosecuting the case to the very best of his ability. A review of the early 1964 record in this case would make the most cynical lawyer respect the preparation, skill, tenacity, and just plain hard work, all accomplished by a dedicated district attorney per-forming his duty in a mostly hostile environment. But even in defeat Waller obtained a victory of sorts. Without these hung juries Byron De La Beckwith would have gone unpunished, since if he had been acquit-ted by either of the 1964 juries, there never could have been another trial because the doctrine of double jeopardy would have prevented it. Mississippi had to wait for history to do its job. But as far as Bill Waller was concerned, he'd done his and he'd done it well.

Beckwith the Mad Bomber

Encouraged by the "go-ahead" signal he got from the juries in the first and second trials, Beckwith decided that his celebrity might enable him to be elected to political office. In 1967 he ran for lieutenant governor and received more than 34,000 votes, allowing him to finish fifth in a field of six.

Sometimes at political rallies he introduced himself as "the man they say shot Medgar Evers." Other times he was more explicit, such as the time he entered a Belzoni store and introduced himself by say-ing, "I'm Byron De La Beckwith, and I'm running for lieutenant gov-ernor. I'm the man who killed Medgar Evers!" For the remainder of the decade, he reveled in his membership in the KKK and attended right-wing rallies, where he ranted about the evils of desegregation. In early 1973 he was seen at Citizens' Council rally in Jackson at which Alabama governor George Wallace was the featured speaker.

A couple of weeks later the FBI office received an informant's tip that Beckwith was planning to bomb the Anti-Defamation League headquarters in downtown New Orleans.⁹ Eight days later, after a brief stop in Jackson, where it was alleged he picked up the bomb, Beckwith was spotted on Highway 49 in his 1968 white-and-blue Oldsmobile 98. Beckwith's route into New Orleans took him over the five-mile span across Lake Pontchartrain. When he reached the other side, the New Orleans police pulled him over. It was a little after midnight. Beckwith got out of his car and was told by police officers to put his hands on the hood. One of the police officers patted him down and discovered a .45-caliber automatic tucked into his pants.

"You're under arrest for carrying a concealed weapon."

"I always carry a .45," Beckwith answered.

The police officer then shined his flashlight into Beckwith's car. On the front seat was a wooden box with a black bag pulled over it. The officer asked Beckwith if he had ever been arrested.

"Yes, sir, I was arrested before," Beckwith said. "They say I killed a nigger in Mississippi."

When the bomb squad arrived and opened the box in Beckwith's car, they found six sticks of regular-strength dynamite and a five-pound cartridge of high-grade dynamite. Into the dynamite had been inserted a blasting cap. Connected to the blasting cap were a ticking alarm clock and an Eveready battery.

Beckwith was taken to the parish jail to await arraignment. As he was moved about the facility, reporters spotted him and shouted out questions to him.

"Are you a member of the KKK?" one reporter asked.

"I've been accused of it," he answered.

When Beckwith's case went to trial in January 1974, it was in federal court, and for the first time he faced a jury that contained blacks and women. Beckwith took the stand in his defense and admitted that the .45-caliber automatic belonged to him, but he said that he had a permit for it. When prosecutors asked him about the bomb, he said he had never seen it before and had no idea how it got into his car.

The jury reached a unanimous verdict: not guilty on all counts.

Beckwith was delighted. He told reporters he was thinking about running for political office in Mississippi—maybe he'd try for a seat in Congress.

Not delighted by the verdict was New Orleans's new district attorney, Harry Connick (father of the popular singer of the same name). After the trial Beckwith left New Orleans, but he did not leave the thoughts of Connick, who brought his law partner, Bill Wessel, into the case and asked him to find a way to prosecute Beckwith on state charges. Under Louisiana law, persons accused of certain misdemeanors could be tried by a five-member jury. Beckwith was still accused of illegally transporting dynamite into Louisiana, a misdemeanor.

Finally, in May 1975, Beckwith went on trial in state court on the dynamite charges. This time, to his horror, the jury consisted of five black women. Beckwith was playful throughout the trial, sparring with the prosecutors, but the jury was not impressed with his good-old-boy routine. After deliberating for only thirty-five minutes, the jury returned a guilty verdict.

Beckwith was given the maximum sentence of five years in prison.

After a two-year delay for appeals, he entered the Louisiana state penitentiary in Angola in 1977. He was kept in a solitary cell just off death row so that guards could protect him from the general population, a large percentage of which was black. In 1980, with two years of his sentence taken off for good behavior, Beckwith was released and allowed to return to Mississippi, where he set up housekeeping in a house trailer near Cruger, a rural community not far from Greenwood. He tried to fade into the kudzu-smothered woodland that surrounded his house trailer, but occasionally newspaper reporters would get directions to his home and, much to Beckwith's displeasure, show up on his doorstep unannounced. He always turned them away with a threatening scowl.

One of the last to knock on his door was a young *Jackson Daily News* reporter named Jim Ewing. As a representative of one of the most conservative dailies in the South, Ewing was hopeful that if anyone could get an interview with the reclusive Beckwith, he could. He was wrong. Beckwith politely turned him away, saying he was afraid he would be misquoted by the "Jewish-owned press." Ewing wrote a story anyway, to mark the twentieth anniversary of Medgar Evers's death. The headline was BYRON DE LA BECKWITH LIVES QUIETLY IN THE DELTA.

Shortly after that encounter with Ewing, Beckwith moved to Tennessee and married Thelma Neff, a retired nurse he'd met after his release from prison. She owned a small house on Signal Mountain just outside Chattanooga. When Beckwith moved in, he hung a large Confederate flag out over the porch. It is not surprising that Thelma, who led a rather routine life as a nurse and mother, shared Beckwith's right-wing views on race and politics. Generally speaking, rural Tennessee leans either to the radical right or the radical left, with not much ground left in the middle. Thelma leaned to the radical right.

As the decade wore on, the Beckwiths shared their love of political activism by working together on an assortment of issues, such as campaigning to get fluoride out of the local water supply. Occasionally they returned to Mississippi, where he introduced Thelma to his friends—and at least one of his former enemies, Bill Waller, whom he happened upon at a campaign rally in Blackhawk, a rural community not far from Greenwood. Beckwith flagged down the startled candidate for governor and introduced him to Thelma. They even shook hands.

The Third Trial

The Beckwiths returned to Signal Mountain and finished out the decade, convinced they were making progress in their quest to elevate Beckwith to the historical place of honor they felt he deserved. Unknown to Beckwith, Hinds County district attorney Ed Peters and assistant district attorney Bobby DeLaughter were looking for ways to prosecute him for Evers's murder a third time.

By the early 1990s, the needed pieces had fallen into place. First, Delmar Dennis, a KKK member who had become an FBI informant, confirmed that he had heard Beckwith say that killing Evers "gave me no more inner discomfort than our wives endure when they give birth to our children." Second, Evers's wife, Myrlie, presented the prosecutors with the 963-page transcript of the first trial. The transcript had mysteriously disappeared from the court records, and the lack of a transcript had often been cited by prosecutors over the years as a reason for not reopening the case. As it turned out, Myrlie had a copy in a trunk of keepsakes.

With the transcript and new evidence, Peters and DeLaughter were anxious to ask for an indictment. But DeLaughter still was concerned about whether he had enough evidence to go before the grand jury.[10] His dogged investigation brought out numerous little admissions, such as the one from Peggy Morgan, who heard Beckwith say that he "had killed a nigger, but nobody was ever able to prove it," and from Mary Ann Adams, to whom Beckwith was introduced as "the man who killed Medgar Evers." DeLaughter and his team were able to locate witnesses lost from the 1964 trial, including a young woman, Frances Harrison, who had seen Beckwith in Jackson around the time of the murder.

After going before the circuit judge to authenticate the court record of the first 1964 trial, DeLaughter was now ready to get this case before the grand jury. He reasoned that if the eighteen grand jurors did not think much of the case, why should one believe that twelve people on the trial jury would view it differently. Grand juries are greatly swayed by the prosecutor. Knowing this, DeLaughter made a more balanced presentation: after putting on the prosecution's witnesses, he called the two Greenwood police officers who would provide the alibi for Beckwith. This is something prosecutors normally would never do, but DeLaughter wanted the grand jury to hear these alibi witnesses because if he could not get an indictment with these police officers swearing they saw Beckwith in Greenwood around the time of the murder of Evers, he would never get a conviction at the trial. This gave DeLaughter a reasonable gauge of his chances of a conviction. Another unusual tactic was to ask Special Assistant Attorney General John Henry to be on hand to answer any questions the grand jury panel of ten blacks and eight whites might have concerning the much-publicized speedy trial issue. After the presentation to the grand jury, the prosecutors left the room for the panel to deliberate.

Later, when the panel left the grand jury room, DeLaughter asked the foreman, Dr. Carl Evers, a professor at the University of Mississippi Medical School, about the vote.[11]

"Seventeen to one," answered Evers.

DeLaughter stood stunned. "Yes, sir, but which way?"

Evers smiled and told DeLaughter he had his indictment and "didn't anybody believe those clowns," referring to the two Greenwood police officers who had provided Beckwith with his alibi. There was one holdout who just did not think the case should be re-prosecuted because of the length of time since the last trial. Evers also told DeLaughter it was very helpful to have Henry available because there were numerous questions concerning the time element.

Close to 8:00 P.M. on Friday, December 14, 1990, Evers handed over the sealed indictment to senior circuit court judge William F. Coleman.

A stunned Beckwith, now seventy, said he would fight extradition to Mississippi. Thelma told reporters he was too ill to withstand another trial. As if to reinforce that point, Beckwith entered a Nashville hospital within a week after the indictment and underwent surgery to clear a blocked carotid artery. "He's been a good man all his life—I'm so mad," Thelma told reporters for the *Clarion-Ledger.* "He's been through hell. He's done more good than any fifty people I know. He's a good Christian and everybody loves him."

Not so sure of that was Mississippi governor Ray Mabus, who signed an extradition request within hours of receiving it and sent it by overnight delivery to Tennessee governor Ned McWherter, who approved the request in quick order. Beckwith challenged the extradition, first in state court, then in federal court, and it was not until October 1991 that Beckwith was returned to Mississippi, where he was held in the Hinds County Detention Center without bail.

Bobby DeLaughter had now turned over a log that exposed the dirty, violent, racist Mississippi history of over a quarter century ago.

The legal war had started with heavy explosions. Peters and DeLaughter had their work cut out for them. No quicker had the jailhouse door closed on Beckwith than his new court-appointed lawyers, Jim Kitchens and Merrida Coxwell, sought his release on bail. This request was vigorously opposed by the prosecutor. They used the hearing not only to keep Beckwith in jail but also to preserve the admissibility of some crucial evidence.

DeLaughter piled on the evidence showing Beckwith's criminal record and tying him to white supremacy groups, and he displayed a multitude of letters from Angola Prison that implicated Beckwith as Evers's murderer. The defense called Beckwith's son, Byron De La Beckwith VII, who testified as to Beckwith's ill health, that his father would not flee, and that he was not a threat to the state. Beckwith VII's testimony was torn apart by the skillful cross-examination of Peters. His young son, Byron De La Beckwith VIII, later appeared at the trial, running around the courtroom, pointing to spectators and asking if they were "a Jew."

Judge Breland Hilburn denied bail, "at least for a while." Beckwith's lawyer asked for reconsideration, filing affidavits by Travis "Cannonball" Buckley, the notorious Klan lawyer who had defended Imperial Wizard Sam Bowers and his successor, L. E. Matthews. After the motion was denied, Beckwith sought relief in the Mississippi Supreme Court, which also refused to release Beckwith.

In Mississippi all criminal trials are conducted in the county where the crime arose. The prosecution cannot ask for a change of venue, but the defendant may make such a request under the proper circumstances. Here, the defense did, arguing that pretrial publicity would deny Beckwith a fair trial. After endless squabbling Judge Hilburn finally ordered that the jury be picked from Panola County, since it had a racial composition equivalent to that of Jackson, and the jury selected would be brought back to Jackson for the trial.

The defense team then filed its blockbuster, its motion to dismiss, claiming that Beckwith had been deprived of his rights to a speedy trial and that his rights against double jeopardy were violated. It was now late summer of 1992, nearly thirty years since this tragic murder.

This was a serious threat, and the prosecutors took it seriously. Although the prosecutors had prevailed in the lower court, Beckwith's lawyers succeeded in getting an emergency appeal to the Mississippi Supreme Court.

The Mississippi Supreme Court did not seem especially enamored of the prosecutor's position but finally rejected Beckwith's double-jeopardy claim outright and, by an eyelash (four to three), decided not to rule on the speedy-trial issue until after the trial.[12] Peters and DeLaughter had dodged a legal bullet that would have ended the case. The court thought bail was proper, and Beckwith was released on a $100,000 bail bond. The three dissenting justices believed that the decision allowing the court to go forward was an "egregious miscarriage of justice." Chief Justice Roy Noble Lee, who had been on the bench since 1976, wrote for the dissenting justices:

> In my view, the majority opinion does violence to the United States Constitution, the Mississippi Constitution and established law and precedent of the United States and the State of Mississippi. I believe it to be erroneous and the worst pronouncement of the law during my tenure on the Mississippi Supreme Court bench, and that it is an egregious miscarriage of justice. Therefore, I emphatically dissent![13]

But the case would go forward with the speedy-trial issue left unresolved—which DeLaughter knew in the back of his mind could come back to haunt him later, even if they got a conviction.

In January 1994 the court staff, Judge Hilburn, Peters, and DeLaughter headed up to Panola County for the jury selection. Panola County is a rural county situated in the northwestern quadrant of the state. Batesville is the principal town. It has a black-majority population of 52 percent. Once again, selecting a jury for this trial was no easy task. Ed Peters, as Hinds County district attorney, had been particularly successful in selecting juries over the years. Surprisingly, an outstanding jury consultant, Dr. Pete Rowland, from the University of Kansas, along with another skilled consultant, Dr. Andrew Sheldon from Atlanta, volunteered to assist. Peters and DeLaughter had never had the luxury of using jury consultants, but the presence of Dr. Rowland and his staff was extremely helpful. Rowland pushed out into the community and discovered attitudes and leanings that would be important to the prosecutors in framing their questions to the prospective jurors. Beckwith, of course, was present, wearing one of his brightly colored sport jackets and the ever-present Confederate-flag lapel pin.

The exclusion process began with the judge asking standard questions, such as whether it would be a hardship to serve.[14] Although the process is dead serious in most cases, some humor cannot be ignored. Several prospective jurors were excused, one because he had "to attend to some cows for a man." Going into the medical excuses, one colloquy went like this:

"I got an ill-deformed baby at home."

"You have a baby with a deformity?"

"Yes, he plays with fires, so I have to watch him."

"Does the child have mental problems?"

"Well, out of one ear."

The panel was finally winnowed down to forty-six jurors, with each party allowed twelve peremptory challenges. With Pete Rowland at their side, Peters and DeLaughter toyed with one combination after another, and it looked as if at least half the jury would be black. The jury and the entire court staff then traveled back to Jackson for the trial to begin. On Thursday, January 27, 1994, DeLaughter began his opening statement to the jury. He opened with a compelling outline of his case: "[This case is] about a man whose life was snuffed out on June the twelfth of 1963, by a bullet that tore through his body. Medgar Evers was shot and killed. He lost his life by a bullet that was aimed out of prejudice, propelled by hatred, and fired by a coward from ambush at night."

After the opening statements by both sides, the prosecution called Myrlie Evers as its first witness. She was eloquent and absolutely credible. Her heartrending testimony concerning the death of her beloved husband suffused the entire courtroom with the soft light of dignity, but at the same time outrage. DeLaughter then began shoveling in his evidence, much as it was presented in 1964: the policemen arriving, the ride to the hospital, the Jackson detectives and their investigation, Beckwith's rifle in the honeysuckle, his fingerprints, the witnesses at the drive-in and grocery store, and the witness who saw Beckwith's Plymouth Valiant.

The evidence clearly pointed to Beckwith's guilt, but it was his numerous outlandish admissions that sealed his fate. Any number of witnesses provided testimony and documentary evidence concerning the racial views of Byron De La Beckwith and his comments regarding the murder. Beckwith's nephew, Reed Massengill, who had corresponded with Beckwith over a period of time, produced a number of Beckwith's startling written admissions, including this revealing statement: "The Negro in our country is as helpful as a boll weevil to cotton. Some of these weevils are puny little runts and can't create the volume of damage that others can. Some are powerful, becoming mad monsters. . . . They must be destroyed, with their retched [sic] remains burned, lest the pure white cotton bolls be destroyed."[15]

Massengill produced a letter from Beckwith to his son that was written on the day President Kennedy was shot, telling him that "whoever shot Kennedy sure did some fancy footwork," and that "I bet ole Medgar Evers told Kennedy when he got down there—I thought you'd be along pretty soon—Haw. Haw. Haw." Mary Ann Adams testified that in 1966, while she was working for the Holmes County Co-Op in Lexington, Mississippi, she was dining at a restaurant near Greenwood when Beckwith walked over to her table with another man and introduced himself, sticking out his hand for a handshake. She told him that he was a murderer and she wasn't interested in shaking his hand. "He got extremely agitated and angry," she recalled. "[He] said he had not killed a man, but a damn chicken-stealing dog, and you know what you have to do with a dog . . . after it's tasted blood"[16]

Adams was then asked if "at any time that you were introduced to this defendant as the man that killed Medgar Evers, what, if any, protest did he make?" She responded, "He made none. He just got angry when I refused to shake his hand."

Peggy Morgan from Greenwood, Mississippi, testified that she had once traveled to the Mississippi State Penitentiary at Parchman,

Mississippi, with Beckwith and her husband to visit her husband's brother, Jimmy Dale Morgan. According to Morgan, Beckwith "started talking about some bombings." She gave the following testimony regarding her conversation with Beckwith:

Q. Tell what he said in reference to the murder or killing of Medgar Evers.

A. Okay. He said that he had killed Medgar Evers, a nigger, and he said if this ever got out, that he wasn't scared to kill again.

Q. Okay. If what ever got out?

A. This trip to the penitentiary.

Q. And if it got out that what? I didn't hear what you said. That if this got out—

A. He wasn't scared to kill again.

Elluard Jenoal (Dick) Davis testified for the state. Davis became involved with the Ku Klux Klan in the 1960s as an infiltrator working for the FBI. On October 21, 1969, he met with Beckwith at a restaurant in Winter Haven, Florida. Davis stated that Beckwith discussed his arrest and imprisonment and also his prior trials. According to Davis, Beckwith never admitted that he was guilty but also never denied it. Davis stated that Beckwith discussed "the term I think he used was 'selective killings' that he thought was necessary . . . a partial solution to the right wing's problem. And I remember very distinctly that he said that he would never ask anyone to do anything that he hadn't already done himself."

Delmar Dennis, from Sevierville, Tennessee, a "small publisher," testified that he was a former pastor of the First Southern Methodist Church of Meridian, Mississippi, and spent seven years as a coordinator for the John Birch Society. He joined the Ku Klux Klan in March 1964 and was a member until June 1964, when he dropped out. Dennis stated that he got out of the Klan when he learned it was a violent organization after attending a Klan meeting in Neshoba County in June 1964. Several months later he infiltrated the Klan for the FBI, where he remained undercover until October 1967.

Dennis stated that the first time he met Beckwith was on August 8, 1965, where he saw Beckwith at a Klan meeting in Byram, Mississippi. Beckwith was the featured speaker, and Dennis remembered that "he was admonishing Klan members to become more involved, to become violent, to kill the enemy. . . . He admonished us to kill from the top down, and he said, 'Killing that nigger didn't cause me any more physical harm than your wives have to have a baby for you.'" Dennis obtained Beckwith's autograph, which was introduced as evidence. Dennis also remembered meeting with Beckwith in 1967 when Beckwith was campaigning for lieutenant governor and promoting a newspaper titled *Southern Review*.

Mark Reiley from Chicago, Illinois, testified that he was a former sergeant at Louisiana State Penitentiary at Angola and that he handled security for Angola inmates who were sent to the Angola ward at Earl K. Long Hospital. He was assigned to guard Beckwith in the hospital. At that time Beckwith was serving a sentence, later vacated, for conviction of illegally transporting explosives in Louisiana. Reiley developed a strong personal relationship with Beckwith, who became a father figure to him. Reiley spent from eight to twelve hours per day for several weeks with Beckwith, who instructed him in the Bible and gave him a book titled *Verbatim*. Beckwith told Reiley that black people were "beasts of the field." He stated, according to Reiley, that white people were "chosen people to rule over the earth and be in charge of the beasts of the field."

Reiley said that he was present when Beckwith rang for a nurse. The nurse appeared, and she happened to be black, and Beckwith began screaming at her.

Q. Do you recall the essence of the conversation and some of the exact words?

A. He was screaming back at her, "If I could get rid of an uppity nigger like Nigger Evers, I would have no problem with a no-account nigger like you."

These admissions and confessions from the very pen and mouth of Beckwith, coming from a wide variety of witnesses in all walks of life, spoke to Beckwith's guilt with shocking clarity. After putting more than thirty witnesses on the stand, the state rested its case. Then the defense began calling its witnesses. The defense relied primarily on the three alibi witnesses who testified that they had seen Beckwith in Greenwood at around the time Evers was murdered. For Roy Jones, a volunteer with the auxiliary police in Greenwood who by now was deceased, his 1964 testimony was read into the record. The same was done for the testimony of Greenwood police lieutenant Hollis Cresswell, who, according to the defense lawyer, was too ill to testify. That left the third alibi witness, James Holley, a Greenwood police officer with a potbelly and a crew cut, to take the witness stand. The courtroom grew ominously quiet as he sauntered up to the witness chair and specifically testified that he had seen Beckwith in Greenwood at about the time of Evers's murder.

Ed Peters had the honor of cross-examining Holley, and he did not disappoint.[17] After rattling Holley on numerous points, including forcing him to admit that although he had seen the Jackson police officers in Greenwood investigating the murder, he had not told them he had seen Beckwith in Greenwood at the time of the murder, even though Beckwith was languishing in jail. Peters asked incredulously, "Why didn't you tell them your buddy Beckwith was in Greenwood and couldn't have committed this dastardly crime?"

Peters continued, What about the DA's office? Did you talk to them? What about the FBI? You didn't tell them when you knew Beckwith could not be responsible? Did you know your buddy Delay was in jail eight months? Ten months? And you never told anyone?

"And you let your buddy Delay stay in jail all that time," Peters asked, "and never once told a single person investigating it, 'You've got the wrong guy in jail'?"

"I did not," answered Holley.

After cross-examining him on a number of other points, Peters confirmed with Holley that they were still friends. Walking away from Holley, along the front of the jury box, Peters suddenly asked, "If I ever get in jail, will you promise not to leave me in there for eight months if you knew where I was at the time of the crime?"[18]

No one heard the answer. The courtroom erupted in laughter while Peters left the witness and took his seat quietly at the counsel table.

The trial ended as it had started, with a brilliant summation by DeLaughter. He concluded with these words:

> From the evidence in this case, the law that you've sworn to apply, it can't be but one way if justice is truly going to be done. And so, on behalf of the State of Mississippi, I ask that you hold this defendant accountable. Find him guilty, simply because it's right, it's just, and Lord knows, it's just time. He has danced to the music for thirty years. Isn't it time that he pay the piper?

> Is it ever too late to do the right thing? For the sake of justice and the hope of us as a civilized society, I sincerely hope and pray that it's not.

The jury began deliberating at 1:30 P.M. on February 4, 1994, and after five hours had not reached a verdict. Jury members retired to their motel for the night to resume deliberations early the next morning, and at 9:35 A.M. they signaled that they had reached a verdict.

DeLaughter later wrote that for a few minutes everything stopped, "My heart, my breath and time itself." Peters asked the court if it would wait a few minutes until Mrs. Evers could get to the courtroom. She quickly arrived with her family.

"All rise," the bailiff thundered.

Judge Hilburn took his place on the bench and warned: "Ladies and Gentlemen, when the verdict is read, there will be no demonstrations or any type of emotional outburst. Bring the jury in."

One by one the members of the jury filed in and stood in a single line before the bench, facing the judge.

"Ladies and Gentlemen of the jury, have you reached a verdict?"

"We have, Your Honor," the black minister spoke, which meant he had been selected foreman by the other jurors.

"The clerk will read the verdict."

How could it take such a terribly long time to hand the yellow piece of paper to the clerk, Barbara Dunn? DeLaughter closed his eyes and felt that "all the world was holding its breath."

Dunn slowly read, "We, the jury, find the defendant guilty, as charged."

There were muffled sounds in the courtroom and then shouts.

"Yes! Sweet Jesus, thank you!"

"Guilty, guilty, guilty!"

Judge Hilburn, with a stern look, quieted the storm and discharged the jury. As they walked out of the courtroom, Thelma Beckwith wailed, "He's not guilty! And ya'll know he's not. The Jews did it."

The court asked Beckwith to come forward, and he did so without his customary smirk and cockiness. "Mr. Beckwith, by mandate of the laws of the State of Mississippi, it is required that I sentence you to a term of life imprisonment."

Thelma sat quietly, watching as the guards led her husband from the courtroom. She wiped away her tears. "He's not guilty and they know it," she sobbed. "He's sick and everything."

Beckwith's attorneys appealed the conviction, but the courts refused to allow him out on bail. Thelma blamed the Anti-Defamation League for her husband's woes, saying the group had framed him in the Louisiana bomb conviction.

Edwin King, who was listed as a witness for the defense but never called, said that although he thought Beckwith was a "despicable sicko" and was guilty of murdering his friend Medgar Evers, he did not believe Beckwith got a fair trial, because of grand jury testimony that he considered incorrect.[19]

The trial was indeed over, but those pesky constitutional issues still hung over the prosecution. An appeal was immediately taken to the Mississippi Supreme Court, the same court that had expressed concerns about constitutional issues, even when it had allowed the case to go forward. Finally, on December 22, 1997, the Mississippi Supreme Court overruled all constitutional objections and affirmed the verdict of the trial jury.

While serving a life term at a Jackson facility, Beckwith was taken on January 21, 2001, to the University of Mississippi Medical Center, where he died at the age of eighty. Five days later he was given a hero's burial by family, friends, and supporters, in Chattanooga, Tennessee, under the supervision of the imperial wizard of the KKK.

Alex A. Alston Jr.:

The Mississippi Appellate Court was created in 1964, and, as president of the Mississippi bar right before its creation, I had worked tirelessly to see to its legislative approval. The court was greatly needed. Before that any appeal went directly to the Mississippi Supreme Court, which was overwhelmed and needed a buffer so it could be more selective in the cases it handled and also more carefully consider each case before it. Like the supreme court, the appellate court is made up of elected judges.

A short time after the jury verdict convicting Beckwith, Bobby DeLaughter stopped by my office for a cup of coffee and a chat. He informed me that he was running for one of the newly established appellate judgeships that contained a district including Hinds County and fourteen surrounding counties. He felt confident that since he was not running against an incumbent, his years of courtroom experience would make him an attractive candidate.

DeLaughter asked if I would serve as his campaign chairman. I was delighted. We went right to work and formed strong contacts in each of the fourteen counties. Our solicitation in this district looked very promising.

Myrlie Evers flew in at her own expense to help DeLaughter campaign in the black districts on the weekend before the election. Author Willie Morris accompanied them as Evers introduced DeLaughter to African American churches, organizations, and radio audiences as a courageous man who had prosecuted her husband's killer.

We were excited and could smell victory from the reports we were receiving from out in the district. His opponent was a conservative, old-line white lawyer-politician whom I thought would not be nearly as attractive as DeLaughter in the campaign

My enthusiasm should have abated somewhat when I heard rumors of campaign literature being thrown back in DeLaughter's face when the voter realized that he was the prosecutor of Byron De La Beckwith, but I also had seen him receive warm congratulatory handshakes, and my calls were well received throughout the district, so I didn't think too much about it.

On the night of the election, friends and family joined DeLaughter and his wife, Peggy, in a motel room to watch the returns. It took only a short time to discover that DeLaughter had been trounced. He lost two to one, and he took it hard. We all took it hard. My heart went out to him and Peggy because I knew how hard they had worked and how much he wanted this judgeship.

After that gloomy night I began poking around in the district to see what had happened. It soon became crystal clear. It was Bobby DeLaughter, after all, who had prosecuted Beckwith for the murder of Medgar Evers. That was enough. Many still resented the fact that he had looked back thirty years to see that racial justice was done. I had no idea that that sentiment was so pervasive in 1994. The flames of racism die hard.

16

Philadelphia Redux: Edgar Ray Killen Raised from the Dead

By 1976 most of the men convicted in the Neshoba County murders of the three civil rights workers were out of prison. Many returned to their hometowns, where they were greeted with backslaps and thoughtful gifts from grateful white residents and fellow Klansmen. Some were hailed as conquering heroes. Others drifted into a type of rancid anonymity.

Sheriff Lawrence Rainey—who was acquitted in the case of Schwerner, Goodman, and Chaney—was welcomed back home after the trial by many people in Philadelphia, but he was unable to hold a job in law enforcement, though he did work for a time as a security guard at a shopping mall. For the remainder of his life, he complained that the FBI prevented him from getting on his feet again. He blamed others for the bad things that happened to him, never accepting responsibility for his actions. He died of throat cancer on November 8, 2002, at the age of seventy-nine.

After serving six years in prison, Cecil Price, the deputy sheriff involved in the case, started driving a truck for an oil company. Unlike many of the others, he seemed to mellow somewhat as the years went by. He once told a reporter that he'd watched the black history television drama *Roots*, a confession that seemed tinged with remorse. He died on May 6, 2001, at a Jackson hospital, three days after a fall in Philadelphia that authorities ruled accidental.

At the time of Price's death, Mississippi attorney general Mike Moore was considering bringing murder charges against some of those involved in the Philadelphia murders, with Price considered a possible witness for the prosecution. Moore is best known for filing a very successful lawsuit against tobacco companies in the 1990s, claiming that they should reimburse the state of Mississippi for having to treat those with smoking-related illnesses. The result was a landmark $246 billion settlement with Mississippi and the other states that joined in the lawsuit. Moore appeared as himself in the 1999 Michael Mann film *The Insider,* which depicted some of the more dramatic aspects of the case.

With Moore distracted by the tobacco lawsuit, the suspects in the Philadelphia murders seemed to drop off the attorney general's radar. Former Klan leader Sam Bowers had returned to his hometown of Laurel, Mississippi, in 1976 after serving six years in prison, and resumed his job with an amusement company. In a 1996 interview with the *Oxford American*, Bowers, then seventy-two, didn't discuss the Neshoba County case, but he did offer his perspective on Christianity: "I'm a Pauline, Galilean, Calvinist, Reformed Lutheran Christian. I believe that the empirical resurrection of Jesus Christ is the one single and central fact of manifested history." It is almost beyond comprehension that a Jew-hating Klansman could twist the teachings of Jesus Christ, the most famous Jew of them all, into a justification for violence against black and Jewish Americans; but that illogic was at the essence of Bowers's interpretation of Mississippi Values.

Shortly after sharing his views about Christianity, Bowers was convicted of the 1966 bombing death of civil rights leader Vernon Dahmer, for which he received a life sentence. While in prison, he did an interview with the Mississippi Department of Archives and History with the understanding that it would not be made available to the public until after his death. In 2004 a Jackson newspaper published portions of the interview, in which Bowers, with customary bravado, said he was delighted to be convicted in the Philadelphia case, since it had allowed the main instigator (Edgar Ray Killen) to go free. Bowers died on November 5, 2006, of a heart attack at Mississippi State Penitentiary Hospital.

Of the major figures in the Philadelphia murders still on the scene in 2005, only Klansmen Billy Wayne Posey, age sixty-nine, and Edgar Ray Killen, age eighty, were still alive. In the mid-1970s, Killen was charged with making death threats against a Newton County private detective who had followed him and a married woman with whom he was having an affair to a motel. The threats were made to the detective's wife, who secretly recorded her conversation with Killen. During the telephone call Killen was recorded as saying, "You tell him that he is exactly right, that he is dead. Tell him that's the first thing I would like for him to do if you get to see him again is prepare to meet his maker."[1] The district attorney who prosecuted him, Marcus Gordon, obtained a conviction, and Killen spent four months in jail for the crime.

As early as 2000, Posey had implicated Killen in the Philadelphia murders but only after receiving a guarantee from prosecutors that they would not use his statements against him if Posey were ever charged with crimes related to the murders. Posey was officially immune to prosecution.

In 2005, a little more than a year after taking office, Mississippi attorney general Jim Hood asked the FBI for help in building a case against Killen. Former FBI agent Jim Ingram was called back into service to help Neshoba County authorities with the investigation. Posey was taken before a Neshoba County grand jury to testify about his knowledge of Killen's involvement in the murders of Schwerner, Goodman, and Chaney. After testifying behind closed doors, Posey was besieged by reporters in the hallway and complained that he thought it was ridiculous for the murders to be reinvestigated after so many years. Thanks, in part, to Posey's reluctant testimony, Killen was indicted for orchestrating the murders of the civil rights workers.

Technically speaking, Hood's success at obtaining an indictment was due to the dogged persistence of his staffers, who discovered a felony manslaughter statute that could be applied to the case. At a deeper level it was due to Hood's upbringing as a prosecutor's son in the red-clay hills of northern Mississippi. He was the first Mississippi attorney general to be educated in an integrated school system, and he carried none of the racist baggage that allowed killers such as Edgar Ray Killen to have immunity.

"Once I got into office, I kept getting asked, 'What are you going to do about that case?'" explained Hood. "Once I met with some of the victims' family members, I realized that these people had never had their day in court. I looked at the facts of the case more closely, and when I realized that it met my threshold for presentation to a grand jury, I let them decide up or down."

Preacher Killen Goes to Court

Killen lived in a ramshackle house surrounded by broken-down cars and trucks on about twenty acres of worn-out land immediately north of Union, a hamlet of about two thousand people, located mostly in Newton County. His little universe was just barely in Neshoba County, in about the center of the southern border. All of this is part of the Mississippi sand-clay hill region, with its soil a mixture of reddish sand and clay that is very susceptible to erosion.

Killen, known as "Preacher" to his neighbors, was physically strong, and his friends said he could do the work of two men. He operated a sawmill and moonlighted as a jackleg preacher in Baptist churches in a hardscrabble area of the state. He officiated at weddings and buried the dead with an unusual wit and gift of gab. One neighbor remarked that when he saw Killen walking up, he knew he would have to miss the long-promised fishing trip with his grandson because sometimes Killen's stories rambled on interminably.

Killen roamed free in Neshoba and Newton counties, with everybody knowing full well he had orchestrated the 1964 murders of the three civil rights workers. In the 1967 federal trial for violation of the civil rights of Chaney, Goodman, and Schwerner, the jury voted eleven to one for Killen's conviction, the lone holdout steadfast in her belief that she just could not convict a preacher. Killen walked freely through the shopping malls and barber shops and mingled with the crowds, sometimes causing all voices to fall silent on his approach.

The massive investigation and the civil rights trial did not deter Preacher Killen from railing against integration and preaching in his county churches that white dominance was the way of the Lord and any opposition must be crushed. When the FBI investigators were questioning him about the murder of Martin Luther King Jr., Killen inquired, "Who did it?" When the FBI asked why he wanted to know, Killen exclaimed, "I want to shake his hand." The two people he most admired were the late governor Ross Barnett and the late senator James O. Eastland, the two who most exemplify the Mississippi resistance to civil rights. Killen kept a big picture of Barnett hanging on his wall and praised Big Jim Eastland for bottling up civil rights legislation for decades. As Howard Ball tells us in *Justice in Mississippi*, Preacher Killen lived in his own corner of Mississippi amid a "culture of impunity." It had now been forty years. When they tried to get him on a civil rights violation in connection with the murders, he'd walked free. Why should he worry now?

In early January 2005, Killen was shocked when a Mississippi grand jury indicted him for orchestrating the 1964 slayings of the three civil rights workers. On January 7, 2005, he pleaded not guilty to the three counts of murder. He now faced the first-ever state charges in these three forty-year-old murders.

The tension in Philadelphia was electrifying, with television and radio networks and print media from around the world pouring into the city. Most locals showed resentment, considering all of these theatrics to be an invasion. On June 13, 2005, Killen returned to the Neshoba County Courthouse in Philadelphia to face his trial. Some of the Klan had gathered. J. J. Harper of Cordele, Georgia, the imperial wizard of the American White Knights of the Ku Klux Klan, was there to greet him, to eagerly shake Killen's hand and to show support for his Christian brother.

Looking a bit like a crazed creature from the dark forest, Killen was pushed into the courthouse in his wheelchair by a deputy, surrounded by a gauntlet of question-shouting reporters. He lashed out at them with sinister clawlike hands that flailed in the sunshine, resembling a mole that'd been dragged from a black hole into the light of day. There was a wild look in his eyes, an expression of rage on his face. Not until he was pushed into the air-conditioned cocoon of the courthouse did he relax, wrapping himself in a cloak of redneck hubris.

As with all criminal trials, the trial started with the selection of the jury. This took a couple of days, June 13 and 14. The judge was Marcus Gordon, a no-nonsense jurist who had grown up in the same small town as Killen and as a district attorney in the mid-1970s had prosecuted Killen for making threats against a private detective. Judge Gordon conducted the trial with fairness and efficiency. He began dismissing jurors, some for not being able to read and write, about twelve for being over age sixty-five, several for being related to Killen, and others for being close friends of Killen's. This was a close-knit community. Almost everybody knew everybody else. As a matter of fact, Preacher Killen had conducted the funeral services for both of Judge Gordon's parents some few years earlier.

The panel selected to hear the case consisted of twelve jurors and five alternates. There were nine white women, four white men, two black women, and two black men—four teachers, two nurses, a librarian, an engineer, a social worker, a homemaker, a few chicken farmers, and laborers of one kind or another. Atlanta jury consultant Andrew Sheldon, who had assisted the prosecutors in the Beckwith trial eleven years earlier, worked with the prosecution.

The prosecutors—Mark Duncan, a newly elected district attorney who was only a toddler when the crimes were committed, and Attorney General Hood, who was not even born when the crimes took place—spent only two days presenting their case. Their efforts were severely restricted by the deaths of many of those who'd participated in the murders and the failure of any of the living Ku Klux Klan members who had a hand in the crimes to come forward and testify. Hood fervently hoped they would do so and even subpoenaed five for trial, but the Klansmen simply would not testify. That left the prosecutors with only the transcript of the 1967 federal conspiracy trial to establish much of the required proof. Jerry Mitchell wrote presciently in the *Clarion-Ledger* that the prosecutors' case would hinge on their ability to "make the dead come to life," and that was indeed what happened.

Although limited to only fifteen minutes for the opening statement, the prosecution came to life when Hood suggested that some of the witnesses would be "speaking from the grave."[2] He told the jury that Killen was a Kleagle, a Klan officer who organized and recruited Klan members. He said that the plans of the Klan were to eliminate Michael Schwerner, and that the Klan burned down the Mount Zion Methodist Church to lure Schwerner back so that they could kill him. Chaney, Goodman, and Schwerner were stopped by Cecil Ray Price and placed in jail so the Klan could be gathered to commit the murders. According to Hood, Killen even went so far as to order the men to obtain plastic gloves for the elimination.[3] When released from jail, the three civil rights workers were chased down and killed on the spot, and their bodies were disposed of fifteen feet under a dam being constructed not far from Philadelphia. Looking at Killen seated in the courtroom, Hood said that not only had Killen planned the murders, but he also told people afterward where the bodies were hidden. He concluded, "You will find the defendant guilty of the three counts of murder."[4]

Killen was represented by Mitch Moran, who at forty-three had no remembrance of the horrors inflicted on blacks during the civil rights era, and James McIntyre, seventy-three, a Jackson attorney who had been in the trenches defending criminal cases all his life. After Hood spoke for the prosecution, Moran surprised the courtroom by admitting that Killen was a member of the Klan and that he recruited

Klan members to kick the three civil rights workers' "butts out of Neshoba County." But Moran emphasized that that does not make Killen guilty of murder. It is not against the law to be a member of the Klan, he argued, and it's certainly not murder to tell someone to kick the butt of another.[5]

The prosecution's case consisted of fourteen witnesses, six of these "from the grave," meaning that their testimony was read from the 1967 transcript because they were deceased at the time of this trial. The prosecution's first witness was the articulate and intelligent wife of Michael Schwerner, Rita Schwerner Bender, who since the 1964 murders had remarried. Her heartrending testimony made a strong opening for the prosecution.[6] The prosecution then piled on the evidence through the testimony of witnesses who outlined the details of the murders.

Hood and Duncan did the best they could with the reading of this testimony. Good trial lawyers know such testimony is terribly dry, and they make great efforts to avoid it. In this case, however, the transcript testimony was essential to place the civil rights workers at the Mount Zion Methodist Church on June 21, 1964, and to prove the admissions of Killen, the burned car of the civil rights workers, and, in general, the details of this tragic event. The eighth to testify was the mother of the murdered Andrew Goodman, who at ninety read the last message she received from her son on a postcard, presumably sent to allay some of her fears:

Dear Mom and Dad,

I have arrived safely in Meridian, Mississippi. This is a wonderful town and the weather is fine. I wish you were here. The people in this city are wonderful and our reception was very good.

All my love,
Andy[7]

The prosecution established that in January 1964, Schwerner and his wife, Rita, traveled from their home in New York to Mississippi to work in the civil rights movement. When the Schwerners arrived in

Meridian, they befriended Chaney, and together they set out to establish a community center to provide African American teens a safe place to meet and visit, and also to provide children access to books. The Schwerners lived in a number of places in Meridian as guests of African American families but had to leave when the families received threats. After this process was repeated several times, they moved into an upstairs apartment with no running water. Each day they went to Young's Hotel to shower but were forced to sneak in the back door because the hotel was owned by an African American who was afraid of what would happen to him if word got out that he was allowing whites to use facilities designated for blacks.

The Schwerners were increasingly subjected to threats.[8] Rita received calls telling her she had better "watch out" or her husband would be killed, and sometimes the caller would tell her that her husband had already been killed. In spite of the threats, the Schwerners continued their work.

Killen, who was the recruiter for both the Neshoba County and Lauderdale County Klan organizations, called Klaverns, recruited Delmar Dennis, the Methodist pastor in Meridian who would later testify in the Beckwith case. Killen explained to Dennis that "there would be things the Klan would need to do, and among those would be the burning [of] crosses, people would need to be beaten, and occasionally there would have to be elimination," which Dennis testified meant killing a person.[9] Schwerner, referred to by the Klan simply as "Goatee," became the subject of discussions at Klan meetings.[10] According to Dennis, Killen stated that the elimination "had already been approved by the state officers of the Klan and had been made a part of their program, and it would be taken care of."

Around Memorial Day 1964, Schwerner and Chaney met with the members of Mount Zion Methodist Church in Neshoba County to seek permission to use the church facilities that summer for a school similar to the community center in Meridian. They also wanted to use the facilities as a place to train volunteers to help African Americans register to vote. Subsequently, Schwerner and Chaney joined Goodman in Ohio.

On June 18 the Schwerners, Chaney, and Goodman received word in Ohio that the church had burned. They decided that Rita would remain in Ohio while Schwerner, Chaney, and Goodman returned to Mississippi to meet with the church members. On Saturday, June 20, Schwerner kissed Rita good-bye and left for Mississippi with Chaney and Goodman in a blue station wagon. It was the last time Rita saw her husband alive. That evening Schwerner called Rita to tell her they had arrived in Meridian and were planning to go to Philadelphia the next day. After the three men were stopped on the way to Philadelphia and placed in the Neshoba County jail, Killen immediately rounded up a gaggle of Klansmen to perform the "elimination."

At about 10:30 P.M., the three men were released. They were followed by the Klansmen on Highway 19 toward Meridian. Deputy Price caught up with them and pulled them over to the side of the road. They were ordered into the backseat of the patrol car and driven back toward Philadelphia. The patrol car turned left onto a graded clay road, where the three were shot and mutilated. Their bodies were then taken to the site of a dam construction, where Klansmen stood guard over the bodies until a bulldozer operator arrived to bury them under the dam.[11]

Killen admitted his guilt on at least two occasions. The day after the killings, he went to Klansman Joseph M. Hatcher for the purpose of delivering a gun. During the transaction Killen readily admitted, "We got rid of those civil rights workers, and you won't have no more trouble out of Goatee."[12] In 1967 young Mike Winstead went to church at Pine Grove Baptist Church. Killen came to church that day, and although Mike was only ten years old at the time, he remembered vividly a conversation Killen had with Mike's grandfather later that day. Mike recalled his grandfather asking Killen if he had had anything to do with the killing of those three civil rights workers, and Killen had responded, yes, and he was proud of it.[13]

Some of the most exciting testimony from the grave came from Delmar Dennis, a Klan informant who explained how the "elimination" was carried out. The belated testimony was a reminder, as William Faulkner once pointed out, that "a mule will labor ten years willingly and patiently for you, for the privilege of kicking you once." Dennis's testimony, even when read in a monotone in open court, whacked Killen where it hurt the most—in juror believability.

Prosecutors always attempt to end with a strong witness and, if possible, one who will tap into the emotions of the jurors. Duncan and Hood did just that with the heartfelt testimony of the mother of the murdered James Chaney, Fannie Lee Chaney, eighty-two at the time of the trial.[14] She testified about James leaving to install a children's library and never coming back and tearfully testified about the treatment she received after James was reported missing. She was threatened, her home was shot at and splattered with eggs thrown by passing cars, and she was unable to find a job of any kind and finally was forced to move her family to New York. With her testimony the prosecution rested.

The defense went to work by placing on the stand Killen's brother and sister, who swore that Killen was with them for a Father's Day party on the day of the event, that he stayed there until 4:00 or 5:00 P.M., and that after that he was at the funeral home to officiate at two wakes.[15] On cross-examination of Killen's brother, District Attorney Duncan asked if he knew that his brother (Edgar Ray Killen) was a member of the Klan. Killen's brother, to the chagrin of Duncan, quickly answered that he didn't know, "but I've heard talk that your daddy and granddaddy was in the Klan more than I have him."[16] Duncan stared at Killen's brother and continued his cross-examination. Not only does everybody in Neshoba County know everybody else, but they even know the foibles of each other's ancestors.

Attorney General Hood began the closing argument for the prosecution with these words: "Evil flourishes when good people sit idly by and do nothing." He pleaded with the jury to do its duty and emphasized that it is never too late to do what is right. He personalized the civil rights workers by emphasizing that they came to Mississippi to do God's work and to help their fellow man. He pleaded that the jury not just let God deal with Killen—because doing so would be "shirking your duty"—and he reminded them that it was Killen who orchestrated the crime and then hid in the funeral home "like a coward."[17]

All during the trial Hood pondered why Killen would commit such a crime.[18] In his own mind he tried to dissect his character and emotional makeup, trying to understand the man. He used logic in an attempt to understand but finally realized that if the crime had been logical, Killen wouldn't have done it. Killen was a preacher, wasn't he? It really bothered Hood that he could commit such a despicable act. He'd buried the judge's parents. Surely, he had some redeeming qualities. Hood could tell by looking at the jury that they were just as puzzled as he was about Killen.

Toward the end of his closing argument, he walked over to Killen and pointed directly at his face. Recalls Hood: "I'd already showed the jury a picture of him as a young man, trying to bring it back to them. I said, 'There evil sits. It's seething behind those glasses.'"

Suddenly, Killen blurted out, "Shut up, you son of a bitch!"[19]

Killen's lawyer swatted at his hand, trying to silence him, but it was too late. He'd shown his true character, and at the worst possible moment. Hood recalls "standing there with my mouth open. The jury's sitting there hearing this stuff." It was then that he realized "there are forces of good and evil in the world—and evil was seething behind those glasses." Hood adds, "I hope one day, before he passes away, that he reads what he's preached all those years."

After Killen's outburst James McIntyre stormed back with his closing argument in Killen's defense. He stressed the state's burden to prove its case beyond a reasonable doubt and explained how the state had failed to meet this burden by calling witnesses who had admittedly lied in the 1967 trial and who were paid FBI informants. He emphasized that the jury must look to justice and fair play and implored the jurors to find his client not guilty.

After the final closing by Duncan for the state, the judge dismissed the five alternate jurors, and the remaining twelve began their deliberation at about 3:30 P.M. on June 20. Two hours later the jury reported back to Judge Gordon that they were divided six to six and could not reach a verdict at that time. Rumors were rampant that the jury was deadlocked and the case would end with a mistrial. Judge Gordon called a recess until the following day.

The next morning the jury began their deliberations again at 11:18 A.M., and in less than three hours the jurors announced they had arrived at a unanimous verdict. The jury marched in and made a semicircle around the judge's bench, and the foreman handed the verdict to Judge Gordon. The courtroom was completely silent as the judge deliberately perused the verdict form and then handed it to the clerk, Patti Duncan Lee, who read the verdict: the jury had rejected the murder charges but found Killen guilty of manslaughter on all three counts. Ironically, the verdict came exactly forty-one years to the day after Chaney, Goodman, and Schwerner were murdered. After the trial former FBI agent Jim Ingram said there was no doubt in his mind about Killen's guilt. "No matter what his family says, [Klan leader] Bowers gave him the nod—get Schwerner."

Two days later Judge Gordon sentenced Killen to serve twenty years on each count, for a total of sixty years. The courtroom sat stunned. No one had expected the maximum. Killen had nothing to say when given the opportunity to speak by Judge Gordon, who then ordered the sheriff to take Killen back to jail to begin his sentence.

There was probably more drama at the bail hearing on August 12, 2005, than at the trial. Under Mississippi law the hearing cannot be held before an appeal is filed with the Supreme Court. Killen clearly wanted bail so that just maybe he could remain free and spew his racial hatred in his churches and to all who would listen. The two questions the trial judge must ponder at such a bail hearing are whether the defendant is a flight risk and whether the defendant would pose a special danger. The courtroom swarmed with members of Killen's family and his friends. The defense attorneys called seven witnesses to prove that Killen was not a flight risk and that, because of his health condition necessitating his continued use of a wheelchair, he could not possibly be a threat to the community.

Two of the witnesses testified that they had known Killen all of his life and that he was their pastor for years.[20] Another testified that he was baptized by Killen, and yet another testified that he was a church member and neighbor of Killen. In addition, three other witnesses testified that Killen was not a flight risk, nor a danger to others.

The testimony of the state was weak, bringing in the jailers who had asked Killen routine questions, one being whether he had any suicidal tendencies.[21] Killen had shot back that he would "kill you [the jailer] before I would kill myself." Killen's lawyers ridiculed these jailers, and all admitted on cross-examination that they really didn't think Killen would rise out of his wheelchair and kill them. The defense put on the sheriff in rebuttal, and he testified that Killen was not a threat to himself or to other prisoners.

After hearing arguments Judge Gordon granted Killen his release on a $600,000 bail bond. The Mississippi Supreme Court, on September 8, 2005, refused to hear the state's appeal of Judge Gordon's ruling on bail. That meant that Killen was able to move around as a free man. But Killen, emboldened by his bond victory, moved around a little too much for a man supposedly confined to a wheelchair. Policemen and friends from other counties saw Killen out of his wheelchair and walking with no problem, filling up his vehicles with gas and otherwise moving about the county freely and without the necessity of a wheelchair. All of this was noted in local newspapers, thus giving the impression that Killen had misrepresented his physical condition to the court. In addition, there was a "Killen Appreciation Day," which was scheduled for September 18, and Killen had expressed his enthusiasm for being present. White supremacist Richard Barrett said, "It's an old-fashioned Mississippi homecoming. It's held for sports figures and beauty queens. Why not for political prisoners?"[22]

Judge Gordon was incensed. At a hearing on September 12, 2005, he expressed his feeling that Killen's miraculous recovery indicated that fraud had been committed on the court and that Killen's enthusiasm to attend the "Killen Appreciation Day" was revolting, since it showed callous disregard for the deaths of the three innocent persons, who died in a cruel, heinous, and atrocious manner. Killen was ordered back to jail, his only hope now being a reversal by the Mississippi Supreme Court.

The Mississippi Supreme Court took its own good time and finally came down with a decision on April 12, 2007. The opinion was astonishing, not for its affirmation of the decision of the lower court that Killen must languish in jail for the rest of his life but for the enlightening and surprising language it used in reaching its decision. In structuring its opinion, a unanimous Mississippi Supreme Court, for the first time in history, found that in the years leading up to 1964, "racial discrimination in Mississippi was rampant and largely unchecked."[23] The court, with obvious passion, stated that rampant racial discrimination "was practiced at all levels of state government, and by many citizens, in varying degrees."

The court reasoned that the White Knights of the Ku Klux Klan "was a violent and radical organization, whose members passionately believed that the white race was superior to other races; that integration of the races violated the laws of God and nature; and that educational and social mingling of the races was to be prevented at all costs." The court continued by observing that the Klan "practiced hatred and violence . . . and was to use whatever force necessary—including harassment, intimidation, physical abuse, and even murder—to maintain racial and social segregation in Mississippi." It continued by finding that few African Americans were registered to vote, that juries were all white, and that there was a complete domination by whites in state and local government, including law enforcement.[24] The court noted that the Klan included among its members and sympathizers law enforcement officers, who provided both protection against prosecution and the appearance that Klan activities were conducted under state law.

The court went even further by recognizing that in the 1960s, racial tensions were high and, even when the FBI became involved in investigating civil rights cases and church bombings, white citizens most often were unwilling to assist, and that in Neshoba County in 1964, the white citizens were hostile to the federal agents and were unhappy they were there. Civil rights workers were viewed and labeled by many whites as "outsiders" and as "troublemakers" who had no business in Mississippi. Some even felt that if the three men had fallen victim to violence, "they had brought it upon themselves." It was against this history that Michael Schwerner, James Chaney, and Andrew Goodman found themselves working together in the civil rights movement in Meridian in 1964.

The Mississippi Supreme Court almost summarily dismissed Killen's legal arguments, including the assignment of error that the trial court had erred in granting the state's request for jury instructions on manslaughter. The high court found that there was more than sufficient evidence supporting manslaughter and that there were no errors in the trial court's instructions. The high court further held that the delay of forty-one years in bringing the indictment did not deny Killen due process of law, nor did it violate his Sixth Amendment right to a speedy trial. The state had pointed out that any delay was preindictment and that the trial took place only five months following indictment. The high court utilized the two-prong test for analysis of preindictment delays, which requires the defendant to show that the preindictment delay prejudiced the defendant and that the delay was an intentional device used by the government to obtain a tactical advantage over the accused. The court held that Killen had failed to meet its burden on both issues.

More perplexing to the court was Killen's argument that he was prejudiced by the trial, since if he had been prosecuted in the 1960s, he likely would have drawn an all-white jury—and that jury would have been reluctant to convict a white man whose only crime was doing harm to a black man (Chaney) and two white civil rights workers (Schwerner and Goodman). In other words Killen was saying that he probably would have been immune from prosecution in 1964 because an all-white jury would not have considered it a crime to kill an African American or a civil rights worker.

The high court was shocked by that argument. It agreed that Killen's premise was accurate in the observation that juries have changed since the 1960s and that the political climate and attitude of the general public was materially different, but Killen's lawyers could cite no authority for their proposition that the verdict should be reversed because the political climate had changed, and the high court refused to entertain this argument. It concluded by stating, "We shall say no more than to add that we find this argument has no merit, and we are surprised it is made."[25]

Whatever immunity Killen possessed for over four decades, granted to him by Mississippi Values, suddenly vanished with that surprising high court decision born of disgust, guilt, and a hope of redemption, leaving him in prison with only his own fears and obsessions to guide him to the other side, which most folks in Mississippi prayed would be a short journey.

For Attorney General Jim Hood, the trial was something that he undertook out of a sense of duty. At its core the case was simple in that the base issue was murder. It was not until months later, when Hood went to a national meeting for attorneys general, that he understood the full impact of the case. Attorneys general approached Hood with comments about how Mississippi had changed, the clear implication being that Mississippi had a terrible past to overcome. Recalls Hood in an interview with the authors: "Most of them were in college when all this occurred, and they knew everything about it. . . . I saw how people perceived us before and then afterward. In the end, I think the trial will help Neshoba County put the matter behind them."

17

James Ford Seale: Time Runs Out for a Killer

The five-page indictment succinctly laid out the charges against James Ford Seale: one count of conspiracy, one count of kidnapping for the abduction of Henry Dee, and one count of kidnapping for the abduction of Charles Moore. The indictment alleged that Seale was a member of the White Knights of the Ku Klux Klan of Mississippi, which "targeted for violence African Americans they believed were involved in civil rights activity." Further, the indictment alleged that Seale abducted Moore and Dee and transported them to the Homochitto National Forest, where the two men were beaten "with switches and tree branches" and then bound with duct tape and taken to the Mississippi River, where they were thrown into the river to drown.

On January 25, 2007, Seale pleaded not guilty before United States magistrate Linda Anderson, who, as was noted earlier, denied bond, stating, "Neither the weight of the crime nor its circumstances have been diminished by the passage of time."

The trial was held in the historic federal courtroom on the fourth floor of the James O. Eastland Courthouse on Capitol Street in Jackson, Mississippi. The courtroom is approximately forty-five feet by a hundred feet, with the judge's imposing bench at the west end and with beautiful wood panels running about halfway up the walls. On the north and east walls, portraits of former federal judges stare down on the participants like prophets from the Old Testament. The lighting is provided by eight large chandeliers, dome lights hanging from the ceiling in two rows.

The courtroom is graced by a large mural that is covered at all times by a curtain. The mural, titled *Pursuits of Life in Mississippi*, extends almost entirely across the west wall behind the judge's bench, incredibly purporting to depict Mississippi pastoral scenes. The people depicted in the painting are neatly segregated, the whites very happy as they play, and the blacks working physically hard but happily playing the banjo and dancing. The mural was painted by a celebrated artist, Simka Simkhovitch, at the end of the Great Depression. Murals such as this are often mistaken for Works Progress Administration art, but they were actually administered by the Procurement Division of the Treasury Department. The artists were chosen by anonymous competitions where the national jurors were often other artists.

Simka Simkhovitch, who was born in Russia and came to New York in 1924, completed this remarkable mural in 1938. The Russian artist was chosen over celebrated Mississippi artist Walter Anderson, who lived as a hermit on the offshore islands and painted beautiful natural scenes of seabirds and sea life. Anderson competed vigorously for the commission, and his rejection caused him great frustration and tribulation. Coupled with illness, family tragedies, and his struggle to make a living with work he detested (manufacturing figurines), the rejection led to a mental breakdown with psychotic episodes.

For many years, presiding in the courtroom, seated beneath the mural, was the infamous Judge William Harold Cox, who was never hesitant to display his racist wrath. In January 1964 a number of blacks in Canton were denied their right to register to vote and filed suit against the circuit clerk, Foote Campbell, to allow registration. Judge Cox referred to the Canton blacks who attempted to register as "a bunch of niggers." Once he told Constance Baker Motley, an African American civil rights activist and lawyer who in 1956 wrote the original complaint in *Brown v. Board of Education*, whose head touched the wall as she leaned back while examining a witness, "Counselor, get your greasy hair off my wall."[1] And thus Judge Cox carried on until his retirement. No attempt at recusal was ever successful.

Monumental changes can take place in forty-two years. When James Ford Seale, wearing prison orange, shuffled into the fourth-floor courtroom to answer the charges for the crimes he'd committed on May 2, 1964, no longer was the racial mural visible across the west wall behind the judge's desk; it was now obscured by a neat blue curtain. No longer was Judge Cox there bellowing his racial wrath from the judge's bench. In his place sat Chief Judge Henry Wingate, a Yale-educated African American appointed in 1985 when he was thirty-eight years of age, who had enjoyed a distinguished career as an Assistant United States Attorney for the Southern District of Mississippi before this appointment. No longer was James Seale a handsome, vigorous twenty-nine-year-old. Although he appeared somewhat impish, he was now a bespectacled seventy-one-year-old man with loose shackles on his feet and hands. The courtroom in which he quietly sat was now not only politically correct but completely reconstructed.

Seale was a long way from his home in Roxie, a tiny town located in southeast Mississippi in Franklin County. In 1960 it had a population of 569 people, about 40 percent white and 59 percent African American. Ironically, the most famous son of Seale's little hamlet is the celebrated author Richard Nathaniel Wright (1908–1960), a grandson of slaves who was born into poverty on a plantation near Roxie. He wrote sixteen books that were highly acclaimed as the greatest books ever written on race and class divisions. His powerful novels reflected the forces of poverty, injustice, evil, and hopelessness—forces that tragically culminated in the brutal deaths of Charles Moore and Henry Dee.

The most infamous son of this hamlet is James Ford Seale, who actually got away with the murders of Charles Moore and Henry Dee for most of his life, that is, until the day he entered the courtroom and sat near the outside wall with his attorneys. On that first day he glanced back at his wife, Jean, but otherwise sat almost at attention, gazing straight ahead.

Judge Wingate mounted the bench as the courtroom deputy called the court to order. Everyone in the courtroom knew who was in charge. It was surely not the lawyers or the participants. Judge Wingate radiates a sense of authority and runs his courtroom with complete control and professional judicial demeanor.

Motions were the issues of the day. The defense attempted to persuade the judge that the bond ruling should be reversed and that the charges should be dismissed because the five-year statute of limitations had expired. The defense struck out on both counts. First, it is unusual for a district judge to reverse a bond ruling of the magistrate, and, second, the judge did not feel there was a statute of limitations that would restrict a charge of kidnapping, since he regarded the act Seale was charged with as a capital crime. Explaining that "kidnapping is typically recognized as a capital offense," Judge Wingate denied the motion and ruled that it did not matter that forty-three years had gone by.

There was other wrangling. The prosecution wanted a long, detailed questionnaire to be submitted to every proposed juror. The defense resisted this proposal, arguing that the questionnaire asked shocking questions about race and that the prosecution was overtly inserting race into the case. The prosecution felt that the questionnaire was essential to understand the proposed jurors' positions on racial issues. Judge Wingate agreed with the prosecution, and the questionnaire was used. Similar questionnaires have been used in a number of high-profile civil rights cases going back to the 1960s.

On April 30, Judge Wingate started hearing the final pretrial motions. The defense had moved to suppress the statements that Seale had made during the two-hour ride from his home to Jackson following his arrest in 1964, and well they should have. The alleged admission was devastating to the defense. ("We know you did it. You know you did it. The Lord above knows you did it."/"Yes, but I'm not going to admit it. You are going to have to prove it.")

The defense attempted to show that Seale was subjected to physical abuse, that he was denied his Miranda rights and did not have a lawyer. The prosecution responded that Seale was not abused, that his statement was entirely voluntary, that the statement made in 1964 was before the requirements of Miranda, and that in any case, Seale never asked for a lawyer. After hearing several witnesses and taking the motion under advisement, Judge Wingate ruled in favor of the prosecution: the admission could be placed in evidence.

The defense also sought to suppress another statement, one of Ernest Gilbert, a deceased FBI informant and a former leader of the KKK. Gilbert had told the FBI that Clyde and James Seale and another Klansman told him they "had picked up the two black kids, took them out to Clyde Seale's farm, beat them, and threw them in the river." It was a substantial blow to the prosecution when Judge Wingate suppressed this statement. Although the reasoning of Judge Wingate is not absolutely clear, it would appear he felt that the statement was hearsay and did not fall within any of the recognized exceptions.

After other legal skirmishes, *voir dire* started on May 30 and lasted for three days. The importance of this phase of the trial cannot be overemphasized. Good lawyers carefully prepare for this phase of the case, knowing that getting the right jurors is essential to a successful outcome. That is why it is so important to have as much information as possible. Early trial books for lawyers emphasized various stereotypes for selection, such as blacks, whites, women, men, nationalities, weight, occupation, etc., as being foremost in the selection. For example, it was thought that all Slavic races would be more sympathetic toward the plaintiff and that Nordic types would be more favorable to the defendant, and that male jurors are better for the defendant as opposed to female jurors. Despite the prevalence of juror stereotyping, psychologists have taught us that it is absolutely incorrect. We have learned that decisions are most often made by the life experiences of the jurors. In other words, each juror views the facts from his or her own lens regardless of race, religion, sex, or nationality, making a thorough *voir dire* extremely important. Lawyers often say that all they want is a "fair and impartial jury." That is not true. What a trial lawyer

worth his or her salt wants is a juror who is prejudiced—but prejudiced in favor of his or her side.

The *voir dire* in the Seale trial was emotional and dramatic.
Seale was now neatly dressed in a carefully pressed blue shirt and
khaki trousers. He sat up straight and listened carefully. Judge Wingate first attempted to weed out jurors who might not be able to
serve. Juror number ten explained that it would be too dangerous for
his brother-in-law to work in the woods alone and leave the cattle
unattended. Juror number seventy-five, a one-armed farmer, said he
could not serve because he had to tend to six chicken houses. Juror
number twenty-five, a white woman wearing a gray "Southern Girl"
T-shirt with a rebel flag on it, could not serve because her father had
just fallen off the roof and she had to take care of him. Juror number
thirty-seven was unable to serve because he had just bought plane
tickets to take his wife to Miami for eye surgery. Juror number
twenty-nine had chronic depression and anxiety. Juror number five,
a white female alcoholic, was suffering from anxiety because she
wished she could be drinking. Juror number fifty-three broke down
in tears telling how nervous she got driving from Lawrence County,
where she lived, and could not sleep thinking about it. Matters got
even more revealing as the process continued. Juror number six
described an incident in which he narrowly avoided being harmed
in a race-motivated church bombing when the KKK rode through
and shot up houses.

The final day of *voir dire* was more of the same. Juror number
sixty-five said she had often heard stories of racial horror from her
family and "my grandmother grew up on a farm, and when white
people came by, they would run away to the woods." Juror number
forty had had a traumatic sexual experience with an older white man:
"He just did things that were not permissible, but I couldn't do anything about it." Juror number forty-nine revealed on the jury questionnaire that her father was a member of the Klan and had abused her
until she was eighteen years old.

At last, on Monday, June 4, 2007, the jury was selected. On the jury
panel there were four blacks and eight whites. Of that number, six were
male and six were female. There were two alternate jurors selected,

both white females. The jury appeared to range from about thirty to fifty years of age. After further dickering over evidentiary matters, the court was ready to begin opening statements at 3:00 P.M.

The lawyers representing the government were Dunn Lampton, United States Attorney for the Southern District of Mississippi; Paige Fitzgerald, Special Litigation Counsel, Civil Rights Division of the Department of Justice; and Trial Attorney Eric Gibson of the Department of Justice. Representing James Ford Seale were George Lucas and Kathy Nester, both lawyers from the Federal Public Defenders' Office located in Jackson.

After the jury was seated, Judge Wingate gave the jury initial instructions, what lawyers sometimes call "boiler plate" instructions. He then slowly and distinctly read the five-page indictment to the jury. At 3:00 P.M., the courtroom was packed and so tense you could cut the air with a knife. Everybody was ready for opening statements. The opening statement is delivered by each side at the beginning of the trial to give the jury an overview of what the evidence will show and to lay it out in a logical manner in order for the jury to follow the testimony more understandably. It is not argument. Argument is reserved for the closing statement when the lawyers can apply all of their rhetorical skills. But this does not mean the opening is not without drama. Lawyers understand the psychological principle of primacy and attempt to construct the facts in such a manner that they will be most persuasive in favor of their client.

A good opening statement that uses the techniques of drama to state the facts in the most persuasive manner and to give the jury a bird's-eye view of what is to come can be likened to a properly conducted musical rendition. Paige Fitzgerald illustrated this as she stood up and made the opening statement for the prosecution. She had emerged as the primary spokesperson for the government. Fitzgerald looked to be about forty and was articulate and quick, with short blond hair and a neatly tailored black suit.

Fitzgerald began her opening statement in a soft voice, looking directly at the jury, and recounted the monstrous murders of Dee and Moore, who were picked up, beaten almost to death, thrown into the trunk of a car, transported to the Mississippi River, weighted down with an engine block and chains, and thrown into the river while still alive. When they were finally fished out of the river, the families of Charles Eddie Moore and Henry Hezekiah Dee "had only bones to bury." She spoke of the upcoming testimony of Charles Edwards, a coconspirator, who would recite in detail the brutal beatings the young nineteen-year-old men received in the Homochitto National Forest. She continued by telling the jury of the exchange between Seale and the FBI agent Leonard Wolf following Seale's arrest, when he admitted guilt but told the agent he'd have to prove it. After a pregnant pause, Fitzpatrick summed it up: "Well, ladies and gentlemen, after forty-three years, we are here to do just that," and then went about telling the jury how they would do so.

Senior federal public defender George Lucas equally demonstrated his skills in crafting a persuasive opening in a difficult case. He could not deny that Moore and Dee had been kidnapped and killed. He could only hope to convince the jury that the government had not proven its case. That was a difficult task after the confession and the passing of forty-three years. He began by expressing his sorrow to the families and recognizing these deaths as a "terrible, horrible incident." He described the deaths as tragic, and he emphasized that one "can't minimize tragedy." Lucas then set out how the government had no credible evidence; it might show Seale was a racist, and the jury "may not like it, but it is not a crime to be a racist," he declared emphatically in defiant terms. Lucas scoffed at the expected evidence of so-called coconspirator Charles Edwards. He detailed to the jury how Edwards had lied about his involvement in this incident "at least nine times," and now that he was under immunity claimed he was telling the truth. Lucas emphasized that "being a member of the Klan is not illegal," and that Seale was not on trial for being a racist. He very persuasively concluded by telling the jury, "[You] cannot find my client guilty to make the family feel better."

The party that has the burden of proof is always allowed to go first. Since the government had the burden of proof, it made the initial opening statement and, after the opening statement for the defense, began to call its witnesses. It poured on the physical evidence. It produced witnesses who testified about finding the decomposed torsos and the personal effects of Moore, including a belt with the letter M inscribed on it. These witnesses further described their findings in almost unspeakable detail, the fact that Moore's ankles were tied together with "baling wire." The witnesses were unanimous, in describing the examination of the parts of the body, that seeing the "baling wire doubled around the ankles, they knew it was not a natural death."

On June 5 the government continued piling on the physical evidence by exhibiting to the jury numerous photographs of the locations and personal items recovered and the wheels, crankshaft, engine block, chains, railroad railings, and other items tied to Moore and Dee in an attempt to keep the bodies down under the river forever.

On the morning of day five of the trial, the people in the crowded courtroom were poking one another and inquiring when Charles Marcus Edwards would testify. He was the prosecution's star witness, the one who had confessed that he had helped beat Moore and Dee in the Homochitto National Forest. The speculation came to an end when one of the attorneys announced that Edwards would be placed on the stand at around 1:30 that afternoon. The courtroom was jam-packed when he took the stand.

Edwards had a white mustache, wore a white open-neck shirt, and was obviously nervous, his sentences slow and halting. The government's case would turn on his credibility. He had to be believed by the jury. Several minutes into his testimony, it was apparent that he was indeed credible. He appeared to tell the truth, although it was very painful. His earlier lies concerning his involvement in these deaths were understandable because he was scared to death of Seale and his gang. Seale would have had no hesitation about killing him, his wife, and their five children. He said that he would not have been able to sleep at night knowing his family wouldn't have a roof over their heads if he'd told the truth all those years ago.

Edwards did not disappoint. He reluctantly told his story, after probing by Fitzgerald. He pointed out that Dee was wearing a black bandana as a potential enemy of the Klan. Moore, he said, was just a victim of circumstances. He continued by stating that he and other Klansmen beat Moore and Dee in the Homochitto National Forest while Seale held a sawed-off shotgun on them, and that later Seale told him he wrapped duct tape around their mouths, bound them down with weights, and threw them into the Mississippi River. Edwards testified that Seale picked up Dee and Moore in his Volkswagen and then Edwards followed in a truck with Klansmen Archie Prather, Curtis Dunn, and Clyde Seale. He said the boys were tied to trees, and he and others beat them with thick switches.

At the end of the cross-examination of this emotional witness, Edwards somberly asked if he could speak to the victims' family members after the jurors had left the courtroom. Judge Wingate granted permission, after which Edwards said, "I can't undo what was done forty years ago, and I'm sorry for that. And I ask for your forgiveness for my part in that crime. That's exactly what I wanted to say to you." Looking at the families of both victims, one could observe tears slowly falling and eyes being softly wiped with tissues and handkerchiefs.

Sorrow next turned into excitement as the attorneys wrangled over the admission of a journal kept by the Reverend Clyde Briggs, minister of the Roxie Colored First Baptist Church. This was the church searched by the Klan, with help from law enforcement officers, after Henry Dee, in an attempt to stop the Klansmen from brutally beating the two men, falsely told them that guns were hidden there.

Judge Wingate allowed not only the three pages dealing with this incident but also the entire journal to go into evidence. Other pages described harassment of the Briggs family by the Klan. Since the entire journal was in, defense attorney Kathy Nester hoped to use it to discredit Briggs as a person with radical associations. On cross-examination she turned to pages written by Briggs's son that criticized the government, which he believed may have helped kill his father back in 1965, and pages describing his father's early involvement in Deacons for Defense, an armed organization formed to counter the Klan.[2]

The atrocities of the Klan continued to be shown by the testimony of the Reverend R. W. Middleton, Seale's pastor at Bunkly Baptist Church for several months in 1963. Middleton testified that Klansman Archie Prather addressed the congregation after it had been told that a "car full of niggers" had followed a white woman home, saying, "Let me ride in the trunk and keep it halfway open. I'll shoot every last one of them niggers." After Middleton suggested that this comment was not appropriate, the Klan ran him out of town. Earlier Seale had come to Rev. Middleton's house to borrow his vise to saw off the barrel of his shotgun. Seale said at the time, "What do you think would happen if I walked into a nigger juke joint and started shooting?"

Thomas Moore took the stand and emotionally testified about his younger, deceased brother, Charles, while the families of Dee and Moore fought back tears.

A good trial lawyer understands the psychological premise of recency and attempts to reserve one of his or her best witnesses as the last. Here again the prosecution did not disappoint. FBI agent Edward Putz, the last government witness, testified hearing James Seale emphatically state, after being told that the agents knew he had committed the kidnapping and murders of Moore and Dee, "Yes, but I'm not going to admit it; you are going to have to prove it." Lawyer Fitzgerald, in order to make sure these words would not be forgotten, repeated them forcefully in closing, declaring that the government had done that very thing. It had proven its case beyond a reasonable doubt.

On Wednesday, June 17, the prosecution rested. On that afternoon the defense started putting on its witnesses. Not surprisingly there was little to say. Don Seale, another of James Seale's brothers, testified that his brother had "sore spots" after he was arrested, and that the house was torn up, the defense apparently using this to show that his admission was not voluntary. Forensic pathologist James Lauridson then took the stand and testified that there was no way to determine the cause of death of the victims. The purpose of this was to convince the jury that Dee and Moore could very well have been killed before their bodies were dumped into the river. If that was so, under the federal kidnapping law it was necessary that they be alive when taken across state lines. On cross-examination, that defense was destroyed by Dr. Lauridson agreeing with the prosecution that "there is no logical reason to bind the feet of a dead body." The final defense witness, James Lynn, of Vicksburg, testified that his father had a barge used to transport cotton and cattle to Davis, near where the bodies were found. The lawyers were trying to show that the crime could reasonably have been committed without crossing state lines.

On this last day, Seale was again neatly dressed in a carefully pressed light blue shirt and dark trousers, seemingly unaware of the attention focused on him by the spectators. At one point the courtroom became even quieter than usual, perhaps anticipating Judge Wingate's critical question to Seale, "Do you elect not to testify?"

Standing and speaking into the microphone for the first time during the trial, Seale succinctly said, "Yes, sir."

The defense then rested, and the trial was now over except for the "shouting and hollering by the lawyers," as some old-timers call closing arguments.

The government is again allowed to make its argument first; it is followed by the defense's closing argument. The prosecution is then given one last shot to reply to the arguments of the defense. So it went in the final arguments in the Seale case. Although U.S. Attorney Dunn Lampton of Jackson had only a small part in the trial thus far, he stood to make the first closing argument for the prosecution. Using his rhetorical skills, which had been honed over the years as a prosecutor, he described Dee and Moore as "well-liked, unobtrusive teenagers" who met their deaths in a most horrible and abominable manner. Lampton described in detail their terrible beatings and being transported in the truck to Parker's Landing to be dumped in the Mississippi River. He described the thoughts that may have gone through Moore's mind as he watched as Henry Dee was drowned first and then as he waited for them to come for him. Lampton made it clear what villainous and wretched murders had taken place.

Kathy Nester, the federal public defender who took the lead role for the defense and questioned the witnesses, first did what all good lawyers do: she went for the weak spot in the prosecution's case. She knew the jurors would not find Seale guilty if they did not believe Edwards's testimony. She attacked it eloquently and with persuasive zeal. "All these years, he's been lying. All of a sudden, he decides to tell the truth," she said, "defining 'truth' as the truth [the prosecution] wanted to hear."

Fitzgerald made the last argument on behalf of the prosecution, bolstering the truthfulness of Edwards's testimony.

Alex A. Alston Jr.:

The courtroom during the 1960s and 1970s was painted a color I would call putrid green. This caused me some consternation in trying cases, because during a trial that lasted several days or more, I would begin to feel a distressing "putrid green," as if I were slightly seasick.

After monitoring the Seale trial, thankfully in a courtroom that was now painted off-white, I felt that the case would turn on two issues. One, whether the jury thought Dee and Moore were taken across the state line while living, and, two, whether the jurors believed the testimony of Edwards and thought he was credible. I believed that the first point concerning state lines was weak for the defense, and I was not convinced whether the jury would even care after hearing days of incredibly emotional testimony concerning the brutal murders of these two young men.

On the second issue, I thought perhaps it was a closer call, but after watching Edwards closely, I came to the conclusion that he was credible. Sure, he had earlier denied involvement in these atrocious murders, but he was deathly afraid, not only concerning what he had done but also about what the KKK would do to him if he ever broke the Klan conspiracy of silence. I concluded that the jury would believe him.

The Verdict

After the closing arguments, Judge Wingate sent the jury out for deliberation and verdict. After approximately two hours, a relatively short time for such a complicated case, the jury returned with a unanimous verdict of guilty on all counts.

After the verdict Seale turned and looked at his wife, seemingly asking if she was all right. Her response was so slight that it was difficult to decipher. The trial was now over, and all that was left was the sentencing.

Former FBI agent Jim Ingram, called back into service yet again by the U.S. Attorney's office, had testified at the trial. Later, when discussing the case with the authors, he said he "looked at the jurors in the Killen trial in 2005 and at the jurors in the Seale trial in 2006, and it was just different." The Seale jury seemed more serious about the proceedings. "When I testified at the Seale trial, I stared straight at the jurors and I could tell. They were taking notes. I walked away feeling different than some of the prosecutors, who thought there might be a hung jury. It renewed my faith in the system in Mississippi." As an afterthought, Ingram added, "James Ford Seale was one of the meanest guys you will ever hope to see."

On August 24, 2007, James Ford Seale entered the historic courtroom one last time, fully shackled and dressed in an orange jumpsuit, to receive the sentence to be imposed by Judge Wingate. Designating the crime as "unspeakable, because only monsters could inflict this," the judge sentenced Seale to three life terms in prison for his role in the killings of Henry Hezekiah Dee and Charles Eddie Moore, adding that the "pulse of this community still throbs with sorrow." This sentence effectively put Seale away for the rest of his life. Judge Wingate appeared to be searching his own heart as he remarked on the "horror" and "ghastliness" of the crime. Since Seale was a cancer patient, Judge Wingate agreed to the defense's recommendation that he serve his sentence in a medical facility.

Those who believed that justice, finally, had been obtained in the murders of Henry Dee and Charles Moore were stunned on September 9, 2008, when a three-judge panel of the U.S. Fifth Circuit Court of Appeals vacated Seale's 2007 conviction on the grounds that the statute of limitations on kidnapping had expired. The three judges—Jerry Smith, age sixty-two, and Harold DeMoss Jr., seventy-eight, both of Texas, and Eugene Davis, seventy-two, of Louisiana—were all older white men, sons of the Old South, appointed by Ronald Reagan and George H. W. Bush, Republican presidents not known for their strong support of civil rights.

At first glance it seems racism was the guiding principle used by the judges; however, a closer reading of their decision makes it clear that they had no choice but to overturn the conviction, thus making it possible for yet another perpetrator of racial murders in Mississippi to go unpunished. However, despite the panel's ruling, the full court denied his release until a hearing could take place in May 2009.

In 1964, when the crimes occurred, kidnapping was a capital offense under federal law, and there was no time limitation on prosecution, but the 1972 amendment to that law established a limitation of five years for prosecution. Seale's 2007 prosecution occurred beyond the statute of limitations. A first-year law student should have seen the reversal coming. Why, then, would the federal government conduct a trial that the Civil Rights Division of the Justice Department had to know would be overturned?

Was Seale's prosecution meant to be a "show trial," a publicity stunt undertaken to bolster a Republican administration's sagging image as a protector of civil rights? If true, that only compounds the tragedy. In 1964 both state and federal authorities had all the evidence that they needed to proceed with a prosecution. Instead, fearing reprisals from racist whites, they allowed the killers to walk. The 2007 prosecution was all flash and no substance, in its own way just as bad as no prosecution at all. Unfortunately, racist killers still are immune to justice in Mississippi.

PART IV

Picking Up the Pieces

18

Atonement in a Haunted Land

For most of the twentieth century, Mississippi was a killing field for state-sponsored terror inflicted on African Americans and whites who participated in the civil rights movement. In retrospect the sheer number of murders, beatings, lynchings, and fire bombings that took place during those years is almost incomprehensible, raising questions about how it is possible for a state to deviate so far from the norm accepted by the rest of the country. It's not enough to blame the Ku Klux Klan, the Mississippi Nazi Party, or the frenzied rednecks that roamed the state with Confederate flags attached to their ramshackle pickup trucks. If that'd been the only source of the problems, the chaos would have been a flicker of short duration.

For what happened in Mississippi to have occurred, every institution in the state charged with leadership had to fail—the news media, the churches, the legal profession, and all three branches of government. Not only did an institutional meltdown have to occur, but there also had to be an overt complicity of everyone involved with the institutions.

In 1964 there were 2,198 lawyers, a little more than 100 district attorneys and county attorneys, and about 500 county, state, and federal judges in the state, 99 percent of them white. They all knew right from wrong, yet only a handful of them did the right thing when called on to do so.

Of the 260 news organizations in Mississippi in the 1960s, employing hundreds of reporters, no television or radio stations and only three newspapers—the Greenville *Delta Democrat-Times*, the *Lexington Advertiser*, and the *Pascagoula Chronicle*—offered leadership through the Dark Days, although it should be noted that those three papers had help from Mississippi native Turner Catledge, managing editor of the *New York Times*. Catledge had arrived at the *New York Times* by way of what is now Mississippi State University, a stint at the *Neshoba Democrat* (Catledge grew up in Philadelphia), and then on to the *Commercial Appeal*, hot on the heels of that newspaper's editorial tussle with the Ku Klux Klan. Acutely aware of the need for honest reporting in the South during the rise of the civil rights movement, he sent a reporter, Claude Sitton, to Atlanta to open a Southern bureau so that the nation would know the truth about what was happening in the South. Without Catledge, a good man, backing up the work of the Mississippians who stood up for what was right, in effect confirming for a national audience the reporting and editorial stands of the *Delta Democrat-Times*, the *Lexington Advertiser*, and the *Pascagoula Chronicle*, it would have been much more difficult for the editors of those newspapers to survive the Dark Days.

Of the nearly five thousand Protestant ministers and Catholic priests in Mississippi in the 1960s that were not run out of the state, there were only a handful of religious leaders who advocated that their congregations adhere to the biblical teachings of their own churches. In an effort to justify human rights abuses against a race they felt to be inferior, most church leaders modified their spiritual guidance to suit the prevailing doctrine of white dominance.

Of all the institutions that should have held firm for justice but didn't, the three branches of government, particularly the judiciary and the prosecutorial arm of the executive branch of state government, experienced the most grievous failure. Prosecutions of hate crimes were extremely rare during the Dark Days, and when they occurred, they invariably ended in dismissed charges, hung juries, or not-guilty verdicts by all-white juries. As a result, those inclined to commit hate crimes were brazenly confident—and with good reason—that they were untouchable.

James L. Dickerson:

One of the interesting things about growing up in a small Mississippi Delta town during the Dark Days is the opportunity it provided to understand the minds of neighbors who were obsessed with racism. Because in small-town America everyone knows everyone else—and everyone else's business—I knew the secrets of most of the town's residents. There was one Klansman, obese with slicked-back hair the color of burnt motor oil, who preyed on little boys when he wasn't spouting the racist line. There was the gentleman farmer, whose life revolved around racist theory, who because he couldn't satisfy his wife, pursued half the women in town, failing to satisfy them as well, I am told. And the belligerent racist redneck who found that the only women that he felt he could satisfy were of black skin color, for they were fearful of him and did not berate him for his failures in bed, a response he mistakenly took as validation of his racial superiority.

Notes Mississippi attorney general Jim Hood, speaking with new-millennium wisdom: "Back then, the hot-button issue was that African American men were going to marry your white daughter. Interracial marriage was their pressure point. I think a lot of people believed that."

One of the most startling things one uncovers when delving into the emotional makeup of men who subscribe to a racist philosophy, especially men who exhibit violent behavior, is the degree of sexual dysfunction that is present. Doesn't it seem a bit odd that when night riders kill a black man, it always seems to involve removing his clothing or touching him in intimate ways?

Emmett Till was stripped naked before he was killed, an indication that sexual gratification was probably a factor in the emotional rush of taking his life. Before he was shot and tossed into the river, Mack Charles Parker was wrestled and beaten by the men who lynched him, the sexual implications of those hands-on interactions obvious both from a latent homosexual perspective and from the desire to literally feel the power of a black man who had been with a white woman, a recurring fantasy of white men in the South. White Mississippians were fearful of black sexual power—and, at the same time, curious about it. Likewise, Charles Moore and Henry Dee were tied to a tree and whipped with branches, a fantasy worthy of the notorious Marquis de Sade, the eighteenth-century Frenchman who inflicted torture on his victims for sexual gratification.

The murder of Medgar Evers falls into another sex-related category—suppressed sexual rage. Thanks to the foresight of Byron De la Beckwith's nephew, Reed Massengill, who wrote a biography about his infamous uncle, we have detailed information about Beckwith's sexual profile that we don't have for other assassins.[1] According to Massengill, who interviewed his Aunt Willie about her husband's sexual habits, we know that he was frequently impotent. Only infrequently were Willie's efforts to help Beckwith achieve an erection successful. Most of the time he was unable to perform. Wrote Massengill: "With each passing year, Beckwith's impotence became a more significant problem. Even more worrisome, to Willie, was that his dominance and sense of power over her seemed inextricably linked to his level of sexual excitement."

The manner in which Beckwith's impotence was manifest in his racism is clearly evident in the racist flyers that he wrote and distributed on street corners in Greenwood. In one flyer he wrote, "The black race in America must not be permitted to enter the white bedchamber through the open doors of the integrated church." Beckwith was obsessed with fears that a black man would do for his wife what he himself could not do—give her pleasure. Those thoughts built day by day, finally escalating into a rage that resulted in cold-blooded murder.

The history of lynching in Mississippi is replete with examples of torture that are textbook examples of sexual emotional displacement. Before they were killed, black men were often stripped and their genitals were mutilated by white men who were obsessed with touching the body parts of a bound black man. Sometimes their genitals were cut off and placed in the mouths of the victims, an obvious sign of latent homosexuality. For that reason lynching was about more than violence or power—it was about sexual gratification. It is difficult for a mental health professional to look at a Klansman in his hood and robe without seeing the sexual implications. The hood is a classic adaptation of the dominatrix mask, while the robe is designed to conceal not only gender but also sexual arousal while inflicting punishment on other men.

Fear of black sexual prowess with white women, sadistic behavior related to various categories of mental illness, and latent homosexuality, with its accompanying guilt (interrogation techniques in which the pistol was inserted into the mouth of a suspected Klansman was a most effective way of obtaining information, primarily because of the homosexual panic the guilt engendered), were at the core of many of the violent killings that took place in Mississippi during the Dark Days.

James C. Coleman, former director of the Psychology Clinic School at the University of California, wrote that some sadistic behavior evolves from what psychologists call castration anxiety. "Many sadists are timid, feminine, undersexed individuals whose sadistic sexual behavior is apparently designed to arouse strong emotions in the sex object. . . . The sadist presumably engages in the infliction of pain as a 'safe' means of achieving sexual stimulation and gratification."[2]

Beneath the surface of racism linger subterranean motives and drives, some darker than others, all reflective of the very essence of Mississippi Values.

Diehard Mississippi Values

Individuals do not commit despicable acts with an expectation that they will go unpunished unless there is a pervasive belief throughout the culture that odious acts can be justified in certain situations. That was—and still is—the case in Mississippi.

The problem is that white Mississippians, as a whole, don't much care for the Declaration of Independence, with its talk about equal rights—and they support only parts of the U.S. Constitution, such as the Second Amendment, which guarantees the right to bear arms. Over the years, Mississippi has opposed the peaceful-assembly wording of the First Amendment; the Thirteenth Amendment, which abolished slavery; the Fifteenth Amendment, which provided equal rights to citizens of color; the Nineteenth Amendment, which gave women the right to vote and was not ratified by Mississippi until 1984; the proposed child labor amendment of 1924, which Mississippi helped defeat; and the Twenty-Fourth Amendment, which barred the poll tax in federal elections and was never ratified by Mississippi.

Until the federal government forced the Voting Rights Act of 1965 on white Mississippians, the political candidate who invariably prevailed was the one who could most convincingly assure voters that their culture of white dominance would remain intact. After 1965, blacks were able to muster enough votes to force the worst of the white politicians to modify their campaign language, discouraging them from using red-flag words and phrases such as *states rights, communism,* and *Southern way of life.*

Today the phrase used most often by race-baiting politicians is *Mississippi Values,* a code phrase for the old way of life—segregation, violence against people of color, and unbridled corporatism, a modern-day substitute for the old plantation system. As recently as 2007 and 2008, when elections were held for offices at the state and federal levels, candidates boldly advertised their support of Mississippi Values over traditional American values of justice and equal rights. In other words they were a "safe" candidate to trust with the old traditions.

The perpetuation of Mississippi Values has made the state the poorest in the nation.[3] Other distinctions—directly related to the imposition of Mississippi Values—have made the state the fattest in the union; the unhealthiest state overall, with the most venereal disease; the state with one of the highest rates of domestic violence; the state with the lowest educational test scores; the most politically corrupt state, based on public corruption convictions; and, perhaps most relevant, a state with a high incidence of mental illness.

Of all the crimes committed over the years by Mississippi state officials, none approach the depravity of the abuse inflicted on the state's children. In 2007, Mississippi settled a lawsuit brought by Children's Rights, a New York organization that went to court to prove that the Mississippi Department of Human Services was guilty of inflicting sexual, physical, and emotional abuse on the state's 3,500 foster children, most of whom are black. The state accepted the terms of a court-ordered settlement placing Human Services under a five-year period of supervision. Incredibly, those officials at Human Services most responsible for the abuse were never prosecuted. On the contrary, they were left in positions of authority, where they are free to continue the abuse.

Alex A. Alston Jr.:

I have lived in Mississippi all of my life except for the four years I spent in the Marine Corps. I adore this state and the genuine friendliness and hospitality of its people. I recall living in Orange County, California, when being released from the armed services, and telling my friends I was returning to Mississippi to enter law school.

I'll never forget the looks on their faces and their comments: "For goodness sake, why?" "Why would you return to that cesspool?" "Why not go to law school here? This is the fastest-growing county in the country [and it was], and you could make loads of money practicing law here."

But Mississippi is like a magnet. Both sides of my family have lived here for over six generations. My wife's family has deep roots here. We both love the free and open countryside, the beautiful rivers and creeks, and, best of all, our friends and family. I especially enjoy the storytelling tradition and the wonderful anecdotes told by my grandmother of the exploits of her father in the Civil War and of him riding his pony, Blackbird, during the Modoc Indian War.

In 1964, when Bill Waller asked the jury during the *voir dire* for the Beckwith trial if it was all right for a white man to kill a black man, it was not an unreasonable question. As a lawyer, if I asked the same question today, some forty-four years later, the judge would be so outraged that he or she would place me in contempt and probably jail me on the spot. Why did Waller insist on making this racist inquiry in 1964? Simply because he had to. Although it is hard to believe, in 1964 many Mississippians believed it was quite all right to kill African Americans. I had friends who never thought any differently.

Despite *Brown v. Board of Education* and the Civil Rights Acts of 1964 and 1965, Mississippi remained a rigidly segregated and oppressive society for blacks. I recall one of my out-of-state friends calling me and telling me that we should build a tall fence around Mississippi and call it our "insane asylum." The racial violence has been quite harmful to my beloved state. In addition to the harm it has caused the blacks, attempting to hold them down for more than one hundred years, even at a time when they constituted over 50 percent of the population, it has caused tremendous economic harm to Mississippi, from which the state has never recovered.

The vote was withheld from blacks in every conceivable way. As late as 1964, only 6.5 percent of the black voting-age population was registered to vote, and in some counties there were no registered black voters, even in counties where there was a heavy black majority. But the blacks did vote. They voted with their feet. They got out of this race-haunted state, and they left in great numbers. In 1900 the African American population in Mississippi was 59 percent. By 2000 it had dropped to 36 percent. The loss to the state has been enormous. In addition to the devastating effect on the remaining black community, it drained the state of some of its most productive people. Because Mississippi is unable to compete with the population figures of other states, it now has only four United States representatives, down from a high of eight in 1931.

Driving through the Mississippi Delta today, one is sickened when observing the ghost towns scattered throughout that area. Entire Delta towns are standing without one store or business open. My hometown of Hollandale brings tears to my eyes when I look down the main street and remember thousands of people laughing, shopping, and playing, and now see nothing but boarded-up stores and restaurants and some mangy-looking dogs looking for something to eat. The same is true of dozens of towns such as Shaw, Delta City, Arcola, and many more.

After living through all of this, I still would live no other place. I love my friends and family right here in Mississippi. I still have an understanding of my friends who were racist; this is the way they were taught. They grew up in the Jim Crow years and thought the system worked extremely well, and they actually enjoyed their white supremacy. Why should they think any differently? Their parents thought the same.

I sometimes think back to the tragic death of President Kennedy. Reports throughout Mississippi speak of the schoolchildren shouting with joy when they heard the news. One grade school girl told her teacher that she "bet her daddy did it," no doubt recalling the frequent bursts of hatred for Kennedy she had heard from her father.

These were not the best of times. If you attempted to express a view contrary to the rule of white supremacy, you were in trouble. If you were a black, you would immediately lose your job, your house, or your lease; be run out of town; or worse. A white in all likelihood would be ostracized, lose his or her business, or be forced to seek sanctuary in another state. Not only did one have to be careful in what was said, even to close friends and confidants, but also one had to be aware that one was being watched with an eagle eye by various state agencies.

When the Sovereignty Commission files were finally opened to the public in 1998, I was surprised to be notified that my name was in the files, along with thousands of others. An opportunity was given by the court to redact one's name from the files if one desired to do so. My first thought was *Why bother? Why did I care?*

Reluctantly, I went to the records and discovered that my name was included because I was the lawyer who represented the "outlaw group" that ended up with the interim license for television station WLBT. My thought was that this spy agency had a lot of free time on its hands if it was following me around to assure that I was not a Communist and that I was not disregarding Mississippi Values.

Mississippi News Media Today

In many ways the Mississippi media have an even weaker moral compass today than they did during the Dark Days. Journalism has gone downhill since the 1960s. Today there is only one progressive newspaper in the entire state. It was Hodding Carter III who began the newspaper shake-ups, when in January 1980 he and his family sold the *Delta Democrat-Times* to the conservative, California-based Freedom Newspaper chain. Two years later the Hederman family announced the sale of the *Clarion-Ledger* and the *Jackson Daily News*, along with six Mississippi weeklies, to the conservative Gannett Company, a mammoth newspaper chain with expansive corporate interests.

In 1984, Jimmy Ward, who had been struggling with throat cancer for several years, retired on his sixty-fifth birthday, completing twenty-six years as editor of the *Jackson Daily News*. A farewell to Ward, published in the Sunday joint edition of the *Clarion-Ledger–Jackson Daily News* was headlined: Fiery Editor's Retirement Ends an Era. Five weeks later Ward was dead. The following year, almost to the day, Tom Hederman died at the age of seventy-three. The two men were the Butch Cassidy and Sundance Kid of Mississippi media.

The *Jackson Daily News* ceased to exist in 1989, when Gannett folded it into the *Clarion-Ledger*. Today you can find little evidence in Jackson that the *Jackson Daily News* ever existed. Back issues have been purged from the city's public library, and the only place that back issues can be found is at the Mississippi Department of Archives and History, where the newspaper has been stored on microfilm.

The post-Hederman *Clarion-Ledger* raised hopes in 1983 when the newspaper was awarded a Pulitzer Prize for its coverage of educational issues in the state, but it turned out to be more of a last-gasp effort for relevancy by the old staff than a promise of good things to come from new corporate ownership. The "new" *Clarion-Ledger* no longer has a racist agenda, but it does have a troubling history of supporting the rights of corporations over the rights of citizens.

Mississippi attorney general Jim Hood longs for the days when mom-and-pop newspapers across the state offered independent voices on the issues. "I'm not a big fan of the corporate news media," he explains. "Look at what happened with the war in Iraq. The media completed failed. In Mississippi, it used to be television that rushed to the scene of an accident to give us tabloid news, but today the situation has reversed and it's the newspapers that are reporting tabloid news." In 2008, while meeting with the *Clarion-Ledger*'s editorial board, Hood suggested they add a Democratic columnist to their staff to balance conservative Republican dominance of the opinion pages. His suggestion was ignored.

After its corporate takeover in 1982, it took six years for the *Clarion-Ledger* to again distinguish itself by publishing a series of articles on the

Sovereignty Commission. The articles were bolstered by strong editorials from editorial page director David Hampton, who had worked as a political writer and columnist for the *Jackson Daily News*.

During the Dark Days, Mississippi had brave, visionary male and female editors such as Hodding Carter, Hodding Carter III, Ira Harkey, and Hazel Brannon Smith all offering progressive leadership. Mississippi also had a string of editors at the *Commercial Appeal* in Memphis, most notably Michael Grehl, a progressive who took a special interest in Mississippi. However, a troublesome void has developed with the loss of those legendary editors and with the movement of the *Commercial Appeal* toward a more right-wing editorial philosophy. The only shining light in the Mississippi media today is the *Jackson Free Press*, a weekly newspaper under the editorship of Mississippi-born Donna Ladd. As the only progressive newspaper in the state, it has distinguished itself with news stories and editorials that have dealt with a wide range of social and political issues, including important investigations of cold-case civil rights murders.

James L. Dickerson:

One of the hardest things for me to reconcile about the corruption of the news media during the Dark Days is how otherwise decent people could get caught up in a mindset that allowed them to rationalize betraying their First Amendment responsibilities by aiding state-supported terror against African Americans.

Jackson Daily News editor Jimmy Ward was literally the voice of racism in Mississippi in the 1950s and 1960s, using not only hurtful words under his own byline but also the power of the newsroom to manipulate news stories in such a way as to deprive readers of the truth. Yet by the 1970s, when I got to know him, he was a personable man with a good sense of humor who never once made a racist comment in my presence.

Hal DeCell was another newsman who was problematic for me. I grew up reading his *Deer Creek Pilot*, a weekly newspaper that focused on community news. I don't recall the newspaper publishing much news about African Americans, but neither do I recall it taking mean-spirited editorial positions against them. Yet DeCell was one of the founding members of the Mississippi Sovereignty Commission, someone who worked day and night to carry out its destructive mission.

Several years ago, in an effort to better understand DeCell, I spoke to one of his sons, Hal Jr., about his father. He said he had childhood memories of hearing his father discuss the commission. "I remember him saying that the files never should have been done. I know my father, and I know he would never do anything to hurt other folks." I would agree with that. In the 1970s, when I started working for the *Delta Democrat-Times*, the *Deer Creek Pilot* reprinted many of my stories, some on the front page.

On the editorial page, where DeCell and his wife, Carolyn, both wrote columns, I was frequently mentioned, and in the most favorable terms imaginable. Their political and social beliefs were the direct opposite of my own—and they knew that full well—yet they put those differences aside to acknowledge my talents as a writer, no small thing in a community where everyone knows everyone else. You can probably imagine the grief it caused me to acknowledge Hal DeCell's commission activities in this book.

Why did so many journalists during the Dark Days abandon their principles, professional and religious, to serve such a nefarious cause? We may never fully understand that. Some like Erle Johnston lived out the betrayal until the bitter end, never acknowledging guilt, though a 1968 hospitalization for stress charitably could be viewed as an unconscious awareness of guilt. Others, such as Hal DeCell, walked away from the commission and never looked back, resuming a life of community usefulness amid quiet moments of regret expressed to family members. DeCell was like most Mississippians, including myself, who love the state even while simultaneously feeling disappointment in its shortcomings.

It Ain't Over, Not Yet

Government sometimes pretends that it has no past, only a glorious future. New elections, new faces, new priorities are supposed to delete the past, as if it never existed, but the new faces are little more than new images painted over the canvas of old disappointments. Government can never rid itself of its past, not entirely.

For three decades Mississippi officials conspired with racial terrorists, yet never has the federal government conducted an investigation into those human rights abuses. Moving on is not an option. There are people in Mississippi today who committed heinous crimes against humanity, and they are walking about enjoying the fruits of democracy, freedoms that others have given their lives to nourish. If there's one thing that should be obvious about the events that have shaped Mississippi's past, it is that there is still much work to be done to right the wrongs.

Presently, Mississippi is busily redacting its past, with the help of the news media and the churches, behaving like an animal covering up its wastes in a befouled nest. There are those in the state who say the past should be left alone. They are fearful the past will tell them something about themselves that they do not want to hear. In some respects Mississippi is like a town that is being terrorized by an obnoxious drunk wandering the streets, firing a revolver at anything that moves. That drunk is racism, and the good people of the state—and there are many fine people in Mississippi—cower behind drawn blinds, whispering among themselves that tomorrow will be a new day.

One of the great ironies of Mississippi is that many of the native sons who brought high accolades to the state—Medgar Evers, William Faulkner, John Grisham, B. B. King, Willie Morris, Elvis Presley, Eudora Welty, Tennessee Williams, Richard Wright, and others—were universally disliked by white Mississippians throughout much of their careers because of their positions on civil rights issues.

Today Mississippi has more black elected officials than any other state. That is a momentous improvement that is directly related to the spiritual endurance of those who stood up to the tyranny of the past. But even that is not what it seems. Not since Reconstruction has Mississippi elected a person of color to a statewide office. The black office-holders who today make Mississippi look good in the eyes of the nation all owe their victories to small, majority-black voting districts. Voters in white-majority voting districts are still reluctant to extend the hand of acceptance to black candidates.

The racial divide was clearly visible in the 2008 presidential race, which saw Republican candidate John McCain, who has family ties to Mississippi, receive 57 percent of the vote in Mississippi, with Democratic candidate Barack Obama receiving 43 percent. Since blacks make up 37 percent of the population in Mississippi, the highest percentage of any state, it is obvious that very few whites voted for Obama, something that surprised no one. Throughout the campaign, Mississippi racists were the dominant voice in the state, using talk radio to accuse Obama of the most irrational things imaginable. In the days following the election, the *Clarion-Ledger* received reports that children were forbidden to mention Obama's name at school, and those who disobeyed were suspended. One person reported being forcibly removed from a state office building because she was wearing an Obama campaign button.

For most of her life, the beloved Mississippi author Eudora Welty lived only a short distance away from the seat of power in Jackson, Mississippi, and around the corner from her neighbor Alex A. Alston.[4] As she walked the streets to run the pedestrian errands of daily life, read the newspapers, shopped at the grocery, and attended church, she witnessed the effects of the Dark Days in countless ways.

Once, while commenting on her work as a WPA photographer during the Great Depression, Welty said, "My wish, my continuing passion, would be not to point the finger in judgment but to part a curtain, that invisible shadow that falls between people, the veil of indifference to each other's presence, each other's wonder, each other's human plight." She might well have been talking about Mississippi's Dark Days and the challenge that lies in parting the Magnolia curtain so that the atrocities they veil can never be repeated under the tattered flag of Mississippi Values.

Acknowledgments

The authors would like to thank Mississippi attorney general Jim Hood; Governor William Winter; Governor Bill Waller; Jim Ingram; Hollis Baugh; Charles Hall, for a wonderful story; Martin Kilpatrick; Donna Ladd; John Waits; the late Joseph Sullivan; George Rogers; the staff at the Alexander Heard Library at Vanderbilt University Library; Rick Abraham; Hal DeCell Jr.; our excellent editor Susan Betz, whose probing questions sometimes kept us up late at night searching for answers; project editor Devon Freeny; the staff at the Memphis/ Shelby County Public Library; Ed Frank at the Mississippi Valley Collection at the University of Memphis; the staff at the Mississippi Department of Archives and History; photographers Steve Gardner, Kate Medley, and Matt Saldana; Samuel M. Davis, dean of the Ole Miss School of Law, who was kind enough to read the first draft of the manuscript and offer copyediting suggestions.

Alex A. Alston Jr. would especially like to thank his wife, Sarah Jane, who encouraged him throughout this endeavor; his lifetime friend Kathryn Dean Bibb, who grew up in Hollandale with him and consulted with him on the early days in Hollandale; his friend and paralegal Pauline Cochran, who put up with him for more than forty years while practicing law and who painstakingly typed large portions of this manuscript from his difficult notes. He is indebted to two outstanding ministers, Dr. T. W. Lewis and the Reverend Keith Tonkel, who inspired him over the years and gave him insight into some of the passages in this work, and also the Reverend Kenneth Dean, who steadfastly kept the faith through some horrific years. His thoughts also go to two great unsung heroes, George Lucus and Kathy Nester, the attorneys who defended James Ford Seale in a difficult and unpopular case and who consulted with him throughout that trial and furnished the authors with all the documents on appeal. Likewise, he would like to thank his friend Judge Bobby DeLaughter, who consulted with him extensively concerning the Byron De La Beckwith trial. His warmest thoughts go to Earl T. Thomas, now deceased, who taught him that lawyering is the noblest of professions; and his friend Walker Watters, who confirmed many of the stories relating to their early practice of law in Jackson.

Notes

2. Emmett Till: A Prelude to Terror

1. William Bradford Huie, "The Shocking Story of Approved Killing in Mississippi," *Look*, January 24, 1956; Centers for Disease Control, www.usgovinfo.about.com/od/healthcare.

2. The background information on Emmett Till, the participants in the killing, and the aftermath were gleaned from several sources, including William Bradford Huie's *Look* article, reports on the trial, a U.S. Department of Justice press release dated May 19, 2004, and two articles written by Jerry Mitchell for the *Clarion-Ledger* (November 14, 2007 and February 11, 2007).

3. The account of what happened inside the store is derived from Alabama-born journalist William Bradford Huie's interviews with Roy Bryant and J. W. Milam and from reports on the trial. Admittedly, it offers only one perspective, which runs counter to the theory that Emmett Till only whistled at Carolyn Bryant, but Huie's account is specific in detail and believable. If Bryant and Milam had fabricated details of the encounter, they likely would have claimed that Till had physically assaulted Carolyn, a claim that would have bolstered their defense.

4. Huie, "Approved Killing in Mississippi."

5. Mississippi Department of Archives and History, Sovereignty Commission files, SCR ID 10-5-0-91-1-1-1, dated October 3, 1956.

3. Mississippi Crosses the Line

1. Roger Greene, "South's Mightiest Champion of White Race," *Commercial Appeal*, February 5, 1956.
2. James Gunter, *Commercial Appeal*, December 29 and 30, 1955.
3. Anthony Lewis, *New York Times*, December 30 and 31, 1955.
4. *Mississippi Code*, vol. 2, title 3 (1972).
5. Author interview with William Winter, 1997.
6. Author interview with George Rogers, 1996.
7. Neil R. McMillen, *The Citizens' Council: Organized Resistance to the Second Reconstruction 1954–1964* (Chicago: University of Illinois Press, 1994), 37.
8. Sovereignty Commission files, Mississippi Department of Archives and History (MDAH).
9. All the details in this chapter of DeCell's travels for the Sovereignty Commission are from Mississippi Sovereignty Commission files and State Auditor files at the MDAH and from the files of Governor Paul B. Johnson at the University of Southern Mississippi.
10. Robert Webb, "Power-Packed Truth Marketed to Nation by State Sovereignty Commission Skill," *Jackson State Times*, May 12, 1956.
11. Information about the FBI's filing system was derived from a number of sources, including Curt Gentry's *J. Edgar Hoover: The Man and the Secrets* (New York: Plume, 1991); the final report (book III) of the Select Committee to Study Governmental Operations (U.S. Senate, 1976); Kenneth O'Reilly's *Hoover and the Un-Americans* (Philadelphia: Temple University Press, 1983); and Athan Theoharis's *From the Secret Files of J. Edgar Hoover* (Chicago: Ivan R. Dee, 1991).
12. Sovereignty Commission files, MDAH, memo from Zack Van Landingham, March 26, 1959.
13. Sovereignty Commission files, MDAH, memo from Zack Van Landingham to the director, May 18, 1959.

4. The Lynching That Shocked the World

1. Howard Smead, *Blood Justice: The Lynching of Mack Charles Parker* (New York: Oxford University Press, 1986). The chronology of events leading up to the rape is faithful to Smead's account, which was based on interviews with James and June Walters (by the time of the interviews, James and June had divorced and she had remarried).
2. Smead, *Blood Justice*. This quotation and all others related to the rape and immediate aftermath are taken from Smead's interviews with June Walters.
3. Jim G. Lucas, "Why the Lynching? Possible Answer," *Memphis Press-Scimitar*, May 22, 1959.
4. FBI files on Mack Charles Parker.
5. Ibid.
6. Ibid.
7. Associated Press, "Red Hot Political Charges Fly in Lynching Case," May 19, 1959.
8. Mississippi Department of Archives and History, Sovereignty Commission files.
9. Smead, *Blood Justice*.

5. The Loose Ends of Government

1. United Press International, *Memphis Press-Scimitar*, November 1959.
2. Associated Press, May 19, 1959.
3. Phil Stroupe, "Choice of Waits Praised," *State Times*, n.d.
4. Sovereignty Commission files, Mississippi Department of Archives and History (MDAH).
5. Armis E. Hawkins, *The Grand Leader* (Jackson, MS: J. Prichard Morris Books, 2007).
6. Sovereignty Commission files, MDAH, report,May 13, 1964.
7. *Jackson Advocate*, May 12, 1962.
8. Lynne Olson, *Freedom's Daughters: The Unsung Heroes of the Civil Rights Movement from 1830 to 1970* (New York: Scribner, 2001), 192.

6. Hoddy Toddy: The Integration of Ole Miss

1. Clyde Kennard, letter to the editor, *Hattiesburg American*, December 6, 1968.
2. Sovereignty Commission files, Mississippi Department of Archives and History (MDAH), report from Zack Van Landingham, December 17, 1959.
3. This account of James Meredith's enrollment at Ole Miss is derived from Meredith's book *Three Years in Mississippi* (Bloomington: University of Indiana Press, 1966); newspaper stories from the *Jackson Daily News, the Memphis Press-Scimitar*, the *Commercial Appeal*, the *Mississippian*, and the *Clarion-Ledger*; David Halberstam's story published in *Esquire*; Sovereignty Commission files, MDAH; and the Kennedy-Barnett tapes, President's Office Files, Presidential Recordings Collection, John F. Kennedy Library.
4. President's Office Files, Presidential Recordings Collection, John F. Kennedy Library, Dictabelt 4A1, cassette A.
5. Sovereignty Commission files, MDAH, report from Tom Scarbrough, May 29, 1963.
6. United Press International, "Cleve McDowell Under Arrest," September 21, 1963; United Press International, "Once Again, Ole Miss Becomes Segregated," September 25, 1963.

7. The Assassination of Medgar Evers

1. Our account of Medgar Evers's assassination was compiled from information obtained from *Jackson Daily News, Clarion-Ledger*, Associated Press, United Press International; Sovereignty Commission reports, Paul B. Johnson Collection, University of Southern Mississippi; and *Ghosts of Mississippi* by Maryanne Vollers (New York: Random House, 1998).
2. Author Interview with the Reverend Edwin King, 1996.
3. Myrlie Evers with William Peters, *For Us, the Living* (Garden City, NY: Doubleday, 1967).

4. Thomas R. West and James W. Moon, eds., *To Redeem a Nation: A History and Anthology of the Civil Rights Movement* (St. James, NY: Brandywine Press, 1993), 137.

5. Adam Nossiter, *Of Long Memory: Mississippi and the Murder of Medgar Evers* (Cambridge, MA: Da Capo Press, 2002).

6. Sovereignty Commission files, Mississippi Department of Archives and History (MDAH).

7. Sovereignty Commission files, MDAH, report from Tom Scarbrough, September 12, 1962.

8. *Commercial Appeal*, March 8, 1963.

9. *New York Times*, July 19, 1963.

8. Philadelphia Burning

1. Sovereignty Commission reports, Paul B. Johnson Collection, University of Southern Mississippi.

2. Ibid.

3. FBI files, memo from A. Rosen to Mr. Belmont, September 18, 1964.

4. Sovereignty Commission reports, Paul B. Johnson Collection.

5. Sovereignty Commission reports, Paul B. Johnson Collection, report to commission members, September 1, 1964.

6. Sovereignty Commission reports, Paul B. Johnson Collection.

7. Ibid.

8. Ibid.

9. FBI memo from A. Rosen, September 21, 1964.

10. Mississippi Department of Archives and History, Sovereignty Commission files, report, December 8, 1964.

11. Sovereignty Commission reports, Paul B. Johnson Collection.

12. FBI files, memo, September 19, 1964.

13. Trial transcript.

9. Charles Moore and Henry Dee

1. Town of Meadville, "History of Meadville," www.meadvillems.com/history.html.
2. Testimony at James Ford Seale murder trial.
3. Jerry Mitchell, "Former Klansman Apologizes to Victims' Kin," *Clarion-Ledger*, June 6, 2007.
4. Testimony of Charles Edwards at James Ford Seale's murder trial.
5. Vernon Lane Wharton, *The Negro in Mississippi 1865–1890* (repr., New York: Harper and Row, 1947), 38–42.
6. Testimony at James Ford Seale's murder trial.
7. Jerry Mitchell, "Witnesses Testify About Finding Body," *Clarion-Ledger*, June 5, 2007.
8. The Reverend Briggs diary, read to jurors at James Ford Seale's murder trial.
9. Donna Ladd, "The Crime: May 2, 1964," *Jackson Free Press*, May 24, 2006.
10. Mississippi Department of Archives and History, Sovereignty Commission files, report, February 20, 1964.
11. Ladd, "The Crime."
12. Ronnie Harper, interview with David Ridgen in *Mississippi Cold Case*.
13. Donna Ladd, "Dredging Up the Past: Why Mississippians Must Tell Our Own Stories," *Jackson Free Press*, May 31, 2007.
14. Donna Ladd, *Jackson Free Press*, July 20, 2005.
15. Ibid.
16. This information was revealed in David Ridgen's documentary *Mississippi Cold Case*, but prior to the airing of the film, unknown to Ridgen, the information was also posted on www.hungryblues.net, a blog written by Benjamin Greenberg.

10. Mississippi's Legal Jungle

1. Vernon Lane Wharton, *The Negro in Mississippi 1865–1890* (repr., New York: Harper and Row, 1947), 137.
2. *Patton v. Mississippi*, 332 U.S. 463 (1947).

3. *Patton v. State*, 201 Miss. 410, 29 So.2d 96 (1947).

4. *Cameron v. State*, 102 So.2d 355, 412 (Miss. 1958).

5. Ibid. at 411.

6. *Harper v. State*, 171 So.2d 129 (Miss. 1965).

7. *Batson v. Kentucky*, 476 U.S. 79 (1986).

8. *McGee v. State*, 953 So.2d 241, 244 (Miss. 2005); *Walker v. State*, 815 So.2d 1209 (Miss. 2002).

9. Julius E. Thompson, *Lynchings in Mississippi* (Jefferson, NC: McFarland, 2007), 100.

10. Neil R. McMillen, *Dark Journey* (Champaign, IL: University of Illinois Press, 1998), 233.

11. Ibid.

12. *Curtis Publishing Co. v. Butts* and *Associated Press v. Walker*, 380 U.S. 130 (1967).

13. *Loftin v. State*, 150 Miss. 228, 116 So. 435 (1928).

14. *Fisher v. State*, 145 Miss. 116, 127, 110 So. 361 (1926).

15. *White v. State*, 129 Miss. 182, 187, 91 So. 903 (1922).

16. Ibid.

17. *Breckenridge v. Time, Inc.*, 179 So.2d 781 (Miss. 1965).

18. Willie Morris, *The Courting of Marcus DuPree* (New York: Doubleday, 1983), 167–168.

19. *Breckenridge v. Time, Inc.*, 179 So.2d 781 (Miss. 1965).

20. The entire rendition of these facts is taken from the Opinion of the Mississippi Supreme Court in *Pruitt v. State*, 163 Miss. 47, 139 So. 861 (1932).

21. Ibid. at 62–64.

22. *Hearings before the United States Commission on Civil Rights*, vol. II, Administration and Justice, hearing held in Jackson, Mississippi, February 16–20, 1965, 306–307.

23. Michael de L. Landon, *The Honor and Dignity of the Profession: A History of the Mississippi State Bar, 1906–1976* (Jackson, MS: University Press of Mississippi, 1979), 158.

24. *United States, ex rel. Goldsby v. Harpole*, 263 F2d 71, 82 (5th Cir. 1959).

25. John Howard, *Men Like That* (Chicago: University of Chicago Press, 1999), 157.
26. *Brown v. State*, 173 Miss. 542, 158 So. 339 (1935).

11. Mississippi Gestapo

1. Sovereignty Commission files, Mississippi Department of Archives and History (MDAH), report, July 10, 1963.
2. Ibid., July 19, 1963.
3. Michael Rejebian, "Eastland Submitted Names for Commission Probes," *Clarion-Ledger*, January 28, 1990.
4. Sovereignty Commission files, MDAH, report, November 29, 1962.
5. Ibid., letter, March 13, 1964; ibid., letter, March 6, 1962.
6. Sovereignty Commission reports, Paul B. Johnson Collection, University of Southern Mississippi.
7. Ibid.
8. Sovereignty Commission files, MDAH.
9. Sovereignty Commission reports, Paul B. Johnson Collection, report from Tom Scarbrough, March 15, 1967; ibid., letter from U.S. Assistant Attorney General John Doar to Governor Warren P. Knowles, March 4, 1967.
10. Position paper prepared by Mississippi Draft Information Service.
11. The information about the James Meredith shooting was obtained from Sovereignty Commission reports in the Paul B. Johnson Collection at the University of Southern Mississippi.
12. Sovereignty Commission files, MDAH, memo from Tom Scarbrough to Erle Johnston, June 20, 1966; ibid., memo from Erle Johnston to Herman Glazier, governor's assistant, June 14, 1966.
13. Author interview with William Winter, 1996.
14. Author interview with George Rogers, 1996.
15. Author interview with Bill Waller, 1996.
16. Author interview with David Ingebretsen, 1996.
17. Author interview with Ed King, 1996.

12. Praise the Lord, but Don't Seat the Blacks

1. Mississippi Department of Archives and History, Sovereignty Commission files, reports of Zack Van Landingham.

2. Randy Sparks, *Religion in Mississippi* (Jackson, MS: University Press of Mississippi and Mississippi Historical Society, 2001), 251–252.

3. See Curtis Wilkie, *Dixie* (New York: Scribner, 2001), 66, for a reflection on revivals in Summit, Mississippi.

4. Ibid.

5. W. J. Cunningham, *Agony at Galloway* (Jackson, MS: University Press of Mississippi, 1980), 13–24.

6. Mark Newman, "The Mississippi Baptist Convention and Desegregation, 1945–1980," *Journal of Mississippi History* 59 (1997), 1.

7. Ibid., 9.

8. Ibid., 17.

9. Sparks, *Religion in Mississippi*, 238–239.

10. Senate Concurrent Resolution No. 615, Mississippi Legislature, Regular Session 2006.

11. Cunningham, *Agony at Galloway*, 7.

12. Sparks, *Religion in Mississippi*, 245.

13. Ann Waldron, *Hodding Carter: The Reconstruction of a Racist* (Chapel Hill, NC: Algonquin Books of Chapel Hill, 1993), 314.

14. Sparks, *Religion in Mississippi*, 229.

15. Marie R. Lowe and J. Clint Morris, "Civil Rights Advocates in the Academy: White Pro-integrationist Faculty at Millsaps College," *Journal of Mississippi History* 69, no. 2 (2007), 121.

16. Will D. Campbell, *Providence* (Atlanta: Longstreet Press, 1992), 16–17.

17. Newman, "Mississippi Baptist Convention and Desegregation," 19.

18. Charles Marsh, *God's Long Summer* (Princeton, NJ: Princeton University Press, 1997), 5.

19. Newman, "Mississippi Baptist Convention and Desegregation," 14.

20. Author interview with Jim Ingram.

13. All the News That's Fit to Print—for White Mississippians

1. R. H. Henry, *Editors I Have Known* (New Orleans: self-published, 1922).
2. Ibid.
3. *Clarion-Ledger/Jackson Daily News*, Sunday ed., November 24, 1957.
4. James Dickerson, "Faulkner's Letters—Revealing," *Delta Democrat-Times*, February 20, 1977.
5. "Lawyer Ads Beneficial," *Delta Democrat-Times*, June 29, 1977.
6. James L. Dickerson, "Life After Life?" *Delta Democrat-Times*, August 29, 1977.
7. Author interview with Charles Evers, 1996.
8. Mississippi Department of Archives and History, Sovereignty Commission files, letter from Erle Johnston, January 7, 1966.
9. Gary McElroy, "Portrait of a Nazi Leader: 'We Are the Old Order,'" *Jackson Daily News*, May 12 and 13, 1980.
10. Ira Harkey, *The Smell of Burning Crosses* (Xlibris, 1967).
11. Runyon, Damon, "Durant Editor, Says Runyon, Is Prettiest Party Delegate," International News Service, July 26, 1940, reprinted, *APF Reporter*, Summer 1983.
12. David R. Davies, *The Press and Race* (Jackson, MS: University Press of Mississippi, 2001).
13. Ibid.

14. Inside the FBI: The Truth About Mississippi

1. Don Whitehead. *The FBI Story* (New York: Random House, 1956).
2. Glenda Elizabeth Gilmore, *Defying Dixie: The Radical Roots of Civil Rights* (New York: W. W. Norton, 2008).
3. Tim Weiner, *Legacy of Ashes: The History of the CIA* (New York: Doubleday, 2007).
4. Sovereignty Commission files, Mississippi Department of Archives and History (MDAH).
5. Sovereignty Commission files, MDAH.

6. Sovereignty Commission files, MDAH, memo from Erle Johnston, November 22, 1965.

7. Sovereignty Commission files, MDAH, memo from John Sullivan, March 4, 1964.

8. Ibid., memo from John Sullivan, March 8, 1964.

9. All information about Webb Burke was obtained from his FBI personnel file, obtained under the Freedom of Information Act; Mississippi Sovereignty Commission files; and interviews with Joseph Sullivan, 1996, and Jim Ingram, 2008.

10. Reid Derr interview with Frank Barber, Center for Oral History and Cultural Heritage, University of Southern Mississippi, May 30, 1990, and June 30, 1993.

11. Author interview with Jim Ingram, 2008.

12. Ibid.

13. Sovereignty Commission files, MDAH, memo from Andy Hopkins, July 22, 1964; memo from Erle Johnston, May 28, 1964; report from "Investigator #51" (Jerry Harrison of Harrison Detectives), May 18, 1964.

14. Author interview with Joseph Sullivan, 1996.

15. Ibid.

15. Byron De La Beckwith: Ordeal by Trial and Error

1. *Jaquith v. Beckwith*, 157 So.2d 403 (Miss. 1963).

2. Bill Waller, *Straight Ahead* (Brandon, MS: Quail Ridge Press, 2007), 69.

3. Original transcript can be found in loose documents of Judge Bobby DeLaughter in the Department of Archives and History, Jackson, Mississippi.

4. Waller, *Straight Ahead*, 72.

5. Adam Nossiter, *Of Long Memory* (Reading, MA: Addison-Wesley, 1994), 154.

6. Waller, Bill. *Straight Ahead*, 75.

7. Ibid., 76–77.

8. Mississippi Department of Archives and History, Sovereignty Commission files.

9. This account of Byron De La Beckwith's New Orleans arrest and trial was compiled from a variety of sources, including Maryanne Vollers's *Ghosts of Mississippi* (New York: Random House, 1998), the *Clarion-Ledger*, and various other newspaper and magazine articles.

10. Author interview with Bobby DeLaughter, 2008.

11. Ibid.; Bobby DeLaughter, *Never Too Late* (New York: Scribner, 2001), 173.

12. DeLaughter, *Never Too Late*; interview with Bobby DeLaughter; *Beckwith v. State*, 615 So.2d 1134 (Miss. 1992).

13. *Beckwith v. State*, 615 So.2d 1134, 1149 (Miss. 1982).

14. DeLaughter, *Never Too Late*, 222–223.

15. *Byron De La Beckwith, VI v. State*, 707 So.2d 547, 561 (Miss. 1997).

16. Ibid. at 562.

17. DeLaughter, *Never Too Late*, 273.

18. Ibid., 270.

19. Author interview with the Reverend Ed King, 1996.

16. Philadelphia Redux: Edgar Ray Killen Raised from the Dead

1. Trial transcript, published May 1, 2005, in the *Clarion-Ledger*.

2. Trial transcript, vol. 6, 522.

3. Ibid., 527.

4. Ibid., 528.

5. Ibid., 528–532.

6. Ibid., 562–582.

7. *Killen v. State*, 958 So.2d 172, 179 (Miss. 2007).

8. Ibid. at 172, 175–176 ¶¶ 11–13 (2007).

9. Ibid. at ¶ 14.

10. Ibid. at *177–178* ¶ 20.

11. Ibid. at 182–183.

12. Ibid. at 182 ¶ 39.

13. Ibid. at 182 ¶ 45.

14. Trial transcript, vol. 8, 850–851.

15. Ibid., 863, 868.

16. Ibid., 873.

17. Ibid.
18. Author interview with Jim Hood, 2008.
19. Ibid.
20. Bond hearing transcript, 4–22.
21. Ibid., 23–36.
22. Jerry Mitchell, *Clarion-Ledger*, August 18, 2005.
23. *Killen v. State*, 958 So.2d 172, 174 ¶ 4 (2007).
24. Ibid. ¶ 7.
25. Ibid. at 191 ¶ 79.

17. James Ford Seale: Times Runs Out for a Killer

1. Constance Baker Motley was the first African American woman elected to the New York State Senate. In 1966, President Lyndon Johnson named her as a United States district judge for the United States District Court for the Southern District of New York, in which capacity she continued serving until her death in 2005.
2. The Deacons for Defense was of recent origin and finally arose out of the frustration of blacks, due to white brutality and the recognition that in order to preserve their lives, they must arm themselves. The best study of that organization is found in Lance Hill's *The Deacons for Defense* (Chapel Hill: University of North Carolina Press, 2004).

18. Atonement in a Haunted Land

1. Reed Massengill, *Portrait of a Racist* (New York: St. Martin's Press, 1994).
2. James C. Coleman, *Abnormal Psychology and Modern Life* (Chicago: Scott, Foresman, 1964).
3. Mississippi rankings in the areas of disease are based on national health statistics; rankings on mental health are based on reporting by Mental Health America (formerly Mental Health Association), specifically reports on the average number of poor mental health days experienced by persons eighteen or older; rankings on educational potential are based on national test scores; Mississippi was named the most politi-

cally corrupt state in a 2004 study conducted by the Corporate Crime Reporter.

4. Malcolm Jones, "Southern Lady, World-Class Storyteller," *Newsweek*, August 6, 2001.

Select Bibliography

Books

Ball, Howard. *Justice in Mississippi: The Murder Trial of Edgar Ray Killen.* Lawrence, KS: University Press of Kansas, 2006.

Bartley, Numan V. *The New South: 1945–1980.* Baton Rouge: Louisiana State University Press, 1995.

———. *The Rise of Massive Resistance.* Baton Rouge: Louisiana State University Press, 1969.

Cagin, Seth. *We Are Not Afraid: The Story of Goodman, Schwerner, and Chaney and the Civil Rights Campaign for Mississippi.* New York: Macmillan, 1988.

Campbell, Will D. *Providence.* Atlanta: Longstreet Press, 1992.

Carter, Hodding. *Southern Legacy.* Baton Rouge: Louisiana State University Press, 1966.

Carter, Hodding (III). *The South Strikes Back.* New York: Doubleday, 1959.

Classen, Steven D. *Watching Jim Crow: The Struggles over Mississippi TV.* Durham, NC: Duke University Press, 2004.

Cobb, James C. *Away Down South.* New York: Oxford University Press, 2005.

Cortner, Richard C. *A "Scottsboro" Case in Mississippi.* Jackson, MS: University Press of Mississippi, 1986.

Crespino, Joseph. *In Search of Another Country.* Princeton, NJ: Princeton University Press, 2007.

349

Cunningham, W. J. *Agony at Galloway*. Jackson, MS: University Press of Mississippi, 1980.

Davies, David R. *The Press and Race: Mississippi Journalists Confront the Movement*. Jackson, MS: University Press of Mississippi, 2001.

DeLaughter, Bobby. *Never Too Late: A Prosecutor's Story of Justice in the Medgar Evers Case*. New York: Scribner, 2001.

Doyle, William. *An American Insurrection*. New York: Doubleday, 2001.

Evers, Charles. *Evers*. New York: World Publishing, 1971.

Feldman, Glenn. *Politics and Religion in the White South*. Lexington, KY: University Press of Kentucky, 2005.

Gentry, Curt. *J. Edgar Hoover: The Man and the Secrets*. New York: Plume, 1991.

Gilmore, Glenda Elizabeth. *Defying Dixie: The Radical Roots of Civil Rights*. New York: W. W. Norton, 2008.

Golden, Harry. *Only in America*. Cleveland, OH: World Publishing, 1958.

Harkey, Ira. *The Smell of Burning Crosses: A White Intergrationist Editor in Mississippi*. Xlibris, 1967.

Hawkins, Armis E. *The Grand Leader*. Jackson, MS: J. Prichard Morris Books, 2007.

Hearings Before the United States Commission on Civil Rights, vol. II, Administration of Justice. Hearings Held in Jackson, Mississippi, February 16–20, 1965.

Henry, R. H. *Editors I Have Known*. New Orleans: E. S. Upton Printing Company, 1922.

Highsaw, Robert B., and Charles N. Fortenberry. *The Government and Administration of Mississippi*. New York: Thomas Y. Crowell, 1954.

Hill, Lance. *The Deacons for Defense*. Chapel Hill, NC: University of North Carolina Press, 2004.

Howard, John. *Men Like That*. Chicago: The University of Chicago Press, 1999.

Johnston, Erle. *Mississippi's Defiant Years: 1953–1973*. Forest, MS: Lake Harbor, 1990.

Key, V. O. *Southern Politics*. New York: Random House, 1949.

Loevy, Robert D. *To End All Segregation: The Politics of the Passage of the Civil Rights Act of 1964.* Lanham, MD: University Press of America, 1990.

Loewen, James W., and Charles Sallis. *Mississippi: Conflict and Change.* New York: Pantheon Books, 1974.

Lord, Walter. *The Past That Would Not Die.* New York: Harper & Row, 1965.

McMillen, Neil R. *The Citizens' Council: Organized Resistance to the Second Reconstruction.* Chicago: University of Illinois Press, 1994.

———. *Dark Journey: Black Mississippians in the Age of Jim Crow.* Champaign, IL: University of Illinois Press, 1998.

Marsh, Charles. *God's Long Summer.* Princeton, NJ: Princeton University Press, 1997.

Massengill, Reed. *Portrait of a Racist.* New York: St. Martin's Press, 1994.

Meredith, James. *Three Years in Mississippi.* Bloomington, IN: University of Indiana Press, 1966.

Mills, Kay. *Changing Channels: The Civil Rights Case That Transformed Television.* Jackson, MS: University Press of Mississippi, 2004.

Morris, Willie. *The Courting of Marcus Dupree.* Garden City, NY: Doubleday, 1983.

———. *The Ghosts of Medgar Evers.* New York: Random House, 1998.

Nash, Jere, and Andy Taggart. *Mississippi Politics.* Jackson, MS: University Press of Mississippi, 2006.

Nelson, Jack. *Terror in the Night.* New York: Simon & Schuster, 1993.

Nossiter, Adam. *Of Long Memory: Mississippi and the Murder of Medgar Evers.* Cambridge, MA: Da Capo Press, 1994.

Olson, Lynne. *Freedom's Daughters: The Unsung Heroes of the Civil Rights Movement from 1830 to 1970.* New York: Scribner, 2001.

O'Reilly, Kenneth. *Hoover and the Un-Americans: The FBI, HUAC, and the Red Menace.* Philadelphia: Temple University Press, 1983.

Parker, Frank R. *Black Votes Count.* Chapel Hill, NC: University of North Carolina Press, 1990.

Payne, Charles M. *I've Got the Light of Freedom.* Berkeley, CA: University of California Press, 1995.

Pyle, Christopher. *Military Surveillance of Civilian Politics.* New York: Garland, 1986.

Raines, Howell. *My Soul Is Rested.* New York: G. P. Putnam's, 1977.

Roberts, Gene, and Hank Klibanoff. *The Race Beat.* New York: Knopf, 2006.

Silver, James W. *Mississippi: The Closed Society.* New York: Harcourt, Brace & World, 1964.

Sims, Patsy. *The Klan.* New York: Stein and Day, 1978.

Smead, Howard. *Blood Justice: The Lynching of Mack Charles Parker.* New York: Oxford University Press, 1986.

Sparks, Randy J. *Religion in Mississippi.* Jackson, MS: University Press of Mississippi, 2001.

Theoharis, Athan. *From the Secret Files of J. Edgar Hoover.* Chicago: Ivan R. Dee, 1991.

Thompson, Julius E. *Lynchings in Mississippi.* Jefferson, NC: McFarland, 2007.

U.S. Government. *Supplementary Detailed Staff Reports on Intelligence Activities and the Rights of Americans.* Select Committee to Study Governmental Operations, Book III (1976).

Vaught, John. *Rebel Coach: My Football Family.* Memphis: Memphis State University Press, 1971.

Vollers, Maryanne. *Ghosts of Mississippi.* Boston: Little, Brown, 1995.

Waldron, Ann. *Hodding Carter.* Chapel Hill, NC: Algonquin, 1993.

Waller, Bill. *Straight Ahead.* Brandon, MS: Quail Ridge Press, 2007.

Weiner, Tim. *Legacy of Ashes: The History of the CIA.* New York: Doubleday, 2007.

Whitehead, Don. *Attack on Terror: The FBI Against the Ku Klux Klan in Mississippi.* New York: Funk & Wagnalls, 1970.

———. *The FBI Story: A Report to the People.* New York: Random House, 1956.

Wilkie, Curtis. *Dixie.* New York: Scribner, 2001.

Winter, William F. *The Measure of Our Days.* Jackson, MS: University Press of Mississippi, 2006.

Journals

Lowe, Maria R., and J. Clint Morris. "Civil Rights Advocates in the Academy: White Pro-integrationist Faculty at Millsaps College." *Journal of Mississippi History* 69, no. 2 (2007).

Newman, Mark. "The Mississippi Baptist Convention and Desegregation, 1945–1980." *Journal of Mississippi History* 59 (1997).

Newspapers and Magazines

Associated Press, "Barnett Stumping with Old Script," April 21, 1967.

———. "Gov. Coleman of Civil Rights Era Dies in Miss," September 29, 1991.

———. "Kennedy Tapes Crackle with Ole Miss Tension," *Commercial Appeal*, June 24, 1983.

———. "Mississippi Civil Rights Files Make Ex-allies Foes," October 3, 1993.

———. "Mississippi Seeks Dismissal of Lawsuit on Secret Files," October 2, 1980.

———. "Sovereignty Commission's Files Unsealed," June 1, 1994.

———. "Sovereignty Group May Be Abolished," March 8, 1958.

Brower, Sinda. "Crowd Cheers Barnett." *The Mississippian*, September 28, 1962.

Brown, David. "Mississippi Citizens Form Councils for Segregation" *Memphis Press-Scimitar*, September 9, 1954.

Brown, LaRaye. "For Families of Victims, Closure After Conviction." *Clarion-Ledger*, June 15, 2007.

Campbell, Sarah. "Files Will Open on Civil Rights Targets." *Commercial Appeal*, September 21, 1993.

———. "Queries Trim Beckwith Jury Pool." *Commercial* Appeal, January 19, 1994.

DeWan, Shaila. "Push to Resolve Fading Killings of Rights Era." *New York Times*, February 3, 2007.

Dickerson, James. "Magnolia Pilgrimage." *Commercial Appeal*, June 19, 1983.

———. "Life After Life?" *Delta Democrat-Times*, August 29, 1977.

———. "More Questions." *Commercial Appeal*, November 2, 1983.

———. "Politics of Squalor." *Commercial Appeal*, October 27, 1983.

———. "Voter Judgment." *Commercial Appeal*, November 6, 1983.

———. "Winter's Record." *Jackson Daily News*, June 30, 1980.

———. "Winter's Voice." *Commercial Appeal*, April 25, 1982.

Editorial. "The Kennedy Strategy." *New Republic*, February 15, 1960.

———. "The Leadership of LBJ." *New Republic*, April 18, 1960.

Friedman, Thomas L. "Generation Q." *New York Times*, October 10, 2007.

Gunter, James. "Unit Is Formed Here to Co-ordinate Aims of Southern Groups. *Commercial* Appeal, December 29, 1955.

Harrison, Selig S. "Kennedy as President." *New Republic*, June 27, 1960.

———. "Lyndon Johnson's World." *New Republic*, June 13, 1960.

Henry, John C. "Bill Would Give Mississippi Highway Patrol Sovereignty Records." *Delta Democrat-Times*, January 6, 1977.

Ladd, Donna. "We're Sorry." *Jackson Free Press*, January 25–31, 2007.

———. Miscellaneous articles. *Jackson Free Press*, July 27, 2005– June 27, 2007.

Lewis, Anthony. "Segregation Group Confers in Secret." *New York Times*, December 30, 1955.

McElroy, Gary. Various articles. *Jackson Daily News*, May 12 and 13, 1980.

Marsh, Charles. "Rendezvous with the Wizard." *Oxford American*, October/ November 1996.

Minor, Bill. "'Civil rights' Also Absent in the 1960s at Local Movie Theaters." *Clarion-Ledger*, June 1, 2007.

———. "Waller Vetoes Funds for Unit." New Orleans *Times-Picayune*, April 19, 1973.

Mitchell, Jerry. "Jackson Papers Were Tools of Spy Commission." *Clarion-Ledger*, January 28, 1994.

———. "Justice on the Way." *Clarion-Ledger*, January 25, 2007.

———. "Hunting the Klan" *The Clarion-Ledger*, January 28, 2007.

———. "Jury Selection Begins Today in Seale Kidnapping Trial." *Clarion-Ledger* May 30, 2007.

———. "Questioning of Potential Jurors over in Seale Trial." *Clarion-Ledger*, June 2, 2007.

———. "Witnesses Testify About Finding Body." *Clarion-Ledger*, June 5, 2007.

———. "Former Klansman Apologizes to Victims' Kin." *Clarion-Ledger*, June 6, 2007.

———. "Witnesses: Seale Admitted His Involvement in the Klan." *Clarion-Ledger*, June 8, 2007.

———. "Guilty on All Counts." *Clarion-Ledger*, June 15, 2007.

Oakley, Robert Edward. "The Victims." *Mississippi* (Winter 1967).

Overby, Charles. "A Mental Confrontation." *The Mississippian* (February 6, 1968).

———. "Protesting the Protesters." *The Mississippian* (1968).

Saggus, James. "Governor's Mansion to Become a Fortress." Associated Press, September 15, 1970.

Sherrill, Robert G. "James Eastland: Child of Scorn." *The Nation*, October 4, 1965.

Spence, John. "200 Turn Out to Help Form Citizens' Council." *Memphis Press-Scimitar*, November 8, 1961.

United Press International, "Coleman Appoints Winter to Tax Collector Post," *Memphis Press-Scimitar*, April 4, 1956.

———. "Five Negroes Shotgunned," *The Mississippian*, June 26, 1963.

———. "Once Again Ole Miss Becomes Segregated," September 25, 1963.

———. "Fiery Flare-up in Political Debate—Barnett, Williams Get Hot," May 16, 1967.

Watkins, Billy. "Seale's Defense Tough to Tackle." *Clarion-Ledger*, June 5, 2007.

Trial Transcripts

Edgar Ray Killen v. State of Mississippi. Case No. 2005-KA-01393-SCT. Record Room, Mississippi Supreme Court.

State of Mississippi v. Byron De La Beckwith. First Trial, 1964. Mississippi Department of Archives and History.

Index

Abraham, Rick, 179

Adams, Mary Ann, 269, 274

Adams County, Mississippi, 208

Alabama, 234

Allen, Louis, 136

Alston, Alex A., Jr., 8–9, 37–39, 41–42, 82–85, 119–20, 151–53, 155–56, 158–60, 163–65, 167–68, 195–98, 203–5, 280–81, 313, 325–27, 332

American Civil Liberties Union (ACLU), 188, 228

Americans for the Preservation of the White Race, 112–13, 143

Anderson, Doug, 187

Anderson, Linda, 143, 301

Anderson, Reuben, 167

Anderson, Walter, 302

Anti-Defamation League, 265–66, 279

Antilynching bills, 154, 216

Arkansas, 106, 216, 240

Arledge, Jimmy, 126, 127

Armistead, Rex, 171, 172

Arnett v. Carol C. and Fred R. Smith, Inc., 159

Associated Press, 155–56

Association of Citizens' Councils of South Carolina, 64

Ball, Howard, 287

Banks, Fred, 167

Baptist Church, 195, 207, 209

Baptist Committee of Concern, 209

Barber, Frank, 243

Barbour, William, 189–90

Barnett, Hop, 123, 124, 126

Barnett, O. H., 158–60, 261

Barnett, Ross, 58, 63, 66, 67, 81, 86, 155, 175, 230, 263, 287

   contempt order against, 78

   and James Meredith, 76–79

   and John F. Kennedy, 78–80

   and Robert F. Kennedy, 78–79, 174

   and Sovereignty Commission, 64

   and states' rights, 65

   support of segregation, 57, 62, 65

Barnette, Horace Doyle, 126–27

Barr, John U., 30

Barrett, Russell, 171

Batson v. Kentucky, 150

Baugh, Hollis, 13–15

Beard, Fred, 220

Beckwith, Byron De La, 97–100, 101, 108, 185, 280–81, 325

   and Anti-Defamation League bombing, 265–67

and Coleman letter, 35, 36, 106
desegregation, obsession with, 105–6
firearms, obsession with, 98, 106
first trial of, 259–64
and KKK, 265–66, 276
marital problems of, 107, 322
and Medgar Evers murder, 97, 269
political aspirations of, 265, 267
racist beliefs of, 262, 276
second trial of, 264–65
third trial of, 270–77, 279
Beckwith, Byron De La, V, 97
Beckwith, Byron De La, VII, 99, 271
Beckwith, Byron De La, VIII, 271
Beckwith, Mary Louise. *See* Williams,
     Mary Louise
Beckwith, Thelma, 268, 270, 279
Belmont, Alan, 31
Belmont Café, 120, 152–53
Beth Israel Congregation, 210
Birdsong, T. B., 240–41, 244, 255
black power, 183
bombings, 89, 129–30, 138, 147, 208–9,
     211
     Byron De La Beckwith and, 265–67
Bonanza (television series), 172
Boren, Hugh, 64
Borinski, Ernst, 206
Bowers, Sam Holloway, Jr., 124, 126,
     127, 156, 208, 211, 254–55, 271,
     284–85
Braden, Anne, 237
Braden, Carl, 237
Brand, Jack, 155
Breckenridge, Charles, 158
Briggs, Clyde, 132, 134, 310
Broome, Vernon, 54
Brown, Charles, 87
Brown, R. Jess, 51

Brown v. Board of Education, 1, 303,
     325
Bryant, Curtis, 129
Bryant, Carolyn, 18–20, 24
Bryant, Roy, 17–23
     arrest, trial, and acquittal of, 24
     confession of, 25–26
Buckley, Horace, 187
Buckley, Travis, 156, 271
Burke, Webb, 185–86, 188, 239–43,
     254, 255
Burrage, Olen, 121
Bush, George H. W., 315

Cain, Mary, 173
Calloway, Marsh, 206–7
Cameron, J. C., 149
Camp, Howard, 88
Campbell, Foote, 302
Campbell, Will, 200–201
Carmichael, Stokely, 181, 183
Carroll County, 177
Carter, Betty, 215, 219
Carter, Esther, 121
Carter, Hodding, 24, 199, 215–18, 230,
     232, 329
Carter, Hodding, III, 218, 220, 226,
     230, 327, 329
Carter, Jimmy, 218
Carter, Philip, 218–19
Catledge, Turner, 320
Central Intelligence Agency (CIA)
     covert activity recruitment, 236
     Intelligence Community division of,
     32
Chaney, Fannie Lee, 293
Chaney, James, 121, 124, 127, 139, 158,
     246, 248, 251–53, 283, 285, 287,
     291, 298

murder of, 118, 122, 289, 292, 295
surveillance and arrest of, 110–11
Chatmon, Sam, 10
Chaze, William, 222
Chisolm, Mrs. Frankie, 117, 120, 121
A Christian View of Segregation
    (Gillespie), 206
churches
    black, 147, 207–9
    support of civil rights, 200–203, 320
    support of segregation, 193–95, 198–
        200, 207
Churchill, Winston, 85
Citizens' Council, 32, 64, 188, 194,
        200–201, 204, 206, 221, 231, 235,
        238, 251
    and Beckwith trial, 260, 264
    and Communist Party, 234
    moderate ministers, targeting of, 205,
        207
    Providence Farms investigation by,
        206
Citizens' Council (newspaper), 34
civil disobedience, 70
Civil Rights Act (1964), 137, 152, 243,
        325
    and public accommodations, 250
    and Title VI, 209
Civil Rights Act (1965), 325
Civil War, 61
Clark, John A., 166–67
Clarion (newspaper), 214
Clarion-Ledger, 204, 214, 220, 223, 224,
        327–28, 332
Clark, Paul, 237–38
Clarksdale, Mississippi, 36, 99
Clegg, J. E., 240
Cleveland, Mississippi, 9
Clinton, Bill, 67

Coleman, J. P., 27–28, 34–36, 41, 43,
        45–46, 52–54, 57–62, 64
    and creation of Sovereignty
        Commission, 31–33
    on racial problems, 31, 39–40
Coleman, James C., 323
Coleman, William F., 270
Commercial Appeal (newspaper), 25,
        29–30, 217, 329
Communist Party, 112
    and civil rights movement, 30,
        234–35
confessions, forcing of, 156–58
Congress of Racial Equality (CORE),
        109, 110, 113–14
Connick, Harry, 267
Constitution. *See* Mississippi
        Constitution; U.S. Constitution
Cope, DeLoach, 59
Cottonmouth Moccasin Gang, 138
Council of Federated Organizations
        (COFO), 67, 130
Counterintelligence Program
        (COINTELPRO), 40, 180, 236–37
Cox, William Harold, 69, 122–27, 188,
        302–3
Coxwell, Merrida, 271
Cresswell, Hollis, 277
Cunningham, E. H., Jr., 260
Cunningham, W. J., 207

Dahmer, Vernon, 156, 284
Dale, Sebe, 51, 52, 55
Davis, Elluard Jenoal, 275
Davis, Eugene, 314
Davis, Jefferson, 133
Davis, Joseph, 133
Deacons for Defense, 310
Dean, Kathryn, 196

Dean, Kenneth L., 204
DeCell, Carolyn, 35, 330
DeCell, Hal, 34, 35–36, 329–30
DeCell, Hal, Jr., 330
Declaration of Independence, 323
Dee, Henry Hezekiah, 130, 138, 143,
    301, 303, 311–12, 313–14, 322
  kidnapping of, 131–32
  murder of, 133–35, 307–10
Deer Creek Pilot (newspaper), 34, 329,
    330
Defying Dixie: The Radical Roots of
    Civil Rights (Gilmore), 234
DeLaughter, Bobby, 280–81
  and Beckwith trial, 268–72, 273–74,
    278–79
DeLaughter, Peggy, 281
Delta Council, 208
Delta Democrat-Times, 216–20, 327
Delta Star (newspaper), 215–16
Democrat-Times, 215
Democratic Party, 39, 62, 65–66
DeMoss, Harold, Jr., 314
Dennis, Delmar, 268–69, 275–76, 291,
    292–93
DeSoto County, Mississippi, 157
Diamond, Dalton, 88–89
Dickerson, James L., 4–8, 15–16,
    41–42, 58–64, 69–72, 87–91, 99–
    105, 114–15, 174–75, 187–88,
    217–19, 224–29, 321–23, 329–30
Dickerson, James Luther "Dick," 5,
    101–5
Doar, John, 77– 78, 113, 124, 126, 178
Dogan, H. H., 26
Downing, Virgil, 64, 184
draft boards, 179, 180
Duckworth, Roman, Jr., 136
Dulles, Allen, 112, 243
Duncan, Mark, 288, 290, 293

Dunn, Barbara, 279
Dunn, Curtis, 310

Eastland, James O. ("Big Jim"), 9, 25,
    27–29, 65–67, 69, 76, 107, 122,
    169–70, 175, 238, 287
  and Supreme Court, 28, 30, 31, 39
Edwards, Charles Marcus, 137, 141–42
  arrest of, 135
  testimony of, 308–10, 312–13
Edwards, Jonathan H., 261
Eisenhower, Dwight, 39, 53, 106
Elle, Sallie Mae, 6–8
Equal Protection Clause, 150
Evans, Medford, 35
Evers, Carl, 270
Evers, Charles, 222, 259
Evers, Medgar, 44, 45, 75, 93–94, 108,
    185, 259, 261, 264–65, 268–69,
    281, 322, 331
  assassination of, 94–95, 260
  funeral of, 95–96
Evers, Myrlie, 93, 94, 269, 273, 278,
    280
Ewing, Jim, 267–68

Farley, Robert, 84
Faulkner, William, 29, 77, 218, 230,
    292–93, 331
Federal Bureau of Investigation (FBI),
    186, 233–34, 243, 246, 250, 255
  and civil rights workers murders,
    117–19, 120–21
  covert activity recruitment, 236
  importance of informants to, 248–49
  and KKK, 123, 275
  monitoring of civil rights leaders,
    30–31, 40, 235
  monitoring of Communist activities,
    234–35

Federation for Constitutional
    Government, 29–30, 41
Fifteenth Amendment, 323
Finger, Homer Ellis, Jr., 206
First Amendment, 323, 329
First Baptist Church in Summit, 198
First Presbyterian Church (Jackson),
    204–5
Fitzgerald, Paige, 307, 311, 313
Florida, 234
Foote, Shelby, 215
Fore, J. W., 225
Forman, Lenox, 135, 137
The Formation of the Negro (Lynch),
    114
Fort-Whiteman, Lovett, 234
Fox, John, 259, 260, 261
Frank, Reuven, 36
Franklin Advocate (newspaper), 142
Franklin County, Mississippi, 130, 132,
    134
Freedom Riders, 66–67, 69–70, 210
    arrests of, 67, 68, 71–72
Freedom's Daughters (Olson), 71
Freeman, Morgan, 99–101
Furr, Jerry, 201, 202

Galloway Memorial Methodist Church,
    198–99, 202
Gandy, Evelyn, 59
Gartin, Carroll, 57, 59
Gentry, Bobbie, 99
Georgia, 234
Gibson, Eric, 307
Gilbert, Ernest, 135, 305
Gillespie, Bob, 155
Gillespie, G. T., Sr., 205–6
Gilmore, Glenda Elizabeth, 234
Golden, Harry, 152
Golding, Boyd, 54, 58

Goodman, Andrew, 110, 113, 121, 124,
    127, 139, 158, 246, 248, 251–53,
    283, 285, 287, 291, 298
    arrest of, 11
    murder of, 118, 122, 289, 292, 295
Gordon, Bob, 226–28
Gordon, Marcus, 285, 288, 294–96
Gore, Ney, 34, 36, 43
Gray, Lloyd, 229
Greene, Percy, 224
Greenville, Mississippi, 3–4, 215–16
Greenwood, Mississippi, 3, 97, 99, 101,
    105, 107
Greenwood Citizens' Council, 36,
    106
Grenada, Mississippi, 176
Grehl, Michael, 329
Grisham, John, 331
Guihard, Paul, 81
Gunter, James, 28–30
Gunter, Walter Ray, 81

Hackman, Gene, 252
Halberstam, David, 76
Hale, Dennis, 169–70
Hallenbeck, John R., 159
Hampton, David, 227
Harkey, Ira, 230, 329
Harper, J. J., 288
Harper, Ronnie, 140
Harrison, Frances, 269
Harrison, Jerry, 252–53
Harvey, Paul, 215
Hatcher, Joseph M., 292
Hawkins, Armis, 65–66
Hederman, Rea, 229
Hederman, Robert, 214
Hederman, Tom, 214, 223, 244, 328
Heffner, Albert, 203
Heffner, Malva, 203

Helms, Richard, 236
Hendrick, Leon, 153, 261, 264
Henry, John, 269–70
Henry, R. H., 213–14
Henson, Jim, 13, 15
Hewitt, Woody, 32
Hickman, C. H., 50
Hicks, Leonard, 34, 35, 40
Higgs, William, 165–66
Hilburn, Breland, 271, 272, 278, 279
Hill, Ester Mikell, 153
Hinds County, Mississippi, 151
Hollandale, Mississippi, 11–13, 15, 37, 69, 326
    black population in, 10, 13, 41
    churches in, 195–97
Holley, James, 277
Hollis, Louis, 35
Hood, Jim, 285–86, 288–90, 293–94, 299, 321, 328
Hoover, J. Edgar, 125, 242–44, 247, 250
    monitoring of civil rights leaders, 30–31, 40, 235
    obsessions of, 233–34
Hopkins, Andrew, 64, 115–18, 121–23, 137, 169, 184, 239, 252–53, 264
House Committee on Un-American Activities, 138, 237
Huie, William Bradford, 25
Humes, H. H., 41, 208
Humphrey, Hubert H., 65, 154
Hurst, E. H., 136
Hutto, Wayne, 137

Ickes, Harold, 67
Illinois, 66
Ingebretsen, David, 188–91
Ingram, Jim, 128, 211, 244, 247–48, 249, 250–51, 255, 285, 314

interracial marriage, 321
Iraq War, 157, 328

Jackson, Andrew, 2–3
Jackson, Mississippi, 67–68, 244–46, 250–51, 271
Jackson Citizens' Council, 34
Jackson Daily News, 204, 214, 220, 223–26, 228, 327–28
Jackson Free Press, 140, 142, 329
Japanese American internment camps, 216
Jews, discrimination against, 89, 111, 210–11, 264, 268, 284
Jim Crow, 37–39. *See also* segregation
Jobe, E. R., 86
John Birch Society, 35
Johnson, Charles, 124
Johnson, James Weldon, 234
Johnson, Lyndon B., 65, 112, 243, 246
Johnson, Paul B., 64–65, 76–78, 109–10, 113, 119, 123, 171, 173, 183, 223, 243, 245–46
Johnson, Thomas E., 200
Johnston, Erle, 86–87, 109, 112–13, 172, 177, 182–85, 238–39, 244–45, 330
    and corruption of the media, 221–24
Jones, Albert, 64, 86, 95
Jones, B. J. "Shorty," 41, 42
Jones, Elnora, 84
Jones, Roy, 277
Jordan, James, 125
judicial system, failures of, 167, 260, 320–21
jury system
    failures of 147–51
    jury selection, 261–62, 264, 272–73, 288, 314
Justice in Mississippi (Ball), 287

Katzenbach, Nicholas, 79
Kelley, Clarence, 242
Kennard, Clyde, 73–75, 88
Kennedy, Ethel, 173
Kennedy, John F., 13, 65–66, 175, 221, 274
    and Ole Miss, 78–80
    reaction to assassination of, 90–91, 326–27
    speech on race, 93
Kennedy, Robert F., 69, 86, 112
    and Ole Miss, 78–79, 81, 173–75
Kershaw, Alvin, 200
Killen, Edgar Ray, 121, 140, 286, 299
    and KKK, 289, 293
    and Philadelphia murders, 285, 287, 291, 292
    release and "Killen Appreciation Day," 296
    trial of, 125–26, 285–88, 293–95, 298, 314
Kilpatrick, Martin, 69–70, 71, 88–89
King, B. B., 331
King, Dick, 45
King, Edwin, 94, 96, 190, 279
King, Martin Luther, Jr., 40, 132, 175, 181–82, 209, 235, 247, 287
    assassination of, 249–50
Kitchens, Jim, 271
Knights of the Great Forest, 172
Knowles, Warren, 178
Kochtitzky, Bob, 204
Kosciusko, Mississippi, 85
Kosciuszko, Tadeusz, 85
Ku Klux Klan, 22, 28, 29, 70, 116, 125–26, 134, 235, 243, 248–49, 251, 265–66, 280, 288–89, 297, 301, 310–11, 313, 320
    and Communist Party, 234
    and draft boards, 179–80
    and FBI, 123, 254, 275
    and Mississippi Highway Patrol, 123, 186, 244, 245
    and Mississippi Sovereignty Commission, 112, 253, 254, 255, 256
    and sexual dysfunction, 322–23
    as terrorist organization, 213

Ladd, Donna, 140–41, 142–43, 329
Lampton, Dunn, 142, 307, 312
Landon, Michael de L., 164
Lauderdale County, Mississippi, 148
Lauridson, James, 311
lawyers
    black, 164
    white, 165–67
Lawyers Committee for Civil Rights Under Law, 164
Lawyers' Constitutional Defense Committee, 164
Lee, George Washington, 24, 135
Lee, Harper, 164
Lee, Herbert, 136
Lee, Patti Duncan, 295
Lee, Roy Noble, 272
Leland, Mississippi, 13, 15
Lewis, Anthony, 30
Lewis, T. W., 204
Life magazine, 158–59
Lincoln, Abraham, 106
Littlejohn, Roy, 129
Lofton, Hines, 156
Long, Betty Jane, 109
Look magazine, 25–26
Lott, Hardy, 260
Lott, Trent, 154
Louisiana, 267
Lucas, George, 307–8
Lyle, Garland, 137

Lynch, L. G., 114, 115
lynchings, 52–53, 153–54, 199
    press responses to, 154, 215–16
    and sexual dysfunction, 322–23
    as social control, 154
    See also specific incidents
Lynn, James, 312

Mabus, Ray, 189, 190, 270
Madison County, Mississippi, 208
Maedke, Janet, 178–79
Malone, Maurice, 43, 64
Marcello, Carlos, 254
Marshall, Thurgood, 69, 75, 122, 220
Martinband, Charles, 200
Massengill, Reed, 274, 322
Mathis, Johnny, 38
Matthews, L. E., 271
McCain, John, 332
McCain, William, 74
McDowell, Cleve, 85–90
McGowen, M. M., 153
McIntyre, James, 289, 294
McKeithen, Bill, 88
McShane, James, 77, 78
McWherter, Ned, 270
Mead, Lynda Lee, 61, 82
Meadville, Mississippi, 130–31, 134,
    141
Medley, Kate, 141
Memphis, Tennessee, 250
Memphis Press-Scimitar, 87
Mendenhall Baptist Church, 198–99
Meredith, James, 86, 88, 113, 155, 165,
    173, 230
    and Ole Miss, 75–81, 82–83, 85, 87,
        89
    shooting of, 180–82
    voting rights march, 180, 224

Middleton, R. W., 310, 311
Milam, J. W., 18–23
    arrest, trial, and acquittal of, 24
    confession of, 25–26
Milam, Juanita, 18–20
Miller, Carlton, 125
Miller, Rush Glen, 197
Millsaps College, 206
Milner, Dumas, 172
Minor, Bill, 150
Miss America, 61, 82
Mississippi Appellate Court, 280
Mississippi Baptist Convention, 209
Mississippi Burning (movie), 252
Mississippi Constitution, 2, 58, 147–48,
    160, 272
Mississippi Delta, 4, 13–14, 38, 39, 193,
    326
Mississippi Highway Patrol, 251
    infiltrated by KKK, 123, 186, 244,
        245
Mississippi Southern College, 73
Mississippi State Penitentiary
    (Parchman Farm), 5, 71–72
Mississippi State Sovereignty
    Commission, 35–36, 55, 67, 86,
        88, 106–7, 121–22, 127, 136, 137,
        142–43, 165, 169, 176–78, 181,
        183–84, 220, 231, 235, 238–39,
        242, 252, 327, 329, 330
    abolition of, 186–87
    arms purchases of, 109–10
    and Beckwith trial, 264
    and Clyde Kennard, 74
    on college campuses, 171
    and Communist Party, 234
    creation of, 31–33
    and draft boards, 179
    and FBI, 245, 246, 253–54

filing system of, 40, 43
informants for, 41, 113–14
intimidation tactics of, 43–44, 170
and KKK, 253, 254, 255, 256
and Medgar Evers, 94–95
media influence of, 40, 221,
    223–24
and NAACP voter registration, 44
secret files of, 186–91
and University of Mississippi, 171
Mississippi Summer Project, 110
Mississippi Supreme Court, 160, 166,
    280, 296
and Beckwith trial, 279
and Killen trial, 297
on qualified electors, 148
on racial discrimination, 297
on water cure, 157
Mississippi Values, 2, 16, 19, 41, 57, 61,
    84, 109, 122, 136–37, 238, 247,
    284, 299, 327, 332
consequences of, 323–25
Mitchell, Jerry, 289
Mize, Sidney, 55
Mobley, Mary Ann, 82
Molpus, Chester A., 200
Money, Mississippi, 17
Montgomery, Benjamin T., 133
Moore, Charles Eddie, 130, 138, 142,
    143, 301, 303, 311–12, 313–14,
    322
    kidnapping of, 131–32
    murder of, 133–35, 307–10
Moore, Mike, 284
Moore, Roy, 123, 245, 255–56
Moore, Thomas, 140–42, 311
Moran, Mitch, 289–90
Morgan, Jimmy Dale, 275
Morgan, Peggy, 269, 274

Morris, Willie, 11, 226, 280, 331
Motley, Constance Baker, 303
Mount Zion United Methodist Church,
    110, 289–91
Muirhead, Jean, 150–51
murals, 302

Nash, Diane, 68–69
National Association for the
    Advancement of Colored People
    (NAACP), 13, 25, 35, 74, 110, 148,
    194, 200–201
    FBI campaign against, 30–31, 237
    Legal Defense Fund of, 164
    voter registration efforts of, 44
National Council of Churches, 201,
    202–3
National Rifle Association, 262
National Socialist White People's Party
    (Nazi Party), 228
National States' Rights Party, 249
Neff, Thelma. See Beckwith, Thelma
Neshoba County, Mississippi, 110, 208,
    248, 286, 293
Nester, Kathy, 307, 310, 312
New Orleans, 250
New York Times, 30
New York Times v. Sullivan, 156
news media
    contemporary media, 327–29
    support of civil rights, 229–32, 320
    support of segregation, 214, 220–24
    See also specific newspapers
Nineteenth Amendment, 324
Nixon, Richard M., 65, 66, 106
North Carolina, 234
Norvell, Aubrey, 180–82
Nussbaum, Areme, 211
Nussbaum, Perry, 210–11

Obama, Barack, 158, 332
Odle, Joe T., 209
Ole Miss. *See* University of Mississippi
Olson, Lynne, 71
Otto, John, 243
Outlook (TV program), 36
Owens, Jesse, 216
Oxford, Mississippi, 84

Palmyra Island, Mississippi, 132
Panola County, Mississippi, 271, 272
Parchman Farm (Mississippi State
    Penitentiary), 5, 71–72
Parker, Mack Charles, 50–51, 55, 321
    lynching of, 52–54, 58
Patterson, Donald P., 205
Patterson, Joe, 43–44, 45, 64, 117, 119,
    244, 255
Patterson, Robert, 263
Patton, Eddie, 148
Patton v. Mississippi, 148
Payne, Charles M., 4
Pearce, Mary Ann, 99
Pendergrass, Edward J., 207
Perez, Leander, 30
Perkins, Oscar, 157
Peters, Ed, 268, 269, 271–73, 277–78
Philadelphia, Mississippi, 110, 117, 158,
    287
Pickett, Fred, 264
Pierson, Robert, 67
Pike County, Mississippi, 129, 131, 147,
    208
population
    decline among blacks, 326
    demographics of early settlers, 2–3
Port Gibson, Mississippi, 37
Posey, Billy Wayne, 126–27, 285–86
Posey, Buford, 111–12
Prather, Archie, 310–11

Presley, Elvis, 38, 331
Price, Cecil Ray, 111, 115, 117–18, 123,
    127, 284
    arrest of, 121
    trial of, 126
Proctor, John, 116, 247, 251–52
Providence Farms, 206
Pruitt, Ervin, 161–63
Pursuits of Life in Mississippi (mural),
    302
Putz, Edward, 311

Quantrill's Raiders, 61
Quinn, James, 228

Rabbit Foot Minstrels, 11, 37
Rainey, Lawrence, 112, 115–18, 123,
    127, 158
    acquittal of, 283
    arrest of, 120–21
    death of, 283
    trial of, 124–26
Rainey, Ma, 38
Ray, James Earl, 247
Reagan, Ronald, 314
Reed, Jimmy, 13
Reiley, Mark, 276
Reily, Marvin W., 167
The Reivers (Faulkner), 230
religion. *See* churches
Republican Party, 106
Ridgen, David, 139–43
Roberts, Alton Wayne, 126–27
Rockefeller, Nelson, 67
Rogers, George, 32–33, 187–88
Rogers, Will, 215
Rowan, Carl, 201
Rowland, Pete, 272
Roxie Colored First Baptist Church, 310
Royster, Vermont, 98

Ruleville, Mississippi, 9
Runyon, Damon, 232
Russia, 234. *See also* Communist Party

Saggus, Jim, 221–22
Salter, John, 190
Sampson, C. E., 107
Sanders, Stanny, 260, 263
Scanlan, T. M., 213
Scarbrough, Tom, 64, 86, 169, 176–79,
    181–82
Schwerner, Michael, 109, 113, 121,
    124–25, 127, 139, 158, 246, 248,
    251–53, 283, 285, 287, 290–91,
    298
  murder of, 118, 122, 289, 292, 295
  surveillance and arrest of, 110–11
Schwerner, Rita, 109, 290–92.
Scott County (Mississippi) Times, 222
Seale, Clyde, 305, 310
Seale, Don, 311
Seale, Jack, 135, 136
Seale, James Ford, 131–33, 136–39,
    141–42
  arrest of, 135
  indictment against, 143, 301
  overturned conviction of, 314–15
  trial of, 302–14
Seale, Jean, 304
Second Amendment, 323
segregation, 1, 2, 6–7, 9, 147, 155, 167,
    325–26. *See also* Jim Crow
Selah, W. B., 197, 202
Senate. *See* U.S. Senate
sexual dysfunction and racism, 321–23
Sheldon, Andrew, 272–73, 288
Sherrill, Robert, 69
Silas Green Show, 11, 37
Sillers, Walter, 29, 58, 64
Silver, James, 82–84, 171

Simkhovitch, Simka, 302
Simmons, William J. "Bill," 34–35, 44,
    46, 64, 194
Singletary, Hale, 115
Sitton, Claude, 320
Slade, Hammond, 50–51
Sloan, Henry S., 241
Smith, Bessie, 38
Smith, Hazel Brannon, 95, 230–32, 329
Smith, Howard K., 171–72
Smith, Jerry, 314
Smith, Lamar, 24, 136
Smith, Mike, 184
Snodgrass, Charles, 137
Snowden, Jimmy, 126–27
South Carolina, 234
Southern Baptists, 195, 207, 209
Southern Christian Leadership
    Conference (SCLC), 40, 110
Southern Conference Educational
    Fund, 237
"Southern Manifesto" (Eastland), 39
Sovereignty Commission. *See*
    Mississippi State Sovereignty
    Commission
Soviet Union. *See* Communist Party;
    Russia
Spencer, James L., 260
Spillane, Mickey, 99
Stainbeck, Ingram, 98
Stauffer, Todd, 140
Stevenson, Adlai, 39
Stevenson, Preston, 200
Stewart, Bill, 54
Stewart, Richard, 166
Stockstill, J. E., 170
Stoner, J. B., 249–50
Student Nonviolent Coordinating
    Committee (SNCC), 107, 110
Sudduth, Charlie, 69–71

Sullens, Frederick, 25, 214–15, 224
Sullivan, Charles, 57
Sullivan, John D., 238–39, 246
Sullivan, Joseph, 246–47, 252, 254–56
Summer in Mississippi (documentary), 139
Sunflower County, Mississippi, 157
Supreme Court of the United States, 166, 190
    and desegregation, 27, 28, 105–6
    and jury system, 148–49
    and Meredith case, 76
    and peremptory challenges, 150
    See also Mississippi Supreme Court

television, 79, 93, 226–27
    Sovereignty Commission and, 36, 41, 171–73, 221–22
    support of civil rights, 95, 113 , 204–5
    support of segregation, 204–5, 220–21, 230
Tennessee, 234, 268
Thirteenth Amendment, 323–24
Thomas, Earl T., 155–56, 159, 163
Thomas, Robert, 64
Thompson, Allen, 95
Thurmond, Strom, 29
Till, Emmett, 17–20, 321
    abduction and murder of, 21–23
    confession to murder of, 25–26
    funeral of, 24
    media reaction to murder of, 25
Till, Louis, 25
Time magazine, 158–59
Tippah County, Mississippi, 208
To Kill a Mockingbird (Lee), 164
Toler, Kenneth, 222
Tonkel, Keith, 201

Tougaloo College, 238
Truman, Harry S., 66, 154–55
Tubb, Tom, 76
Turcotte, W. H., 225
Turner, Audie, 5, 39
Turner, Juanita, 4
Turner, Rex, 217
Turner, Steve, 58
Twenty-Fourth Amendment, 324

United States Commission on Civil Rights, 208
University of Mississippi (Ole Miss)
    Cleve McDowell at, 85–88
    football team at, 81–82
    James Meredith at, 75–81, 82–83, 85, 87, 89
    reaction to John F. Kennedy assassination, 90–91
    riot at, 80–81, 83–84
    Robert F. Kennedy address at, 173–75
    Sovereignty Commission and, 172
University of Mississippi School of Law, 82
U.S. Constitution, 25, 31, 106, 272, 323. *See also* Equal Protection Clause; *specific amendments*
US Press Association, 223
U.S. Senate, 154. *See also* Eastland, James O.

Van Landingham, Zack, 34, 40, 43–45, 54, 74, 194–95, 236–38
Vaught, John, 81
Vietnam War, 139
violence against blacks, 129–31, 135–36, 326. *See also* bombings; lynchings; *specific incidents*

Virginia, 234
voting
    patterns, 331–32
    rights of blacks, 326
    rights of women, 151
Voting Rights Act of 1965, 324

Waits, Hilton, 58–61
Walker, Clinton, 136
Walker, Edwin, 83, 155–56, 263
Wallace, George, 265
Waller, William L., 185–88
    and Beckwith trials, 259–65, 325
Walters, Debbie Carol, 47–49
Walters, Jimmy, 47–49, 55
Walters, June, 47, 52, 55, 58
    assault of, 48–50
Ward, Jimmy, 214–15, 222, 224–26,
    229, 244, 328, 329
Wasson, Ben, 218
waterboarding/water cure, 157–58
Waters, Muddy, 27
Watters, Walker, 120
WBBM Radio, 222
Webb, David, 143
Webb, Mary Lou, 142–43
Webb, William, 98
Weir, Laurel G., 159
Wells, W. Calvin, III, 120
Welty, Eudora, 331, 332
Wessel, Bill, 267
White, Ben Chester, 138
White, Hugh, 240–41
White Citizens' Council. See Citizens'
    Council
White Knights of the Ku Klux Klan.
    See Ku Klux Klan

WJTV-TV, 220
Wildmon, Donald, 227
Wilkins, Roy, 44–46
William Carey College, 209
Williams, John Bell, 29, 40, 184–85,
    223
Williams, Mary Louise "Willie," 98–99,
    107, 322
Williams, Tennessee, 331
Williams, Walter, 61
Williamson, Frank, 160–62
Williamson, James Walton, 161
Williamson, Luella, 160–63
Winfrey, Oprah, 85
Wingate, Henry, 303–7, 310, 312–14
Winstead, Mike, 292
Winter, William, 32–33, 186–87, 191,
    223
Wisner, Frank, 235–36
WLBT-TV, 95, 204–5, 220, 327
Wolf, Leonard, 135, 308
Women for Constitutional Government
    (WCG), 173
Works Progress Administration (WPA),
    302
Wright, Elizabeth, 21–22
Wright, Fielding L., 27–29, 98
Wright, Preacher, 20–22
Wright, Richard, 303, 331
Wright, Simeon, 18–19, 21
Wyckoff, Elizabeth, 71

Yerger, Susie, 97
Yerger, Wirt, Jr., 106